"The project of 'renewal' in Catholic theology has been underway for almost two generations. Since the early twentieth century, theologians have been yearning for the revitalization of their sacred discipline. And yet, arguably, clarity about the precise essence of such a renewed theology remains elusive. Thus, the pressing question remains: What is authentic Catholic theology? With subtlety and nuance, the essays in this volume collectively invite readers to revisit this crucial question. These authors (representing a diverse range of academic backgrounds and spiritual traditions) identify key principles that always inform Catholic theology—even as they model its authentic practice. This volume describes what 'faith seeking understanding' looks like, and why authentic theology is always possible and is still needed (even in the twenty-first century). I am grateful for this book. It points toward something that the contemporary practice of Catholic theology eagerly awaits: 'a renewal of the renewal.'"

CAJETAN CUDDY, O.P.
Dominican House of Studies
Washington, D.C.

"This important book is a masterful treatment of some of the major problems with contemporary theology that deviates from the Catholic tradition. Its contributors are among the best qualified scholars to comment upon the defects of progressivist theology and to offer explanations for some of the most important approaches to orthodox Catholic theology. Among the relevant theological topics covered the magisterium, Scripture, the *sensus fidelium*, councils and synods of bishops, heresy, and the development of doctrine. Each of these topics is relevant to the theological crises that the Church is facing today. No other book to my knowledge tackles these contemporary theological issues with such expertise. This book should be required reading for all seminarians and for students of theology."

CARDINAL GERHARD LUDWIG MÜLLER
Former Prefect of the Congregation for the Doctrine of the Faith

"Christians today are divided between those who are servants of the Word, accepting Revelation as godly, and those who see themselves as masters of the apostolic tradition, able to change the deposit of faith and morals. One cannot belong to both camps. This superb collection of essays, sometimes blunt and regularly demanding, merits the effort required of the reader. It examines the philosophical presuppositions of the revolutionaries, then analyses and answers their arguments striving to separate ought from is and theology from Scripture. The authors take us to the heart of the mighty struggles that have continued for decades, sometimes hidden, sometimes openly in synods, which have already destroyed national communities and might yet provoke a German schism while certainly hastening its decline."

CARDINAL GEORGE PELL
Archbishop Emeritus of Sydney, Australia

"If the bearers of the Catholic Magisterium are, at the present time, sailing, more or less open-eyed, into a whirlpool, it would be a mistake to ascribe this simply to the machinations of progressive Jesuits or even to the heady mix of cultural populism, moral individualism, and global politics that dominates the Western media. Below the turbulent surface of current ecclesial life lie the deep currents which the contributors to this book seek to plumb. They show how, without a robust metaphysics, an objective ethics, and an epistemology suited to both— none of which can be absolutely guaranteed in later-twentieth-century Church intellectuals, Catholic philosophy cannot safely take on board any worthwhile wares the cargo of modern thought might contain. Likewise, without a steady gaze on the fixed stars of canon, creed, and crozier by which the Church, historically, has read the map of the Christian life (that is: an authoritative Bible, a Tradition doctrinally understood, and a practice of episcopacy—including papacy—self-consciously faithful to the apostolic deposit), Catholic theologians, and their epigones in high places, will inevitably hole the side of the Barque of Peter."

AIDAN NICHOLS, O.P.
Former John Paul II Memorial Visiting Lecturer at the University of Oxford

THE FAITH ONCE FOR ALL
DELIVERED

THE FAITH ONCE FOR ALL
DELIVERED

Doctrinal Authority in Catholic Theology

Edited by Kevin L. Flannery, S.J.

EMMAUS
ACADEMIC
Steubenville, Ohio

EMMAUS
ACADEMIC

Steubenville, Ohio
A Division of The St. Paul Center for Biblical Theology
Editor-in-Chief: Scott Hahn
1468 Parkview Circle
Steubenville, Ohio 43952

Library of Congress Cataloging-in-Publication Data applied for
ISBNs: 978-1-64585-293-3 hc / 978-1-64585-294-0 pb / 978-1-64585-295-7 eb

Cover design and layout by Allison Merrick and Emily Morelli

Cover credit: *Christ Handing Keys to St. Peter* by Giambattista Pittoni, 18th century

Dear friends, I wanted very much to write to you concerning the salvation we share. Instead, I must write to urge you to contend for the faith which was once for all delivered to God's holy people.

Epistle of St. Jude, verse 3

We may understand, then, why the Catholic Church, both yesterday and today, gives so much importance to the rigorous conservation of true Revelation, considering it an inviolable treasure, and why it bears such a rigorous sense of its fundamental duty in defending and transmitting the doctrine of the faith in unequivocal terms; orthodoxy is its first concern; the pastoral Magisterium its primary and providential function; the apostolic teaching affirms in fact the canons of its preaching; and the mandate of the Apostle Paul, Depositum custodi *[Guard what has been entrusted to you] (1 Tim 6:20; cf. 2 Tim 1:14), constitutes such a commitment for it, that its violation would be a betrayal. The teaching Church does not invent its doctrine; it is a witness, it is an interpreter, a mediator; and regarding the truths pertaining to the Christian message, it could be called conservative, intransigent; to those who request it to make the faith easier, more adapted to the caprice of the changing mentality of the times, it responds together with the Apostles: "Non possumus, we cannot" (Acts 4:20).*

Pope Saint Paul VI, General Audience, January 19, 1972

TABLE OF CONTENTS

CONTRIBUTORS

RAYMOND LEO CARDINAL BURKE, Prefect Emeritus of the Supreme Tribunal of the Apostolic Signatura.

ROBERT DODARO, O.S.A., Member of the Augustinians at Our Lady of Grace Monastery, King City, Ontario, Canada.

EDUARDO ECHEVERRIA, Professor of Philosophy and Theology, Sacred Heart Major Seminary, Detroit, Michigan.

EDWARD FESER, Professor of Philosophy, Pasadena City College, Pasadena, California.

KEVIN L. FLANNERY, S.J., Emeritus Professor of Philosophy, Pontifical Gregorian University, Rome.

JOHN FINNIS, Fellow of the British Academy; Professor Emeritus, University of Oxford; Professor Emeritus, University of Notre Dame, Notre Dame, Indiana.

CHRISTOPHER J. MALLOY, Associate Professor of Theology, The University of Dallas, Irving, Texas.

GUY MANSINI, O.S.B., Max Seckler Chair of Fundamental Theology, Ave Maria University, Ave Maria, Florida.

C. C. PECKNOLD, Associate Professor of Theology, The Catholic University of America; Theologian-in-Residence, The Basilica of St. Mary, Alexandria, Virginia.

JOHN M. RIST, Emeritus Professor of Classics and Philosophy, University of Toronto, Toronto, Ontario.

CONTRIBUTORS

ROBERT CARDINAL SARAH, Prefect Emeritus of the Congregation for Divine Worship and the Discipline of the Sacraments, Rome, Italy.

THOMAS HEINRICH STARK, Professor of Philosophy, Philosophisch-Theologische Hochschule St. Pölten, St. Pölten, Austria; Professor of Philosophy, Philosophisch-Theologische Hochschule Benedikt XVI., Heiligenkreuz, Austria.

EDMUND WALDSTEIN, O.CIST., Lecturer in Moral Theology, Philosophisch-Theologische Hochschule Benedikt XVI., Heiligenkreuz, Austria.

FOREWORD

Raymond Leo Cardinal Burke

Blessed Pope Pius IX, in the bull *Ineffabilis Deus*, by which he defined the dogma of the Immaculate Conception of the Blessed Virgin Mary, made clear that he was not presenting any new teaching but rather defining what the Church has always believed. Making reference to the teaching of Saint Vincent of Lérins, he wrote:

> Indeed, the Church of Christ, watchful guardian and protector of the dogmas deposited within her, never changes anything, never diminishes anything, never adds anything to these, but with complete diligence, she faithfully and wisely draws upon those things shaped from antiquity and sown by the faith of the Fathers; and, in this way, she strives to refine and polish them so that these ancient dogmas of heavenly instruction may attain clarity, light, and precision, but they still retain their fullness, integrity, and proper character, and they grow according to their own nature, namely within the same dogma and in the same sense and the same meaning.[1]

---

[1] "Christi enim Ecclesia, sedula depositorum apud se dogmatum custos et vindex, nihil in his umquam permutat, nihil minuit, nihil addit, sed omni industria vetera fideliter sapienterque tractando si qua antiquitus informata sunt et Patrum fides sevit, ita limare, expolire studet, ut prisca illa caelestis doctrinae dogmata accipiant evidentiam, lucem, distinctionem, sed retineant plenitudinem, integritatem, proprietatem, ac in suo tantum genere crescant, in eodem scilicet dogmate, eodem sensu eademque sententia." Peter Hünermann and Helmut Hoping (eds.) for the Latin text, and Robert Fastiggi and Anne Englund Nash (eds.) for the English text of Henrich Denzinger, *Enchiridion symbolorum definitionum et declarationum de rebus fidei et morum,* 43rd ed., *Compendium of Creeds, Definitions, and Declarations on Faith and Morals* (San Francisco: Ignatius Press, 2012), 574, no. 2802.

What Blessed Pius IX wrote expresses an essential aspect of the living presence of Christ Our Lord with us in the Church.

Christ dwells with us always in the Church, most fully and perfectly through the sacred liturgy, above all, the Holy Eucharist. In the Holy Eucharist, the priest acting in the person of Christ makes new his sacrifice on Calvary and its incomparable fruit, his Body and Blood as the spiritual food for our earthly pilgrimage. Christ, the fullness of the revelation of God to us, is also present with us in the authentic teaching of the Church, so that all that he has taught remains alive for us, leading us into an ever-deeper knowledge of the truth about God and his plan for our eternal salvation.[2] It is in the sacred liturgy, in fact, that we encounter that truth, even as it is through the teaching authority of the Church that we are led to encounter Christ in the sacraments. According to the ancient wisdom expressed by Prosper of Aquitaine, "The law of praying establishes the law of believing."[3] In other words, the truth of the faith finds its highest and most perfect expression in the sacred liturgy. Christ never fails to hand down to us in the Church the saving truth which he revealed once and for all time by the mystery of his redemptive Incarnation. Through Sacred Tradition and Sacred Scripture, always intimately united to one another, Christ continues to be our living teacher in the Church (CCC §80). The dogmas of the faith invite us to enter ever more deeply into the truth they contain, the truth handed down to us by Our Lord.

Studying the history of the Church, we find many examples of the living Christ preserving the Church in the unchanging truth and leading her to "grasp its full significance over the course of the centuries" (CCC §60). In every age of the Church, there have always been those who would betray the truth in order to advance a certain ideology or personal agenda. Instead of turning to Christ and to the truth which he unfailingly teaches in the Church, they have followed their own wisdom, a worldly wisdom which has led them into apostasy, heresy, and schism. Saint Paul, in his instruction and exhortation to Saint Timothy as a bishop, addressed the situation as it was already manifesting itself in the first years of the Church's life:

> I charge you in the presence of God and of Christ Jesus who is
> to judge the living and the dead, and by his appearing and his

---

[2] Cf. Catechism of the Catholic Church, §50.

[3] "Legem credendi lex statuat supplicandi." A. G. Martimort, *L'Église en prière: Introduction à la liturgie*, 3rd ed. (Paris: Desclée, 1965), 231.

kingdom: preach the word, be urgent in season and out of season, convince, rebuke, and exhort, be unfailing in patience and in teaching. For the time is coming when people will not endure sound teaching, but having itching ears they will accumulate for themselves teachers to suit their own likings, and will turn away from listening to the truth and wander into myths. (2 Tim 4:1–4)

In every century of Church history, the phenomenon has manifested itself. When it has, faithful popes and bishops—for example, Popes Leo the Great, Gregory the Great, Gregory VII, Pius V, and Pius X and Bishops Ambrose, Athanasius, Augustine of Hippo, and John Chrysostom—have tirelessly defended the truth, in accord with Saint Paul's admonition to Saint Timothy, even at the cost of exile and martyrdom.

Saint Paul, for instance, when he encountered the aberrations which the early Christians had introduced into the Eucharistic sacrifice, disciplined the situation immediately and unequivocally, not by inventing something new but by presenting what he had received through the apostolic tradition. He declared:

For I received from the Lord what I also delivered to you, that the Lord Jesus on the night when he was betrayed took bread, and when he had given thanks, he broke it, and said, "This is my body which is for you. Do this in remembrance of me." In the same way also the chalice, after supper, saying, "This chalice is the new covenant in my blood. Do this, as often as you drink it, in remembrance of me." For as often as you eat this bread and drink the chalice, you proclaim the Lord's death until he comes. (1 Cor 11:23–26)

It is Our Lord himself, alive in the Church, who declares the truth about the Holy Eucharist through his apostle Paul. Thus, Saint Paul does not hesitate to discipline the Christians at Corinth with these words: "Whoever, therefore, eats the bread or drinks the cup of the Lord in an unworthy manner will be guilty of profaning the body and blood of the Lord" (1 Cor 11:27).

In the same way, Saint Jude the Apostle, brother of Saint James the Less, Bishop of Jerusalem, confronted certain heresies, for example, Gnosticism, which were leading many of the faithful away from Christ and his truth. Saint Jude begins his letter to the faithful making clear that salvation is from Christ alone in his holy Church. He writes: "Beloved, being very eager to write to you of our common salvation, I found it necessary to write appealing to you to contend for the faith which was once for all delivered to the saints" (Jude 1:3). Saint Jude, in strong terms, describes the confusion, error, and spiritual devastation wrought by heresy. He then concludes his exhortation with these words:

> Now to him who is able to keep you from falling and to present you without blemish before the presence of his glory with rejoicing, to the only God, our Savior through Jesus Christ our Lord, be glory, majesty, dominion, and authority, before all time and now and for ever. Amen. (Jude 1:24–25)

In accord with Saint Jude's divinely inspired words, when confronting the mission of the Church in every age and the particular challenges to the mission presented by each age, Christ alone, alive in the Church, is "the way, and the truth, and the life" (John 14:6). Turning to him, he leads us into the truth which he has revealed and which alone is our salvation, the salvation of the world. To the question of Saint Thomas the Apostle, "Thomas said to him, 'Lord, we do not know where you are going; how can we know the way?' Jesus said to him, 'I am the way, and the truth, and the life; no one comes to the Father, but by me'" (John 14:5–6). Our Lord remains with us, as he promised, "always, to the close of the age" (Matt 28:20).

In our time, there are those who announce a "paradigm shift" in the Church, as if the Church should now abandon her divinely given nature to meet the challenges of the present age. Instead of turning to the truths of the faith as they have been unfailingly taught in the Church, the heralds of a revolution in the Church use a host of ill-defined or undefined slogans, most of which enjoy no history in Sacred Tradition, to advance their agenda. They would have us believe that we can discover the truth in popular sentiments and trends of the time. They also use traditional theological categories, for example, the Magisterium, conscience, development of doctrine, and the sense of the faithful, without respect for their proper nature. The slogan "synodal way" has emerged, yet its proponents openly admit has nothing to do with the perennial canonical institute of the synod—a process developed to assist the Roman pontiff and bishops in teaching the unchanging truths of the faith and in applying the discipline which safeguards those truths—but rather "puts everything on the table" for eventual change.

Today, when so much confusion, error and division beset the Church, it is essential to understand the false philosophies which lead to the betrayal of the truth of the Church's doctrine and discipline and to understand the fundamental theological categories which have assisted the Church to remain always in the truth of Christ (cf. John 8:31–32), all along the Christian centuries. The present volume, entitled after the words of the exhortation of Saint Jude, *The Faith Once for All Delivered*, provides the essential tools for the understanding of the philosophical errors which generate confusion and error regarding the truth and for the understanding of the theological tools which help us to remain in the unchanging truth as Christ hands it down to us in the Church. For that reason, I am honored to present to the reader the excellent essays which comprise *The Faith Once for All Delivered*. They are prepared by scholars of philosophy and theology in service of the Church in our time.

In writing this foreword, I express heartfelt gratitude to the authors and, in a particular way, to Father Kevin Flannery, S.J., the editor of the volume, for his tireless work in bringing together the important essays contained in it. I thank all the authors for their vital work on the critical categories, the sense of the faithful, and the development of doctrine, theological matters which are subject to so much confused interpretation. May the labors of all who have made this volume assist the Roman pontiff and the bishops in fulfilling their responsibility, as Saint Paul, under the inspiration of the Holy Spirit, expressed it to Saint Timothy: "preach the word, be urgent in season and out of season, convince, rebuke, and exhort, be unfailing in patience and in teaching" (2 Tim 4:2). May they also assist the faithful to exercise their right and indeed their responsibility "to manifest to their pastors their opinion on matters which pertain to the good of the Church and to make their opinion known to the rest of the Christian faithful, without prejudice to the integrity of the faith and morals, with reverence toward their pastors, and attentive to common advantage and the dignity of persons."[4] May *Faith Once for All Delivered* serve Christ our teacher and his truth which dispels confusion and error and heals division, bringing all of the faithful to him who alone makes us one.

Raymond Leo Cardinal Burke
September 29, 2021

---

[4] Code of Canon Law, can. 212, §3.

INTRODUCTION

The purpose of this book is twofold. In the first part, the authors look at the philosophical roots of modern progressivist Catholic theology dating back to the Enlightenment and discuss the incompatibility of this theology with the Catholic tradition. In the second part, the authors examine five traditional sources of theology (*fontes theologiae*) and offer explanations of correct and incorrect ways of treating them within theological discourse in order to remain in the Catholic tradition and avoid the errors inherent in progressivist theology and biblical exegesis.

In the first essay, C. C. Pecknold presents a general overview of the movement from the philosophies of Kant and Hegel into the so-called "*nouvelle théologie*" of the twentieth century. Pecknold introduces the term "historicism" into his discussion, defining it as "a kind of relativism which makes the truth conditional upon historical context," an error which both Pope Pius XII and French theologian Réginald Garrigou-Lagrange identified with this "new theology." He concludes that Jacques Maritain's "early worry that 'the new theologians' were playing the early Church Fathers to the music of Hegel has proven prescient." In his conclusion, Pecknold draws out the errors of Hegelian historicism into the basic assumptions grounding much of modern Catholic theology, assumptions which set these theologies at odds with the Catholic tradition dating back to the Church Fathers.

Following Pecknold, Christopher J. Malloy examines Karl Rahner's theology in depth and critically. Malloy traces Rahner's transcendental anthropology from its basis in Kant, "identifying how man questions and listens, so as to determine the conditions of credibility for Christianity." He shows how, because of Rahner's wish to avoid finitizing God, it is therefore impossible to "name God." He suggests that among the troubling pastoral implications of Rahner's views on God and grace, "these claims dissuade us from seeking the face of God, . . . the height of human aspiration," while they also result in "[obscuring] the distinction of the first and second commandments (Matt 22:37–40)," with

1

the consequence that certain theologians and even bishops today "[reduce] the greatest commandment [to] the love of neighbor." Moreover, Rahner's theology decentralizes Christianity as the privileged revealed religion. Malloy then traces the basis of Rahner's notion of the "supernatural existential" with reference to Heidegger's philosophy. He defines the supernatural existential in Rahner's terms as "the self-communication of God *in the mode of offer*" that is given to every human being at conception. This offer is not to be identified with sanctifying grace. It is not part of human nature. Malloy also shows that Rahner's concepts of the Trinity and Jesus Christ are out of place in the Catholic tradition, proceeding as they do along Hegelian lines. Rahner's position on the sacraments also deviates from the Catholic tradition. Whereas the tradition holds that sacraments communicate grace to the recipient, in Rahner's view, sacraments symbolize grace that is already present in the world. Thus, for example, the Eucharist expresses the communion with Christ that recipients already enjoy by living in the world. Malloy objects that in the Catholic tradition "the Eucharist is nourishment, not a bill of health," as Rahner would have it. He traces the consequences of Rahner's theology for pastoral activity. Rahner would render baptism unnecessary as a remedy for original sin; he views the Church as the full historical manifestation of grace already present in the world, a view which puts into question the Church's missionary activity aimed at evangelization. As a result of Rahner's views on the Church, "in her sacraments, the Church does not bring new grace to a needy world; rather, she offers signs of the grace of the *world*."

Thomas Heinrich Stark investigates Walter Kasper's theology along Hegelian lines, and in doing so critiques Kasper's linkage between theological truth and historicity. Stark notes that large segments of modern theology have separated themselves from a philosophical basis in Scholasticism, substituting it with an odd mixture of Kant, Hegel, and Husserl, with the result that "theology has for some time been using somewhat softer, more literary-essayistic forms of philosophy or has adopted borrowings from them, for example from Nietzsche, Heidegger, existentialism, and recently postmodernism." Stark contends that "the basic problem of Kasper's theology lies in its dependence on certain philosophical positions of German Idealism." Kasper's reliance upon history as a medium for theology leads him to consider both the Church and Scripture merely as a "historical event." As a consequence, he maintains that the New Testament does not "succeed everywhere to the same extent in capturing the truth and reality of Jesus Christ." Moreover, the Church, in the words of Kasper, "does not simply have the truth, but must seek it anew over and over again," so that "a pure Denzinger theology becomes a thing of the past." Dogmatic credal formulae, such as the Nicene-Constantinopolitan Creed, are only "indispensable signs and symbols for the faith, but not actually the 'object' of the faith." Again, in the words of Kasper, "tradition is not 'the continual repetition of the original truth in its unhistorical form, but rather the continual reproduction of this truth in ever new historical forms.'" But Kasper allows these new historical forms to depart radically from the original apostolic word, provided they retain what he refers to as the apostolic "spirit." "Not every dogma can be reintroduced into every new overall scheme," Kasper argues. Dogmatic formulations can thus outlive their utility and even die. The Magisterium, too, is subject to the principles of Hegelian dialectic. Magisterial propositions, in Kasper's view, must accord with a consensus within the Church, one that takes into account its distinct groupings. To this argument, Stark replies, "it is by no means the case that communication and consensus-building constitute or transform the truth according to constantly changing contextual conditions or according to the demands of some 'pastoral praxis' or other." Stark neatly summarizes the consequences of Kasper's line of thinking by concluding that "in theology politics is slowly replacing philosophy." Stark observes ominously that "it is hard to avoid the impression that leading forces in the Church are currently pursuing the aim of pushing through a reform of the Church along Kasper's lines, in which changing the Church's moral teaching is just the beginning—albeit a weighty one." To Kasper's assertion that infallibility applies to "living historical authorities" and not to "lifeless" and "rigid" propositions, Stark replies that "the Church does indeed teach the infallibility of certain statements, i.e., of certain propositions." Stark comments, "the dogma that Jesus 'is wholly God and wholly human' is for Kasper not only 'in need of interpretation'—which goes without saying—but also 'capable of being superseded'. This spontaneously raises the question: *superseded with what* and, above all, *to what end*?" But for Kasper, the Christian is the person who "holds the whole faith in a fundamental way even if he does not espouse all the conclusions that the Church has drawn from this message over the course of almost two millennia," to which Stark replies, "If that really is all, then we have a serious problem."

Rahner and Kasper are two examples of dogmatic theologians whose adherence to German idealism dislodges their theologies from the Catholic tradition.

Bernhard Häring, on the other hand, could be called the father of post-Vatican II moral theology. Häring's influence on the course of modern moral theology has been tremendous. Edmund Waldstein, O.Cist., offers a critical assessment of Häring's theology. He does so initially by drawing a contrast between the moral theology of Häring and that found in the Catechism of the Catholic Church: "the approach of the moral part of the *Catechism* represents a path in post-conciliar theology distinct from that taken by Häring." Specifically, Waldstein argues, "one of the most important differences between the two approaches is discernible in the way in which they use philosophy, and particularly in the way in which they see the relation between nature and human history." Whereas the Thomist tradition at the base of the Catechism understands nature "as the impression in things of the eternal wisdom of God, serving as a principle of movement towards the good," Häring "tends to relativize such insights as being too tied to the obsolete 'static' categories of Greek metaphysical thought and thinks they have to be modified or replaced by a more dynamic and 'historicist' understanding of nature, and a more 'personalistic' understanding of moral good." In Waldstein's view, the historicist and personalistic approaches of Häring "lead him into serious errors, such as the denial of the Church's perennial teaching on the immorality of artificial contraception." Waldstein argues that theologians "who try to be 'biblical' without philosophical reflection are indeed condemned to read Scripture in the light of the implicit philosophy that they imbibe from the intellectual climate of their own time." Häring criticizes seventeenth-century moral theology as narrowly focused on sin, but for Waldstein, "that narrow focus was also the result of that epoch's lack of a full account of natural teleology," a crisis that "consisted above all in the rejection of Aristotle's philosophy of nature." As a consequence, Häring's moral theology lacks any appreciation for the philosophical underpinnings of natural law, "the moral law written in the hearts of men by the Creator." Häring, in Waldstein's view, "tries to replace a moral theology that involves law with a moral theology of the free response of the Christian to the love of God given in Christ." He thus exalts the role of the individual's conscience, "which might initially be an erring conscience, but which will gradually lead him to a better understanding of what God's love calls him to." Häring thus concludes, in the words of Waldstein, that in terms of an individual following the Church's moral teachings, "even if the Church is right about the matter in hand, it is better for authorities not to apply any pressure on someone who disagrees in conscience—as if following an erroneous conscience is necessarily sinless." For Waldstein, Häring "thinks that there are cases where conscience is in fact right and the 'objective norm' laid down by the Church is wrong." Waldstein concludes, "one can see here the influence of modern romanticism and historicism on Häring's thought." Here one can also find the influence of Hegel on Häring, for whom "history is the judge of which social developments are in accordance with the flourishing of human freedom and which are not." Waldstein observes that "the current craze for 'sex change' operations is an example of this. A man determines through listening to the voice of inner desire that he is in fact a woman, and then rationalist technology is brought to bear on the *res extensa* of his body to change it to a female body, so that he can live 'authentically.'" In the end, Häring "thinks that the proper response to God's love is worked out slowly through history, and that the Church, by listening to the prophetic voice of persons who stand up to her in conscience, learns that certain things impede our making a proper response to God's love." Finally, for Waldstein, Häring concludes that "the resistance of the popes to his theology" as, for example, in the encyclical letter of Pope Saint John Paul II, *Veritatis splendor*, "was a sign of their betrayal of the Second Vatican Council's dynamic vision of reality." In concluding his essay, Waldstein argues that "the truly 'prophetic' role of conscience is not to insist on private opinion, backed up by the custom of our time, against the perennial teachings of the Church. Rather, the truly prophetic act of conscience is to allow oneself to be led by the perennial teaching of the eternal truth."

In the final essay of this first part of the book, John M. Rist examines the concept of heresy as it has been understood in the past and as it operates in the Church today. He points out that heresies may be "conservative" or "liberal"; conservative heresies arise from internal struggles in the Church over conservation of the "faith of our fathers," whereas liberal heresies arise over interactions with external forces aiming to pressure the Church to conform to anti-Catholic observances. Today's heresies are more "moral" than "dogmatic," Rist argues, although the foundations of moral heresies often involve dogmatic positions such as the denial of Christ's divinity (Arianism) or of the effects of original sin on human nature (Pelagianism). For Rist, "the history of Christianity may be viewed as a recurring disentanglement of Christian thought from the cultural and intellectual assumptions of its times: or rather a gradual discernment of what in the cultural environment is compatible with Christianity." Rist observes that many patterns of thought in the West are based today in "thinkers hostile

5

to Catholic doctrine" such as Kant and other Enlightenment philosophers responsible for advancing the concept of human autonomy—a position that finds its religious correlation in Pelagianism. Autonomy gives birth to "choice," as it does in the pro-abortion option in society, and this pressure for human autonomy in society makes it difficult for certain "Catholics" to distance themselves from the pro-abortion position. With choice comes "individualism," wherein "individual choices are authoritative," a view that leads to the "rejection of legitimate authority" and the relativizing of truth along Hegelian lines. "With truth relativized, there can be no fundamental authority other than the power of those able to call the moral, social, political, and ecclesiastical shots." European and North American churchmen are immersed in just this environment, and for this reason the Church has become "indecisive about moral standards where the secular world energetically denies them." Rist sees that the pressure to camouflage deviation in moral norms with an appeal to the "signs of the times" is "exerted at the highest levels of the hierarchical Church." Part of the reason for this demoralizing situation, in Rist's view, is the existence of a papal court along with courtiers eager to please the pope, creating thereby a new variation of ultramontanism. Rist observes that this subservience to the views of the pope was clearly exhibited by the behavior of the Maltese bishops over *Amoris laetitia*. Rist traces some responsibility for this development back to the First Vatican Council's definition of papal infallibility, a doctrine so little understood that it has served to bolster any and all papal pronouncements into a form of truth, thus providing individual bishops and bishops' conferences with cover for their own lack of courage to disagree with the pope. Rist faults modern media along with the tendencies of popes to broadcast their every viewpoint through the media, even granting interviews with the press during papal air flights, for distortions in Catholic teaching. He is also critical of the rhetorical device whereby the pope says one thing one day to placate conservatives while liberals are free to interpret his statement as a sop to their opponents. But such papal "ambiguity" can also be a strategy to bring about subversive changes in Church doctrine. Rist then turns his attention to the sexual revolution beginning in the 1960s. On the issue of the liberation of women, the Second Vatican Council "was sadly unprepared, and when 'enlightened,' inclined to naïveté, forgetting the ubiquity of original sin." Rist holds that those ecclesiastical debates involving a "revolutionary" dynamic will result in the extreme position winning out over the moderate position. Divorce, remarriage, contraception, abortion, and homosexual relations are all examples of this dynamic at work in modern Catholicism. "Homosexual acts, . . . once damnable, were now by no tiny a group of influential theologians and bishops—ever keen to appease if not actually to practice—held to be blessable." Rist also avers that "after Vatican II many Catholic universities, recognizing their own intellectual failings, supposed they had to choose between being Catholic and being intellectual—and chose to remain Catholic only in name and shame." He concludes, "failure to conform to the new *Zeitgeist* leads to extreme unpopularity both within and without the Catholic (indeed the wider Christian) community. We are the new prudes, the new merciless; how can we expect to be loved by the media and its clients?" He adds, "if a bishop or pope is loved and approved by our secular media, he is probably not doing his job; for to *keep* them on side he will have to let it be known that abortion should be put 'on the back burner': as well as that he loves the poor and the environment: as he should—and as he knows will win him secular, if often hypocritical, plaudits." Rist criticizes the "Scripture studies guild" in the Catholic Church for altogether dismissing or rewriting the direct teachings of Jesus on marriage and sexual morality, leading to the kind of relativizing of Catholic doctrine by which "we can all construct our own morality in the 'spirit' of the Gospels." Rist concludes, "though the Church has often been less than merciful in the treatment meted out to sin, yet no doctrinal 'improvement' is acceptable which entails denying Christ's specific commands, hence in effect denying his authority and divinity. Neither pope nor council can authorize forgiveness without demanding avoidance—or at least sincere attempt at avoidance—of the sins forgiven."

Rist's essay concludes the first part of this book concerning the negative effects of German idealism on Catholic theology throughout the twentieth century, in particular, of the doctrinal and moral relativism produced by the influence of historicism. The second part of the book looks at five traditional sources of theology: magisterial teachings, the deposit of faith *as* developed, the sense of the faithful, Scripture, and Church councils, and distinguishes orthodox treatments of these sources from heterodox treatments. Hence, whereas the first part of the book responds to the question of what went wrong with Catholic theology since the Second Vatican Council, the second part of the book indicates how Catholic doctrinal and moral theology can maintain orthodoxy.

Edward Feser begins his essay with an examination of the nature of the Magisterium. The magisterial authority of the Church is "the infallible organ through which Christ's revelation is communicated to the human race." It is "the successors of the Apostles—the bishops, led by Peter's successor, the pope" who inherit the commission that Christ gave to the apostles. "Documents, whether they be conciliar decrees, encyclical letters, catechisms, or what have you, are 'magisterial' because they express the mind of the Church as the moral person through whom Christ speaks." But not all Church documents have equal weight, "because the Church does not always intend to teach with the same degree of finality." Feser goes on to explain the differences between definitive and non-definitive teaching as also between ordinary and extraordinary Magisterium. He then turns his attention to explaining how and why it can sometimes be justifiable for the faithful to correct the Church's pastors. "Bishops, including popes, have no authority, then, either to invent novel doctrines or to contradict the deliverances of Scripture and Tradition. Their duty is rather to preserve and proclaim the deliverances of Scripture and Tradition." What this means in practice is that popes and bishops have no authority when it comes to "*contradicting* Scripture and Tradition, or *manufacturing out of whole cloth* some teaching that has no basis in Scripture or Tradition." Feser then summarizes the five categories of magisterial statements along with the degree of submission that they require from the faithful. He pays particular attention to a 1990 document from the Congregation for the Doctrine of the Faith entitled *Instruction on the Ecclesial Vocation of the Theologian*, which is also known by its Latin title, *Donum veritatis*. This document explicitly details the conditions under which theologians may make suggestions concerning the revision of magisterial teachings. Feser also discusses at length "prudential judgments" in magisterial teachings that are advisory rather than binding. In this connection, he also examines the question of whether and under which conditions a theologian who dissents from magisterial teaching may publicize his objections in appropriate media. He goes on to demonstrate "the historical precedent of errant pastors, including even popes, who have been rebuked by the faithful for failing to uphold traditional teaching." In this section of his essay, Feser treats Saint Thomas Aquinas's discussion in the *Summa theologiae* of this kind of fraternal correction of pastors, including popes. Feser also finds support for the fraternal correction of bishops and popes from several authorities throughout the Church's history, including in the writings of Saint Robert Bellarmine and Saint John Henry Newman.

The issue of development of doctrine is so essential to this wider discussion and so hotly debated within the Church today that the second part of this book dedicates two essays to the matter. The first, by Eduardo Echeverria, traces the issue back to the patristic writer Saint Vincent of Lérins in his chief work, the *Commonitorium* (AD 434). The central question addressed by Saint Vincent in this work is "if true development is possible, then, how does one distinguish it from corruptions of the faith?" Significant to Vincent's discussion is "the principle that development of doctrine should preserve 'what has been believed everywhere, always, and by all' (*quod ubique, quod semper, quod ab omnibus creditum est*)." Along with this principle, Vincent comments "on the way that development should be organic: 'growth of religion in the soul should be like the growth of the body, which in the course of years develops and unfolds, yet remains the same as it was.'" In terms of this development, "differing expressions of the propositional truths of faith must keep the same meaning and the same judgment": "*in eodem scilicet dogmate, eodem sensu eademque sententia.*" Echeverria points out that while Saint Vincent only considered definitive teachings, it is possible to examine in a manner consonant with Vincent's principles "the matter of alterations with respect to non-definitive teaching." In this connection, Echeverria examines some of the teachings of the Second Vatican Council with respect to Saint Vincent's theory of development of doctrine.

The second essay concerning development of doctrine examines the writings of Saint John Henry Newman, who is almost always cited by progressivist theologians as an advocate for a theory of development that results in their own erroneous expressions of Church doctrine, something that Newman opposes vigorously. Kevin L. Flannery, S.J., explains the genesis in Newman's earlier writings of the mature expression of his thought on this issue in his 1848 work, *An Essay on the Development of Christian Doctrine* (revised in 1878), and in 1870 in *An Essay in Aid of the Grammar of Assent*. Flannery shows a continuity between Newman's thought on this subject and that expressed in 434 by Saint Vincent of Lérins whereby "ideas might remain in essence the same even when elaborated logically." In the second part of the 1878 edition of *Development of Doctrine*, Newman treats "doctrinal developments viewed relatively to doctrinal corruptions." It is here that one finds his famous seven "notes" concerning the proper sense of doctrinal development. Flannery offers an explanation of each of these notes in the same order in which Newman discusses them: (1) preservation of type or species, (2) continuity of principles, (3) assimilative power, (4) logical sequence, (5) anticipation of its future, (6) conservative action on its past, and (7) chronic vigor. In regard to the second note, "the basic idea is that a proposed development's espousal of a principle inconsistent with what Newman identifies as the 'continuous principles' of Christianity is indicative that the proposed development is actually a corruption." Concerning the fourth note, Newman refers to "the way in which certain practices follow logically from more basic Christian ideas, although not necessarily as conclusions follow from premises in a syllogism." In terms of the fifth note, Newman means that "our finding in the Church's first centuries practices and ideas corresponding to later practices and ideas constitutes evidence that these latter are genuine developments." Newman, in the sixth note, "says that certain developments appear 'at first sight to contradict that out of which they grew' but are in fact their 'protection or illustration.'" As an example of this note, Newman argues that devotion to the Mother of God does not detract from, but rather strengthens, devotion to Christ. Taken together, all of these notes distance the thought of Saint John Henry Newman from the abuses of his teaching committed by those progressivist theologians who wish to cite him in favor of changes to Church doctrine that are not compatible with these criteria for faithful development.

Robert Dodaro, O.S.A., offers an explanation of the correct way to understand three terms in theology—"sense of the faith" (*sensus fidei*), "sense of the faithful" (*sensus fidelium*), and "consensus of the faithful" (*consensus fidelium*)—according to the teaching of the Catholic Church. He argues that "such a clarification is necessary because of the abuse of these terms—especially 'sense of the faithful'—by many theologians who misuse them as an argument in favor of changing defined Church teachings." Following a set of definitions for these terms, he discusses "sense of the faithful" in relation to public opinion polls that are frequently used erroneously in order to argue for changes in Church doctrine and practice. Public opinion polls, Dodaro argues, are the "crux of the difficulty" with any contemporary use of the term "sense of the faithful." Warnings about mistaking majority opinion for the sense of the faithful are common in magisterial writings, in particular, in Pope Saint John Paul II's document *Familiaris consortio*. In conjunction with this examination, Dodaro discusses "the specious concept of 'the faithful' in some theological treatments of the term." He then treats the question of how precisely the Church can consult the lay faithful on matters of doctrine and the risks inherent in doing so. This essay focuses great attention on the Magisterium's rejection of public opinion polls as a means of gauging the sense of the faithful, as well as the Church's preferred means of consulting the laity over doctrinal matters.

In an essay on the apostolicity and historicity of Scripture, author John Finnis calls "the Church's teaching about the truth of the Gospels" a "model of developed doctrine." Finnis distinguishes his use of the term "historicity" from that generated by German idealism and says that by it he means *historically true*, corresponding to *what really happened*." He takes the term, thus defined, from the Second Vatican Council's key document concerning divine revelation, *Dei Verbum*. Not only does the Council thus affirm the historical truth of the events recorded in the four Gospels, it teaches that they "*authentically* transmit the oral teaching and preaching of the Apostles." Based as it is in this conciliar teaching affirmed throughout *Dei Verbum*, but especially in chapters 18 and 19, Finnis's essay, with meticulous documentation concerning the genesis of this document, runs counter to the findings of most modern New Testament exegesis. The apostles, Finnis argues, "spoke truly and sincerely—with probity, with honesty—about *what they as eyewitnesses remembered*, or what they had been told by others who likewise saw, heard, and remembered." Hence Finnis pours scorn on "the burial of the developed doctrine as soon as its affirmation of the historical truth of the Gospels had been solemnly taught by the Council." He shows how postconciliar exegetes set aside this dogmatic teaching of the Council in favor of a portrayal of the "Gospels and their formation not so much as developments as, to an extent now unascertainable, substitutions." "In the name of historical criticism, all such biblical scholarship and teaching ignores and defies the Church's definitive doctrine." Finnis calls this commonplace error in interpretation of the Gospels "doctrinal error of the gravest kind, but it is also, and first, bad history—defective because insufficiently critical." Finnis explains the charge that modern Gospel exegesis represents "bad history" by means of copious references to the biblical texts themselves, supported by a series of affirmations throughout *Dei Verbum* of the truth and apostolicity of the record of events and teachings of Jesus found in New Testament passages, affirmations that he states are sorely lacking in most magisterial documents since the promulgation of *Dei Verbum*.

In the final essay in this second part of the book, Guy Mansini, O.S.B., examines the pertinent question of the "teaching authority of national conferences of bishops," along with regional synods, an issue rekindled of late by the fact that "national conferences are thought by some to be a possible instrument unto the end of a renewed Church." Mansini begins his study with reference to the sacramental welcome that the Church extends to all people "because the Church is a sacramental reality." He notes that there are several challenges to this welcome, characterized by the rising number of divorced and remarried Catholics, by homosexual unions, by different religious evaluations of marriage and celibacy, and by the disproportionate number of women as compared to men who are religiously interested. For these reasons and others that he enumerates, Mansini points out that "regional assemblies of bishops, bishops who listen to the voice of their faithful people, can be expected to be centers for that adaptation of Church practice and Church teaching that will make the Church contemporary." He describes the existing canonical legislation concerning episcopal conferences as presented in *Apostolos suos*, a document issued by Pope Saint John Paul II in 1998. Mansini explains that "this legislation rather keeps the national conferences tied relatively strictly to the Roman center." Mansini defends this status quo on historical and theological grounds, stemming from the role of Saint Peter codified by Christ in the Gospels and the fact that the pope is regarded as the successor of Peter while the bishops are seen as successors of the apostles. The Second Vatican Council clarified the concept of the "college" of bishops with the pope as the head of the college. Mansini then turns to the central question of the current debate: "Can the encouragement of the council extend to giving such conferences, or regional synods, an authority to teach, like that of the entire college of bishops with and under the pope, in such a way as to bind everyone to the same teaching?" He replies succinctly, "The answer is no." "The answer is no because no national group of bishops can exercise authority in the same way as can the entire college of bishops when they find themselves to be in moral unanimity on the truth of some teaching." Moreover, as *Apostolos suos* argues, "the moral unanimity of a local episcopal assembly *can* be resisted by dissenters, however few they may be." In line with this principle, Mansini clarifies on Eucharistic theological grounds that "each particular Church is under strict obligation to be open to all the other particular churches." To the argument that the different cultures within the Church can be understood as different sources of theology, Mansini responds that "insofar as different cultures produce contradictory and therefore divisive views of reality, however, they cannot be subsumed into the effort to express Christian truth without correction and emendation," and "that the Gospel corrects, it is not corrected by, cultures." Concerning the authority of local synods and councils, Mansini points out that "the sign that the teaching was authentic and of God was the reception of this teaching by the whole Church, Rome included. Nothing has changed." He concludes, "episcopal conferences and synods ... by their nature as partial gatherings of episcopal authority, cannot usurp the voice of the whole, or pretend to speak to their local churches, nationally or regionally gathered, in the way the whole of the college can speak to the whole Church."

The editor of this volume and I are grateful to His Eminence Robert Cardinal Sarah for the Afterword he has contributed to the book. His words and encouragement enrich the offering of essays accomplished in this work.

PART ONE

THE RISE AND FALL OF MODERN CATHOLIC THEOLOGY

C. C. Pecknold

Contemporary Catholic theologians tend to divide up theology historically, as if the patristic, medieval, and modern "periods" give us some privileged way of categorizing thought and understanding reality. Yet, this tendency betrays a certain kind of relativism which has made its way into modern Catholic theology. More precisely, it is a sophisticated and subtle form of skepticism sometimes called "historicism." Historicism says that theology must always be understood and assessed "in context," according to the exigencies of the time and place in which those theologies arose and, therefore, in a way that cuts them off from the larger context of the Church's Tradition since it holds that defined doctrine is subject to historical change. In this essay, I seek to identify this as one of the fundamental characteristics of modern Catholic thought. I will show how this tendency arose philosophically, how it entered into Catholic theology, and what it has cost the Church.

PHILOSOPHICAL BACKGROUND

Skepticism is not, of course, a uniquely modern problem. In the days leading up to his baptism, in philosophical discussion with friends and pupils at Cassiciacum, Saint Augustine treats one of the last great obstacles to the Catholic faith: skepticism. In *Contra academicos*, Augustine refutes those who "hold that everything is a matter of doubt" and who believe that "we can know nothing for certain" as laughable.[1] No one, not even the skeptics, really lives in a skeptical way. The traveler looking for his destination is unlikely to arrive at it by way of "doubting everything." Rather, we are rational creatures who are made to know the truth, to be united to wisdom itself! This alone can make the rational soul happy. Augustine never tires of showing that skepticism is an enemy of morality because it throws up obstacles before the intellect that also impede us from living the good life. Augustine offered in place of skepticism a metaphysical realism that believed that the world was intelligible and that our rational souls were made to know the world through sense images, about which we could make judgments and reason to true conclusions. This was standard among the early Church Fathers, and certainly the medieval schoolman, until the rise in the fourteenth century of a new skepticism called nominalism.

The metaphysical realists of the thirteenth century—such as Saint Thomas Aquinas and Blessed John Duns Scotus—understood that the world was intelligible and that it corresponded to heavenly perfections they called "universals." That is to say, the metaphysical realists all believed that the intelligibility of this world was derived not from us but from the Creator. Both the high Platonic realism of Scotus and the more moderate Aristotelian realism of Aquinas believed that we could come to know the eternal principles, the universals, through the particular things which God has made. William of Ockham (1287–1347) attempted to obliterate this metaphysical realism with a denial of universals altogether. Ockham's famous "razor"—"do not multiply entities beyond necessity"—was intended to cut the particular off from correspondence to universals. Ockham introduced *haecitas*—the "thisness" of particulars—as a new philosophical foundation. Having rejected universals, all that remained were particulars and how we name (*nominare*) them. Thus, "nominalism" was a new constructivist metaphysics in which the individual alone exists as one who names particular things. The individual can name resemblances between things, but those resemblances are not real. Since there are no universals or any correspondence between created things and universal realities, what we call ideas or concepts or natures are really just names (*nomina*) which we have given to them.

An illustration of nominalism that is often given is paper currency. The paper on which a five-dollar bill and a one-hundred-dollar bill are printed is worth the same—in fact, it is worth almost nothing—but what makes these

---

[1] Augustine, *Retractiones*, bk. 1, ch. 1, a. 1.

bills different is the value or name that we give to them. Now, this is perfectly true about paper currency, but the nominalist thinks this is just how the whole of reality is known by us. The nominalist will not say that John and Peter both partake of a common human nature; rather, to speak of a common human nature is just extrinsically to give a name to their common resemblances. Thus, in the strict sense, the nominalist can only recognize the particular individual as real, not human nature as such. This represents a profound skepticism which emerges in the fourteenth century and sets off a series of reactions, first with Luther's post-nominalist protest in the sixteenth century, and then with the so-called Enlightenment of Kant in the eighteenth century. Luther's rejection of philosophy and Kant's rejection of our intellectual capacity to know the invisible God through the things which have been made are direct descendants of this fundamental reduction of metaphysical realism.

While it is true that Immanuel Kant (1724–1804) is rightly seen as the father of modern thought, we should remember that his thought was largely made possible by the metaphysical skepticism of Ockham. Kant's revolution in philosophy was, like Ockham's nominalism, highly sophisticated. Rather than offer a nominalist conventionalism about "naming," Kant argued that human understanding is the source of all our knowledge of the ideas, principles, or general laws of nature that, in turn, shape our experience of the world. While the Catholic Ockham still believed that God reveals the moral law by divine decree, Kant believed that the moral law comes to us by way of reason alone. Most important for our purposes, however, is to see that Kant famously denied traditional demonstrations of God's existence which classical, metaphysically realist philosophers had offered over the course of history: both the ontological argument of Saint Anselm and much of what is summarized by Saint Thomas's "five ways."

Kant's rejection of the ontological argument of Anselm is similar to objections which had been made before him by even Aquinas himself. Anselm had argued that even one who did not believe in God could at least agree that it was possible to conceive of the existence of such a "nothing greater" and that, since it was something greater to exist in reality than in the mind only, "the fool" must admit that God must exist in reality and not only as a concept.[2] Kant says that the argument is circular because it includes the judgment that God exists in the premise that God is "that than which nothing greater can

---

[2] Anselm, *Proslogion*, ch. 2.

be thought." Since the concept of existence is utterly derived from our own experience of the world, Kant thinks that it does not deliver our understanding to the transcendent reality but only to our creaturely concept of existence. As such, it fails as a demonstration of God's existence. Kant similarly dismisses the cosmological argument, or rather the argument from contingency and necessity, as wholly dependent on the ontological argument. While he admires arguments from design, such as Saint Thomas's teleological argument, he does not think even that argument truly brings the mind to knowledge of God as Creator. While not a nominalist in the strict sense, Kant effectively argues that there are no demonstrations of God's existence which escape our categories or lead to certain knowledge of the true God, and thus he remains agnostic about what the natural intellect can know about God's existence and nature. Kant does believe that there is a transcending dimension in our experience of phenomena; however, although he is agnostic about what reason can know of God, he does believe that we do know something of God in the furthest reaches of the transcendent horizon of our experience. In this way, not unlike Ockham himself, Kant remained a skeptic in his philosophy and a pietist in his theology.

Kant's view that God is so transcendent as to be inaccessible within the bounds of reason finds a harmonic counterpoint in Georg Wilhelm Friedrich Hegel (1770–1831). Simply put, Hegel argues the opposite: God was radically immanent in the unfolding of human history, known to us in and through our communal experience of time. As a response to Enlightenment rationalism, Hegel "dialectically" both accepts and rejects Kant's infinitely transcendent God, even as he dialectically accepts and rejects the romantic subjectivity which flowed from it. Where Kant might lead to an individualistic and pietistic conclusion concerning our knowledge of God (by way of *Gefühl*, or religious feeling), Hegel argues that the best argument for God was demonstrably experienced in the unfolding of history.

For Hegel, God is "absolute" and Christianity is an "absolute religion." Abstracting from the doctrine of the Trinity, Hegel imagines that God is the absolute in the process of coming to greater self-understanding through a dialectical unfolding of his divine love in human history. The absolute, or universal, chooses to move out of itself to the historically particular—a kenotic movement which non-identically recurs as God pours out this divine love into a common life of *Geist*, which must be represented by cult, sacrifice, and a *Sittlichkeit* or moral order. This is, of course, an *ek-stasis* which is supposed

THE RISE AND FALL OF MODERN CATHOLIC THEOLOGY

to mirror philosophically the Christian faith in the Incarnation of the Son, as well as mirror his death and resurrection which opens the way to Pentecost and the creation of the Church.

But Hegel universalized this as idealist philosophy. And in the process, he radically transformed the orthodox Christian understanding of the Triune God into something quite different. Hegel does not see God as "the true font of light and wisdom and the primal origin raised high beyond things," because in the most dramatic way possible, Hegel believes that "God is not God without the world."[3]

To some, especially Protestant theologians, it could seem that Hegel was saving Christian theology from the rationalism of the Enlightenment, which had made God so transcendent as to be radically inaccessible to us. Now, these theologians would argue, Hegel has reversed this trend and made God very close to us. Yet, in truth, Hegel subverts orthodox Christian teaching. Instead of thinking about God raised "high beyond all things," Hegel would now have us think of the interdependence of God and the world. For Hegel, there is no real gratuity at all. God needs the world, and the world needs God. In this way there is never the possibility of thanking God for a gift that need not have been given. God must give himself ecstatically to the world, which is other than himself, but which is also becoming himself through the movement of history.

Charles Taylor notes that Hegel could be considered the original "death of God" theologian. Citing a Lutheran hymn, "God himself is dead," Hegel argues that God unites death to his nature.[4] This is so radical that whenever we encounter suffering and death, we can say that we taste the particularities of the eternal divine "history." As Hegel puts it, "This is not a single act but the eternal divine history: it is a moment in the nature of God himself; it has taken place in God himself."[5] We might say that, for Hegel, God's immanence in history is so total that the divine nature is itself historical, or rather an eternal divine history. While Hegel is notoriously difficult to understand, not least in his lectures on religion, what he says about Christ's suffering is illuminating: the Cross discloses the eternal reality—namely, that the ecstatic suffering of self-disruption is necessary for God to be God. Later Protestant

---

[3] Georg Wilhelm Friedrich Hegel, *Lectures on the Philosophy of Religion* (Berlin: Duncker and Humblot, 1832); cf. Charles Taylor, *Hegel* (Cambridge: Cambridge University Press, 1975).

[4] Taylor, *Hegel*, 326.

[5] Taylor, *Hegel*.

theologians, such as Jürgen Moltmann, will take this self-disruption to be not simply the "self-emptying" of the Second Person of the Trinity in his missions; but rather, Christ's death on the Cross would be understood as disclosing an eternal intra-Trinitarian suffering. The Hegelian theologian argues that God suffers in us, just as "we participate in the Trinitarian process of God's history," for in the dialectical unfolding of history which enables our inclusion in the divine life "even Auschwitz is in God himself."[6] This collapsing of the eternal Trinity into the economy of the Trinitarian missions in creation is a kind of panentheism that gives us a God who suffers but not one who really saves. Hegel's God does not save the world so much as reveal his identity with it. His philosophy cannot be said to solve the Kantian problem of God's transcendence; it instead creates a new Hegelian problem of divine immanence and a false divinization of the world through history.

As we have seen, the modern philosophical challenge to metaphysical realism either tended to make God utterly inaccessible to the natural light of human intellect, as with Immanuel Kant, or it tended to make God so utterly immanent within time as to deny that God truly is raised high beyond all things. As a result, modern philosophy tended to return to familiar pagan propensities to make God either the soul of the world or to make him utterly unknowable. This left theologians wanting "dialogue" with modern philosophy to reckon with an entirely new set of categories that, wherever adopted, introduced confusion and obscurity into how theologians understood the Church's teaching. The effects of such philosophical errors can be seen in fundamental and dogmatic theology alike.

THE RISE AND FALL OF *LA NOUVELLE THÉOLOGIE*

Many of these modern philosophical trends influenced a complex phenomenon in twentieth-century theology which came to be called "*la nouvelle théologie.*" "The new theology" was not a repetition of modern metaphysical errors, nor was it a simple theological embrace of modernity. It is fair to say that such a diverse movement is difficult to categorize and summarize. Yet one of the first great critics of *nouvelle théologie*, Réginald Garrigou-Lagrange (who also coined the phrase), argued that whatever the merits of any individual theologian, the

---

[6] Jürgen Moltmann, *The Crucified God: The Cross of Christ as the Foundation and Criticism of Christian Theology* (New York: Harper and Row, 1974), 255, 277.

movement itself had certain common characteristics that were entirely too influenced by a historicist and relativist view of truth.

Sympathetic critics, such as Jacques Maritain, had already worried that some of the new theologians were "reinventing the Fathers of the Church to the music of Hegel."[7] In 1946, Pope Pius XII asked the Jesuits at their General Congregation, "If we were to accept [the new theology] what would become of the unchangeable dogmas of the Catholic Faith; and what would become of the unity and stability of that Faith?"[8] As an advisor to the Holy Office, Garrigou-Lagrange sought to answer that question in his 1946 essay "La Nouvelle Théologie où va-t-elle?" in the *Revue Thomiste*.

Garrigou-Lagrange begins his essay with the words of a prominent Jesuit theologian, Henri Bouillard: "As the mind evolves, *an unchangeable truth* cannot be preserved except by virtue of a simultaneous and correlative evolution of all concepts, which retain a stable and recognizable relationship to that truth. *A theology that is not up-to-date is a false theology*."[9] Bouillard's deepest claim was that modern thought had abandoned Aristotelian metaphysics, and so theology must be brought "up-to-date" to reflect the "unchangeable truths" of Christianity with new concepts. Garrigou-Lagrange asks, "How are we to avoid the conclusion that if the theology of St. Thomas is no longer up-to-date, it is therefore a false theology?" Are the teachings of popes and councils also now false because they are now not "up-to-date"? Without metaphysically realist accounts of nature and substance, for example, must we now say that "transubstantiation" is a false Eucharistic theology? Are we to conclude that new evolutionary accounts of "being as becoming" must update our understanding of the hypostatic union of Christ's two natures defined by the Council of Chalcedon?[10] Garrigou-Lagrange is certain that whatever his good intentions, Bouillard shows us a fundamental problem with *la nouvelle théologie*: it has exchanged the traditional definition of truth (conformity of one's judgment to extra-mental reality and its unchangeable laws) for a philosophy that requires an ever-evolving or "historicist" definition of truth.

Pope Pius XII would shortly thereafter, in his 1950 encyclical *Humani*

---

[7] Quoted in Aidan Nichols, "Thomism and the Nouvelle Théologie," *The Thomist* 64 (2000): 1–19, at 7.

[8] Pope Pius XII, Address *"Quamvis inquieti"* to the Fathers of the Society of Jesus Delegates in General Congregation XXIX (1946).

[9] Réginald Garrigou-Lagrange, "La nouvelle théologie où va-t-elle?," *Angelicum* 23 (1946): 126–45.

[10] Garrigou-Lagrange, "La nouvelle théologie."

Generis, condemn "a certain historicism, which attributing value only to the events of man's life, overthrows the foundation of all truth and absolute law, both on the level of philosophical speculations and especially to Christian dogmas."[11] This "historicism," which we highlighted at the opening of this essay as a kind of relativism that makes the truth conditional upon historical context, is precisely what Garrigou-Lagrange thought was at work in the new theology. It was not that the new theologians were arriving at clearly heretical claims at every turn, but rather that their tacit adoption of relativizing conceptual systems lauded their treatment of the truths of the faith, whether they were turning to patristic and medieval *ressourcement* or contemporary *aggiornamento.* He saw that the notion of truth itself was at stake. He feared that theologians were exchanging a moderately realist, correspondence view of truth—"the adequation of the mind to reality"—for a philosophy of action (or history) in which the mind never conforms to extra-mental, transcendent reality but rather only ever conforms itself to the constantly changing exigencies of human experience. The worry of both Pius XII and Garrigou-Lagrange was that the new theologians had exchanged an objective view of truth as that which has been given with a subjective view in which truth is that which is always in the process of becoming. This historicism betrays a skepticism in which the truth is never known because it is always being deferred to some ever-receding horizon. Such a skepticism would finally mean that the eternal truths of revelation, both those derived from Scripture and Tradition, could never be known as such.

Garrigou-Lagrange saw a large number of Catholic theologians falling into this trap. Some of them were his own students at the Angelicum in Rome. He saw in his student and confrere Marie-Dominique Chenu a prime example of the problem. Garrigou-Lagrange takes to task Chenu's view that "theology is nothing more than religious experience having found its intellectual expression."[12] This makes human experience the source and norm for theology rather than eternal truths and immutable laws of revelation. Similarly, he sees Hegelian thought in Teilhard de Chardin's view that the Incarnation is a "moment" in the evolution of the universe, and that original sin is not so much a voluntary fault of our primal parents but a "relational discord" which impedes our "spiritual

---

[11] Pius XII, Encyclical Letter Concerning Some False Opinions Threatening to Undermine the Foundations of Catholic Doctrine *Humani Generis* (August 12, 1950), §7.

[12] Garrigou-Lagrange, "La nouvelle théologie."

evolution."[13] Garrigou-Lagrange thinks that the influence of these relativizing conceptual systems, such as the Kantian turn to the subject or the Hegelian turn to history, reduces the faith to "a collection of probable opinions" that can always give way to new opinions.[14]

We have already mentioned the diversity of the "new opinions" of *nouvelle théologie*. Yet, the new opinions do not always fall so neatly into Garrigou-Lagrange's critique. Rahner is often associated with the *aggiornamento* side of updating theology to the existential metaphysics of Martin Heidegger. He can also be quite traditional in his use of Thomistic categories.

Karl Rahner

Karl Rahner (1904–1984) is the theologian who is most often, and credibly, charged not with relativism but with "supernaturalizing the natural." What does this mean? Rahner had been initially influenced by Joseph Maréchal's attempt to reconcile Aquinas and Kant (the origins of transcendental Thomism), but Rahner then turned to the highly influential existentialist metaphysics of Martin Heidegger. Heidegger's massively complex work *Being and Time* (1927) had reworked the classical metaphysics of Aristotle to mount a rejection of the "metaphysics of substance," which posits Being Itself raised high beyond all things, and instead sees Being (*Sein*) as that movement of becoming or "a way of life" shared by members of a community. This is fundamentally to think of being in terms of action, energy, and movement rather than in terms of the classical metaphysical terms of substance and accident, redefining potency and act in the more phenomenological terms of openness and becoming. Even in his earliest work, Heidegger distinguishes between the "existentiell," which is everything that exists that has limits, and the "existential," which permeates all things and cannot be delimited. It is this existentialist distinction which helps gives birth to Karl Rahner's idea of "the supernatural existential."

Rahner wanted to find a way to bring modern man into more intimate contact with the supernatural graces. Rather than the "grace extrinsicism" of Aristotelian-Thomism, Rahner was searching for a "grace intrinsicism" which shows the fundamental nearness of God to human existence and humanity's experience of the transcendent. Just as Heidegger had argued that being was self-communicative in time, so Rahner argued that the Incarnation is the

---

[13] Garrigou-Lagrange, "La nouvelle théologie."
[14] Garrigou-Lagrange, "La nouvelle théologie."

self-communication of God in time which discloses for all time the reality of human nature. Jesus Christ reveals to man *what he already is* and must become. This is not because nature is unchanged by this divine self-disclosure; rather, Rahner argued that this is only true because the Incarnation has "permanently modified" human nature. It is not that John or Peter must be born from above, must be transfigured in conformity to Christ. Rather, it is that human nature itself has already been born from above and has already been "permanently modified." What John or Peter must do is discover who they already are in the disclosure of Jesus Christ in their experience. The Incarnation is a "seed of grace" which has been implanted in our nature, and we must recognize and receive this grace which is intrinsic to graced nature in order to reach our own authentic fulfillment. Rahner saw in this a "quasi-formal causality," a form set up within human nature that he called "the supernatural existential," which is either stagnant in inauthenticity or spiraling toward the transcendent horizons of our experience. This led Rahner to develop classical concepts about "implicit faith" into a kind of grace-intrinsicism which posits that man cannot help but to be "an anonymous Christian" who is constantly living in the presence of the Trinity. "Conversion" can only mean a heightened awareness of what is already there. Yet, this risks a kind of total collapse of what conversion really means. Rahner's supernatural existentialism requires no movement from one state to another but entails a spiraling movement in ever-increasing degrees of moving from implicit faith to explicit expression. This stems not only from how Rahner understands the Incarnation and Christian anthropology but it is also a consequence of the way he thinks about the Trinity.

Traditional teaching on the Trinity entails a distinction between God's eternal nature and his missions to his creation. Thus, students will learn about the production and eternal processions of the three hypostases as subsistent relations in the one *ousia* of God, and they will also learn about the appropriate missions of the Trinity in the "economic" or temporal order. Rahner simplifies these categories into the "immanent" and "economic" Trinity. He then proposes what he calls his fundamental axiom, or *Grundaxiom*. He formulates it this way: "The 'economic' Trinity is the 'immanent' Trinity and the 'immanent' Trinity is the 'economic' Trinity."[15] On the surface, this formulation appears unproblematic. After all, it seems to say nothing other than "God is God." Or at least it aims to affirm that God's eternal nature is not other than what he

---

[15] Karl Rahner, *The Trinity*, trans. Joseph Donceel (New York: Herder and Herder, 1970), 22.

has revealed it to be. Yet, the axiom nevertheless has garnered criticism for the subtle way in which it can also seem to collapse the eternal "immanent" order into the temporal "economic" order by making these identical without reserve, qualification, or distinction. By arguing that "the economic Trinity *is* the immanent Trinity," Rahner stresses the way "the Trinity itself is with us" through our experience of the supernatural existential.[16] He tries to guard divine transcendence with appeals to the absolute mystery of the Trinity, but the axiom of identity between God *in se* and God *pro nobis* is so powerful as to have the effect of bringing the "total communication" of the "absolute mystery" all onto one accessible, historical, temporal level. Like Kant, Rahner stresses divine transcendence, but like Hegel and Heidegger, Rahner finds a dialectical identity between transcendence and immanence that risks the same sort of relativism with which this essay began. Instead of a mere "evolutionary" view of history, Rahner gives us a "Trinitarian" one which is generated by God and so "constitutes the future as something open and new."[17] History is generated by God, and it is the means of his self-communication. Therefore, it is hard for Rahner to avoid a rather Heideggerian type of formulation such as "God's being is in becoming," wherein God is continually "begetting himself" in us, in time.

Almost all the difficulties with "modern theology" can be found here. Without greater precision, Rahner's fundamental axiom conflates the divine, eternal order and the economic order of space and time. By arguing for the "identity" of the immanent and economic Trinity, at least in one direction Rahner implies that the "economic self-communication" constitutes the Trinity! This is contrary to the truth. God does not need us. He is necessary; we are contingent and not at all necessary. There is nothing about divine revelation in time that could ever be said to "constitute" the eternal divine nature. To say otherwise would be to deny that the divine nature is eternal. As Gilles Emery notes, "The Father does not become Father by his relation with us in Christ, but rather he is Father from all eternity."[18] Rahner's conflation of the eternal Trinity with our knowledge and experience of the Trinity in time does not preserve the "absolute mystery," as he intends, but rather mystifies history as absolutely Trinitarian. Our experience of the Trinity can never be anything but partial in this present life. We await the beatific vision in which we will see the Trinity

---

[16] See Rahner, *The Trinity*.

[17] Rahner, *The Trinity*, 94.

[18] Gilles Emery, *The Trinity: An Introduction to Catholic Doctrine on the Triune God*, trans. Matthew Levering (Washington, DC: The Catholic University of America Press, 2011), 177.

face to face. Then "we will know as we are known" in God's comprehensive embrace of us. Yet even then we will not be able to say that our knowledge and experience of the Trinity constitute the Trinity. Even then we will not be able to affirm Rahner's *Grundaxiom* because even in the city of God there remains a distinction between the Creator and creation.

THE TEMPTATIONS OF HISTORY

Maritain's early worry that "the new theologians" were playing the early Church Fathers to the music of Hegel has proven prescient. The Councils of Ephesus and Chalcedon had worked out all these questions in such a way as to articulate that the "impassible God" had entered into a passible, changeable human nature "in the economy of the flesh."[19] These were not abstract, idealized, or paradoxical distinctions for the Church Fathers. They were not to be "dialectically worked out" in Hegelian fashion. Rather, the early Church Fathers and the councils sought distinctions which preserved the confession that Christ was fully human and fully divine without confusion. This is our constant need.

Nevertheless, much of modern theology has struggled mightily with the temptations of the Hegelian historicizing of God. Hegel appeals to our modern therapeutic sense of empathy and compassion. It allows God to change, but not us. God always affirms us, whatever sin we actually are experiencing right now, so much so that our sins are implicitly part of our communion with God. This God is "absolute" in his very relativity. Being constituted by his relation to us means that his mercy is nothing other than union with our weakness and suffering. Hegel's God is near to us precisely in the dialectical unfolding of our lives: we must necessarily encounter the God who has negated his absolute existence to become a "fellow sufferer," uniting us in a communion of sympathy for our fellow man.

Finally, Hegel tempted modern theologians to project our times, our suffering, our identity, our limitations onto God, onto Christ and his holy Church—and in doing so, to transform God, Christ, and the Church into an ever-evolving, heightened version of ourselves. Hegel tempts modern theologians to see sins—in our lives and as they unfold in human history—not as a turning away from God but as a kind of dialectical "moment" in which God suffers and dwells with us in our suffering, extending always his mercy

---

[19] Cf. Cyril of Alexandria, *On the Unity of Christ.*

to sinners. Hegelianism can be dressed up to sound Christian. But it actually hides a post-Christian "projectionism" in which God is nothing other than ourselves writ large.

Imagine a house on fire. People are crying out for help from the top floor, unable to escape. Crowds gather, yet feel helpless against the expansive flames. People on the street begin crying, weeping, showing great compassion and solidarity with the suffering of the people trapped. Suddenly, a man appears from nowhere. He throws a heavy jacket on and barrels into the burning house, at great risk to himself, runs up the stairs, and breaks down the locked door that prevented the victims' escape. This man saved the people trapped in that burning house. He was, in fact, much more compassionate, even though he did not indulge in the street-level empathy. Like Christ, the man subjected himself to suffering not in order to dwell in it but in order to rescue human beings from death.

God's mercy flows from the costly sacrifice of his Son in the economy of the flesh. God's plan is not to suffer with us in our sins but to rescue us from them. This means that divine mercy can only flow to contrite hearts by being lifted out of sin, not by being left in it.

For all the relativizing tendencies of modern theology, there is a kind of historical determinism at play in much of it. Whatever happens has happened in God. That includes our sins, which will not, after all, prevent us from being eternally united to God's life. We can see the pastoral implications of the dogmatic conclusions all around us in a kind of libertine acceptance of every sexual sin.

The trouble with this is that it is not the Gospel. It forestalls the possibility of conversion to Jesus Christ; it ensures that there is no movement from the state of original sin to human nature in a state of grace; it ensures that there is never to be a transfiguration of our wounds; and it ensures that whatever tears we cry in this life will not so much be wiped away as shared by God eternally. In the name of mercy, Hegelianism translates the Apostle Paul's "all things are possible" into "all things are permitted" within the unfolding of authentic human and divine experience.

The other trouble with the historicizing temptation is that it is not actually the authentic mercy that the Church teaches us. The *vita apostolica* of the Church is a call to exercise "the missionary option," where openness to the world can never mean conformity to the world. Rather, the mercy of the Church is always a rescue mission, where the mercy of Christ condemns sin and heals the sinners. Authentic mercy can never condone sin, for that is to abandon souls to a spiritual burden that leads to death. If we renounce a throwaway culture, a culture of death, decay, and destruction, we must also understand mercy as a call to repentance and conversion to Christ who is mercy, joy, peace, and life eternal. The Church bids us to turn away from the devil, to confess our sin, and to turn to the divine mercy; and the Church has the power to break our bondage to sin. Simply put, mercy flows not from sympathy with sin, or the mere appearance of human empathy with suffering, but from conversion to Christ Jesus. This is the mercy which is most pastorally necessary because it is precisely freedom from sin through conformity to Jesus Christ and his Church which liberates. Too much of modern Catholic theology has made mercy into self-justification, where we simply project our own permissiveness and license onto God's own life and then call down mercy and peace as if we were doing favors for ourselves. This is the danger of the Hegelian tendency in theology. But as the psalmist understood, it is only when peace kisses justice, and only when mercy enters into communion with truth (Ps 85:10) that our human nature can be saved from sin, cleansed and purified for union with the divine nature. Divine mercy does not dwell with us in our sin but rescues us from it.

RAHNER: THE WITHERING OF FAITH

Christopher J. Malloy

Not infrequently, the student so struggles to comprehend the thought of Karl Rahner that he forgets to ask whether Rahner's claims are *true*. It is certainly an achievement to understand a brilliant thinker—but one must also ask whether he is on the mark.

Asking this question of Rahner is essential and urgent, as I hope to demonstrate. Some have raised concerns, but Rahner's work continues to evade incisive assessment. Meanwhile, his disciples march on, lacking restraint. Rahner consistently presented himself as an orthodox theologian. Appreciative of Rahner, Stephen Duffy was nonetheless disturbed by Rahner's "obeisance to dogma" and wondered whether Rahner deceptively employed "a strategy to hold at bay Roman bounty hunters."[1] Rahner's influence in academia is unmatched, and his thought has also greatly impacted the pastoral sphere. At the pastoral level in particular, few are equipped to deal with the erroneous elements of his thought. As a result, priests and pastoral laborers unwittingly put these into practice. We thus encounter concrete problems such as the following: a loss of the sense of original sin, ignorance of the sacrificial character of Christ's death, ignorance of the divinity of Christ, a profound disregard for the efficacy of the sacraments, an abandonment of the missionary task, an embrace of false religions, etc.

Rahner's laudable goal was to articulate the Christian faith in a credible manner.[2] In the end, however, his theological ventures led to the distortion of the

---

[1] Stephen J. Duffy, *The Dynamics of Grace* (Eugene, OR: Wipf and Stock Publishers, 1993), 336.

[2] Karl Rahner, *Foundations of Christian Faith: An Introduction to the Idea of Christianity*, trans. William V. Dych (New York: Crossroad, 1990), 12.

deposit of faith. So wary of a sacrifice of the intellect, Rahner compromised the faith. Among the reasons for this deviation were his roots in Kant, Hegel, and Heidegger. Rahner utilized theologically the philosophies of these thinkers. This chapter briefly sketches these philosophical roots and their deleterious effects in Rahner's thought. The critique is organized not according to chronological development but according to a suitable presentation of Rahner's theological use of these philosophical influences.

In the first section, I treat Rahner's adaptation of Kant, who demanded that metaphysics demonstrate its credentials before making claims. Similarly, Rahner first examined the human subject, identifying how man questions and listens, so as to determine the conditions of credibility for Christianity. This section adverts chiefly to natural structures of human action, even though grace concretely colors them. The second section treats Rahner's use of Heidegger's phenomenology; Rahner postulated a "supernatural existential" as God's grace on offer universally. This postulate served as foundation for much of Rahner's other work, including his theories about Christ and sacramentality. Each of these theories employs a Hegelian notion of development. The third section treats this Hegelian dimension of Rahner's sacramentality and Christology.

KANT AND RAHNER'S TRANSCENDENTAL ANTHROPOLOGY

Kant

Like many great thinkers, Kant lamented that philosophers disagree so frequently and vehemently. His prescription was that the philosopher should first take stock of his own competence. This undertaking should be critical; that is, it should consist in reason's disciplined recognition of its own limits. Then, the philosopher can confine remarks to his competence.

Kant reported that, after reading David Hume, he awoke from his "dogmatic slumber." The slumber was his failure to see that metaphysics, as it then stood, was in a dilemma. Its practitioners always hoped (a) to make progress and (b) to be absolutely certain. Kant claimed that, on the classical conception of knowledge, these goals could not both be met. According to the classical conception, "truth" is the correspondence of a human mind with the world. If I assert, "It is raining," my judgment is true *if* it is raining. The world measures the truth of human knowledge. Kant came to hold the reverse, that our knowledge measures the world.

Hume convinced Kant that the experience of things "out there" can never produce certainty, only an approximation of a "universally true" claim. For example, seeing a thousand white swans, I expect the next swan to be white. The constant conjunction of swan and white disposes me to have this expectation, but it is not necessary that a swan be white. Hume thought, and Kant agreed, that all inference from experience is limited to the "approximately universal" at best.

Now, Kant applied this opinion to the following commonly held analysis of truth claims. Every truth claim is a proposition of the structure "S (subject) is P (predicate)." A truth claim relates a predicate to a subject. For example, "man is a rational animal" and "the cat is in the hat." The commonly held position was that every truth claim is either analytic or synthetic. A claim is analytic if the predicate simply repeats, overtly or covertly, the subject or part of it. A claim is synthetic if the predicate introduces something not already contained in the subject. The claim that "man is a rational animal" is an analytic claim because the predicate "rational animal" is the very content of the concept "man." In short, the predicate is contained in the subject. So what? Analytic statements, Kant alleges, function like *uninformative* tautologies. We can appreciate the point if we reword the statement as follows: "A rational animal is a rational animal." This statement is obviously true and equally worthless. (Note that the rewording does not reflect the same judgment as "man is a rational animal." Self-evident truths are not banal trivialities; they reflect the order in difference among human insights, but that is a story for another day. Back to Kant.) By contrast, a synthetic statement expresses an advance in human knowledge because the predicate is not already contained in the subject. In the claim "the cat is in the hat," the concept "cat" does not include the predicate "in the hat." It is an informative statement.

This division of propositions touches on Kant's problem. All analytic propositions are self-evidently true apart from empirical verification. Thus, they have the mark the metaphysician seeks: certainty. The drawback is that we learn nothing from such propositions. Thus, if metaphysics consisted only in analytic propositions, it could not be a growing, informative body of thought. It would merely help us to organize our terms, definitions, and claims. What about synthetic propositions? As it seemed to Hume, following Leibniz, every synthetic proposition is contingent (not necessarily true) because the predicate is not contained in the subject. According to Leibniz, to verify a synthetic proposition, one must consult experience. *Is* the cat in the hat? Take a look to find out. But, as Hume taught, experience of things never yields certainty. A naïve intellect jumps to the conclusion that an empirically universal truth is a necessary truth; a wise man holds his tongue. For Kant, the chaos of disputes in philosophy was largely due to naïve confidence.

Still, Kant was not satisfied with Hume's skepticism. After all, he observed, Newton explained with certainty the laws of motion in an informative way. How can this be? Is it possible to know some synthetic (hence, informative) propositions to be true apart from experience? What we know from experience we know *a posteriori*. What we know apart from experience we know *a priori*. So, Kant was asking whether synthetic *a priori* propositions are possible. He claimed they are, adducing arithmetic and geometry as evidence. Kant argued that both sciences are *a priori* because each is certain. He argued for their synthetic character as follows. Take the proposition (or, rather, equation), "Five hundred nineteen (X) plus thirty-seven (Y) equals five hundred fifty-six (Z)." Kant submitted that the proposition is not analytic because the concept of the subject (X+Y) does not contain the concept of the predicate (Z), no matter how long we gaze at the subject. But the answer is absolutely, not just empirically, certain. Thus, arithmetic actually consists in synthetic *a priori* propositions.

Kant then asked the pivotal question: What are the conditions that make synthetic *a priori* propositions possible? Here, he undertook his "transcendental method," a study not of things "out there" but of our manner of knowing. Since these claims (he held) cannot be judged true from experience, by what are we able to verify them? What is the "glue" that for us binds the predicate to the subject? Kant replied: *our intuition*. I verify the equation by *counting*. When I count, I intuit, as it were, the progress from the first number, through the second, to the third. Hence, I supply the glue by my inescapable manner of thinking. Geometry is similar. Geometrical truths are utterly certain laws of spatial relationships. Since (for Kant) experience cannot give us this certainty, the necessity of these laws cannot be "something out there" that we come to know. Whence comes the necessity? Our own *way* of intuiting or picturing spatial relations must constitute the necessity. Because we by necessity intuit space as we do, whatever we experience in space and time must conform to these laws, necessarily and universally. In short, we do not discover the laws empirically; *we put these laws into things*. The truth of both arithmetic and geometry, therefore, is conformity not of the (human) mind to the world but of the experienced world to the mind. This is Kant's "Copernican Revolution": the naïve view of truth as a correspondence of the mind to reality must be reversed.

The same must be said of the natural sciences. In this connection, Kant turned to the concepts of the mind. Of these concepts or categories, some are clearly derived from experience. Think of "guacamole." What about key notions of the natural and philosophical sciences, such as "cause"? Kant agreed with Hume that no amount of experience can justify the notion of "cause." The reason is that "cause" implies an infallible connection of cause and effect, but no number of experiences justifies the concept of an infallible connection between things we encounter. Still, Newton brought together items of experience under universally true judgments, such as his laws of mechanics. How is this possible? Kant concluded: Newton must have employed concepts that he knew *a priori*, not from experience. By employing such concepts, one can construct a natural science, conceiving a connection of appearances as universal and necessary.

At this juncture, we note a final crucial element in Kant. He held that all our categories of thought are geared to the understanding solely of objects that can appear in time and space. We need these categories to understand what appears; otherwise, our experience would be blind. Yet, we can use such categories to understand only what appears, since otherwise they would be empty. So, whatever cannot be experienced in time and space cannot be understood through our categories. Now, God, the soul, and freedom do not *appear* in space and time. Thus, we cannot understand God, the soul, and freedom. We can put content into these empty concepts only with reference to *practical* reason. Thus, so he thought, Kant roused philosophy from its dogmatic slumber.

Rahner on the a priori *Structures* of Man

Rahner put Kant to creative use. Developing a path pioneered by Pierre Rousselot and Joseph Maréchal, Rahner pursued a Kantian method while attempting to retrieve the "realism" Kant denied, especially its ability to offer an intellectual reflection on God. Rahner also retained the anthropocentric turn of modernity. He aimed to present Christianity in a manner that is credible for those living after this turn. So, he studied the conditions for the possibility of hearing God's Word. What is man like such that Christianity can be meaningful?

This mode of inquiry constitutes the "transcendental" character of Rahner's theology. It is transcendental in method and in content.[3] Methodologically, Rahner adopted Kant's search for *a priori* structures of knowing. He investigated our very manner of being subjects, identifying *a priori* structures of knowing that are always operative. Such a method *transcends* particular objects that we contingently encounter (Christ, sacraments, etc.). Rahner's theology is also transcendental in content in that one key *a priori* structure that he identified is the power of human subjectivity to transcend that which it encounters. Let us unpack this point.

Speaking broadly, Rahner described man as embodied "spirit in the world"; man is situated historically yet lives this situated character in a *transcending* way. The power of transcendence is both cognitive and appetitive, but here we must focus on the cognitive aspect. In any act of knowing, we target (what I describe as) an object of "focal awareness." The analogy is visual: objects that we consider come before our "visual field," so to speak. We grasp an object of focal awareness in a *transcending* way because we situate it within a wider context. It is not that we *leave it behind* on a journey upward to a higher target, the "real" target. Rather, we approach a particular object in a manner that exhibits our already having reached beyond it in our very approach to it. A sign of this is that we *name* the object. We say, for example, "This is a 'tree.'" This act of predication displays that we encounter the tree as having "reached" beyond it with the category "tree." This category is a universal. In applying it to *this* thing, we implicitly recognize that there could be another such individual, indeed, infinitely many possible individuals of that kind. Moreover, the very category "tree" can become in its own way an object of consideration. We can think about "treeness," treating it as an object of focal awareness.[4] In doing so, we reach beyond it by appeal to the more universal notion "living thing." Once again, we implicitly recognize the infinite field of possible "living things." Further, we implicitly recognize the infinite field of "non-living things." Again, we can go beyond "living things" to "physical things," etc. This ever-surpassing reach of our approach goes to the most universal limits, to "being itself." Rahner calls this reach the

---

[3] See Karen Kilby, "Transcendental," in *Karl Rahner: Theology and Philosophy* (London: Routledge, 2004), 32–48; and Rahner, *Foundations*, 20.

[4] More precisely, we think of some singular individual under the category "treeness" as a particular in relation to the predicate.

"pre-apprehension" of being.[5] The "object" of this pre-apprehension is the infinite field of whatever is or can be. Rahner held that our approach to any particular thing always implicitly bears in itself a reach toward this infinite field of possibilities.

Rahner insisted that only this reach toward the infinite accounts for the fact that we encounter whatever we encounter only *as* particular and finite. For Rahner, we can grasp the finite *as* finite only by contrast with the infinite. So, in approaching an object of focal awareness as finite, we must already have some sense of the infinite.

But *how* do we have this sense? Can the infinite field of possibilities be an object of encounter? No. For Rahner, it is *a priori* true that we can encounter only finite objects. If the field is infinite, we cannot encounter it as object. If we attempted to approach the infinite field as an object of consideration, we would try to reach beyond it. But there is no reaching *beyond* the infinite field of possible beings. So, the infinite field cannot be known as object.

Can the field be named? Yes and no. Rahner called the field "horizon," but this is no ordinary name. We attend to an object of focal awareness only against the "backdrop" of a horizon. Extending out indefinitely, the horizon is the backdrop, not the thing seen. Similarly, Rahner held, every cognitive act has as its ultimate horizon the field of possible or actual beings. We cannot grasp this field as object. If we aim to track "being" down as object, it eludes us, receding before us. So, the horizon can never become an object of focal awareness. Consequently, "horizon" does not function as a normal generic name, a universal predicate applied to a particular. Rather, it is somewhat like an "ostensive" indicator. It indicates *not* an object but the limitlessness of the transcending *way* that we experience particulars: we approach particular objects within a field that ever grows on account of the "vector" of our inquiry, reaching out in an ever-transcending fashion.[6]

Is the horizon God? As described above, the horizon is not God but only the infinite *field of possibilities*. In this respect, the horizon is what classical philosophy calls a "potential infinity." A "potential infinity" is not an actuality but the limitless character of possibility, of what "can be." Numbers offer

---

5 Karl Rahner, *Spirit in the World*, trans. William Dych (New York, NY: Continuum Publishing Company, 1994), 142.

6 See Rahner, *Spirit in the World*, 144–45. It can help if we initially picture the vector as having an expanding conical shape. But ultimately, the vector is not circumscribed; its reach is being as such, outside of which there is nothing.

an example. Take any *actual* number, no matter how large. You can always go beyond that number by addition, multiplication, etc. The feature "can go beyond" is an infinite or endless potentiality of every number. Similarly, the horizon so described is but a *potential* infinity. Now, in contrast to what is only *potentially* infinite, God is *actually* infinite; he is not just what "can be" but what already is real. Thus, the horizon is not God. When at his best, Rahner distinguished God and the horizon, but he sometimes called God the horizon.[7]

If the horizon is not God, is human thought ultimately adrift toward the merely *possible*, which seems indistinguishable from *nothingness*? A theist, Rahner answered, "No." He began with the premises (a) that the pre-apprehension of being *affirms* any possible object and (b) that "Absolute Being would completely fill up" this possible field. He added (c) that Absolute Being "cannot be grasped as merely possible."[8] Thus, he concluded, the pre-apprehension implicitly affirms the existence of Absolute Being. This reasoning resembles the ontological argument, which moves from the possible to the actual. Now, to argue from the possible to the actual is invalid. Aware of this difficulty, Rahner downplayed the resemblance, but astute critics note a weakness requiring investigation.[9] Perhaps Rahner's optimism and Christian faith, rather than his transcendental method, helped him jump the hurdle from potentiality to actuality. At any rate, his argument is not a causal demonstration of God's existence. Furthermore, he insisted that such demonstrations only echo conceptually the primordial *experience* that our power of transcendence must have Infinite Being as *final* term. And again, Infinite Being is term not as object but as the ultimate "whither" of our transcending way of targeting particular objects. The danger here is that the God Rahner affirmed resembles a potential infinity.

Crucial for us are the conclusions Rahner drew about knowing and naming God. If the horizon cannot be named, much less can God, who "grounds and sustains" all things within the horizon. Just as the name "horizon" is only an indicator pointing not to an object but to our "transcendental experience" and its reach, so the name "God" is but an indicator of the unnameable author of

---

[7] I trust that those quite familiar with Rahner require no references for these claims. For a set of references in Rahner's first two major works and scholarly references as well, see Patrick Burke, *Reinterpreting Rahner* (New York: Fordham University Press, 2002), 26n72.

[8] Rahner, *Spirit in the World*, 181.

[9] See Denis Bradley, "Rahner's *Spirit in the World*: Aquinas or Hegel?," *The Thomist* 41, no. 2 (April 1977): 167–99, esp. 195–99.

being: "It says nothing about what it means, nor can it simply function like an index finger which points to something encountered immediately outside of the word. . . . It means the 'silent one' who is always there, and yet can always be overlooked, unheard, and, because it expresses the whole in its unity and totality, can be passed over as meaningless."[10] Rahner recognized the practice of naming God by analogy, but he reduced this practice to a matter of secondary concern.[11] What is primary is the experience of God simply as ultimate "whither" of our transcending way. So, Rahner favored the name "Mystery" for God, since this term preserves God from finitization, the errant conception of God as one being within the infinite field of possible beings. Rahner wished above all to avoid finitizing God. This wish the Church's mystical tradition shares. Consider how monk and nun meditate so as to perceive God in absolutely everything and to order every thought, word, and gesture to him. Still, this tradition also seeks the face of God. But for Rahner, can man seek the face of God?

Application of the a priori Structures

Having identified the *a priori* structures of human subjectivity, Rahner asked what man's ultimate activity is. His fullest answer involves God's gift of grace, the focus of the second section. Regarding the finality of man as such, his claim is twofold. First, Rahner upheld as possible a merely natural end. On this thesis, the human subject in its ultimate activity ponders the question: "Will God speak?" The very question indicates a contemplative stance that is theocentric, ready to be hopeful, but already meaningful, even were God to remain silent. Was Rahner saying that man seeks the face of God? To answer, we must turn to Rahner's second claim.

Second, for Rahner, our ultimate activity is *pragmatic*, albeit in a transcending manner. This latter response situates the former within the context of man's *a priori* structures. What do I mean by "pragmatic"? For Rahner, man can have focal concern only for objects within the world: things and other persons. Man can *never* treat God as an object of focal concern. So, we should not read the first answer as describing a natural contemplative trying to bend his mind to the contemplation of God as object. Instead, man's concern regards the things of this world. Rahner's pragmatism entails, in the end, that God is not our direct object of concern. Despite his attempt to strike a balance, Rahner too readily

---

[10] Rahner, *Foundations*, 46.

[11] See Rahner, *Foundations*, 61–65 and 71–73.

slipped into conceiving God's presence to a man simply as a function of the condition for the possibility of his dealing with the world: "The presence of the term of transcendence is the presence of this transcendence, which is only present as the condition of possibility for categorical knowledge, and not by itself [*nicht für sich allein gegeben ist*]."[12] To be sure, he attempted to strike what he saw as a balance, namely, that our categorical or conceptual knowledge about God should reflect a tension between God's function in our experience and God's own reality, affirming that "[God's] reality is not simply the function of being the horizon for our existence."[13] Nonetheless, Rahner ultimately buckled in his effort to maintain the value of the conceptual.[14]

Though Rahner did not prescribe utter silence about God, he reduced speech about God to indications of him "only as the term of transcendence," which "takes place only in a categorical encounter in freedom and in knowledge with concrete reality."[15] As for the term "God," although it may once have indicated *a* deity within the world, it is now useful *because* it "has become faceless."[16] The one we name God is the term of transcendence, which "gives itself only insofar as it points wordlessly to something else, to something finite as the object we see directly and as the immediate object of our action."[17] This passage recalls to us that Rahner's analysis of our transcendence applies not only to cognition but to appetite and love. Accordingly, man's love reaches out to particular things, albeit in a transcending manner. So, God is not the "object" of that love; rather, he is the ultimate term of the transcending power of love that targets finite things. Apropos of this, Rahner remarked, "The tendency today to talk not about God, but about one's neighbor, to preach not about the love of God, but about the love of neighbor, and to use not the term 'God,' but 'world' and 'responsibility for the world' . . . has an absolutely solid foundation."[18]

We should pause to reflect on the troublesome pastoral implications of this line of thought. First, these claims dissuade us from seeking the face of

---

[12] Rahner, *Foundations*, 64. German edition: *Grundkurs des Glaubens: Einführung in den Begriff des Christentums* (Freiburg: Herder, 1976), 73 (hereafter, G).

[13] Rahner, *Foundations*, 71.

[14] See Burke's sympathetic critique in *Reinterpreting Rahner*, 240 and 296f. Burke's criticism of Rahner's notion of dogma and dogmatic development, at 285–97, shows some of the grave consequences of this buckling.

[15] Rahner, *Foundations*, 64.

[16] Rahner, *Foundations*, 46.

[17] Rahner, *Foundations*, 65.

[18] Rahner, *Foundations*, 64.

God, yet such a search is the height of human aspiration and the center of true spirituality. Second, these claims obscure the distinction between the first and second commandments (Matt 22:37–40). The ultimate trajectory of this conflation is the identification of the greatest commandment with the love of neighbor; even high-ranking prelates have struggled along these lines.[19] Third, these claims set the stage for the *prioritization* of historical praxis over the deposit of faith and the worship of God. Liberation theology carried out this implication with dreadful effect.

What is true *theism* for Rahner? The original, truest affirmation of God is not the conceptually grounded judgment "God exists." Such a judgment Rahner labels "categorical theism." The original and truest affirmation of God is, rather, "transcendental theism," which is the affirmation of the term of transcendence.[20] How does one affirm this term? Rahner suggested various signs of transcendental theism, such as radical commitment to neighbor, absolute adherence to conscience, etc. In each of these acts, Rahner posited, one *embraces oneself*, affirming one's very power of transcendence and therefore also its term.[21] To embrace oneself as the historical subject of transcending power is the truest theism. To embrace oneself! What about the old approach of "finding God"? Such an approach Rahner described as categorical theism, and he alleged that it cannot give us an object that we affirm as God but only a reflection on the conceptual order that points back to transcendental theism. So, it is even possible to be a transcendental theist while being a categorical or conceptual atheist.[22] That is, the same person can at once embrace conscience radically (thus being a transcendental theist) and yet (mistakenly) think conceptually, "God does not exist" (thus being a categorical atheist). As we shall see, Rahner held that transcendental theism is, in the concrete order, supernatural faith.

---

[19] *Gaudium et spes*, art. 24 (Heinrich Denzinger, *Compendium of Creeds, Definitions on Matters of Faith and Morals*, ed. Peter Hünermann [San Francisco: Ignatius Press, 2012], 4324; hereafter, cited as DH), does not distinguish the second commandment from the first. Pope Francis describes the love of neighbor *as* the first and greatest commandment in *Evangelii gaudium*, art. 161. We can endeavor to interpret these statements in a good light, but they evidently lack helpful precision, since we love our neighbor rightly only when our love is ordered, as to its ultimate end, to God.

[20] This claim appears abundantly in Rahner's corpus; for an explicit use of this phrase, see Karl Rahner, "Atheism and Implicit Christianity," *Theological Investigations*, vol. 9, *Writings of 1965–7, Part 1*, trans. Graham Harrison (New York: Seabury Press, 1972), 156 (hereafter, cited as TI).

[21] See Karl Rahner, "On the Theology of the Incarnation," *Theological Investigations*, vol. 4, *More Recent Writings*, trans. Kevin Smyth (Baltimore: Helicon Press, 1966), 108 and 119; Rahner, "Observations on the Problem of the 'Anonymous Christian,'" *Theological Investigations*, vol. 14, *Ecclesiology, Questions of the Church, the Church in the World*, trans. David Bourke (New York: Seabury Press, 1976), 290; and Rahner, *Foundations*, 228.

[22] Rahner, "Atheism and Implicit Christianity," TI 9, 155–57.

Let's consider the pastoral implications. The tradition holds that grace presupposes nature. So, the tradition holds that a person who cognitively commits to the judgment "God does not exist" cannot simultaneously have supernatural faith. This tradition is biblical: "whoever would draw near to God must believe *that* he exists and that he rewards those who seek him" (Heb 11:6; emphasis mine). The tradition also holds that (1) faith comes from hearing a message proposed by a preacher; and (2) faith involves a cognitive affirmation of the truth enunciated through that message, inspired and assisted by the Holy Spirit (Rom 10:14; 1 Cor 12:3).[23] The tradition also holds that (3) through this affirmation a supernatural relationship with God commences. Rahner's true theism, by contrast, is a nebulous affirmation of oneself, God serving as the condition for the possibility of such an act. What the tradition calls true faith Rahner relegated to "categorical theism."[24] The pastoral implications extend to Rahner's notion of religion, because the foregoing reflections claim to identify the conditions for the possibility of any confessional religion.

According to Rahner, the movement of transcendence inclusive of faith can occur in an encounter with any object, no matter how base or banal: "Transcendental experience and its orientation to God can be mediated by every categorical existent."[25] To be sure, the tradition affirms that no matter what the external circumstances are (prison, poverty, war, etc.), true worship of God is possible. Further, all things can be turned toward God. But while Rahner of course agrees, that is not his point here. He is rather asserting that any categorical object is a sort of *means* of supernatural revelation because it engages one's transcendental experience. The specific object (a devotional item or a trivial item of interest) does not matter in that respect. For Rahner, non-religious categorical objects mediate a relation to God, albeit in an "unthematic" way. Explicitly religious objects do so "thematically," because they conceptually announce the religious theme. Religions other than ancient Judaism and Christianity offer such thematic objects as idols, alleged gods of sundry places, etc. These objects, Rahner held, can mediate God to man because God, as the silent horizon, "is present as such in every assertion, in

---

[23] DH 1526, 4009.

[24] His "fundamental option" theory shares a similar fate. Rahner bifurcates action into two realms, practically banishing from the categorical realm all that is of great moral significance. He thus obfuscates reflection on the moral object, the locus of intrinsically evil acts.

[25] Rahner, *Foundations*, 84.

all knowledge, and in every action."[26] Still, Rahner judged such objects to be of mixed value thematically; only Christianity and ancient Judaism present specially protected interpretations of revelation, Christ being the high point of revelation. Duffy's remarks are pertinent: these affirmations of Rahner were derived not from his transcendental method but from his remnant commitment to tradition. But erosion was settling in. Rahner came to believe it possible that non-Jewish precursors to Christianity are "positively willed by providence" despite their faulty elements.[27] In the pastoral sphere, someone might use this claim to justify the erroneous notion that God positively wills the diversity of religions, just as he positively wills a variety of goods in the created order, such as the binary division of humans into male and female. Thus, the notion of Christianity as *the* way to God is displaced by that of Christianity as the privileged way to God.

In fact, matters are worse. Rahner's *a priori* foundations of theology undermine his profession of Christian faith. They make the very notion of a thematically true categorical object of religion oxymoronic. Why so? A historical, revealed religion "declares phenomena existing within our experience as definite and exclusive objectifications and manifestations of God."[28] Think of Elijah challenging the worshippers of Baal (1 Kings 18:21). Rahner worried that this incarnational element "seems incompatible with our transcendental starting point."[29] Recall that Kant held that we cannot understand God even analogically; Rahner held that no object of focal awareness can be the very term of transcendence. So, anything that Christianity can possibly present before men, even Jesus Christ, is radically unable to make God present as an object of encounter. Rahner is well aware of the problem: Christianity "experiences its most fundamental and universal threat from this difficulty."[30] But, we must ask, how well do Rahner's transcendental conditions harmonize with Our Lord's teaching: "unless you eat the flesh of the Son of man and drink his blood, you have no life in you" (John 6:53)? And why did Our Lord permit the disciples to worship him (Matt 28:17)?

If, on the one hand, any categorical object will do, and on the other hand,

---

[26] Rahner, *Foundations*, 77.

[27] Karl Rahner, "History of the World and Salvation-History," *Theological Investigations*, vol. 5, *Later Writings*, trans. Karl-H. Kruger (Baltimore: Helicon Press, 1966), 106.

[28] Rahner, *Foundations*, 82.

[29] Rahner, *Foundations*, 82.

[30] Rahner, *Foundations*, 83.

no categorical object can do, what contribution can Christianity even offer? For Rahner, it is "still not clear why and to what extent this kind of mediation should belong to one particular categorical existent rather than to another."[31] He suggested two possible and compatible solutions. In the first solution, he regards religion as natural (as distinguished from graced). Considered thus, religion is simply "man's devotion to and respect for the world," albeit in the mode of transcendence.[32] We witness the pragmatism again but with a distinct result. Acknowledging that different people would live this world-respect differently, Rahner suggested as an example that "one person would worship nature as divine."[33] Rahner thus presented nature worship as natural. On such grounds, someone might welcome the worship of an earth goddess. But St. Paul preaches, "The wrath of God is revealed from heaven against all ungodliness" (Rom 1:18–32; cf. Wis 12:23–13:9). Did St. Paul burden world history with needless anxiety about merely "categorical" idolatry?

A second solution opens up, Rahner indicated, if God decides to *offer himself* to man. (Here we step into the theme of grace explicitly.) What did Rahner mean by God "offering himself" to man? Did he conceive of God as making himself present as someone to be encountered, as a face whom to behold? No.[34] For Rahner, God makes himself present in the very *principle* of human subjectivity. A critical observation is in order. The psalmist chants, "In your light do we see light" (Ps 36:9). Accordingly, the tradition has held and ever holds that God enlightens our mind ("in your light") so that we can encounter God now ("we see light"). Granted, this encounter now occurs dimly through faith and analogy, but it is real and it blossoms eternally in the beatific vision. For Rahner, by contrast, we do not encounter God; rather, through God ("in your light") we encounter the *world*.

So, for Rahner, what changes as a result of God's gracious offer? We experience differently the very same things we would experience were God not present. The world "out there" remains the same because it is a tight system of causes. Every event is in one sense exhaustively explicable by this causal nexus.[35]

---

[31] Rahner, *Foundations*, 84.

[32] Rahner, *Foundations*, 84.

[33] Rahner, *Foundations*, 85.

[34] Rahner, *Foundations*, 85. If Thomas Sheehan is right, we never encounter God as object. See Thomas Sheehan, *Karl Rahner: The Philosophical Foundations* (Athens, OH: Ohio University Press, 1987), 184, 192.

[35] See Rahner, *Foundations*, 87–88.

In another sense, everything does change in relation to man, since *man* brings to every encounter this new presence of God within his subjectivity: "The world is our mediation to God in his self-communication in grace."[36]

We can now return to Rahner's notion of world religions in light of this claim about grace. The history of world religions is a history of the genuine essence of supernatural religion in the mode of the transcendental acceptance of God's self-communication. The same history is also this religion's "anti-essence" (*Unwesen*) in the mode of transcendental rejection.[37] In short, Rahner claimed that wherever there is the state of grace, there is true religion and supernatural revelation. A criticism is in order. The Catholic Church certainly acknowledges that non-Catholics can be in the state of grace. But she also holds that the Catholic religion (and, in a preparatory phase, ancient Judaism) is the one true religion of the one true Church. She does not affirm that supernatural revelation and grace come through false religions.[38] Elijah's challenge to the prophets of Baal would be the height of arrogance and folly if supernatural revelation were present always and everywhere.[39] If Rahner were right, Elijah should have celebrated transcendental theism by inviting Baal's prophets and categorical idols into God's temple. Paul VI rejected such misbegotten conceptions of world religions: The Church "causes an encounter with the mystery of divine paternity that bends over towards humanity. In other words, our religion effectively establishes with God an authentic and living relationship which the other religions do not succeed in doing, even though they have, as it were, their arms stretched out towards heaven."[40]

Rahner's *a priori* conditions stymied the theological flowering of his faith. Christianity proclaims God's special interventions in history. Rahner balked, intruding the question: how is a "special intervention" even possible? He asked his readers to consider how any event, even a good thought, can come about. According to his notion of physical causality, every event in its categorical dimension is causally explicable in relation to other such events. No "special intervention" of God, not even a good thought, rises above such causal

---

[36] Rahner, *Foundations*, 151.

[37] Rahner, *Foundations*, 146 [G, 150f].

[38] DH 854, 2921, 3014, 3176; Leo XIII, Encyclical Letter *Humanum genus* (April 20, 1884), §16; John XXIII, Encyclical Letter *Ad Petri cathedram* (June 29, 1959), §17; Paul VI, Encyclical Letter *Ecclesiam suam* (August 6, 1964), §107; CCC §2105.

[39] Rahner, *Foundations*, 149–58.

[40] Paul VI, Apostolic Exhortation *Evangelii nuntiandi* (December 8, 1975), §53.

connections on the categorical level. How, then, does an ordinary event become a "special" objectification of God's gracious presence? It does so "the moment I experience myself as a transcendental subject in my orientation to God and accept it."[41] Once again, *our subjectivity* is what changes, not the world.[42] Rahner anticipated the objection that therefore "everything can be regarded as a special providence" provided only that I accept my concrete life and its power of transcendence. Rahner retorted, Why not?[43]

To test Rahner's *a priori* machinery, we can confront it with events such as the solar miracle at Fatima, witnessed by seventy thousand people and even from thirty kilometers away. Did transcendental subjectivity dry up the rain? Physicist Stanley Jaki's remarks for naysayers are apropos: "Since the event witnessed was undeniable, unbelievers may have felt that it was best to follow the example of such great scoffers at miracles as Hume and Voltaire. They both thought it best not to focus on facts, lest they start looming large and dwarf their inept theories about them."[44] Rahner's understandable wariness about crude accounts of miracles does not justify *a priori* elimination of objective miracles, the reduction of miracles to a changed subjectivity. Affirmation of secondary causes need not entail paralysis of God's arm. Just as God instills natural inclinations, so his hand can delicately and internally draw creatures to higher and different patterns of action, yielding miracles. The solar miracle and Fatima's message serve as stumbling blocks to Rahner's theology.

We have explicitly broached the topic of grace and have implicitly touched it all along. Rahner conceived God's offer of grace with a creative use of Heidegger's notion of "existentials." To this we now turn.

HEIDEGGER AND RAHNER'S SUPERNATURAL EXISTENTIAL

Background: The Dispute on Nature and Grace

We can understand the theory of the supernatural existential only in light of

---

[41] Rahner, *Foundations*, 88.

[42] This notion of an airtight causal connection was surely an outdated aberration Rahner would have rejected upon closer scrutiny. It did, however, contribute to the pressure he felt to resolve the difficulty of accounting for miracles in just the way he did, namely, by reducing them to a subjective condition of experience.

[43] Rahner, *Foundations*, 89.

[44] Stanley Jaki, *God and the Sun at Fatima* (New Hope, KY: Real View Books, 1999), 32.

perennial issues concerning nature and grace. Two principles are at stake in this dispute: the gratuity of grace and the supreme relevance of grace. A key question is pertinent. Does human nature as such tend unconditionally to a natural end or to a supernatural end? In Rahner's day, two major schools offered incompatible answers. Rahner both agreed and disagreed with each. Both schools, and Rahner also, considered this question apart from the concrete issues of original sin and actual sin.

One school, the "natural end" school, held that human nature as such tends unconditionally to a natural end which (1) is attainable by human powers as moved by God's providence proper to the natural order and (2) can make life meaningful by making one genuinely happy. Proponents held this view for two reasons: God is wise, and grace is free. First, they insisted that God's power is wed to his wisdom, which orders things well by directing them to appropriate ends. So, God would not create a rational creature without ordering it to an end that gives it meaning by making it happy. Similarly, a wise and honest lover will not initiate signs of affection if he has no intention of forming a genuine and lasting relationship, lest he be guilty of teasing. Were God not to direct his rational creatures to a proper end, making life meaningful for them, his creative action would be unwise and unjust. So, with respect to God, ordering persons to an end is a *sequela creationis*, something that necessarily attends or follows the creative act. With respect to the rational creature, this ordering is something that is due, a *debitum naturae*. Whereas the act of creation is utterly free, the wisdom of God is such that on the supposition of that act certain things are due.

Is grace, which is necessary to obtain a supernatural end, a *debitum naturae*? No. Grace is *uniquely* gratuitous precisely because it is not among the things due to a created person.[45] God can refuse grace to his rational creatures, but God never acts unwisely.[46] If God can refuse grace without being unwise, then human nature as such tends unconditionally to a naturally attainable end that can make life meaningful. So, the unconditional desire for beatific union with God must not arise from human nature as such. To affirm the contradictory would imply one of two errors. Either (1) God owes grace *because* he always acts wisely and acting wisely means directing things to their fitting ends; or (2) God can create rational creatures that are necessarily and without any

---

[45] DH 1921, 2435.
[46] DH 3891.

fault of theirs on course to misery *because* grace is not a *debitum naturae*. The former alternative is heretical. The latter alternative is blasphemous, smacking of the worst voluntarism. Since these implications are unacceptable, we must hold that human nature as such tends unconditionally to a naturally attainable natural end that can make life meaningful. Now, one can sketch only general features of the natural end, such as loving contemplation of God, friendships, traditions of inquiry, play and art, etc. This end would no doubt include the desire to know who God is, even though only grace can fulfill such a desire. Yet, such desire would not yield despair but a marveling wonder that virtuously remains content. Whatever its details, the natural end would have to suffice to make a man genuinely happy. Only thus can the offer of grace be free, something that God can refuse to make without unwisely rendering creation meaningless and the creature ineluctably wretched. The "natural end" school secured the gratuity of grace. Did it secure the supreme relevance of grace? The second school thought not.

The second, or "supernatural end," school held that our concrete human nature tends unconditionally to a supernatural end, so that no natural end can make us happy. This school accused the former school of making grace and beatific union with God irrelevant, optional, and "extrinsic" because of its depiction of a satisfying natural end. The two schools of thought were thus contradictory.

Henri de Lubac was a major proponent of this second school. For de Lubac, permanent unfulfillment of the natural, unconditional desire for beatific union would cause the greatest suffering possible, the pain of the damned.[47] This assumption makes grace supremely relevant. Does it preserve the gratuity of grace? Both Rahner and the first school thought that it did not.

Rahner agreed with the first school that God's wisdom guides his creative action. According to Rahner, *if* man had an unconditional natural desire for beatific union with God, grace would be due.[48] Rahner rejected the second school on this score. He, however, joined the second school in critiquing the "natural end" school because, as he and the second school alleged, it portrayed grace as an extrinsic layer, added on to nature almost as an afterthought. Rahner expanded on this objection in his own way. On the first school's conception, the man who is not yet "in" the state of grace would

---

[47] Henri de Lubac, *The Mystery of the Supernatural* (New York: Crossroad, 1998), 54.

[48] Karl Rahner, "Concerning the Relationship between Nature and Grace," *Theological Investigations*, vol. 1, *God, Christ, Mary, and Grace*, trans. Cornelius Ernst (New York, NY: Crossroad Publishing Company, 1982), 304–309.

desire beatific union unconditionally only because of the external activity of "actual graces." We should note that actual graces are momentary acts that occur and are gone, such as a good thought or deed. Actual graces are distinguished from habitual graces, which are dispositions that abide in a stable way. Rahner held that the first school portrayed God as addressing a natural man by extrinsic interferences (actual graces) both momentary and random. Rahner appreciated that the first school depicted someone in the state of grace as having a stable disposition toward a beatific end, but he rejected the school's conception of the state of grace as merely an inhering accident. To Rahner, "accident" sounded shallow and peripheral; he wanted grace to be deeper and central. To elaborate his own proposal, he drew on Martin Heidegger's notion of an "existential."

The Postulate of the Supernatural Existential

Heidegger followed his teacher Edmund Husserl in an effort to break out of what Robert Sokolowski has called the "egocentric predicament."[49] The predicament is the difficulty philosophers have had in getting to "the real" since Descartes's turn to the subject. Following Husserl, Heidegger held that from the beginning our thoughts and actions are all about beings. We are already in the world, dealing with things. Heidegger developed his own kind of phenomenology. He did not engage in categorical studies of "things out there." He thus parted from Aristotle's philosophy, which identified categories and traced causal relations. Heidegger trained his eye on the abiding structural features of the way we "ex-ist" in the present, from out of a past, and toward the future. Such features he called "existentials." Crucially, an existential is not an Aristotelian accident distinguishable from substance and susceptible to causal analysis. An example of an existential is that we exist in a mode of projection. We, as it were, project ourselves forward, with aims about things to be developed or achieved. In light of these aims, things show up for us in certain ways; in one way, things show up as "equipment" to be used. We do not, for example, primordially ponder our keyboards as items of "objective" interest, staring at them; rather, we employ them. Correlatively, things show up primordially as "equipment" or as "useful for." For Heidegger, this is really *how* these things *are*. A realist need not object at this point, for Heidegger is bringing to light real features

---

[49] Robert Sokolowski, *Introduction to Phenomenology* (Cambridge: Cambridge University Press, 2000), 9.

of our *living*, and we live with things, approaching them in various manners. One can appreciate Heidegger's phenomenological approach as disclosive and yet also affirm classical realism. Still, one must distinguish Heidegger's analysis from causal analysis and an existential from an Aristotelian accident. How did Rahner wield the concept "existential"?

As noted in the first section, Rahner held that God, who remains the mysterious horizon, freely decided from the outset to offer himself in supernatural self-communication to every human person. God makes this offer to each person not through momentary, random acts, but at all times and abidingly. From the moment of conception, everyone receives God's self-communication, *at least in the mode of offer.* By describing this self-communication as "at least in the mode of an offer," Rahner distinguished it from sanctifying grace, which actually sanctifies the one who has it.[50] Rahner added that every person who has acted in freedom has either accepted or rejected this offer, precisely by embracing or not embracing his own power of transcendence as colored by this offer. So, for those who have acted freely, the self-communication exists *not only* in the mode of offer *but also* in the mode of acceptance or rejection. For the person who accepts it, the existential becomes sanctifying, but the person who rejects it is in the state of mortal sin. Rahner dubbed the self-communication of God *in the mode of offer* the "supernatural existential."[51] The offer is "supernatural" since it is neither part of human nature as such nor something due to an existing human being. It utterly surpasses nature's capacity. Thus, the "supernatural existential" pertains to the realm of gift; it is not a *debitum naturae*. Everything that unfolds on this foundation, grace and beatific union, is likewise gift. Notwithstanding, as an "existential," the offer is an abiding structural feature of man, part of the makeup of his *ex-isting*. Indeed, it is the *inmost* of such features. By describing the offer as an "existential," Rahner at once avoided (1) claiming that it is part of human nature and (2) "relegating" it to an accident or a series of "actual graces" that strike man from the outside. Rahner was able to think of it as inmost and deepest in man and yet not as a natural feature.

If Rahner's theory is correct, the "problem" of nature and grace is resolved. Grace is utterly free, since it is neither a natural feature nor due to nature. But,

---

[50] Rahner, *Foundations*, 127.

[51] Rahner, *Foundations*, 126. See also Rahner, "Concerning the Relationship between Nature and Grace," TI 1, 313.

since the existential is deepest in man, it orients him most deeply to beatific union with God. Grace becomes supremely relevant because true happiness is impossible without beatific union, which requires grace.

A crucial inquiry remains. Is Rahner's postulate *true*? Does it imply any false claims? I treat the first question in this section and the second question in the course of the third section.

Evaluation

If there really is a supernatural existential, what *is* it or what *is* its proximate causal basis?[52] We can tackle this inquiry in two ways. First, we can survey the field of being inductively, searching for an answer by the process of elimination. Second, we can take stock of the phenomenological roots of the notion.

Inductively, we proceed as follows. If the supernatural existential (or its proximate causal basis) is real, it will be something. Is it something created or something uncreated? If it were uncreated, it would not come to be in time and it would not be contingent. Since the existential is contingent and comes to be in time, it cannot be uncreated. If it is created, it must belong either to the realm of nature or to the realm of grace. Obviously, it cannot belong to the realm of nature, since it is gratuitous and supernatural. Thus, if it exists, it must belong to the realm of created grace. Now, created graces are twofold, habitual and actual. Is it either of these?

Habitual graces are stable dispositions of the human person which are infused by God and which inhere in that person's essence and powers. Habitual graces are of two kinds, those that are ordered to the sanctification of their possessor (sanctifying) and those that are not.[53] The supernatural existential can only belong to the former kind, since it is ordered to the sanctification of its possessor. Let us consider whether the existential is one of the three theological virtues or sanctifying grace itself. Since all other habitual graces oriented toward the sanctification of their possessor are premised on these, if the existential is none of these it cannot be any habitual grace. Is the existential charity or sanctifying grace? Well, Rahner asserted that *everyone* has the existential. So, if it were charity or sanctifying grace, everyone would be in the state of grace from

---

[52] For fuller treatment, see my essay, "Karl Rahner's Supernatural Existential: What Is It?" *Freiburger Zeitschrift für Philosophie und Theologie* 63 (2016): 402–21.

[53] Of these, none actually sanctify unless charity also is present. However, if charity is present, the other infused habits of grace become sanctifying. Further, even without charity, these other virtues orient man toward sanctification.

the moment of conception, and neither mortal sin nor damnation would be possible. These implications contradict the faith and smack of naïve optimism about human sinfulness. Unfortunately, Rahner sometimes conflated the existential with sanctifying grace (or faith operating through charity), unwittingly inviting these problems.[54] But at his best, Rahner conceived it as *in the mode of offer*, distinguishing it from sanctifying grace. Thus, the existential is neither charity nor sanctifying grace. Is it theological hope? If it were hope, everyone would always have hope in God and despair would be impossible. But Rahner acknowledged, and the Church teaches, that despair is possible. Is the existential faith? If it were faith, each person's power of transcendence would be so colored that no one could fail to be a transcendental theist; unbelief would be impossible, except at the "categorical" level. Once again, this implication contradicts the faith and constitutes a false basis for pastoral work, which must face the contagious phenomenon of real unbelief. Unfortunately, Rahner sometimes moved in this direction, portraying the existential as constituting a new formal object of man's transcendentality.[55] It is difficult to discern how such a new formal object would not be tantamount to faith. But in any case, Rahner at his best wanted to distinguish faith from the existential.[56] So, the existential is neither faith nor any habitual grace. Finally, Rahner himself denied that the existential is an infused habit or accident.[57]

Could the existential be an actual grace or set of actual graces? Rahner emphatically rejected the idea. Actual graces are momentary acts, such as a salutary thought or a holy deed. The human pilgrim is not always in act, but also sleeps and rests. Actual graces do not amount to an abiding feature of the way the pilgrim, because of God's call, approaches things in the world. Further, actual graces are gifts given from the outside by God's efficient causality. For Rahner, the offer of grace cannot consist in actual graces. He wants this offer to

---

[54] See Rahner, "History of the World and Salvation-History," TI 5, 103; Karl Rahner, "The Sin of Adam," in *Theological Investigations*, vol. 11, *Confrontations* 1, trans. David Bourke (New York: Seabury Press, 1974), 255; Karl Rahner, "Brief Theological Observations on the 'State of Fallen Nature,'" *Theological Investigations*, vol. 19, *Faith and Ministry*, trans. Edward Quinn (New York: Crossroad, 1983), 47; Rahner, *Foundations*, 143.

[55] See Karl Rahner, "Faith and Sacrament," *Theological Investigations*, vol. 23, *Final Writings*, trans. Joseph Donceel and Hugh M. Riley (New York: Crossroad, 1992), 184; Rahner, "Observations on the Problem of the 'Anonymous Christian,'" TI 14, 287ff; Rahner, *Foundations*, 149–50.

[56] Rahner, "History of the World and Salvation-History," TI 5, 104.

[57] See Rahner, *Foundations*, 123.

be "the innermost constitutive element of man."[58] The existential is "precisely what man *is*."[59] So, the existential is not even a set of actual graces.

What then *is* the existential or on what basis does it arise? We have eliminated all possibilities: it is neither God, nor created nature, nor created grace. There is nothing left. The supernatural existential cannot be anything. It is therefore an empty name.

What is more, this problem is rooted in the very nature of the postulate. The perennial issue of nature and grace regards the question, *whence* arises our unconditional desire for beatific union with God? Does it emanate from nature or is it awoken by grace? The question is *causal*. Existential phenomenology refuses to pursue causal inquiry. So, Rahner's postulate *silences* the very question it is intended to answer. This evasion is not satisfying for several reasons. (1) The very desire to know gives rise to causal inquiry. (2) Both the "natural end" school and the "supernatural end" school are committed to such inquiry. (3) Rahner was also committed to the causal question since he distinguished the existential from human nature (*Natur*). His evasion of the question leaves his postulate devoid of content, a theory in name only.

Importantly, the postulate serves as foundation for much of Rahner's theology. If the former trembles, the latter founders. Turning to Rahner's use of Hegel, we encounter, among other problems, erroneous implications of the supernatural existential.

HEGEL AND RAHNER'S NOTION OF THE "REAL SYMBOL"

Rahner employed Hegel's thought with remarkable creativity and not without fruit, especially Hegel's recovery of teleology and dynamism. All things are dynamic. Growth is the *way* they are. Hegel worked out this insight in penetrating ways. A theist might describe Hegel as working from the top down and from the bottom up. He worked from the top down in that he began with the notion of Being Itself and maintained that this notion is in itself empty because absolutely indescribable. On inspection, Being seems identical with Nothing! This contradiction is unstable and leads toward a resolution, namely, Becoming. Becoming is a continuous process describable with respect to the

[58] Rahner, *Foundations*, 116.
[59] Rahner, "Concerning the Relationship between Nature and Grace," TI 1, 302.

aforesaid notions. More precisely, the universal develops by becoming particular. The tension between universal and particular leads to a resolution, which again raises a tension that must be resolved and is resolved, etc. This is the movement conceived, as it were, from top to bottom. Along these lines, Hegel seemed to say that "God" had to create the world. On the other hand, there is the movement from the bottom up. From sheer potentiality, there is a movement toward actuality. There is growth from the lowest simple things to more complex things, and in this growth there is greater and greater actuality, achieved through the resolutions of tensions that arise in the process. In both movements, one becomes what one was meant to be.

Rahner did not subscribe to the "Hegelian" theses that God had to make the world and that "God" (Being Itself?) was originally empty, although as we saw he claimed the concept of "God" was "faceless" and easily overlooked as meaningless. Rahner thought through Christian revelation in Hegelian fashion. The Son, for Rahner, is the self-expression of the Father, who remains mysterious. There are fruitful potentials here (Johannine "Word," Pauline "Image," and Hebrew "*Shekinah*"). But Rahner's actual performance also suffered defects. Infamously, Rahner rejected as Tritheistic the notion that the eternal Son is an "I" who faces the Father as a "Thou."[60] This rejection implicitly demolishes the rich structure of Trinitarian faith. Jesus, however, addressed the Father as "you" (Matt 11:25). How did Rahner account for this form of discourse? He asserted that Jesus spoke these words according to the assumed humanity.[61] This reply makes matters worse. First, it does not repair the demolition of Trinitarian doctrine. In fact, it tramples over the scriptural data. In Scripture, the Father says to the Son, "From the womb of the morning I begot you" (Ps 110:3) and "You, Lord, founded the earth in the beginning" (Heb 1:10). Conversely, the Son says to his Father, "glorify me in your own presence with the glory which I had with you *before* the world was made" (John 17:5; emphasis mine). As is obvious, the Trinitarian dialogue is eternal and uncreated, not merely temporal or related to events in the world, such as the Incarnation. Second, Rahner's reply constitutes a newfangled Nestorianism. Nestorius distinguished the "I" of the man Jesus, son of David, from the "I" of the eternal Son of God. Similarly, Rahner distinguished an "I" of the humanity from the "I" of the deity, except that the "I" of this deity is

---

[60] Karl Rahner, *The Trinity*, trans. Joseph Donceel (New York: Crossroad, 1997), 75–76, no. 30, and 106–107.

[61] Rahner, *The Trinity*, 75–76, no. 30, and 106–107. See also Karl Rahner, "Current Problems in Christology," TI 1, 156ff; Rahner, *The Trinity*, 61–63.

not an "I" distinct from that of the Father! One might say that Rahner's thought is Nestorianism robbed of the Trinity. For Rahner, the human I "faces the eternal Word . . . in obedience."[62] Even sympathetic readers have found an unwitting Nestorianism here.[63] Rahner's dawn darkened too quickly.

Another potentially fruitful use of Hegel is Rahner's insight that Jesus's humanity in its particularity expresses the Word. This use resonates with Vatican II's notion of Christ as being revelational in "his presence and self-manifestation."[64] It also resonates with contemplatives such as Bonaventure and John the Evangelist. Again, we see Rahner's connection with the mystical tradition. Unfortunately, Rahner conjured necessity out of fittingness. He rejected the claim of robust Cyrillian Christology that the hypostatic union *itself* is a cause both sufficient and necessary to render the humanity to be *the very humanity of the Son*. According to this orthodox line of thought, the Son could have produced a different particular instance of humanity because the union itself renders the humanity *truly* the Son's. We can think, for example, of Jesus being taller and with eyes more widely set apart, etc. These possibilities fall within the limits of possible instances of humanity. Why, then, did the Son choose the very particular features that he had? The robust theological tradition is content contemplating the fittingness in the Son's choice, but it bends its knees to the power of God. It confesses that the hypostatic union truly makes the individual humanity of Jesus to be that of the eternal Son and that this particular instantiation is unspeakably fitting but not strictly necessary on the supposition of the incarnation.

Rahner objected. Fittingness was not enough for him; he wanted necessity. He feared that this Cyrillian line of thought makes the Incarnation a masquerade.[65] He alleged that it implies that the particular humanity of Jesus was "chosen at random" and thus renders the humanity "alien" to the Son.[66] Rahner proposed instead that "when God, expressing himself, exteriorizes himself, that very thing appears which we call the humanity of the Logos."[67] What did Rahner

---

[62] Rahner, "Current Problems in Christology," TI 1, 158.

[63] See Walter Kasper, *The God of Jesus Christ*, trans. Matthew J. O'Connell (New York: Crossroad, 1992), 302–303; and Burke, *Reinterpreting Rahner*, 157 and 274–76.

[64] Second Vatican Council, Dogmatic Constitution on Divine Revelation *Dei Verbum* (November 18, 1965), §4.

[65] Rahner, "On the Theology of the Incarnation," TI 4, 116.

[66] Karl Rahner, "The Theology of the Symbol," TI 4, 237–38.

[67] Rahner, "The Theology of the Symbol," TI 4, 239.

mean? Let us bypass in this venue Rahner's dance with divine mutability.[68] Was Rahner asserting that if the Son is to *express* himself, he can only do so by assuming that very instantiation of human nature which he did assume because the hypostatic union would not suffice to make any other possible instantiation of human nature truly that of the Logos? If not, what then does he mean? If so, Rahner straightjacketed God, transgressing his initial, correct thesis that God should not be finitized! How so? As all Catholics hold, no finite reality can exhaustively express the infinite God. Each creature expresses God in some ways yet leaves him unexpressed in other ways so that another creature can add to the richness of the iconic splendor of God. Consequently, no instance of humanity can be the only possible self-expression of the Son, *if* he is divine. Rahner's discomfort with the category of fittingness made him reach for *a priori* necessity, which suffocates divine freedom.[69]

What about Rahner's use of Hegel in sacramental theology? Rahner conceived sacraments as "symbols." How did he understand this term? For Rahner, a symbol is a being's self-expression by which it becomes what it is or was meant to be. We have brushed against the notion already: the Son is "symbol" of the Father and Jesus's humanity is "symbol" of the Son. Rahner saw all reality as "symbolic," as having a tendency to express itself "exteriorly" in order to become itself. For example, the zygote continually expresses itself beyond its current level of articulation, producing the "exteriorization" that *it itself* will be. To be more precise, the substantial form of the zygote expresses itself in the "other" of its own corporeality. For Rahner, self-exteriorization in the symbol

---

[68] For Rahner, a symbol in general is "the self-realization of a being in the other, which is constitutive of its essence." See "The Theology of the Symbol," TI 4, 234. There is no doubt this notion of symbol is rich. However, one must take caution to avoid ascribing to God what would circumscribe him, mutability. Did Rahner take adequate precaution when he wrote, "The being of the Logos—considered of course *as* that which is received by procession from the Father—must be thought of as exteriorizing itself, so that without detriment to its immutability in itself and of itself, it becomes *itself* in truth the existence of a created reality" ("The Theology of the Symbol," TI 4, 238)? On the root of this problem, see Guy Mansini, "Quasi-formal Causality and 'Change in the Other': A Note on Karl Rahner's Christology," in Guy Mansini, *The Word Has Dwelt among Us: Explorations in Theology* (Ave Maria, FL: Sapientia Press, 2008), 15–26.

[69] There is a parallel between the absurdity of a core thesis in Neoplatonism and Rahner's impossible transmutation of fittingness into necessity. The Nous allegedly is the non-contingent emanation from the One; the Nous is the realm of pure thought and of the divine ideas. But, we can ask, are the ideas infinite or finite in number? If infinite in number, the Nous is unordered. Neoplatonists will not want to say the ideas are numerically infinite. But if they are numerically finite, how is the determination of limit made? Is the One able to be mirrored on the level of thought *only* in these ways? Then the One is also finite. Does the One choose? No Neoplatonist will say "yes." There simply is no such thing as the only possible first effect of Infinite Being. Nor is there any such thing as the only possible human instantiation of the Logos.

is the condition for the possibility of self-knowledge.[70] Hence, the primordial reason a being generates its symbol is for itself.[71] Now, any other being can have knowledge of what generates a symbol only by encountering the generated symbol. I know another only by encountering the other's self-expression. I know the sun, for example, by studying its effects; I know my spouse only through encountering her through her gestures, words, and facial expressions. Rahner used the word "symbol" because a symbol makes known to others that which generates it. Someone might wonder, "But don't we encounter things *as* they really are?" Rahner would reply that if you wanted, so to speak, to get behind the symbol to the "thing in itself," you would be abandoning the only way to encounter a "thing in itself." Picture a lover wanting to get to the "real truth" of his beloved by forgetting her face and burrowing into her head. Bad idea. We can only *be with* another through the other's symbolic self-expression. The "thing in itself" truly is present in the symbol but *as expressed*. Thus, a symbol is, precisely as a sign, the very presence of what it signifies. Rahner's phrase "*real* symbol" shows that his notion cannot be likened to a "billboard," which merely indicates something else that is extrinsic. In a real symbol, the signified is *in* the sign. Now to the question: How are sacraments "real symbols"?

Typical of Rahner's starting point is a caricature of the tradition which itself is to be effectively dismissed. In the present case as in other cases, Rahner's caricature is unworthy of an undergraduate paper. Rahner gave the impression that, before him, sacraments had been seen as the *only* way that grace enters the world; further, said world was depicted as being, apart from the sacraments, thoroughly profane and godless. Of course, he rejected the picture: "Man does not enter a temple, a [shrine] which encloses the holy and cuts it off from a godless and secular world which remains outside."[72] What replaces the caricature? Rahner's Copernican Revolution is the replacement. We used to think that grace comes to us through or because of the sacraments; that conception was due to our geocentric benightedness. Now, however, we must recognize that *we* bring the grace to the sacraments.[73] As his disciple Herbert Vorgrimler said, sacraments are simply "manifestations of what the world and human

---

[70] See Rahner, "The Theology of the Symbol," TI 4, 229.

[71] See Rahner, "The Theology of the Symbol," TI 4, 225.

[72] Karl Rahner, "Considerations on the Active Role of the Person in the Sacramental Event," TI 14, 169.

[73] Rahner, "Considerations on the Active Role of the Person in the Sacramental Event," TI 14, 162–69.

history already are."[74] Rahner thus cast out the demon of Catholic ignorance and privilege.

In short, Rahner claimed, the sacraments are "real symbols" of grace; they are *thematically correct* categorical self-expressions of already present grace. There are several aspects to this theory. (1) The theory rests on the premise of the supernatural existential, by which grace is already present at least in the mode of offer. (2) Sacraments are types of categorical objects. Recall that any categorical object "mediates" grace. But recall how Rahner conceived of mediation. Objects do not mediate grace as channels through which grace flows into a person; rather, they serve as *material* for the activity of transcendence as colored by the alleged existential. (3) When such categorical objects are explicitly religious, they "mediate" grace in a *thematic* way. (4) The Catholic sacraments are thematically correct, unlike the rites of other religions, which can really be effective but are not guaranteed to be thematically correct.

Let us take the Eucharist to illustrate Rahner's claim. The Church teaches that the Eucharist is a source of additional grace and nourishment, which come into us from the outside.[75] Hence, a suspension of Masses deprives the faithful of many graces, even though, of course, God can and does also supply grace outside of the sacraments and feeds his children who are in difficult circumstances. Rahner agreed that God acts outside of the sacraments, but he did not agree that God gives grace through or on account of them. For him, the world and human persons are already swimming with grace. The Eucharist does not bring grace to the world; rather, the Eucharist *announces* categorically that the world is already abounding in grace. The Eucharist "constitutes a small sign, necessary, reasonable and indispensable, within the infinitude of the world as permeated by God. It is the sign which reminds *us* of this limitlessness of the presence of divine grace, and *in this sense* and in no other, precisely in *this particular* kind of anamnesis, is intended to be an event of grace."[76]

A general evaluation is in order. First, what was Rahner affirming? He affirmed that sacraments express already present grace. This affirmation is true for some sacraments, sometimes, and in some ways. For example, those who receive the Eucharist in the state of grace express the communion with Christ that they enjoy. Again, an adult catechumen best approaches baptism if

---

[74] Herbert Vorgrimler, *Sacramental Theology*, trans. Linda M. Maloney (Collegeville, MN: Liturgical Press, 1992), 39.

[75] CCC §§1392, 1394.

[76] Rahner, "Considerations on the Active Role of the Person in the Sacramental Event," TI 14, 169.

already in the state of grace. So, some sacraments are *in some ways* like climactic moments or "final causes." However, even this affirmation must be qualified in light of the very *sign* character of the sacraments. In each sacrament the *very signification* of the sacrament indicates *conferral*, not merely "recognition," of grace. The priest says, "I absolve you," not "I declare you already absolved." Perfect contrition may already have taken place, but the sacrament is signified as an effective action. The Eucharist is nourishment, not a bill of health. Rahner's theory contradicts this sign character. Further, some sacraments have effects that can only be newly produced through them. For example, baptism produces character, a real quality in the soul. The very waters of baptism also signify a cleansing that is being accomplished, not merely acknowledged, such as the uniquely gratuitous remission of all punishment for sin. And even for an adult who is justified through baptism of desire, there is no doubt that baptism confers an increase in grace.[77] Again, as experience proves, Holy Orders are not the self-expression of grace latent within a seminarian.

Second, what was Rahner denying? The Church dogmatically teaches that the seven sacraments "both contain grace and communicate it."[78] They are not merely "external signs of the grace or justice received through faith."[79] In short, "In the liturgy the sanctification of the man is signified by signs perceptible to the senses *and is effected in a way that corresponds with each of these signs*."[80] Sacraments are not simply signs but also causes. Rahner, by contrast, wanted them to be causes only as signs. If Rahner were correct, the sacraments would not be fonts of grace. But Vatican II declares the liturgy to be both the "summit" and also "the font from which all [the Church's] power flows."[81] Furthermore, if Rahner were correct, the Mosaic rites would have had an efficacy of the same kind as the sacraments, albeit preparatory and of lesser degree. The Church, however, *qualitatively* distinguishes the efficacy of the sacraments from that of the Mosaic rites, which "did not cause grace."[82] Finally, for Rahner, the sacraments do not give us *more* grace, however analogously we use the notion of measure. Instead, Rahner held that in the sacraments the already present grace

---

[77] But Rahner scoffs, "This explanation seems to be rather artificial," in "Baptism and the Renewal of Baptism," TI 23, 199.

[78] DH 1310.

[79] DH 1606.

[80] DH 4007; emphasis mine.

[81] DH 4010.

[82] DH 1310.

comes to mature self-expression, that is, to categorical appreciation. Similarly, consider a man and a woman who, after months of common virtuous activities, tell each other, "I love you." No doubt, this self-expression brings about an increase in the love they bear for one another. Rahner *reduced* the increase of grace achieved through the sacraments to such kinds of self-expression.[83] But to the contrary, grace is not a natural skill that increases through human activity. Its effects in us can take root more deeply through our cooperation, but the sacraments are not our works. They are God's work upon us. Nor can our work produce more grace within. Still, we can in our lives enjoy an increase in the very grace of justification. We do so in two ways. First, we can through good works merit that God efficiently grant us an increase in this grace.[84] Second and above all, we enjoy an increase in grace through our participation in the sacramentals. As the Church teaches, the Eucharist causes an "increase of grace."[85] In neither of these ways is an already-present grace increased in the manner of self-expression. Instead, in each of these ways God efficiently produces in our soul a greater share in his grace. So, is Holy Mother the Church simply dragging behind her the dogmatic weight of an outdated Ptolemaic worldview?

Other problems come to light when we consider Rahner's treatment of infant baptism, which calls to mind the following dogmas:

1. The original sin in which we are conceived and born is a state of unrighteousness, the absence of justice and holiness, which Adam lost for us.[86]

2. Original sin disqualifies anyone who dies in this state from everlasting life.[87]

3. This loss is passed down by propagation; we inherit it by being begotten of Adam, so that it becomes proper to each of us. Thus, the Church condemns the notion of original sin as something we pick up by way of imitation of the bad example of others. A

---

[83] Rahner, "Baptism and the Renewal of Baptism," TI 23, 199–200.
[84] DH 1535 and 1574.
[85] DH 1322.
[86] DH 1511–12.
[87] DH 780, 858, 926, 1306.

bad example is a situation or a temptation, but original sin is the inherited *loss* of original justice.[88]

4. Original sin is removed in the rebirth of justification, whereby we receive sanctifying grace.[89]

5. For infants, baptism is *the* event in which they who are "born unrighteous" now "become just."[90]

How did Rahner treat these truths? Concerning the second dogma, Rahner wrote, "No man is excluded from salvation simply because of so-called original sin."[91] This passage appears to contradict the dogma that those who die "with original sin only . . . go down immediately to hell."[92] But Rahner was clever in his formula. Notice its *de facto* character: no one *is* excluded. Since the expression is only *de facto*, Rahner could, if scrutinized, claim he was not directly contradicting the dogma even though he seemed to be doing so. Perhaps, he could point out, there is hope for a non-sacramental remedy. Of course, such a remedy is possible to God's power, even though it is not promised in revelation. Importantly, if it exists, it is "known only to God" as Vatican II taught.[93] But Rahner presumed to know how such a remedy is offered: the supernatural existential, which can be operative in any action regarding any categorical object.[94] Moreover, Rahner's formula treats the second dogma with brazen flippancy as though it is of no consequence. It is not surprising that pastoral initiatives rooted in his thought treat original sin lightly. Finally, in some places, Rahner shed the careful formula of a merely *de facto* denial of the second dogma, claiming *de iure* that salvation "*cannot* be denied" except for mortal sin.[95] How can this be reconciled with the second dogma?

Moreover, Rahner's opinion on the first dogma devolved. In his early works, he affirmed that infants are conceived without grace. Even so, he balked at the

---

[88] DH 1349, 1513–14, 1523.

[89] DH 1514–15, 1523–24, 1528–30.

[90] DH 184, 219, 223, 780, 1349, 1514, 1523, 2536, 3330. See also CCC §1250.

[91] Karl Rahner, "The One Christ and the Universality of Salvation," *Theological Investigations*, vol. 16, *Experience of the Spirit: Source of Theology*, trans. David Morland (New York: Seabury Press, 1979), 200. See also Rahner, "Faith and Sacrament," TI 23, 188.

[92] DH 1306.

[93] DH 4322.

[94] Rahner, "Atheism and Implicit Christianity," TI 9, 147–52.

[95] Rahner, *Foundations*, 198; emphasis mine. See also Rahner, "Observations on the Problem of the 'Anonymous Christian,'" TI 14, 286; and Rahner, "Faith and Sacrament," TI 23, 188.

scriptural teaching that they are "children of wrath."[96] Further, he even entertained the idea of a "supratemporal" region in which God's love and original sin simultaneously *belong* to the infant, remarking that the temporal moment in which God's love takes effect in the infant (baptism) is "not after all very important."[97] Pastorally, this opinion supports a cavalier attitude toward the scheduling of baptisms, even though the Church warns about the gravity of delay.[98] If the second dogma is immaterial for Rahner, it is no surprise.

Things got worse. Rahner soon made clear that the supernatural existential begins at conception.[99] Further, he came to teach that the existential "*ipso facto* sanctifies [man] prior to any moral decision on man's own part."[100] The necessary implication is that from conception infants are in the state of grace. Consequently, original sin and grace "do not, properly speaking, follow one upon another in a temporal succession."[101] So, Rahner's knowledge of the inscrutable ways of God emboldened him implicitly to reject the first dogma, that infants are conceived in the state of the absence of grace, receiving sanctifying grace sometime later in life.[102] St. Paul, by contrast, described us all as "children of wrath" (Eph 2:3).[103] A Catholic examination of conscience is required here: have we imbibed this euphoric denial of human sinfulness? Do we, like Rahner, make bold to ignore the second dogma as though it were of no consequence and the first as if it did not exist? If so, how do our Lutheran brothers judge such Pelagian presumption? Rahner's rejection of the first dogma was implicit, not explicit, but we must be clear on what this means. His theory, if true, implies the very rejection of this dogma.

Concerning the third dogma, Rahner presented a caricature of the dogma and dismissed it. The dogma indicates—and responsible theologians hold—that Adam passed on *not personal fault* but the death of the soul (loss of grace) and that he did so by way of propagation. But Rahner was ever anxious to console his reader that original sin "in no way means that the moral quality of the actions of the first person or persons is transmitted to us, whether this

---

[96] See Karl Rahner, "The Immaculate Conception," TI 1, 207.

[97] Rahner, "The Immaculate Conception," TI 1, 208.

[98] DH 1349. See also Paul VI, Apostolic Letter *Solemni hac liturgia* (*Credo of the People of God*) (June 30, 1968), §18; *Acta Apostolicae Sedis*, vol. 60 (1968): 440.

[99] Rahner, "Brief Theological Observations on the 'State of Fallen Nature,'" TI 19, 47.

[100] Rahner, "The Sin of Adam," TI 11, 255.

[101] Rahner, "The Sin of Adam," TI 11, 259.

[102] Rahner, "Brief Theological Observations on the 'State of Fallen Nature,'" TI 19, 43–44.

[103] DH 1521.

be through a juridical imputation by God or through some kind of biological heredity, however conceived."[104] He diverted attention from the dogma and sound theology by distracting the reader with (a) the chimera of an inherited personal act, (b) the voluntaristic theory of imputation, and (c) the Lamarckian idea of an acquired biological "tic." What, then, substitutes for such a gross caricature? Original sin is a negative existential of freedom: it is a "present, universal and ineradicable situation of our freedom as co-determined by guilt."[105] What does this theory mean? In a nutshell, it means that original sin is not the loss of grace in our nature passed down through inheritance but rather the negative aspects of our situation, which inescapably condition us when we act, albeit without destining us to sin. Presenting original sin as an existential, the theory evades causal claims, providing (merely apparent) camouflage for the implicit but real denial of the first dogma. Allegedly, we acquire this existential not by inheritance but by living in a situation that includes, anterior to our freedom, the objectifications of the guilt of others. These objectifications negatively impact the circumstances of our freedom. We can work to improve on the situation, but we cannot overcome it. The existential is permanent and aboriginal; thus, all our labor is negatively marked, even though we are not predetermined to sin. Now, the Pelagians deny that original sin is the absence of original justice and holiness. They hold that original sin becomes ours not by generation from Adam but by imitation of Adam's example. Coupled with the implicit but real denial of the first dogma, Rahner's existential theory resembles the condemned Pelagian theory of imitation. Vorgrimler more boldly stated that one bears guilt for original sin only when one "consciously adopts it as his or her own."[106] Now, if original sin simply were this negative existential of our freedom, then any human living in our situation would bear this negative existential. How, then, could Our Lady and Our Lord Jesus Christ, who exercised freedom in the same situation as we, exist without any trace of original sin?

Concerning the fourth dogma, Rahner really implied that original sin is not removed by justification. As an existential, original sin must abide ineradicably. Else, being in the situation of the objectification of the guilt of others would not constitute, as Rahner insisted it does, one's existing in original sin.

---

[104] Rahner, *Foundations*, 111.

[105] Rahner, *Foundations*, 114.

[106] Vorgrimler, *Sacramental Theology*, 115.

Accordingly, one can simultaneously suffer original sin and yet be sanctified. To be sure, Rahner did not assert the contradictory presence and absence of grace. He did, however, hold that every sanctified pilgrim simultaneously has this negative existential. The supernatural existential and original sin exist in "dialectical" tension.[107] This tension is not a contradiction *because* Rahner implicitly denied the first dogma, that original sin is a state involving the absence of sanctifying grace. But contrary to Rahner's implicit but real rejection of the fourth dogma, the Church dogmatically teaches that original sin is removed in justification, which is "a transition from the state in which man is born a son of the first Adam to the state of grace and adoption as sons of God."[108]

Given the foregoing, it only makes sense that Rahner implicitly but really rejected the fifth dogma—that for an infant, justification occurs precisely at baptism, which brings about the forgiveness of original sin. According to Rahner, infants already have the supernatural existential: "At the moment of calling them into existence, God has already in free love, inserted himself with all his reality in each person as innermost strength and as final end."[109] In the infants, this existential sanctifies since it is sanctifying except for those who resolutely sin against conscience.[110] Because the infants cannot sin, they must be holy even before baptism. Hence, for Rahner, baptism is not the precise event in which an infant is sanctified. He implicitly but really rejects the fifth dogma. So, then, *why* baptize? According to Rahner, the already-present grace "wants to embody itself in all the dimensions of humanity and to become manifest as a divine and 'Christian' reality." Baptism is the "real symbol" or the thematically correct "embodiment and manifestation" of the grace already present.[111]

As is manifest, Rahner's Copernican Revolution turns the Church's faith in baptism inside out. We used to think that baptism brings grace to the infant and effects the forgiveness of original sin. Rahner exorcized that idea and promised that the infant brings grace to baptism, running afoul of the Church's teaching that "even children who of themselves cannot have yet committed any sin are truly baptized for the remission of sins."[112]

---

[107] Rahner, "The Sin of Adam," TI 11, 259; Rahner, "Brief Theological Observations on the 'State of Fallen Nature,'" TI 19, 48.

[108] DH 1524.

[109] Rahner, "Baptism and the Renewal of Baptism," TI 23, 196.

[110] Rahner, "Observations on the Problem of the 'Anonymous Christian,'" TI 14, 294; Rahner, *Foundations*, 198.

[111] Rahner, "Baptism and the Renewal of Baptism," TI 23, 197.

[112] DH 1514.

Rahner's description of the sacraments is echoed in his description of the Church. Just as the sacraments merely express the grace that is already deep within us, so the Church is simply the "full historical manifestation" of the grace already hidden in the world transcendentally.[113] In her sacraments, the Church does not bring new grace to a needy world; rather, she offers "signs of the grace of the *world*."[114] Could such a theory ever inspire an Italian Francis to journey to a sultan and a Navarrese Francis to journey to Japan, each eager to bring God's remedies to the needy? No, but such a theory could easily put a chill on missionary zeal. It could prompt a European missionary to boast about never baptizing indigenous persons of the Amazon in fifty years.[115]

What did Rahner say about the saving work of the greatest missionary, Our Lord? The Church proclaims that Christ merited the offer of grace and salvation.[116] Eternally loving the world, God sent his Son to be the cause on account of which redeeming grace is offered (Rom 3:25). Rahner caricatured this claim and rejected it: the Cross "cannot be the cause of the uncaused salvific will of God. . . . God is not transformed from a God of anger and justice into a God of mercy and love by the cross."[117] Witness again the strategy of deception and evasion. Rahner denied an absurd caricature of dogma and substituted an inadequate theory. His substitute theory is Christ as ultimate "real symbol." The fullness of salvation is in Christ because he is the historical climax of two movements: God's downward offer of salvation and man's upward movement of acceptance. Thus, Christ displays to the world God's irrevocable offer of grace and its definitive acceptance on our part. Now, this Hegelian dimension of Christology has promising potential, but its flower quickly faded in Rahner's care. First, Rahner invited his reader to conceive of Christ as a "marriage" of God and man.[118] Since a marriage implies two persons, such a Christ is reduced to a Marian figure, a person in whom God superabundantly dwells.[119] Second, relatedly, Rahner placed Christ in a receptive role vis-à-vis redeeming grace.

---

[113] Rahner, "Considerations on the Active Role of the Person in the Sacramental Event," TI 14, 180.

[114] Rahner, "Considerations on the Active Role of the Person in the Sacramental Event," TI 14, 181.

[115] See Luis Miguel Modino, "Corrado Dalmonego: Los indígenas pueden ayudar a la Iglesia a limpiarse," *Religión*, December 20, 2018.

[116] DH 1025, 1529, 1690, 3891; Second Vatican Council, Pastoral Constitution on the Church in the Modern World *Gaudium et spes* (December 7, 1965), §22.

[117] Rahner, "The One Christ and the Universality of Salvation," TI 16, 207.

[118] Karl Rahner, "Probleme heutiger Mariologie," in *Aus der Theologie der Zeit*, ed. Gottlieb Söhngen (Regensburg: Pustet, 1948), 98, no. 102.

[119] See Walter Kasper, *Jesus the Christ* (Mahwah, NJ: Paulist Press, 1976), 51–52.

Ultimately, Rahner unintentionally blasphemed, writing that Jesus "has been saved by God."[120] Third, Rahner insisted that a real symbol is *not* a cause of grace except *as* pregnant sign. So, he denied that Christ's work causes the offer of grace, either as secondary efficient cause or as meritorious cause.[121] Instead, Christ's cross is only "the consequence and not the cause"[122] of this offer. The pious Christian will object, citing the following passages in Scripture among others. Paul proclaimed Christ as "an expiation by his blood" (Rom 3:25; see also 1 John 2:2). Jesus claimed to gave "his life as a ransom for many" (Matt 20:28; see also 1 Tim 2:6). Paul celebrated Christ as the Paschal Lamb who "has been sacrificed" (1 Cor 5:7) and rejoiced that God made him "to be sin" (2 Cor 5:21). As the Church teaches, Paul meant that Christ became a "sacrifice for our sins."[123] For Rahner, suchlike dictums are only "secondary notions which must be explained in light of the primary and original data of Scripture."[124] Rahner thus relegated a matter of central concern, a set of inspired teachings, to the category of "secondary notion." A few years later, he insinuated the invalidity of the notion: "At that time the idea of propitiating the divinity by means of a sacrifice was a current notion which could be presupposed to be valid." Today, however, it "offers little help to us."[125] So, what was Rahner's understanding of the primary data? "The death of Jesus *means something* for the salvation of all men."[126] The death of God Incarnate "means something." Now there's a savior before whom one can fall to one's knees!

CONCLUSION

The promise of Rahner's brilliance was darkened by his sacrifice of faith upon the altar of modern reason. The buds of his insight withered under the tyranny of *a priori* necessity. He resisted the path of great theologians who begin with God's works and strive to fathom the fittingness thereof. Instead, after the briefest acknowledgement of having already encountered and embraced the Christian starting point, Rahner focused on deducing transcendental conditions of the

---

[120] Rahner, *Foundations*, 284.

[121] Rahner, "The One Christ and the Universality of Salvation," TI 16, 212–15.

[122] Rahner, "The One Christ and the Universality of Salvation," TI 16, 211.

[123] DH 539.

[124] Rahner, "The One Christ and the Universality of Salvation," TI 16, 211.

[125] Rahner, *Foundations*, 282.

[126] Rahner, "The One Christ and the Universality of Salvation," TI 16, 212.

possibility of being Christian. He then reworked the Catholic faith according to those conditions as though they were unquestionably legitimate. Knowing the tradition, he dismissed caricatures of it and substituted his own theories that fail to express the substance of the faith. The result was erosion and distortion of the faith. While affirming one truth, he denied another. We can recall some of these tragedies here.

Rightly confessing that there are not three Gods, Rahner absconded with the Father's only-begotten "Thou." His Trinity collapses into modalism: the Son as non-personal self-expression of the Father.

Rightly wary of the errors of voluntarism, Rahner clipped God's wings. He knew that the light of God radiates through the face of Christ, yet he was too impatient to affirm that divine freedom might have orchestrated things otherwise.

Rightly confident that God pursues pagans, Rahner smiled upon idols as effective mediations of grace. Of course, he rejected "categorical" idolatry as such, but he did not much mind the ritual practices of idolaters, which are only thematically incorrect. Moreover, he found the very notion of a "thematically correct" object troubling. Since no categorical object is ever adequate anyway, the notion of a thematically correct one appears hauntingly oxymoronic. Consider, then, how a committed Rahnerian might react to the practice of Eucharistic adoration. He might coin the blasphemous phrase "cookie worship," a phrase that once sullied mouths at my alma mater.

Indeed, rightly holding that the King of Glory also works beyond the sacraments, Rahner refused him entry through these ancient doors. Rahner was quick to insist that they are not "barren" but pregnant signs. This protest is of no avail. The Eucharist is not merely a pregnant indication of the surfeit of grace already coursing through our veins. It is the heavenly food come down from heaven to nourish famished pilgrims. But, on Rahner's reading, could not a live-streamed Mass be a sufficient embodiment of grace? How great of a trial would suspension of the sacraments really prove to be?

Rightly believing that God wills salvation, Rahner refused to hear about "children of wrath." For him, everyone has the supernatural existential from conception, and this is effectively sanctifying unless one sins mortally. So, for the infants, baptism is not a victorious transition from sin to grace but merely the cultic expression of the grace within. No sense in rushing this, especially in the midst of a pandemic.

Rightly holding that in Christ dwells the fullness of deity, Rahner stripped him of merit and mopped away his expiatory blood. Rahner sold the price of our salvation to the naysayers, only to behold a man who is but a Theotokos—and a redeemed one at that.

Rightly insisting that God is infinite and unfathomable, Rahner banished his face from human eyes. Every pious person confesses with Augustine that God cannot be exhaustively known. Yet, we strive to know of God even now, dimly through a mirror, and we hope someday to behold him face to face (1 Cor 13:12). When we fail to seek his face in right worship, we end up prioritizing historical progress and neglecting the higher things. But Our Lord said that one thing is necessary, and the very stones of Scripture still cry out, "Blessed are the pure of heart, for they shall see God" (Matt 5:8). To say, as Rahner did, that God is simply nested within our subjectivity as the condition of the possibility of gracious acts of self-expression does not feed the hungry heart. It is true that God is the light *in which* we see light. But he is also the Threefold Light whom we hope to see. Lovers search for their beloved and long to behold him: "'Your face, LORD, do I seek.' Hide not your face from me" (Ps 27:8).

THE HISTORICITY OF TRUTH: ON THE PREMISES AND FOUNDATIONS OF WALTER KASPER'S THEOLOGY

*Thomas Heinrich Stark**

The God who is enthroned above the world and history as an unchanging being represents a challenge for man. He must be denied for man's sake because he claims for himself the dignity and honour that are properly due to man. . . . A God who is only alongside and above history, who is not himself history, that God is a finite God. . . . Such a God corresponds to a rigid world view; he is the guarantor of the existing and the enemy of the new.[1]

Walter Kasper

The subject of the present essay is the philosophical, that is, pre-theological, foundations of Walter Kasper's theology, which—as the axiomatic basis of this theology—determine its basic structure. Lying at the heart of this axiomatic basis is—in my opinion—how Kasper defines the relationship between truth and historicity.

Following Ernst Troeltsch,[2] Kasper is convinced that the encounter currently taking place between theology and history brings with it far greater

---

* Translation by Susan Johnson. A German-language version of this essay with extended notes appears as "Die Geschichtlichkeit der Wahrheit—Zu den Voraussetzungen und Grundlagen der Theologie Walter Kaspers," *Divinitas*, new series, no. 1 (2021): 211–57.
[1] Walter Kasper, "Gott in der Geschichte," in *Gott heute. 15 Beiträge zur Gottesfrage*, ed. N. Kutschki (Mainz: Matthias-Grünewald-Verlag, 1967), 139–51, 148.
[2] Ernst Troeltsch, "Über historische und dogmatische Methode in der Theologie," in *Zur religiösen Lage, Religionsphilosophie und Ethik* (Tübingen: J. C. B. Mohr, 1913), 729–53.

problems than the encounter that took place long since between theology and the natural sciences.[3] Kasper illustrates this conviction with a fundamental experience of contemporary humanity. He writes: "At present we are experiencing a radical historicization of all areas of reality. Everything is in a state of upheaval and change; there is hardly anything fixed and constant anymore. This historical change has also seized the Church and her understanding of the faith."[4]

The origins of the radical historicization of all areas of reality asserted by Kasper lie in the actual course of European intellectual history, the latter being at the same time an illustration of the change it has brought about. Kasper writes:

> The Church and her fundamental creeds had, after all, taken shape in antiquity. Antiquity assumed that there was a fixed set of essential laws [*Wesensgesetzlichkeiten*] governing reality as a whole, as well as an eternal order governing all processes of change. History was a phenomenon within the framework of an encompassing order.

As a result of this, history did not become a central problem in ancient times. The situation is, however, different in modern times and in the historicism characterizing them, which—the way having been prepared by humanism—began to finally break ground in Romanticism and German idealism from the turn of the nineteenth century onwards. Kasper describes the result of this paradigm shift, which he terms a "revolution," as follows:

> For modern thinking . . . history is not a moment within an encompassing order; rather, every order is a moment within a history that immediately relativizes it. Here reality does not have a history; it is itself profoundly history.[5]

The revolution of historical consciousness was, of course, based on a necessary precondition: "History could not be experienced as history until the historical tradition was no longer an automatically lived reality, but was instead felt to be a past that had been overcome and which people strove critically to get

---

3 Walter Kasper, *Einführung in den Glauben* (Mainz: Matthias-Grünewald-Verlag, 1972), 134. In English: Walter Kasper, *An Introduction to Christian Faith*, trans. V. Green (London: Burns and Oates, 1980), hereafter, *Introduction*. The quotations in the present text have been translated directly from the German as the published English translation is often very free. The page numbers nevertheless refer to the published English edition.

4 Kasper, *Einführung*, 134; *Introduction*, 155.

5 Kasper, *Einführung*, 135; *Introduction*, 156. Cf. Walter Kasper, *Das Absolute in der Geschichte. Philosophie und Theologie der Geschichte in der Spätphilosophie Schellings* (Mainz: Matthias-Grünewald, 1965); Walter Kasper, *Glaube und Geschichte* (Mainz: Matthias-Grünewald, 1970).

beyond. . . . This meant a relativization of the previous argument from authority and fundamentally challenged the absolute validity of sacred documents."[6]

Accepting without contradiction this historical finding as he interprets it, Kasper now ascribes a normative significance to it when he states: "The things that happen in history are theologically not merely the surface phenomena of an eternal ground of being, not fleeting shadows of the eternal, but rather the actual nature of 'things' themselves. There is no metaphysical ordering structure that could be disentangled from all the concretion in history and salvation history." For, "history is the last horizon of all reality."[7] From this it follows: "An historical view of the world therefore states that reality does not represent an objectively existing entity, that instead the subject enters into the constitution of the world, as, conversely, the subject is mediated by the world. So the constitution of reality takes place in the dialectical interplay of world and man."[8] Of course, in the final analysis man cannot be excluded from this historicization either; in fact, not even nature can. For, "what was said of the absolute spirit in idealistic thinking is said of man in existentialist thinking. Man does not live only in a history that remains somehow external to him; history is instead . . . man's constitution. . . . Man is profoundly historical."[9] Indeed, given these premises, even cosmic reality undergoes a thoroughgoing historicization. Kasper asks: "What kind of reality is it that we have to have in our sights when articulating the faith today?" And he replies: "Today this is obviously not a given nature and a cosmos encompassing us; it is instead a reality that human labour, civilisation and technology are helping to shape. Human activity enters this reality as a constitutive component of its makeup. It is a societally mediated reality."[10] The following theory points in exactly the

---

[6] Kasper, *Einführung*, 136; *Introduction*, 157.

[7] Kasper, *Einführung*, 144; *Introduction*, 165.

[8] Here Kasper is quoting Walter Schulz, *Philosophie in der veränderten Welt* (Pfullingen: Neske/ Buechergilde Guetenberg, 1972), 10, 143f, 470ff, 602ff, 841ff, quoted in Walter Kasper, *Der Gott Jesu Christi*, Gesammelte Schriften, vol. 4 (Freiburg im Breisgau: Herder, 2008), 194. Kasper describes this constructivist position (in the same paragraph) as being in accordance with the scholastic tradition—which it recognizably is not—since Scholasticism assumed a decidedly realistic standpoint. As an epistemological justification of his position, Kasper argues as follows: "Experience embraces both objective experience and subjective feelings. It arises from the interplay of objective reality and subjective intercourse with the natural and social environment. . . . So experience has a dialectical structure; and that means it is historical. For 'history' means the reciprocal interaction between man and world." Kasper, *Der Gott Jesu Christi*, 159; in English: *The God of Jesus Christ*, trans. Matthew J. O'Connell (London: SCM, 1984), 82.

[9] Kasper, *Einführung*, 135f; *Introduction*, 156f.

[10] Kasper, *Einführung*, 108; *Introduction*, 121.

same direction: "So the world is not finished but involved in a continuous process in which man and the world mutually change and determine each other. It is not an eternal natural order but an historical world."[11] This means that there is no unappealable objectivity in the sense of the classical concept of *physis* (nature); rather, material reality and its order, too, are the product of historical processes. (This, incidentally, is a central thesis of the postmodern gender theorist Judith Butler.)

But if history is in such a radical way the last horizon of all reality, this cannot remain without consequences for the concept of truth. And so, Kasper approvingly cites Hegel's three most famous statements about the concept of truth: "For Hegel, the True is the whole. 'However, the whole is only the essence consummating itself through its development.' 'The True is thus the Bacchanalian revel in which no member is not drunk.'"[12] Admittedly—as Kasper rightly points out—Hegel's concept of truth stands in the tradition of the modern conceptualization of truth: "In contrast to patristic and high scholastic teaching, the modern age is no longer familiar with the givenness of the truth mediated by tradition. Now the truth results instead from the process of history. Truth is not merely mediated historically; it is history and historical. With this, one can either reconcile everything and join Hegel in sublating all historical spirits into one absolute spirit, or else one can revolutionise everything and subordinate truth to the tradition of the respective praxis and the goal of history that is striven for in it."[13]

"The historical thinking of the modern age did not," according to Kasper, "come about without the influence of the biblical belief in history; it represents, so to speak, its secularized consequence."[14] Therefore, it is also closer than classical philosophy to the "scriptural understanding of truth."[15] "In contrast to an otherwise widespread understanding of truth, truth in the biblical sense," so Kasper argues, "is not simply the agreement between thinking and reality

---

[11] Kasper, *Einführung*, 136; *Introduction*, 157. On Kasper's theory that reality as such is not merely historical but rather itself entirely history, see also: *Evangelium und Dogma. Grundlegung der Dogmatik*, Gesammelte Schriften, vol. 7 (Freiburg im Breisgau: Herder, 2015), 625f.

[12] Kasper, *Einführung*, 135; *Introduction*, 156. Here Kasper is quoting G. W. F. Hegel, *Phänomenologie des Geistes*, ed. Johann Hofmeister, 6th ed. (Hamburg: Meiner, 1952), 21, 39. Kasper's translator uses Hegel, *Phenomenology of Spirit*, trans. A. V. Miller (Oxford: Oxford University Press, 1977), 11, 27.

[13] Kasper, *Evangelium und Dogma*, 524f.

[14] Kasper, *Einführung*, 145; *Introduction*, 166.

[15] On the supposed convergence between modern and "biblical" thinking, cf. Kasper, *Der Gott Jesu Christi*, 255–61.

(*adaequatio rei et intellectus*).[16] Truth is rather an event, and it is only in the execution of it that the original presupposition is proved valid. Truth cannot be captured; rather, truth emerges. Truth and history belong directly together here."[17] Consequently, Kasper can also assert: "There are no propositions that are *a priori* true and infallible, that is, no propositions that, detached from any reference to a situation, concretely convey truth simply by being uttered as such."[18] It is this historicization of truth that leads Kasper to believe that prophetic proclamation calls for "the ever new shattering of hitherto held concrete conceptions of hope." He then continues: "Inner-historically truth always remains promise; it can never be adequately captured in propositions, but is open to God's ever greater future. Truth as it is understood in Scripture possesses the element of being surprising, new and surpassing."[19]

On the one hand, Kasper warns against what he calls a "banal criticism of propositional truths,"[20] only to contradict this warning a little later—in a way that is typical of him—when he explains:

> Nevertheless, such propositions[21] should not—as Rahner does in a way that actually contradicts the rest of his theory—be called infallible. It is only the orientation towards truth that is infallible; the articulation of this orientation can also miss, misrepresent or misinterpret the truth. This is linked to a basic insight of the post-Hegelian philosophy of history, which states that the per se infallible anticipation of the absolute is in essence indeterminately open and therefore variously determinable. The Absolute that shines forth from all cognition [*Erkenntnis*] is the absolutely

---

[16] Thomas Aquinas, *Summa theologiae* I, q. 16, aa. 1–2: "Quod autem dicitur quod veritas est adæquatio rei et intellectus potest ad utrumque pertinere." "Et propter hoc per conformitatem intellectus et rei veritas definitur. Unde conformitatem istam cognoscere, est cognoscere veritatem."

[17] Kasper, *Einführung*, 61; *Introduction*, 59.

[18] Kasper, *Evangelium und Dogma*, 809.

[19] Kasper, *Evangelium und Dogma*, 102.

[20] Kasper, *Evangelium und Dogma*, 189.

[21] In the preceding paragraph, Kasper explicates the propositions he is referring to here as follows: "After all, man does not exist in any other way than in language. Only in and through language does he extend into that sphere of unconditional truth. That is why in every language there are propositions that make an absolute claim, for example the statement that all human life is to be unconditionally protected. This basic insight of the philosophy of language was intended to prevent any banal criticism of propositional truths of the kind that sometimes plays a role in the infallibility debate." Kasper, *Evangelium und Dogma*, 189.

Open and as such the space of freedom. The absolute truth engages man absolutely and at the same time sets him free.[22]

Kasper tries to legitimize his fluidization of the classical concept of truth through what he calls the "eschatological character of theological truth": "Truth is a path, and faith means setting out on that path trusting that due to God's faithfulness the truth will turn out to be what it promises."[23] Since Kasper is well aware that his historicized concept of truth contradicts the magisterial tradition, he regards himself as entitled and called upon to reject statements by the Magisterium connected to this: "Precisely in order to ensure that the truth remains the same in different conditions of understanding it must be expressed differently. Those statements in the encyclicals *Humani generis* and *Mysterium fidei* which refuse to accept this historical character of dogmas fail to be convincing."[24] But since the (supposedly) biblically inspired and secularized historicity of Hegel to which Kasper refers pertains to world history, he, Kasper, is able to conclude: "World history and salvation history cannot . . . be cleanly separated." We learn what is meant by this statement from its justification:

All reality is subject to the call and offer of God's grace and is therefore potentially salvation history. That is why there are holy pagans and pagan prophets. If a theological distinction is nevertheless made between salvation history in the narrower sense and salvation history in the broader sense, this is because we as Christians assume that in the history of Israel, which was perfected and surpassed in Jesus of Nazareth, the word of God "infallibly" reached its goal, was received "purely" and testified to "correctly," that here God's dialogue with man was "successful" and that we here possess a yardstick against which we can judge all history.[25]

So how does the history of Israel become salvation history in the narrower sense? It is not because God, at a particular place and time, chose a certain people to be his own and, as the sovereign Lord of history, guides the destiny of his people on the ways of salvation. According to Kasper, the reason salvation history is the history of the people of Israel is rather that in it God's dialogue

---

22 Kasper, *Evangelium und Dogma*, 190.

23 Kasper, *Evangelium und Dogma*, 734.

24 Kasper, *Evangelium und Dogma*, 809.

25 Kasper, *Einführung*, 141; *Introduction*, 162.

with mankind has succeeded in an exemplary way; this is because certain people, namely the members of the people of Israel, have received the Word of God purely and because they have testified correctly to the success of the dialogue with God. Consequently, the behavior of human beings is as much a cause of salvation history's coming about as the action of God. That is why the history of Israel is not salvation history in a substantial and therefore unique sense either. Rather, it is merely the *yardstick* by which to judge when and where else world history actualizes its potential to be salvation history. It should therefore be possible for what has happened to the people of Israel to happen analogously in other places, at other times, to other peoples, for example to the peoples of the Amazon region.

According to this interpretation, the history of Israel would then not be the unsubstitutable foundation of salvation history, but merely an example of it. What kind of concept of the relationship and the "dialogue" between God and man lies behind this historical-theological construction becomes clear when we call to mind how Kasper characterizes what is specifically Christian in comparison to the history of Israel. "The Christian," according to Kasper, "reveals itself to us as an historical dialogue between God and man; it takes place in principle wherever people engage with the transcendence that opens up to them in their freedom."[26]

So, to recapitulate: in one human faculty, namely freedom—that is, in the immanence of the human spirit—a transcendence opens up (in whatever way). And when man "engages" with this transcendence (whatever that may mean), this is where the historical dialogue with God takes place. This historical dialogue in turn reveals "the Christian"—that is, what is Christian. But since this dialogue takes place in principle wherever people "engage" with their immanent transcendence, "the Christian" must—so the logical conclusion—also be able to reveal itself outside "the Christian" (whatever that, once again, is supposed to mean).

It actually goes without saying that such speculations and their consequences cannot remain without consequences for the understanding of the Church and the understanding of Sacred Scripture. Although for Kasper the Church is also an institution, she is nevertheless to his way of thinking "primarily event; she is something happening."[27] Scripture, too, then becomes, so

---

[26] Kasper, *Einführung*, 140; *Introduction*, 162.
[27] Kasper, *Einführung*, 123; *Introduction*, 139.

to speak, a historical event. For salvation history "in turn has a history of its own in which it first becomes itself. Hence it should come as no surprise to us to find mythological, polytheistic and pagan elements persisting in the Old Testament that are at odds with both the New Testament and our enlightened consciousness. Nor does the New Testament succeed everywhere to the same extent in capturing the truth and reality of Jesus Christ."[28]

So, if even Sacred Scripture—since it is not always completely "successful"—is not simply the word of God but first has to work its way up historically to this height, then how much less can the word of the Church be the word of God? "Therefore the word of the Church is not simply and in every respect the word of God; the Church is only ever journeying anew towards it."[29] Therefore, "the Church must go beyond herself over and over again into her own future; she virtually lives through proclaiming her own provisionality (Karl Rahner). She does not simply have the truth, but must seek it anew over and over again. This is done by paying patient and courageous attention to the 'signs of the times.'"[30]

Here exegesis has an important role to play since "the interpretation of Sacred Scripture becomes, as it were, the 'soul of the whole of theology.'"[31] In this context Kasper distinguishes a "dogmatic" from a "historical-critical reason."[32] Whatever may be hidden behind these catchwords with their pretended technical terminological precision, Kasper at any rate opts for a priority of the historical-critical method since "the historical-critical method has meanwhile established its self-evident 'right of abode' not only in exegesis but also in dogmatics. All more recent dogmatic drafts strive to include exegetical findings."[33] "This recognises in principle the critical function of Scripture in relation to the dogmatic tradition and a pure Denzinger theology becomes a thing of the past."[34] This means that the "critical function of Scripture" should be taken into account here against "dogmatic tradition." However, since—as we have heard—the Scriptures have not always completely "succeeded" in "capturing the truth and reality" of Jesus Christ, this deficit of the Scriptures must be compensated for by their historical-critical interpretation. It is therefore not surprising that

---

[28] Kasper, *Einführung*, 141f; *Introduction*, 170.

[29] Kasper, *Einführung*, 143; *Introduction*, 164.

[30] Kasper, *Einführung*, 142; *Introduction*, 163.

[31] Kasper, *Evangelium und Dogma*, 650.

[32] Kasper, *Evangelium und Dogma*, 651.

[33] Kasper, *Evangelium und Dogma*, 650.

[34] Kasper, *Evangelium und Dogma*, 651.

Kasper forthrightly admits: "The historical-critical method is, after all, not a neutral instrument, but rather a revolutionarily new way of thinking that permeates, problematizes and relativizes everything like leaven."[35]

And the Church must "respond to the signs of the times"—although it is clear that she "does not have these answers 'ready-made' to hand, but that the questions of the day demand a new and deeper penetration of the Gospel, in this way giving rise to new answers that are not simply an abstract conclusion drawn from what has gone before."[36] The Church, therefore, has "not to represent a system of abstract truths or a general worldview, but rather to proclaim God's mighty deeds in history and to make them present through word and sacrament."[37] "The dogmatic credal formulae should bear witness to God's historical fidelity. They are therefore indispensable signs and symbols for the faith, but not actually the 'object' ['*Sache*'] of the faith."[38] Kasper therefore calls for a "theological theology," citing Saint Thomas Aquinas[39]—as always, questionably—in support of his assertion that "the object of theology is therefore neither dogma nor the exegetical history of Scripture, but God; all other reality, however, is an object of theology inasmuch as it is related to God as its origin and objective."[40] The dogmas of the early Church frequently took the form of liturgical doxologies. "Dogma, according to this understanding, is not an abstract doctrine that is considered true, but rather a personal statement of faith whose goal is not so much the proposition itself as the 'object' it refers to, namely God himself, to whom the praise is addressed."[41] For this reason Kasper criticizes an understanding of dogmas as "officially presented propositional truths."[42] "In principle, truth can never be expressed in *one* sentence. Hence a theological question is never settled once and for all with one dogma."[43] "Dogmatic knowledge, too, is piecemeal knowledge. Dogmatic statements, too, are subject to the eschatological reservation."[44] "Dogmas can therefore only be stations along the way, but never the goal. Therefore they must remain

---

[35] Kasper, *Evangelium und Dogma*, 651.

[36] Kasper, *Einführung*, 142f; *Introduction*, 164.

[37] Kasper, *Einführung*, 138; *Introduction*, 159.

[38] Kasper, *Evangelium und Dogma*, 655.

[39] Thomas Aquinas, *Summa theologiae* I, q. 1, a. 6.

[40] Kasper, *Evangelium und Dogma*, 656.

[41] Kasper, *Evangelium und Dogma*, 733.

[42] Kasper, *Evangelium und Dogma*, 176.

[43] Kasper, *Einführung*, 43; *Introduction*, 170.

[44] Kasper, *Evangelium und Dogma*, 191.

fundamentally open to the Church's further historical journey. They are not just the conclusion of a particular historical development; they are always at the same time a new beginning, too."[45]

With Kasper there is a clearly recognizable tendency to understand dogmas as the result of a social contract within the Church since dogmas result—in his opinion—from the communal nature of the Church and the concomitant need to formulate common credal statements. "Dogmas are therefore a kind of disciplinary language regulation in the Church. In many cases they could in principle be stated differently."[46] According to Kasper, the disciplinary aspect of the dogmatization process referred to here also produces a one-sidedness in the way dogmas are formulated since dogmatization often takes place as a rejection of heretical-because-one-sided interpretations of the faith. "If the Church opposes an interpretation, she dogmatizes what she believes in a targeted manner. She then expresses this belief with a certain one-sidedness that results from the error being condemned."[47] In this way, Kasper argues, the alleged one-sidedness of dogmatized magisterial statements reflects the complementary one-sidedness of the heresies that the Magisterium is condemning.

Kasper caps this all off when he speaks out in favor of a clearly Gnostic-inspired, pessimistic assessment of finiteness and historicity by equating the latter with a "sinful closedness" (probably toward the truth) in the following formulation: "Not only the finiteness of human language, but also its historicity—and that also means its sinful closedness—are at work. It is therefore possible for dogmatic propositions to be formulated in an overhasty, superficial, arrogant, interest-based or unloving manner. They are therefore—as Heinrich Schlier has put it—abidingly *denkwürdig*."[48] In this context, the term "*denkwürdig*" (memorable, noteworthy) is probably to be understood as a synonym for "*fragwürdig*" (questionable, dubious) since "it is perfectly possible for dogmas to be one-sided, superficial, opinionated, stupid and overhasty."[49] That is why "in the history of dogma there is also a history of forgetting, of impotence and of failure."[50]

---

[45] Kasper, *Evangelium und Dogma*, 734. Admittedly, Kasper does not concede such a new beginning to the Marian dogmas of 1854 and 1950 since, to his way of thinking, they represent a "furthest extreme." "They are more the end product of a development than a new beginning with future promise" (176).

[46] Kasper, *Evangelium und Dogma*, 735.

[47] Kasper, *Evangelium und Dogma*, 733.

[48] Kasper, *Evangelium und Dogma*, 192.

[49] Kasper, *Einführung*, 148; *Introduction*, 170.

[50] Kasper, *Einführung*, 143; *Introduction*, 164.

Therefore, the Church must "daily confess her guilt, her falling short of the goal."[51] For, "sociological and historical findings make many outward forms and structural elements of the Church appear conditioned by their respective times and the corresponding doctrines suspiciously like ideology, i.e. like the super-structure and canonization of a particular historical and sociological status. The upheaval is most striking in moral theology."[52] And Kasper provides an example of this: "The citing of a dogma is where the real problem begins, namely that of interpreting it for the respective time. Merely citing the doctrinal provisions of the Council of Trent on, for instance, the indissolubility of marriage—however true and important these statements continue to be today—says very little about the concrete pastoral 'treatment' of people in second marriages."[53]

We can probably only understand Kasper's position by setting it against the background of one of his remarks on political theology, namely: "Proclaiming the faith realistically today means articulating it in a socially relevant way."[54] This is why, for him, the "question of the social efficacy of the faith" is certainly of theological significance.[55] But how is the social relevance and efficacy of the faith to be ensured? In light of everything we have noted so far, Kasper's answer would probably have to go something like this: this is done by evaluating the implications for salvation history of the factual course of history and of those "signs of the times" that point to these implications. But then, as Kasper notes, there is a "history of human freedom, in which the dignity of the personal con-science is being increasingly discovered," something he doubtlessly interprets as such a sign of the times.[56] As far as ecclesiastical politics is concerned, this assessment is then spelled out as follows:

> If discrepancies arise between the Church's official doctrine and the everyday faith experience of the faithful—as is widely the case today—then such conflicts cannot be resolved by simply reiterating and re-inculcating the traditional formulae of the faith without any kind of discussion. It is only in the consensus of everyone that the truth of the gospel can emerge. The ecclesiality of faith

---

[51] Kasper, *Einführung*, 144; *Introduction*, 164.
[52] Kasper, *Einführung*, 144; *Introduction*, 158.
[53] Kasper, *Evangelium und Dogma*, 809.
[54] Kasper, *Einführung*, 108; *Introduction*, 121.
[55] Kasper, *Einführung*, 108; *Introduction*, 122.
[56] Kasper, *Einführung*, 137; *Introduction*, 158.

is not expressed primarily in an attitude of obedience towards ecclesiastical authority.[57]

For, according to Kasper, ecclesiastical obedience is a reciprocal relationship; he maintains: "Obedience in the Church can never be described as one-way; it is something that occurs mutually."[58] This would mean that not only do the people of the Church have a duty of obedience toward the Magisterium, but that vice versa the Magisterium has one toward the people of the Church.

For Kasper, infallibility is therefore "a relative, or better: . . . a relational concept."[59] "Infallibly proclaimed dogmas are relational in the sense that real symbols are relational. The point of them is to make something else really present and thus point beyond themselves."[60]

> Tradition is [therefore] not to be confused with the apostolic *symbolum* or any other expression of Christian truth; it is rather "the meaning and thought, the objective spirit of the Christian truth, which keeps on creating new expressions of itself and manifests itself in the most diverse directions, but always as the same spirit." It is "not just the apostolic word as such, as a definitely formulated content"; rather it is at the same time "the apostolic spirit" which was handed on to the Church and lives on in her. Thus tradition is not "the continual repetition of the original truth in its unhistorical form, but rather the continual reproduction of this truth in ever new historical forms."[61]

"In dealing with tradition, a 'surplus' repeatedly announces itself that has not been adopted in the implementation. By taking tradition at its word, one is led again and again to criticize the traditions that represent it and to redesign them in a creative way."[62] With regard to the historical mediation of tradition, Kasper refers to Hegel, stating: "Hegel's philosophy [can] be extremely helpful when it comes to taking intellectual responsibility for this historical mediation and thus better conceptualizing the essence of tradition."[63]

---

[57] Kasper, *Einführung*, 125; *Introduction*, 142f.

[58] Kasper, *Einführung*, 126; *Introduction*, 143.

[59] Kasper, *Evangelium und Dogma*, 194.

[60] Kasper, *Evangelium und Dogma*, 194.

[61] Kasper, *Evangelium und Dogma*, 498f.

[62] Kasper, *Evangelium und Dogma*, 499.

[63] Kasper, *Evangelium und Dogma*, 527. Here we learn how Kasper intends to use Hegel's philosophy in

What Kasper intends to conceptualize here with the help of Hegel is, for instance, the distinction made in classical theology—which he refers to disparagingly as "*Schultheologie*" (scholastic theology)—between tradition as *actus tradendi (id quo traditor)* and as *traditum (id quod traditor)*. The unity of these two aspects of the connectedness of tradition (*Traditionszusammenhang*) creates

a comprehensive connectedness between the people involved in the process of tradition. . . . The subject of tradition is therefore a "we," theologically speaking, the "we" of the ecclesial community of faith. This traditional statement can be better understood by making critical use of Hegel's philosophy. With Hegel's help, Church tradition understood as an act-being unity can be thought of and conceptualized as the concrete place of truth, as the presence of the Spirit of God and thus as the principle of theological knowledge [*Erkenntnis*]. The current discussion about the theory of truth points in the same direction. For it has shown that truth asserts itself in the process of communication and consensus-building.[64]

With regard to tradition and its infallibility, Kasper therefore concludes: "So it is not a matter of the infallibility of lifeless and rigid propositions, but rather of the infallibility of living historical authorities. Depending on the

---

determining the identity and continuity of the context of tradition (*Traditionszusammenhang*) in the Church's proclamation of doctrine. Hegel, he says, created with respect to the "historically dynamic understanding of truth" the ingenious concept of "definite negation" (Hegel, *Phänomenologie des Geistes* no. pp. 92, 68f, 74). Cf. on this above all H.-G. Gadamer, *Wahrheit und Methode. Grundzuge einer philosophischen Hermeneutik*, 2nd ed. (Tübingen: Mohr Siebeck, 1965), 335–40 (no. 32); T. W. Adorno, *Drei Studien zu Hegel* (Frankfurt am Main: Suhrkamp Verlag, 1969), a concept that can be of significant assistance in solving our question of identity and continuity amid all the variability and discontinuity. He assumes that we can recognize each thing only in contradistinction to another. Truth is therefore only possible via negation, through refinement of the original experience, through insight into the untruth of previous knowledge. This "self-consummating scepticism" does not, however, lead to "pure nothingness." It is not a total negation, but rather a determinate negation. The nothingness is a determinate nothingness and has its content. It is "the nothingness from which it itself has resulted." "In that negation the transition has been made by virtue of which the progression through the complete series of shapes comes about on its own accord" [Hegel, *Phänomenologie des Geistes* (at n. 92), 68f.]. The new object contains in each case "the nullity of the first"; but it is also "what experience has learned about it" [ibid., 73] and in this respect the new object is the truth about the old one. So it is precisely in the negative-critical mediation that continuity is maintained. The "tremendous power of the negative" [ibid., 29] necessarily includes a positive. "The result of Dialectic is positive, because it has a definite content, or because its result is not empty and abstract nothingness but the negation of certain specific propositions which are contained in the result" [*Enzyklopädie der philosophischen Wissenschaften im Grundrisse,* ed. G. W. F. Hegel, F. Nicolin & O. Pöggeler, 6th ed. (Hamburg: Feliz Meiner Verlag, 1959), 103] (Kasper, Evangelium und Dogma, 788).

[64] Kasper, *Evangelium und Dogma*, 528.

situation, they may in some circumstances be able to historically reinterpret their earlier statements."[65]

Certainly, such a new understanding of "infallibility" then also brings with it "a new, substantially more open and dynamic form of orthodoxy."[66] Walking further along Hegelian paths, Kasper explains:

> From this dynamic understanding of orthodoxy arises . . . the legit-imate right to, indeed the need for dogma criticism. As we have seen, the historical appropriation and reception of tradition is only possible critically. It is only through critical mediation that tradition arrives at its own truth. Only when the one-sided, his-torically conditioned, limited and in this respect also false and untrue aspects of the dogmas are pointed out, only when what is not true about them is also stated, only then is "the truth" about them told. This formulation is deliberately ambiguous. It means that the truth of the dogmas also includes their relative untruth and one-sidedness, but also that dogma criticism, like any other criticism of tradition, is only legitimate if it sticks to "the matter in hand" and engages with the immanent truth in such a way as to take the propositional intention and pinnacle of meaning [Sinnspitze] immanent in them as a starting point and lead beyond these. So one must interpret dogmas dialectically; then criticism is an element of the thing-in-itself and not a reasoning brought in from outside.[67]

When you try to make this sort of dialectical omelette, eggs will, of course, be broken, since "not every statement is possible in every context. Not every dogma can be reintroduced into every new overall scheme. It definitely did have its function and its truth within the old system; it does not simply become false even today. But in some circumstances it can simply be dead within a new way of thinking and facing new problems. Dogmas can die if they are no longer assimilated in a living way and faithfully put into practice."[68] "Orthodoxy

---

[65] Kasper, Einführung, 149; Introduction, 171. Cf. in this connection Kasper, Evangelium und Dogma, 790: "So we must not relate infallibility to individual propositions but rather to the fact that with Jesus Christ God's truth came definitively and infallibly into the world."

[66] Kasper, Evangelium und Dogma, 792.

[67] Kasper, Evangelium und Dogma, 791.

[68] Kasper, Evangelium und Dogma, 791. And this, to Kasper's way of thinking, is precisely what is happening at the present time, for "today we are experiencing an enormous upheaval in all the

must therefore be understood as a dynamic event and as an open process. It is the binding and obligatory context of dialogue between the contemporary Church and Tradition, and between the different groups and tendencies within the Church of today."[69] For, "the authority that gives concrete expression to the Gospel with a claim to being definitive is the Church as a whole. It is the real subject of infallibility. . . . The infallibility of the Magisterium thus remains integrated in the infallibility of the whole Church."[70] Thus, the authority of the Magisterium would be dependent on the above-mentioned consensus. A Church built in every respect on dialogue and consensus would cease to be a "system of unfreedom and fear." It is, Kasper argues, not acceptable "to maintain an absolutist regime [in the Church]. It is only possible to demonstrate the credibility of the faith, especially today, by at the same time supporting a serious reform of the Church."[71] And it is hard to avoid the impression that leading forces in the Church are currently pursuing the aim of pushing through a reform of the Church along Kasper's lines, in which changing the Church's moral teaching is just the beginning—albeit a weighty one.

Of particular interest and central importance in this context is the ecclesiological foundation with which Kasper backs up the position he takes on Church politics and in which historicity once again plays a central role.

Kasper defines the Church as the "sacrament of the Spirit"[72] and admits frankly with respect to this that "the definition of the Church as the sacrament of the Spirit is not at all as harmless as it appears at first sight. What it basically amounts to is a determined correction of the view, originating from Augustine and last reiterated on the part of the Magisterium by Pius XII in the encyclical 'Mystici corporis' (1943), according to which the Holy Spirit is the soul of the body of the Church."[73] A good hundred pages later, however, Kasper—arguing in precisely the opposite direction—praises the Tübingen School for their "criticism of the narrow view of the Church as a sociological and hierarchical

---

socio-cultural conditions of our lives. The changes are so all-embracing and so breathtaking that most people's consciousnesses can scarcely keep up with them. This gives rise to an extremely great non-simultaneity of consciousness" (*Evangelium und Dogma*, 791).

[69] Kasper, *Evangelium und Dogma*, 806.

[70] Kasper, *Einführung*, 150; *Introduction*, 171f.

[71] Kasper, *Einführung*, 64; *Introduction*, 62.

[72] Cf. Walter Kasper, *Die Kirche Jesu Christi. Schriften zur Ekklesiologie I*, Gesammelte Schriften, vol. 11, ed. George Augustin and Klaus Krämer (Freiburg im Breisgau: Herder, 2008), 295–305. Originally, "Die Kirche als Sakrament des Geistes," in Walter Kasper and Gerhard Sauter, ed., *Glaube im Prozess: Christsein nach dem II. Vatikanum: Für Karl Rahner* (Freiburg im Breisgau: Herder, 1984), 221–39.

[73] Kasper, *Die Kirche Jesu Christi*, 298.

THE FAITH ONCE FOR ALL DELIVERED

structure" and applauds them for the fact that Möhler and "likewise John Henry
Newman and Matthias Josef Scheeben, who started off in the Roman School,
. . . once more looked upon the Church, primarily from the viewpoint of her
inner life, as a living organism,"[74] that is, as a body. This, it must be added, is
precisely how a tradition stretching from Saint Augustine to Pope Pius XII
understood her.[75]

However, of far more crucial significance than the contradiction that
emerges here is the following statement of Kasper's: "The Church is an intermediate reality which, in a similar way to the Old Testament law, has 'come
between' until the visible dawning of the eschatological kingdom of God. The
Church is thus by her very nature pointed beyond herself. She is an anticipatory
sign of the rule of God, which is one day meant to encompass the whole of
reality and which is secretly breaking through everywhere, including outside
the Church."[76] Kasper is asserting two things here. First, that the Church, that
is, the Mystical Body of Christ and the concrete form of the New Covenant,
will one day be overcome in just the same way as the Old Covenant. Secondly,
contrary to what the Church has always and irrevocably taught, he is saying
that the Church is not the exclusive instrument used by God to spread his
dominion over the whole of creation and that, in this specific sense, there is
no salvation outside the Church. Rather, he says, God's salvific work is also
"secretly" at work outside the Church—and is so "everywhere"—from which
the logical conclusion is that participation in the life of the body of the Church
is but one among countless other ways to salvation, which makes conversion
to the one and only Church of Christ dispensable, if not even making mission
in the final analysis an affront (*Ärgernis*).[77]

The eschatological aspects of Kasper's thinking that are discernible here

---

[74] Kasper, *Die Kirche Jesu Christi*, 433.

[75] The contradiction that emerges in these statements becomes particularly evident when one recalls
Kasper's firm option for a definition of the Church as *communio*; cf. Kasper, *Die Kirche Jesu Christi*,
397–522. For every *communio*—once it reaches a certain size—is by nature primarily a social and
juridical, institutional, and consequently administrative entity, making it in the Aristotelian sense
a political one, too. And that is indeed exactly how the Church presents herself in the spiritually
emaciated German-speaking countries. In the overstaffed and structurally fossilized corporation-like
"*communio*" of the German-speaking churches, with their network of institutions, committees, and
councils and their way of acting as if they were national churches, there is little sign of any animate
and therefore living-sensual embodiedness.

[76] Walter Kasper, *Katholische Kirche. Wesen, Wirklichkeit, Sendung* (Freiburg: Herder, 2011), 299.

[77] Let us recall that it has already been pointed out above that in Kasper's view "that which is Christian
. . . reveals itself—in a mysterious way—outside the Church as well." Cf. Kasper, *Einführung*, 140;
Introduction, 162.

then take on a clearer form in his pneumatology, and he in fact defines ecclesiology as "function" of pneumatology. The starting point for this pneumatological ecclesiology is once again Kasper's understanding of the eschatological character of the Church:

> The Church as an eschatological phenomenon virtually lives from the proclamation of her provisionality (Karl Rahner). She is orientated not only towards a salvation-historical past but also towards a salvation-historical future in which she will one day be obsolete.... The Church bears the shape of history (Vatican II); she, too, is subject to the law of history. She, too, does not simply have the truth; she must first be guided into all truth by the Holy Spirit (Jn 16:13). The word of the Church is not simply and in every respect the word of God; the will of the Church is not simply the will of God; the respective spirit prevailing in the Church is not simply identical with the Holy Spirit. The Church is only on her way to all this, forever embarking on it anew.[78]

But because the Church does not "simply" embody the truth and the will of God, instead always merely being—under the guidance of the Spirit—on her way to the truth and will of God, "that is why ecclesiology falls within the framework of pneumatology." Kasper describes it—as already noted above—as a "function of pneumatology."[79] But—and the following point really cannot be emphasized enough—"here the spirit is," as Kasper puts it, "not first of all the third divine person, but rather the power through which God's saving action in Jesus Christ becomes present in history."[80] But what does this spiritual "power," which is not the third divine Person, bring about? After everything we have heard so far, it would seem to be that this "power" guides the Church along her historical path. But where does this path of the Church lead? "The historical path of the Church is where the beginnings of a return of the whole of history to God take place.... Rather, right from the very beginning the whole reality of creation is created for Christ (Col 1:16; Eph 1:10) and related to salvation history. Thus the reality of creation, too, is deep down historically determined."[81]

---

[78] Walter Kasper, *Glaube und Geschichte* (Mainz: Matthias-Grünewald, 1970), 55.

[79] Cf. Walter Kasper and Gerhard Sauter, *Kirche, Ort des Geistes* (Freiburg im Breisgau: Herder, 1976); Kasper, *Katholische Kirche*.

[80] Kasper, *Einführung*, 121; *Introduction*, 138.

[81] Kasper, *Einführung*, 144; *Introduction*, 165.

At this point Kasper now refers in a footnote to Pierre Teilhard de Chardin, stating, "Above all Pierre Teilhard de Chardin has repeatedly pointed out the significance of an evolutionary view of the world for the Christian faith."[82]

What we have before us now is the crux of the matter. For the question arises as to who or what that ominous "spirit" actually is by whose power "God's saving action in Jesus Christ becomes present in history," if he is not the third divine Person? The answer to that question can be deduced from Kasper's reference to Teilhard de Chardin. The fact is that Teilhard's eschatology of the Omega Point describes a return of the world and history to God, doing so as the result of an evolutionary process of perfection that takes place in history. It is therefore not surprising that Kasper, in following Teilhard, is forced to reject the classical doctrine of original sin as obsolete and claim that "a new understanding of the traditional doctrine of original sin has been arrived at."[83] He goes on to say: "Thus, for example, there is no longer any place for the classical teaching on man's original state in its previous form within an evolutionary-historical world view. Nevertheless, the identity and continuity of the one message is not necessarily jeopardized by all this."[84] It will, however, hardly be possible to accept this assessment since Teilhard's historical-philosophical interpretive model corresponds structurally to that of German idealism, especially to that of Hegel's philosophy of spirit/mind (*Geist*). According to Hegel, history is in fact a process of perfection in which the absolute spirit comes to itself by sublating its being-in-itself and its being-for-itself into its being-in-and-for-itself, and in the end—returning to itself—apprehends itself as the true, which is the real. We know from revelation, however, that the end of history is not characterized by the final self-perfection of creation, but by its ultimate falling away from God and the ultimate catastrophe of human history that accompanies it. It has often been pointed out that it is impossible to tell how Teilhard's eschatology is supposed to be compatible with that of Sacred Scripture and the Tradition of the Church that is based on it.[85] And so it does not seem to me too far-fetched,

---

[82] Kasper, *Einführung*, 144; *Introduction*, 165n10. In other places, Kasper has attempted to mediate between Teilhard's position and others that contradict it, albeit in a way that is difficult to follow. On this see, e.g., Kasper, *Glaube und Geschichte*, 68, 155; Kasper, *Das Absolute in der Geschichte*, Gesammelte Schriften, vol. 2 (Freiburg im Breisgau: Herder, 2010), 547.

[83] Kasper, *Evangelium und Dogma*, 786f.

[84] Kasper, *Evangelium und Dogma*, 787.

[85] From the perspective of what is our main interest here—namely, philosophy, see in this context: Hans-Eduard Hengstenberg, *Evolution und Schöpfung. Eine Antwort auf den Evolutionismus Teilhard de Chardins* (München: Pustet, 1963); Hengstenberg, *Mensch und Materie. Zur Problematik Teilhard*

given the quotations I have cited above, to express the suspicion that the basic problem of Kasper's theology lies in its dependence on certain philosophical positions of German idealism.[86] In support of this view, it is also possible to adduce the fact that Kasper places himself in the tradition of the Tübingen School, which is known to have attempted to rebuild Catholic intellectual life on the basis of German idealism.[87] The pneumatology Kasper talks about, of which ecclesiology is said to be a function, would thus have as its object a spirit which, if it is not—as Kasper himself says—identical with the Third Divine Person, would be far more reminiscent of Hegel's absolute spirit, which comes to itself in a historical process, sublating its dialectical opposites within itself, and thus develops into that whole which is the true.

It therefore seems to me a quite reliable hypothesis to attribute the positions that Kasper has taken up again just recently in the fields of moral theology and sacramental ministry to the dependence of his theology on the positions taken on the philosophy of history by leading representatives of German idealism. Let me conclude by illustrating this hypothesis with a number of individual problems, which are, however—as will become apparent—closely connected.

When Kasper claims that the understanding of truth in Sacred Scripture is not congruent with that of classical philosophy, what is correct about this is that the concept of truth—especially in the New Testament—certainly implies more

---

de Chardins (Stuttgart: W. Kohlhammer, 1965); Dietrich von Hildebrand, *Das trojanische Pferd in der Stadt Gottes* (Regensburg: Verlag Josef Habbel, 1968), 339–75.

[86] Interestingly, Kasper accuses Ratzinger (his longtime adversary) of all people of being attached to an idealistic position shaped by Schelling and Hegel, and he identifies this in turn with the essence and the basic thought models of "Greek" philosophy (Walter Kasper, "Das Wesen des Christlichen," *Theologische Revue* 65 (1969): 182–88, at 184). The deceitfulness of this attack is twofold: firstly, the "idealism" of Attic philosophy (i.e., starting with Socrates and based on Plato and Aristotle), which has always been regarded as an indispensable tool by truly Catholic theology, implements a fundamentally different thought model from that of the "idealism" of Teutonic provenance. In Schelling and Hegel, it is not Socrates who rears his head again but rather Heraclitus, just as in Spinoza and Fichte (under Spinoza's influence) it is Parmenides redivivus. So, what does "Greek" mean here? Incidentally, the (nota bene: Protestant) theory of the alleged "Hellenization of Christianity" to be detected in the background here is so banal and has been so often refuted that—given the complexity of the actual circumstances—it is not necessary to waste a single further word on it. Secondly, with his attack on Ratzinger, Kasper disguises his own dependence—in this case actually provable—on what is this time not Attic idealism but rather German idealism of a Romanticist-Gnostic nature, which (in Heidegger's case in particular) shrouds the Mediterranean lucidity of Greek and Latin thinking in a Teutonic fog. So, after the dastardly deed is done, Kasper points a finger at Ratzinger and cries out: "Stop, thief!"

[87] On the Tübingen School, cf. Kasper, *Die Kirche Jesu Christi*, 18–22, 432f; Michael Kessel and Ottmar Fuchs, ed., *Theologie als Instanz der Moderne. Beiträge und Studien zu Johannes Sebastian Drey und zur Katholischen Tübinger Schule* (Tübingen: Francke Verlag, 2005); Stefan Warthmann, *Die Katholische Tübinger Schule. Zur Geschichte ihrer Wahrnehmung* (Stuttgart: Franz Steiner Verlag, 2011).

than the conformity of thinking or a statement with reality.[88] Needless to say, it does imply this conformity *too*. Indeed, the conformity between thinking or a statement and reality constitutes the only possible semantic basis of any concept of truth at all, including, of course, that found in the New Testament. All other implications of the New Testament concept of truth only become comprehensible when they are related to an *adaequatio rei et intellectus*. The only possible alternative interpretation would be to see Scripture as a myth that tells "what never was and always is."[89] But the Gospel of Jesus Christ is not a myth; it means exactly what it says. To be sure, not everyone is obliged to believe this.

When Kasper further claims that truth can in principle never be expressed in *one* sentence,[90] then that is simply wrong. For the *one* sentence, "It is snowing," is true, and is so precisely *when it is snowing* (as Alfred Tarski succinctly puts it).[91] Admittedly, the *whole* truth about a situation, even one so banal as the fact that it is snowing, cannot be expressed in a single statement; but then, no one has ever claimed that it can. When Kasper furthermore not only denies that individual propositions can be true but likewise maintains that truth can in principle "never be adequately captured in propositions," this would seem to mean that truth is simply not expressible, which in turn would mean that it is also not knowable.[92] But then, of course, the truth of this very proposition could not be stated with any claim to truth.

In addition to this, Kasper's view that there are "no *a priori* true and infallible propositions"[93] is simply false, too, since all true logical and mathematical judgments are *a priori* true (and, if you like, infallible), as are all true analytical judgments, for it belongs to the definition of analytical judgments that they are *a priori*. Dogmatic statements are not *a priori* true because they refer to facts of experience. However, their truth in no way depends on some ominous "situational reference" but only on the fact that they are adequate to the object that is predicated, that is, that they accurately reflect concrete facts.[94] The "situational reference" only comes into play in the hermeneutical mediation of

---

88   Kasper, *Einführung*, 145; *Introduction*, 166.
89   Thus, the classical definition of myth in Sallustius, *De diis et mundo* 4.
90   Kasper, *Einführung*, 149; *Introduction*, 170.
91   A. Tarski, "Der Wahrheitsbegriff in den formalisierten Sprachen," *Studia Philosophica* 1 (1936): 268.
92   Kasper, *Die Kirche Jesu Christi*, 194. Of course, it also still needs to be clarified here what exactly the term *"einfangen"* (capture) is supposed to mean in this context.
93   Kasper, *Evangelium und Dogma*, 809.
94   Kasper, *Evangelium und Dogma*, 809.

dogmatic statements; this, however, has no influence on the assertoric content of the statements.

And when Kasper furthermore asserts that infallibility does not apply to lifeless and rigid propositions but rather to living historical authorities,[95] then this assertion—if we delete the adjectives contained in it—is contrary to the infallible teaching of the Church, as anyone can easily confirm by consulting Denzinger or Ott.[96] For the Church does indeed teach the infallibility of certain statements, that is, of certain propositions.

Hence it is also wrong when Kasper claims that the Church does not have a system of abstract truths or a general worldview to represent since it goes without saying that dogmatics—when considered formally—is in fact a coherent system of abstract truths.[97] The simple reason for this is that dogmatics consists of statements in the form of descriptive propositions, and propositions are constructed from terms which, as general terms, are known to be abstract in nature. In the proposition "Jesus is the Christ," which Kasper sees as encapsulating the entire Christian message, the general and therefore abstract term "Christ" is predicated on the singular term "Jesus." This is—as everyone knows—simply the way language works.

However, if the dogmatic teaching of the Church is—when considered formally—a system of descriptive propositions, then it is also wrong to assert that the answers that the Church has to give in each respective case cannot be abstract conclusions drawn from previous answers.[98] For, with the correct application of the rules of logic, it is very well possible to derive from true propositions further true propositions, which can then serve as answers to questions that are currently topical. A theology that forgoes this possibility has renounced reason.

If, on the other hand, a theology decides not to renounce reason but rather to apply it, it will not be able to avoid developing a system of statements that meets the formal criteria of a worldview. And naturally, such a worldview—contrary to Kasper's opinion—will very well have to be the subject of the Church's proclamation as long as the Church is prepared to base her missionary activity on rational discourse rather than on suggestion and group dynamics.

---

[95] Kasper, *Einführung*, 149; *Introduction*, 171. Cf. in this connection Kasper, *Evangelium und Dogma*, 790: "So we must not relate infallibility to individual propositions but rather to the fact that with Jesus Christ God's truth came definitively and infallibly into the world."

[96] Faith is indeed *also* the accepting as true of propositions: DH 3008, 3009, 3011, 3033, 3034.

[97] Kasper, *Einführung*, 138; *Introduction*, 159.

[98] Kasper, *Einführung*, 142f; *Introduction*, 164.

When Kasper further advances the thesis that "infallible propositions are not propositions . . . which when detached from their situation and use can contain no error at all," this raises the question of what exactly he means by it. So let us hear how he justifies his thesis: "Dogmas are subject to the historicity of all human speech and are concretely true only in relation to the corresponding context. This means that they must be repeatedly re-interpreted and translated to meet new situations."[99] This is either banal or fundamentally wrong. For, on the one hand, it goes without saying that statements that were made several centuries ago have to be interpreted from the spiritual context of their times and "translated" in the quite literal sense but also, where necessary, in the figurative sense, too. This translation process is, however, only possible because the *most comprehensive* context and last horizon of dogmatic statements is that of human reason; human reason, though, is only capable of performing the required translation precisely because it is grounded in its participation in the eternal Logos and as such is not subject to historical change. But Kasper does not seem to have this banal fact in mind when he writes a little later that the certainty of faith must be "liberated from an anxious clinging to old forms and formulas" into "a tutiorism of risk (Karl Rahner)," because "in the present upheaval, it is not caution but responsible risk that is the safest thing." These remarks all sound very much like Heidegger's "resoluteness" (*Entschlossenheit*), but then they do after all take a seemingly pious biblical turn: "If infallibility is understood in this way as the infallibility of hope, then it is in the best sense of the word an evangelical truth."[100]

But what is the relationship between the truth of the Gospels and the truth of dogmatic statements? In a dispute with Hans Küng in 1975, Kasper speaks of the "epochal upheavals in the horizon of understanding" between "the apostolic and the post-apostolic tradition," only to go on to state: "With such continuity in discontinuity, it goes without saying that the Christ dogma of the early and medieval Church is not the organic development of biblical Christology, but is instead its historical realization, which can in turn serve as a model for the task of translating the Christian message that faces the Church today."[101] Kasper therefore advocates a "typological hermeneutics," which he characterizes as

---

[99] Kasper, *Einführung*, 148; *Introduction*, 170.

[100] Kasper, *Einführung*, 151; *Introduction*, 173.

[101] Walter Kasper, "Für eine Christologie in geschichtlicher Perspektive. Replik auf die Anmerkungen von Hans Küng," in *Grundfragen der Christologie heute*, ed. Heinrich Fries and Leo Scheffczyk (Freiburg im Breisgau: Herder, 1975), 179–83, at 180.

follows: "Statements of belief from the past must be understood as types and as models. We cannot simply repeat them today; but they must serve us as models for an independent solution to our present problems of faith."[102]

In compliance with this hermeneutical instruction, Kasper now claims that although "dogmatic credal formulae" are "indispensable signs and symbols of the faith, they are not actually the 'subject' ['*Sache*'] of faith."[103] This raises the question of what "'subject' ('*Sache*') of faith" actually means here. Dogmatic credal formulae are at all events an object of faith inasmuch as their propositional content is a content that is to be believed. Faith is not merely some kind of mood or attitude; nor is it merely an anthropological existential. Instead, faith is necessarily grounded in holding quite specific objective facts along with the assertoric statements that name them to be true. And these facts persist independently of our communication about them since this is precisely what constitutes the essence of objective facts. When, however, Kasper maintains that "faith does not, after all, consist just in holding objective facts of salvation to be true,"[104] then the answer to this must be that it *does indeed also* consist in a holding to be true of such facts that have been communicated to us through a tradition that has preserved the semantic integrity of the descriptive statements of the apostolic faith right down to the present day. If this were not so, faith would have no foundation in reality. Referring to the fact that in the early Church dogmas often had the formal form of liturgical doxologies, Kasper then proceeds to argue: "According to this understanding, dogma is not an abstract doctrinal statement that is considered to be true, but rather a personal statement of faith."[105] The reply to this must be that the praise is offered in the form of a descriptive statement whose naturally abstract content belongs, of course, to the Church's binding teaching; and the praise obviously presupposes that the content of the statement is held to be true since it would otherwise degenerate into a hollow compliment.

It is, of course, correct that "truth *establishes its validity* in the process of communication and consensus-building,"[106] for where else is it supposed to do so, after all? Validity is normative and therefore only perdures within the

---

[102] Kasper, *Evangelium und Dogma*, 790. On the "typological hermeneutics" mentioned here cf. *Evangelium und Dogma*, 789f.

[103] Kasper, *Evangelium und Dogma*, 655.

[104] Kasper, *Einführung*, 139.

[105] Kasper, *Evangelium und Dogma*, 733.

[106] Kasper, *Evangelium und Dogma*, 528.

framework of communicative interaction. However, it is by no means the case that communication and consensus-building constitute or transform the truth according to constantly changing contextual conditions or according to the demands of some "pastoral praxis" or other. For if one wished to "subordinate the truth to the tradition of the respective praxis and the goal of history aimed at in it," then the question would arise of where to take the yardstick with which to measure the suitability of the respective praxis.[107]

Dogmas are therefore by no means—as Kasper maintains—"answers of the Church to the word of God"; rather, they are answers to the questions of the faithful which affirm the word of God in a way that interprets it.[108] It is furthermore totally unclear what a dogmatic answer to the word of God on the part of the Church is in any way supposed to be. Hence it is also incorrect to state that "what was professed at that time must be understood as a guide for what we profess today."[109] For it would by no means be possible "today"—guided by a past "answer to the word of God"—to give a different answer, one resulting from the "signs of the times," that was analogous to the past answer yet diverged from it. And this is the case for the simple reason that dogmas are precisely not answers to the word of God, but rather an interpretation of a certain aspect of faith, which, once given, remains definitively valid and must be incorporated unchanged into the foundations of all subsequent interpretations.

Kasper's position, on the other hand, is entirely different, derived as it is from a "pneumatology" that does not involve the third divine Person but rather some other "spirit." Let us recall:

> Tradition is [therefore] not to be confused with the apostolic *symbolum* or any other expression of Christian truth; it is rather "the meaning and thought, the objective spirit of the Christian truth, which keeps on creating new expressions of itself and manifests itself in the most diverse directions, but always as the same spirit." It is "not just the apostolic word as such, as a definitely formulated content"; rather it is at the same time "the apostolic spirit" which was handed on to the Church and lives on in her. Thus tradition is not "the continual repetition of the original truth in its unhistorical

---

[107] Kasper, *Evangelium und Dogma*, 524f.
[108] Kasper, *Evangelium und Dogma*, 653.
[109] Kasper, *Evangelium und Dogma*, 653.

form, but rather the continual reproduction of this truth in ever new historical forms."[110]

Admittedly, statements—as linguistic entities—point beyond themselves in that, or to the extent that, they point to extra-linguistic facts and circumstances.[111] So far this statement remains trivial as regards propositional logic since it merely names the simple reference function. However, in fulfilling the reference function, assertoric statements have a truth value, that is, they are either true (i.e., adequate representations of their extra-linguistic reference objects) or untrue (i.e., inadequate representations of their extra-linguistic reference objects). Consequently, they can either be confirmed or disproved, that is, overcome by other statements on the basis of new insights. By no means, however, does a statement (without changing its reference object and thus becoming a different statement) point beyond itself in such a way that, in the course of being handed on and as a result of the changing contextual conditions during the very process of Tradition, it could evoke statements that are antithetical to it or dialectically cancel it by means of the determinate negation of Hegelian logic. Yet this is precisely Kasper's position—or rather, it is the logical consequence of the position he has taken, a consequence that he admittedly highlights with sufficient openness. Kasper conceives of a context of Tradition in which the truth of the statements being handed down in it is ensured solely by the *factual* course and the uninterruptedness of a *reception history* in the course of which the semantic content of the statements passed down can, however, change—by means of the application of determinate negation—and indeed must do so in order to remain true despite constantly changing contextual conditions. However, if—as Kasper seems to imply—the development of Catholic doctrine that takes place in Tradition does not represent an organic further development of its origin, then the continuity of the development of this doctrine does not lie in the continuity of the immutable validity of certain semantic contents but rather in the continuity of the application of a certain exemplary model of linguistification or inculturation so as to make present . . . well, what, actually?

The model of continuity presented here does not, then, need to worry about an integrity of semantic content that survives over time; indeed, it makes the possibility of such an integrity inevitably appear to be an illusion. But because under these circumstances it is no longer possible to discern *what* the *object* of

---

[110] Kasper, *Evangelium und Dogma*, 498f.

[111] Kasper, *Evangelium und Dogma*, 194.

the Christian faith actually is, the Church has never taught any such thing. For Christ is the same yesterday, today, and forever (Heb 13:8). And because human beings possess a reason that can be enlightened by grace, they are capable of understanding this, and the Church is able to teach this understanding of the faith continuously and unchangingly.[112]

Since all this is so, the Church is indeed always on a journey, but not—as Kasper says—on the way to a truth that she constantly has to seek anew;[113] rather, she is on the way to an ever-deeper *grasp* and more comprehensive *realization* of a truth that she has already *found*, that is to say, found in Christ. Nor is the "truth" itself by any means, as Kasper alleges, a "way."[114] There certainly are ways that lead to the truth, but there are also those that fail to reach this goal. And when Kasper further claims that the truth is an event, this claim only makes sense if the concept of truth is structurally conceived in the same way as, for example, Hegel conceives it.[115] However, things are somewhat more complex with Hegel than with Kasper. Moreover, the concept of truth in Sacred Scripture certainly does not imply Hegel's concept of truth—as opposed to that of classical philosophy, whose metaphysical insights have served theology as indispensable tools from its earliest beginnings.

When Kasper now states that there is no metaphysical ordering structure to be extricated from all the historical and salvation-historical concretion, then he is either stating a truism in that it has always been clear, at least for the Aristotelian tradition, that metaphysical ordering structures only have continued ontological existence when they manifest themselves in the physical world, that is, in a material and thus spatially and temporally structured reality, and that these manifestations definitely can turn out quite differently over time;[116] or else, Kasper means something quite different, namely this: "The world . . . is not an eternal natural order, but rather an historical world."[117] Kasper here replaces the classical metaphysical view of the world with a "historical view of

---

[112] When Kasper argues against the modern understanding of Tradition, represented above all by Hegel, saying, "Theology must start from the given truth of God in Jesus Christ. It can therefore speak of the historical mediation of the truth but not, however, of the historicity of the truth itself" (*Evangelium und Dogma*, 527), then—after everything we have presented so far—this objection can be at most just lip service, if not even a diversionary tactic.

[113] Kasper, *Einführung*, 143; *Introduction*, 164.

[114] Kasper, *Evangelium und Dogma*, 734.

[115] Kasper, *Einführung*, 61; *Introduction*, 59.

[116] Kasper, *Einführung*, 144; *Introduction*, 165.

[117] Kasper, *Einführung*, 136; *Introduction*, 157. On Kasper's thesis that reality as such is not merely historical but is itself wholly history, see Kasper, *Evangelium und Dogma*, 625f.

the world" but in so doing neglects to take into account that because the subject actively appropriates reality in experience taking place historically, this in no way means that the activity of the subject constitutes the world.[118] What the subject actively constitutes is instead his or her *conception* of reality. However, not every conception of reality is (equally) appropriate to reality. Conceptions of reality can also be false, which would not be possible if the activity of the cognizing subject constituted not only the conception of reality but also the reality itself, that is, that which is represented by the conception. In this case, every conception of reality would be *a priori* adequate to reality itself.

With his denial of an eternal natural order, however, Kasper also denies the objective existence of a time-transcending *physis*, thus opening the door to constructivism. This position can, however, invoke neither classical philosophy, nor Hegel, nor Schelling, but at most postmodernists cast in the mold of a Jacques Derrida or a Judith Butler, who followed Derrida. Yet it should actually be clear—at the latest since Heraclitus and the Logos speculation that began with him—that processes of change can only be thought of and recognized against the background of an immutable basic structure that regulates all processuality—which is what Heraclitus terms Logos.

Therefore, Kasper is also wrong with his assertion: "Not nature and not the depths of the human soul, but history is the dimension in which we as Christians encounter God."[119] However, since creation is Logos-shaped, this means that the human mind/spirit, which participates in the divine Logos, is quite capable of knowing (*erkennen*) its divine Creator from creation, which means from nature. This is what the First Vatican Council teaches infallibly. But knowledge (*Erkenntnis*) is the indispensable basis of every encounter, for someone I do not know (*erkennen*) is someone I cannot encounter, either. And it has been taught by the entire mystical Tradition of the Church, alongside Augustine, that the depths of the human soul are also a privileged place for encountering God.

Finally, the following must be taken into consideration: the existence of an unchanging natural order, that is, a nature (*physis*) that is, as it were, logically ordered, together with the cognizability of this order is an indispensable precondition for the possibility of natural science as the science of the physical world. Furthermore, the existence of a *physis* in the classical sense is an indispensable

---

[118] Kasper, *Der Gott Jesu Christi*, 194.
[119] Kasper, *Einführung*, 138; *Introduction*, 159.

precondition of all metaphysics of whatever kind; then, as a metaphysics of nature, it also acquires *normative* significance in the shape of natural law. But within the framework of Kasper's theology, sliding as it does into baseless speculations, it is impossible to found morality in natural law. This explains the strange positions he takes in the field of teaching on the family, sexual ethics, and sacramental ministry.

If we now ask ourselves what basic understanding of Christianity underlies Walter Kasper's theology, it will probably be necessary to turn to his Christology, which offers a classic example of the application of his theological principles and methods as they have been presented so far. And here we come upon Kasper's astonishing notion that Christology cannot be based on the statement that Jesus is the Christ, that is to say, on the very statement which—according to Kasper—encapsulates the entire Christian message. This is because—so he states—"most exegetes in German-speaking countries" are of the opinion that the "titles of Christ are not statements made by the earthly Jesus himself but rather professions of faith of the post-paschal Church"; and so, it is impossible to start from the titles of Christ when laying the foundations for Christology.[120] "According to the Synoptic Gospels, Christ never calls himself the Son of God. This clearly identifies the statement about being the Son of God as a profession of faith by the Church."[121] "So he presumably did not refer to himself as Messiah, or Servant of God, or Son of God, and probably not as Son of Man either."[122] Furthermore—according to Kasper—the New Testament authors use terms like sacrifice, atonement, satisfaction, and substitution as "mere interpretations of actual reality."[123] Which, of course, then raises the question of what this "reality" is.

It actually goes without saying that such an approach to Christology cannot fail to have consequences for Trinitarian theology. So there is an inner consistency to this when Kasper's Christology does in fact leave its mark on his Trinitarian theology, for in his opinion not only the statements about Christ's preexistence but also those on the immanent Trinity in general are "not direct statements of faith but rather statements of theological

[120] Walter Kasper, "Neuansätze gegenwärtiger Christologie," in *Christologische Schwerpunkte* (Düsseldorf: Patmos-Verlag, 1980), 17–36, 27.

[121] Kasper, *Jesus der Christus*, 129.

[122] Walter Kasper, "Jesus und der Glaube," in Walter Kasper and Jürgen Moltmann, *Jesus ja—Kirche nein?* (Zurich: Benziger-Verlag, 1973), 9–35, 20.

[123] Kasper, *Einführung*, 115.

reflection."[124] This then results in analogous shifts of meaning with regard to Jesus's sonship. For—according to Kasper—Jesus is the Son of God because he is "in his free human obedience, wholly an empty form (*Leerform*) and instrument for God's existence and activity in history."[125] Here the human nature is affirmed, but the divine nature and the divine Person subsisting in the two natures is (at least implicitly) denied. Paul Hacker observes correctly: "What Kasper says here about Christ is according to Catholic teaching also true of Mary. What is special about the divine Person is tacitly denied."[126] Hence the dogma that Jesus "is wholly God and wholly human" is for Kasper not only "in need of interpretation"—which goes without saying—but also "capable of being superseded (*überholbar*)."[127] This spontaneously raises the question: *superseded with what* and, above all, *to what end*? Presumably, to any end you like, since according to Kasper the words "Amen, amen, I say to you" imply "an entire Christology."[128]

So it is not really surprising then that Jesus's resurrection is for Kasper "not an historical fact that can be objectively and neutrally established."[129] "The Resurrection itself is not historically verifiable, but only the faith in it of the first witnesses and possibly the empty tomb."[130] Even so, regarding the angel speaking at the empty tomb Kasper explains: "This ancient tradition is not an historical account of the discovery of the empty tomb, but evidence of faith."[131] On what is in his opinion the oldest account of Easter (Mark 16:1–8), Kasper says that these are "not historical details but ... stylistic devices intended to attract attention and raise excitement."[132] Also, the touching of the Risen One and the eating together with him (Luke 24:36–43; John 20:24–29) are for Kasper merely literary "stylistic devices."[133] After all this, it really hardly matters

---

[124] Kasper, *Einführung*, 96; *Introduction*, 105.

[125] Kasper, *Einführung*, 54; *Introduction*, 51.

[126] P. Hacker, "Walter Kasper, der Verteidiger Kesslers," *Theologisches* 153 (1983): 5018, http://www.theologisches.net/files/1983_Nr.153.pdf.

[127] Kasper, *Einführung*, 55; *Introduction*, 51.

[128] Kasper, *Einführung*, 53; *Introduction*, 49.

[129] Kasper, *Einführung*, 59; *Introduction*, 57.

[130] Kasper, *Jesus der Christus*, 155; *Jesus the Christ*, trans. V. Green (London: Burns and Oates, 1976), 131. (The English translation has confused *u.U.* and *u.a.* here!)

[131] Kasper, *Jesus der Christus*, 150; *Jesus the Christ*, 127.

[132] Kasper, *Jesus der Christus*, 149; *Jesus the Christ*, 127.

[133] Kasper, *Jesus der Christus*, 166; *Jesus the Christ*, 139.

anymore when Kasper states that "the probability is that we need not take the so-called 'nature miracles' as historical."[134]

On the relationship between objective historical facts and events and the faith that is based on the accounts of such facts and events, Kasper explains: "The decisive question is not what 'objectively' took place, but whether we are ready, as the first disciples were, to give ourselves to be taken over (*in Beschlag nehmen*) by Jesus Christ."[135] Here the question arises of why we should let Jesus Christ "take us over" (whatever that is supposed to mean, incidentally) if what the Gospels recount and what the Church has always believed and confessed as a historical reality is not exactly what objectively took place. What did or did not happen is of all-important significance. For something that did not happen cannot have any meaning, either. All spiritual meaning exists only in its being attached to a material carrier of meaning. This is one of the rudimentary insights of modern symbol theory.[136] All creeds and testimonies of faith as well as all theological "interpretations" and "statements of reflection" are (in the literal sense) completely "objectless" if they do not refer to objective facts. As is very clear to see here, the historicization of the truth leads in the final analysis to a turning away from the objective historical facts, or to the complete dissolution of all objective facts in their entirety in a free-floating discourse and in the hermeneutical processing of the form of the historical course it takes, which thus increasingly takes on self-referential features. Welcome to postmodernism!

So let us now conclude.

For a long time, theology was based on a hard philosophy, namely Scholasticism, which can be described as the analytical philosophy of the Middle Ages or else as a use of natural human reason that is thoroughly streamlined at the highest level. In the modern age, large parts of theology have then detached themselves from Scholasticism, but without basing themselves on a different, modern variant of a hard philosophy such as Neo-Kantianism, Husserlian phenomenology, or analytical philosophy (however, one would have to evaluate such a new base). Instead of this, however, theology has for some time been using somewhat softer, more literary-essayistic forms of philosophy or has adopted borrowings from them, for example from Nietzsche, Heidegger, existentialism, and recently from postmodernism, combining these

---

[134] Kasper, *Jesus der Christus*, 107; *Jesus the Christ*, 91.

[135] Kasper, *Jesus der Christus*, 167; *Jesus the Christ*, 140.

[136] Cf., for example, Thomas Stark, *Symbol, Bedeutung, Transzendenz. Der Religionsbegriff in der Kulturphilosophie Ernst Cassirers*, Teil 1, "Das Symbol" (Würzburg: Echter, 1997).

with the theorems of Kant and Hegel and then occasionally reading them into Saint Thomas Aquinas.

The language of this kind of theology is a strange language of compromise. Bits of theory that are logically scarcely compatible with one another are here dressed in the outward form of a supposed dialectic. This brings about an argumentative pendulum movement, which in the past decades has repeatedly allowed numerous theologians skillfully to make critical inquiries on the part of the Magisterium swing to a standstill. But the language of compromise is the language of politics. And so, in theology politics is slowly replacing philosophy. The result of all this is a strange special discourse of its own which—quite unlike the theological tracts of the nineteenth or earlier centuries—is not received outside the ecclesiastical milieu. Thus, contemporary theological discourse turns into a milieu discourse. And this is the reason why the supposed reaching out to the world ends up with the message of theology no longer getting through to the world. Instead, the standards of the world appear to be gaining an increasing influence on theology.

Kasper therefore also advocates "a new, substantially more open and dynamic form of orthodoxy" which "can no longer be measured by mere adherence to certain propositions" but which "takes its bearings first and foremost from the centre and foundation of the faith."[137] But what is this "centre and foundation of the faith," and what is the "open and dynamic orthodoxy" that is built on this foundation? Kasper explains this—in his usual hazy manner—as follows:

> Here the individual remains in the true faith as long as he is open to the wider whole of the Church community, as long as he does not allow the thread of conversation to be broken even though he has to honestly confess that he can no longer go along with various things in the Church's tradition. This emphasis on the center and the foundation could, despite such partial identification, justify the hope that Vatican II attached to emphasizing the hierarchy of truths, namely that the Church today will be granted a deeper penetration into the "riches of the Spirit."[138]

But what—we must ask ourselves in conclusion—is left after all this of the Christian message? Not very much, it would seem. On the penultimate

---

[137] Kasper, *Evangelium und Dogma*, 792.
[138] Kasper, *Evangelium und Dogma*, 792f.

page of his book *An Introduction to Christian Faith*, Kasper cites as "the basic idea behind everything I have said up to now" the following: "The message of God's being God as the ground that makes possible man's existence as man. It is the secret longing of history; the centre of Jesus' message of the kingdom of God; and the epitome of the Church's salvific mission."[139] Furthermore, toward the beginning of *An Introduction*, Kasper already expresses the view that the question of God must be asked entirely from the perspective of man and his search for "happiness, fulfilment and meaning" and from "his search for the humanity of his being human."[140] And again on the penultimate page of the same work we read: "Whoever believes that in Christ hope is opened up to us and to all people, and whoever accepts this and displays concrete commitment in making himself a figure of hope for others, this person is a Christian. Such a person holds the whole faith in a fundamental way even if he does not espouse all the conclusions that the Church has drawn from this message over the course of almost two millennia."[141]

If that really is all, then we have a serious problem.

So let us at the very end give the floor once more to Walter Kasper—this time, for once, with our full approval:

> Without the courage, one could almost say without the temerity to make definitive decisions and statements, the Christian faith would give itself up. But this is exactly where its strength and power lie, too. It can promise and accord man definitive meaning. A Church that no longer possesses the strength to do so would richly deserve it if no one any longer took any interest in her preaching, which would have degenerated into idle chatter.[142]

---

[139] Kasper, *Einführung*, 168; *Introduction*, 194.
[140] Kasper, *Einführung*, 27; *Introduction*, 16.
[141] Kasper, *Einführung*, 168; *Introduction*, 169.
[142] Kasper, *Einführung*, 148; *Introduction*, 169.

BERNHARD HÄRING'S
MORAL THEOLOGY

Edmund Waldstein, O.Cist.

Father Bernhard Häring, C.Ss.R. (1912–1998), was one of the most influential moral theologians of the twentieth century. He is often seen as a key figure in overcoming the narrow casuistry of the manuals of moral theology used in seminaries before Vatican II and as an important influence on Vatican II's vision of moral theology. In an audience with the General Congregation of the Society of Jesus in 2016, Pope Francis decried the "decadent scholasticism" of his own seminary formation, which had a casuistic approach, a legalistic reductionism that neglected the crucial role of discernment in the moral life. The Holy Father then praised Häring as "the first to start looking for a new way to help moral theology to flourish again."[1] After praising Häring, Pope Francis went on to praise the great Church doctors of the High Scholastic period, Saint Thomas Aquinas and Saint Bonaventure, and to note that their method of moral discernment was used by the Catechism of the Catholic Church.

Certainly, the Holy Father is right to praise Häring for having seen some of the limitations of preconciliar moral theology. A fuller examination of Häring, however, shows that he sometimes exaggerated and misunderstood the limitations of preconciliar theology, and that his own new approach suffered from serious weaknesses. The Holy Father's praise of the Catechism as returning to the sapiential theology of Saint Thomas and Saint Bonaventure

---

[1]   Pope Francis, "To Have Courage and Prophetic Audacity," Dialogue with the Jesuits Gathered in the 36th General Congregation (October 24, 2016).

THE FAITH ONCE FOR ALL DELIVERED

is instructive here. In important ways the approach of the moral part of the Catechism represents a path in postconciliar theology distinct from that taken by Häring. It is a path represented by Saint John Paul II and by the Thomist theologian Servais Pinckaers (one of the chief drafters of the third part of the Catechism). One of the most important differences between the two approaches is discernible in the way in which they use philosophy, and particularly in the way in which they see the relation between nature and human history. While Thomists such as Pinckaers defend the permanent validity of Saint Thomas's understanding of nature as the impression in things of the eternal wisdom of God, serving as a principle of movement toward the good, Häring's approach tends to relativize such insights as being too tied to the obsolete "static" categories of Greek metaphysical thought and thinks they have to be modified or replaced by a more dynamic and "historicist" understanding of nature and a more "personalistic" understanding of moral good. Häring's historicism and personalism lead him into serious errors, such as the denial of the Church's perennial teaching on the immorality of artificial contraception.

Invoking a principle which he formulates as "time is greater than space," Pope Francis has called for social action that initiates processes rather than possessing spaces.[2] Häring's historicist theology might seem to provide a worthy theoretical underpinning for such a theology—that is to say, a theology that takes into consideration time. And, yet, the way in which his theology develops undermines that very consideration. A deeper philosophy of nature as reflective of the divine law—which law governs not only history as it unfolds in any one epoch but ensures continuity over time—would provide a better grounding for an analysis of the processes that truly lead to the goal that divine wisdom implanted in human nature at its creation. Thus, despite Pope Francis's explicit praise of Häring, an adequate moral theology for our time would do well to look to other guides.

---

2 See Francis, Apostolic Exhortation on the Proclamation of the Gospel in Today's World *Evangelii gaudium* (November 24, 2013), §§222–23; Francis, Post-Synodal Apostolic Exhortation on Love in the Family *Amoris laetitia* (March 19, 2016), §3. Unfortunately, the Holy Father appears to understand time, insofar as it is greater than space, as pertaining solely to the future and not embracing also the past. In *Evangelii gaudium* §222 he says of time that it "has to do with fullness as an expression of the horizon which constantly opens before us" and that "people live poised between each individual moment and the greater, brighter horizon of the utopian future as the final cause which draws us to itself." And in *Evangelii gaudium* §223 he says: "Time governs spaces, illumines them and makes them links in a constantly expanding chain, with no possibility of return."

HÄRING'S LIFE AND INFLUENCE

Häring was born on November 10, 1912, in the small town of Böttingen in southwestern Germany. He was the eleventh of twelve children in a family to which he would always look back as a haven of peace and exemplary faith. His father, a prosperous farmer, went to Mass daily. Häring wanted to become a missionary and, at first, thought of entering the Jesuits. He changed his mind when he heard that the most talented Jesuits usually became professors. Having no desire to be an academic, he entered the Redemptorists in 1934. He studied in the Redemptorist seminary in Gars am Inn, Bavaria. Moral theology was his least favorite subject in seminary. He considered the approach of his teachers and the textbooks they employed arid and unfruitful. But, on his own time, he read some theologians—such as Fritz Tillmann—who had been trying to develop a more biblical and Christocentric vision of moral theology. He also developed an enthusiasm for the phenomenological ethics of value that was being developed by philosophers such as Max Scheler and Dietrich von Hildebrand.

In 1939, Häring was ordained a priest, hoping to be sent to Brazil as a missionary. But, to his great disappointment, his superiors decided that he should do a doctorate in moral theology at the University of Tübingen since they needed a moral theologian for their seminary.

Häring's studies were interrupted by the Second World War. He was conscripted in 1940, and served as a medical orderly from 1941–1945 on the Eastern front. He was wounded at the Second Battle of Kharkov in 1942, being left with a piece of shrapnel in his head that would remain as a perpetual reminder of the war. As Häring himself would later say, the experience of the war years gave him a certain mistrust of obedience to authority: "I also experienced the most absurd obedience by Christians—God have mercy—toward a criminal regime. And that too radically affected my thinking and acting as a moral theologian."[3] Häring would carry this mistrust of authority into his relationship with the hierarchy of the Church; he would try to develop a moral theology of responsibility rather than of obedience.

After the war, Häring continued his studies in Tübingen, writing his dissertation under Theodor Steinbüchel, a disciple of Fritz Tillmann. His dissertation was entitled "The Holy and the Good," and it examined the relation

---

[3] Bernhard Häring, *My Witness for the Church*, trans. Leonard Swidler (New York: Paulist Press, 1992), 23.

of faith and morality in three modern philosophers (Immanuel Kant, Nicolai Hartmann, and Max Scheler) and in three Protestant theologians (Friedrich Schleiermacher, Rudolf Otto, and Emil Brunner). It was clear that he was not content to work within the existing framework of Catholic moral theology and scholastic philosophy but wanted to expand the framework through dialogue with authors outside that tradition. During his time in Tübingen, Häring also attended the lectures of the Protestant ethicist Helmut Thielicke.

Häring began teaching at the Redemptorist seminary in Gars am Inn. Soon he was sent to Rome to help set up the Alphonsianum, the Redemptorist institute for higher studies in moral theology. The Alphonsianum was meant to train professors of moral theology from all around the world, and Häring realized at once the opportunities for influencing the course of moral theology in the Church that this presented. Häring threw himself into his work with great energy. The many students that he formed were soon spreading his ideas throughout the Church. But, not content with indirect influence, Häring soon began traveling the world himself giving lectures in various languages. Above all, he spread his ideas through an astonishing stream of articles and books, including two multi-volume textbooks of moral theology: *The Law of Christ,* written before Vatican II, and *Free and Faithful in Christ,* written after.

At Vatican II itself, Häring was active as a theological expert, particularly in the drafting of the Constitution on the Church in the Modern World, *Gaudium et spes.* Not all of Häring's suggestions for that document were accepted, however. He wanted the section on marriage to include a softening of the Church's teaching on artificial contraception, which was not forthcoming. This question would come to occupy him much in the following years. He was deeply disappointed by Pope Saint Paul VI's reiteration of the Church's teaching on contraception in *Humanae vitae,* and became one of the most vociferous dissenters from it. In the remaining decades of his life, before his death in 1998, he was much involved in controversies over Church teaching on sexual matters. "I find it absolutely laughable and at the same time frustrating," he would say in the 1980s, "that at my age I still have to pour out so much energy on questions like flexibility and inflexibility concerning the forbidding of contraception and in the struggle against sexual rigorism."[4]

---

[4] Häring, *My Witness,* 24.

MORAL THEOLOGY AND THE CRISIS OF PHILOSOPHY

In a 1963 paper on the renewal of moral theology, Häring points out some of the weaknesses of the type of moral theology that had come to maturity in the seventeenth century, when moral theology was more clearly separated from the rest of theology, and which had been developed subsequently.[5] This type of moral theology was meant mainly as a guide to confessors in the Sacrament of Penance. It was therefore narrowly focused upon sin. It had developed a subtle and differentiated system for determining the sinfulness of acts from both objective and subjective viewpoints. The objective viewpoint was given by the law, the subjective by various factors, such as ignorance and passion, affecting the degree to which someone was culpable for breaking the law. Häring called for moral theology to be reintegrated into the greater whole of theology itself. He wanted it to show how the new creation in Christ (treated in dogmatic theology) is realized in our moral actions. He wanted to draw more on Sacred Scripture and the Fathers of the Church than had been the case up until then. He wanted moral theology to concern itself not so much with the avoidance of sin but rather with the perfection of charity, which until then had been the preserve of ascetic and mystical theology.

With all this I can fully agree, but problems emerge whenever Häring brings up the relationship between moral theology and philosophy. In the context of calling for moral theology to draw more deeply on Scripture, Häring writes:

> One must be able to see at first glance that a Catholic moral theology's form and content and structure of thought is marked more by Sacred Scripture than by any code of law or philosophical system, whether contemporary or Aristotelian. One would gravely wrong St. Augustine or St. Thomas if one thought one could be faithful to them simply by adopting their Platonic or Aristotelian conceptual tools.[6]

Häring is certainly right that the soul of theology should be Scripture and the deposit of faith it articulates, but there is a subtle error in the way he presents philosophy here. Philosophy is not a neutral "tool," such that different philosophical systems could be equally useful in helping to expound the truths

---

[5] Bernhard Häring, "Heutige Bestrebungen zur Vertiefung und Erneuerung der Moraltheologie," *Studia Moralia* 1 (1963): 11–48, especially at 17. Translations from this essay are my own.

[6] Häring, "Heutige Bestrebungen," 14.

revealed in Scripture—as though different philosophies were like different typefaces in which a printer can set the same text. Rather, philosophies make specific claims about reality, claims which can be true or false. A theologian infected by false philosophical claims will inevitably misinterpret Scripture and so the content of the faith. Nor can the problem be avoided by trying to make sure that one's worldview is primarily biblical rather than philosophical. Biblical revelation presupposes the knowledge of reality that comes from our natural contact with the world. Theologians who try to be biblical without philosophical reflection are indeed condemned to read Scripture in the light of the implicit philosophy that they imbibe from the intellectual climate of their own time. The use by the great Fathers and doctors of the Church of the Socratic tradition of philosophy as developed by Platonism and Aristotelianism was not the use of a mere "tool"; it was part of the providential and intrinsically necessary "rapprochement between Biblical faith and Greek inquiry" that began already in the New Testament itself.[7]

What Häring's analysis of the limitations of moral theology from the seventeenth century to Vatican II lacks is any awareness of the degree to which those limitations were in fact brought about by the great crisis of philosophy of the seventeenth century, in which modern philosophy rejected the Socratic—and so also Platonic and Aristotelian—tradition of inquiry. Certainly, the narrow focus of early modern moral theology was largely determined by its aim of providing guidance for confessors, in itself not an unworthy goal. But that narrow focus was also the result of that epoch's lack of a full account of natural teleology. That crisis consisted above all in the rejection of Aristotle's philosophy of nature. Since this philosophy of nature was essential to an adequate understanding of "natural law," the moral law written in the hearts of men by the Creator, its rejection could not fail to have an influence on moral theology. While the Aristotelian view of nature was carried on by some Catholic—especially Dominican—commentators on Saint Thomas, others came to present the precepts of natural law without any of its philosophical underpinnings.

Many of the central insights of the Socratic tradition of philosophy— insights into the nature of reason, being, and the good—had been appropriated and purified by the Fathers of the Church in their dialogue with the Platonists.

---

[7] Benedict XVI, Lecture with the Representatives of Science at the University of Regensburg, "Faith, Reason and the University: Memories and Reflections" (September 12, 2006).

But it was not until Saint Thomas Aquinas in the thirteenth century that the full breadth of Aristotle's philosophy of nature was brought into synthesis with the biblical account of creation.

Aristotle had noted that in our common experience we see that some things are natural and some things artificial.[8] Animals, plants, rivers, and rocks come to be "by nature," whereas houses, roads, and cars are made by human artifice. The concept "nature," as expressed both in Greek (*physis*) and in Latin (*natura*, from which we derive the English word), is related to birth (in Greek, *phyein*; in Latin, *nasci*). Living things are not made from the outside, but come to be from an internal principle of motion. This is true not only of animals like dogs that are "born" in the literal sense but also, analogously, of plants that come to be from seed. It is even true, in a weaker sense, of nonliving things like rivers and rocks; they are not built by other things. Hence, Aristotle defines nature as an internal principle of motion in a thing.[9] There is something inside a tree, say, on account of which the tree takes in water and light and grows toward a certain complete and flourishing state of being a tree and doing what a tree does.

Nature, Aristotle clarifies, is not any principle of motion that happens to be in a thing (for example, a disease), but rather a principle that is in the thing *fundamentally* and *essentially*. In fact, this fundamental principle of motion and change within a thing is what makes a thing to be what it is. Hence nature also means the "whatness" (quiddity) of a thing: that which makes a thing to be what it is. Note that this is not true of artificial things. A wooden boat does not have a principle of motion fundamentally and essentially interior to it. A boat is made up of different parts, each with its own intrinsic nature, and these parts are related to each other in an extrinsic manner, resulting in a certain common way of acting—or, to be more precise, being acted upon. If one buried a boat and, by chance, something sprouted and grew from it, what might sprout would be a tree, not a boat.[10] Insofar as a boat can be said to have a characteristic motion, that motion does not come from a principle *intrinsic* to the boat but is made possible by the external action of a shipwright and the subsequent external action of a pilot.

Aristotle argues that natural things are composed of what he calls "matter"

---

[8] The following paragraphs are based on my essay "Natural Things," in *Catholicism and the Natural World*, ed. Thomas Storck (Waterloo, ON: Arouca Press, forthcoming).

[9] Aristotle, *Physics* 2.1, 192b20–23.

[10] See Aristotle, *Physics* 2.1, 193a10.

and "form." Matter is the *ability* or *potential* to be a thing, but it is not (in Aristotle's account) itself a thing. Form is what *makes a thing to be what it is*. A natural thing is matter determined by form. A natural thing is *one single thing*, the union or *concretion* of matter and form. When a dog is conceived, the form of a dog is coming to be in the matter where the form of sperm and ovum were before; when a dog dies, the form of rotting flesh is coming to be where the form of dog was before. In a human being, to take a more important example, the matter of the body and the form that is the soul do not exist as two separate things but as one concrete thing. The body is totally suffused and formed by the soul, which gives it its meaning and makes it to be a living *body* rather than an inert thing. Aristotle argues that matter is for the sake of form. That is, matter has a purpose that is fulfilled when it is "actualized" by form. At times, Aristotle even speaks of matter *desiring* form.[11]

In its most basic principles, nature is *purposive, teleological*; it is aiming at something good. Aristotle argues that this purposiveness of nature characterizes all natural activity. Nature is an intrinsic principle of motion, and this motion is aimed at the fullness of being and activity of a natural thing. When a tree grows and stretches out its branches, it is acting with a purpose, for the full actualization of tree-nature, the perfection of tree-life. This purposiveness of natural activity is not random, not by chance; it is a stable inclination within natural things. Aristotle manifests this by comparing craft to nature and nature to craft: both nature and craft are for an end.[12] This is especially clear in cases where craft is used to help nature toward an end to which it already seemed to be striving. For example, when a physician uses his craft to heal a patient, he is really helping the natural process of healing within the patient. Hence, it is clear that the patient's nature was already aimed at the goal of health. This is also clear in natural things that go through a set of ordered actions terminating in something beneficial to them. For example, a spider goes through a set sequence of actions to spin a web, a web which ends up being useful to the spider. There appears to be something almost like intelligence in the spider's actions. "Whence some people are at a loss as to whether spiders and ants and such things work by mind or by something else."[13] And yet, spiders clearly do not act by deliberating or planning in their *own* minds. They act instinctively.

---

[11] Aristotle, *Physics* 2.9, 192a20–23.

[12] Aristotle, *Physics* 2.8, 199a8–20.

[13] Aristotle, *Physics* 2.8, 199a21–23.

There seems, therefore, to be a wisdom in the purposiveness of natural things that is not the wisdom of their own minds.

Saint Thomas Aquinas takes this Aristotelian account and develops it further. He argues that to act for an end necessarily presupposes some kind of intelligence. So, he argues, natures are (as it were) impressions of the divine intelligence on creatures; the nature of each thing is a participation in the divine wisdom by which that thing is directed toward its end:

> For nature seems to differ from art only because nature is an intrinsic principle and art is an extrinsic principle. For if the art of ship building were intrinsic to wood, a ship would have been made by nature in the same way as it is made by art. . . . Hence, it is clear that nature is nothing but the reason [*ratio*] of a certain kind of art, i.e., the divine art, impressed upon things, by which these things are moved to a determinate end. It is as if the shipbuilder were able to give to timbers that by which they would move themselves to take the form of a ship.[14]

This view of nature has far-reaching implications for the understanding of the moral life. The moral life is concerned with fulfilling the tendency toward the good that God inscribed in our innermost nature. The new creation in Christ heals our nature and elevates it to be able to attain even greater goods, but it does not replace nature. Actions are good when they are in accord with our natural tendency toward the good; they are evil when they run counter to it.

Take the example of contraception. Contraception runs counter to the natural teleological tendency of our reproductive faculties. The divine wisdom, inscribed in the sexual act, directs that act toward the giving on of human life. A truly human sexual act is an expression of love, but not of just any kind of love: it is the expression of that very specific kind of love that is the root of the family, where human life is passed on. Contraception, by artificially excluding the natural end of the act, changes the kind of act that is taking place. It is no longer the *kind* of act that is ordered to passing on life. Contraception is therefore like a lie that contradicts what the divine wisdom is speaking through us. In contrast,

---

14   Thomas Aquinas, *Commentary on Aristotle's Physics*, trans. Richard J. Blackwell, Richard J. Spath, and W. Edmund Thirlkel (New Haven: Yale University Press, 1963), lec. 14, no. 268 (p. 124) (translation slightly modified). Cf. Francis, Encyclical Letter on Care for Our Common Home *Laudato si'* (May 24, 2015), §80.

periodic abstinence for the sake of avoiding pregnancy in certain circumstances is like silence rather than a lie. Natural Family Planning (NFP) does not violate the nature of the sexual act. NFP restricts the sexual act to certain times but does not change the kind of action being done. An act of sexual intercourse at a time known to be infertile is still the *kind* of action that is directed to giving on life.[15]

The teleological vision of nature was rejected by philosophers such as Francis Bacon and René Descartes in the seventeenth century. Descartes developed a so-called "mechanical" philosophy of nature that reduced all of physical reality to its quantitative, measurable aspect. Nature was *res extensa*, extended thing, subject to external forces, but without any *intrinsic* principle directing it to an end. The human soul, on the other hand, was *res cogitans*, thinking thing, entirely different from the natural world. Human beings were entirely free to manipulate physical reality in any way that seemed to serve their convenience. And it was this manipulation (technology) that became the goal of Cartesian natural science.

In philosophical ethics, the influence of Cartesian natural philosophy can be seen in the various attempts by Enlightenment philosophers to ground morality without teleology. Thus, Scottish philosophers (such as David Hume and Adam Smith) tended to ground morality in moral sentiments, whereas continental philosophers such as Immanuel Kant grounded it in the nature of reason itself. None of these attempts were entirely satisfactory, and they provoked a philosophical reaction, often called "romanticism," which seemed in some ways to be a return to nature as an intrinsic principle but in fact ended up intensifying the Enlightenment rejection of teleology. This romantic reaction is particularly crucial to understanding Häring's theology.

In Catholic moral theology, an indirect effect of the Cartesian revolution can perhaps be detected in a reversal of the relation between law and virtue that seems to lay less stress on intrinsic teleology. For Saint Thomas, one of the primary functions of laws laid down by the authority in a community is to foster virtue within the subjects of the law. Virtues are the habits that perfect a person's natural faculties, helping them to reach their natural end. So, the function of law is to help its subjects become good by reaching the goal to which the intrinsic principle of their nature is already leading them.[16] Moral

---

[15] See my essay "Natures as Words, Contraception as a Lie," Ethika Politika (website), September 17, 2014, accessed July 15, 2020, https://ethikapolitika.org/2014/09/17/natures-words-contraception-lie.

[16] Thomas Aquinas, *Summa theologiae* Ia-IIae, qq. 92, 96.

theologians of the period from the seventeenth to the early twentieth century, however, often reversed the relation. Thus, Heribert Jone, a German moral theologian of the twentieth century, writes:

> Man must attain to his last end by personal activity in conformity with the remote (objective) and proximate (subjective) norms of moral action, namely, law and conscience. These norms are violated by sin; their observance is made easy by the virtues.[17]

Here the primary consideration is law (and conscience, which applies law to particular cases). The function of virtue is to make law easy to follow. In other words, instead of law being for the sake of virtue, and thus of the fulfillment of natural teleology, virtue is for the sake of the fulfillment of law.

CONSCIENCE AND THE *ZEITGEIST*: HÄRING'S HISTORICISM AND HERDER'S ROMANTICISM

Had Häring possessed a deeper understanding of natural teleology, he might have tried to restore the Thomistic relation between law and virtue—understanding the former as for the sake of the latter. Instead, Häring reacted to what he saw as the legalistic rigorism and inflexibility of Catholic moral theology with a kind of antinomianism that no longer sees much good in law at all.

Häring tries to replace a moral theology that involves law with a moral theology of the free response of the Christian to the love of God given in Christ. He sees this response as a dynamic process in which the Christian learns ever more what an adequate response would be. In this process the Christian must follow his conscience, which might initially be an erring conscience, but which will gradually lead him to a better understanding of what God's love calls him to. Häring liked to quote a dictum of Saint John Henry Newman's: "I have always contended that obedience even to an erring conscience was the way to gain light."[18] This dictum, however, takes on a somewhat different meaning in Häring than it had in Newman. In the larger passage from which the quoted sentence is taken, Newman says that his rejection of arguments that he had put forward earlier—that is, his "inconsistency" in converting from Anglicanism,

---

[17] Heribert Jone, *Moral Theology,* trans. Urban Adelman (Cork: Mercier Press, 1961), no. 3.

[18] John Henry Newman, *Apologia Pro Vita Sua,* ed. David J. DeLaura (New York: Norton, 1968), 162.

which he had defended with great zeal, to Catholicism—does not "unsettle one's confidence in truth and falsehood as external things." He writes:

> For is it not one's duty, instead of beginning with criticism, to throw oneself generously into that form of religion which is providentially put before one? Is it right, or is it wrong, to begin with private judgment? May we not, on the other hand, look for a blessing *through* obedience even to an erroneous system, and a guidance even by means of it out of it? Were those who were strict and conscientious in their Judaism, or those who were lukewarm and sceptical, more likely to be led into Christianity, when Christ came? Yet in proportion to their previous zeal, would be their appearance of inconsistency. Certainly, I have always contended that obedience even to an erring conscience was the way to gain light, and that it mattered not where a man began, so that he began on what came to hand, and in faith; and that anything might become a divine method of Truth; that to the pure all things are pure, and have a self-correcting virtue and a power of germinating.[19]

Newman holds that zealously following an erring conscience can bring a person to the truth. It does this, however, because the person zealously delving into the "erroneous system" eventually perceives its inherent inadequacies. As he says here, one's obedience with respect even to an erroneous system can become "a guidance even by means of it [i.e., that system] *out* of it." A few lines before the quoted passage, Newman says that it is not conversion that puts into doubt "the objectiveness of Truth," raising the suspicion "that one thing and another were equally pleasing to our Maker, where men were sincere," but rather failing to repudiate erroneous ideas once they are identified as such.[20] For Newman, the reason why following zealously even an erroneous conscience is good is that it leads to the truth, as it led the zealous pharisee Saint Paul to embrace Christ. Not to embrace the truth once it is seen would be sinful.

This is quite different from what we find in Bernhard Häring. He argues that, even if the Church is right about the matter at hand, it is better for authorities not to apply any pressure on someone who disagrees in conscience—as

---

19 Newman, *Apologia*, 161–62.
20 Newman, *Apologia*, 161.

if following an erroneous conscience is necessarily sinless. Häring writes as follows:

> From an objective, abstract point of view, we might, as outsiders, say that the person's conscience is erring, but existentially it might indicate the best possible step in the direction towards more light. It would be a most serious fault against the dignity of the conscience if a pastor, a confessor, or anyone else were to press the person to act against his sincere conscience, or indiscreetly try to inculcate the objective norm if this would disturb the person who simply cannot accept a particular precept or norm.[21]

Newman would probably agree with the first sentence of this passage. But he would strongly disagree with the rest of it. The Church, including its pastors and confessors, is obliged to speak the full truth of the Gospel in the hope that the person possessed of an erroneous conscience might indeed *be* disturbed and so come to see and to overcome its inadequacies.

But there is another reason why Häring thinks it so important to respect conscience in the way he advocates. He thinks that there are cases where conscience is in fact right and the "objective norm" laid down by the Church is wrong. One can see here the influence of modern romanticism and historicism on Häring's thought.

"There are legitimate reciprocal influences between moral theology and the zeitgeist," wrote Häring in 1963.[22] By zeitgeist Häring means the "spirit" informing a particular "historical period"— the tendency of opinion, will, and feeling that forms the thought and life of the people of that period. He appeals for this understanding to the work of the German romantic (or proto-romantic) philosopher Johann Gottfried Herder (1744–1803).[23]

Herder's philosophy was in large part a reaction against the arid rationalism of the Enlightenment. Herder wants to see nature as an inner source of meaning with things. As Charles Taylor explains:

> Herder offered a picture of nature as a great current of sympathy, running through all things. . . . "See the whole of nature, behold

---

[21] Bernhard Häring, *Free and Faithful in Christ: Moral Theology for Clergy and Laity*, vol. 1 (New York: Seabury Press, 1978), 241.

[22] Häring, "Heutige Bestrebungen," 21.

[23] Häring, "Heutige Bestrebungen," 20.

the great analogy of creation. Everything feels itself and its like, life reverberates to life." Man is the creature who can become aware of this and bring it to expression. . . . It is an inner impulse or conviction which tells us of the importance of our own natural fulfilment and of solidarity with our fellow creatures in theirs.[24]

Superficially, this seems like a return to the Aristotelian idea of nature as an intrinsic, teleological principle. But the resemblance is deceptive. To quote Taylor again:

This conception reflects the return in force of biological models of growth, as against the mechanistic ones of association, in the account of human mental development, models which Herder articulated so well and so effectively in this period. This obviously owes a great deal to Aristotle's idea of nature which actualizes its potential. But there is an importantly different twist. Where Aristotle speaks of the nature of a thing tending towards its complete form, Herder sees growth as the manifestation of an inner power (he speaks of "Kräfte"), striving to realize itself externally. . . . In fact, the Aristotelian concepts have been interwoven with the modern notion of expression as an articulation which both manifests and defines. This is closely tied to the idea of a self, a subject. It is no longer some impersonal "Form" or "nature" which comes to actuality, but a being capable of self-articulation. . . . Expressivism was the basis for a new and fuller individuation. This is the idea which grows in the late eighteenth century that each individual is different and original, and that this originality determines how he or she ought to live. . . . What the voice of nature calls us to cannot be fully known outside of and prior to our articulation/definition of it. We can only know what realizing our deep nature is when we have done it.[25]

What is going on here, in other words, is a reversal of the relation of potential and act. As we saw, for Aristotle the potentiality of matter is for the sake of its own actualization through form. Hence, the good is something objective: it is the actuality toward which a thing is directed by its nature. But for Herder

---

[24] Charles Taylor, *Sources of the Self: The Making of the Modern Identity* (Cambridge, MA: Harvard University Press, 1989), 369–70.

[25] Taylor, *Sources of the Self*, 375–76.

the opposite is the case. The good is now something radically subjective. We have here an inversion of teleology in which the "inner power" of desire is the source of goodness rather than goodness eliciting and calling forth desire.

The result is an ethics of "authenticity" and a politics of "identity." Persons and groups find and realize their authentic identities by expressing the inner power of desire and fashioning objects suited to it. The zeitgeist is the authentic expression of the identity of a particular time and place. The goodness of a particular way of life, and of particular kinds of actions, stems from their authenticity in expressing the vital inner élan of "nature." Although this way of thinking arose in opposition to Cartesian rationalism, in practice it has proved complementary to it. The ethics of authenticity serves as a source of goals to be realized through the rationalist domination of nature. The current craze for "sex change" operations is an example of this. A man determines through listening to the voice of inner desire that he is in fact a woman, and then rationalist technology is brought to bear on the *res extensa* of his body to change it to a female body so that he can live "authentically."

Herder's thought was a key influence on modern historicism—especially through the work of Georg Wilhelm Friedrich Hegel (1770–1831), who was deeply influenced by Herder. History is the judge of which social developments are in accordance with the flourishing of human freedom and which are not. Hence the ubiquity in modernity of talk about "the judgment of history."

Häring's theology proposes something similar for the life of the Church. He thinks that the proper response to God's love is worked out slowly through history, and that the Church, by listening to the prophetic voice of persons who stand up to her in conscience, learns that certain things impede our making a proper response to God's love.[26]

For Häring, one of the essential achievements of Vatican II is that it opened up the Church to a more historical understanding of reality, and therefore of morality. As he puts it:

> In an approach to the ethical problems [of our time] there is a fundamental choice between a static and a dynamic view of human history and nature. Most of our moral principles and our teaching about natural law have traditionally been based on a rather static vision of history and human nature. But the Second Vatican

---

[26] Häring, *Free and Faithful in Christ*, 1:281.

Council, after exploring major cultural changes, new insights into human history, and the new powers of the various sciences, asserts: "History itself speeds along on so rapid a course that an individual person can scarcely keep abreast of it. The destiny of the human community has become all of a piece, where once the various groups of man had a kind of private history of their own. Thus the human race has passed from a rather static concept of reality to a more dynamic, evolutionary one. In consequence, there has arisen a new series of problems, a series as important as can be, calling for new efforts of analysis and synthesis" (*Gaudium et spes*, 5). Moral theology has to draw its conclusion from this statement or be sincere enough to reject it. . . . Creation is an unfinished work that calls for man's cooperation to bring it to greater perfection. And man himself is an unfinished work, called to become an ever better image of God. Therefore he can be faithful to himself and to his Creator only by striving for progress in a creative way. He is a cultural being. He never simply adjusts himself to nature. Rather, as co-creator and co-revealer with God, he has to take nature into his hands to transform it in accordance with his goal to grow in his capacity to reciprocate love and to discern what enhances human dignity and what blocks it.[27]

On Häring's view, therefore, the Second Vatican Council is calling for a view of reality that is so historicist that man can be called a co-creator, bringing new realities and moral values into existence. The problem with this view is that man is a creature, not the creator. Man's nature is not something that he makes himself but rather the impress of the eternal and unchangeable wisdom of God in him.

HÄRING'S RHETORICAL APPROACH TO PHILOSOPHY

Another difficulty in interpreting Häring's thought stems from the inconsistent way in which he uses philosophy. As suggested above, Häring saw philosophy as a tool that theology uses as a printer might use different typefaces—to suit stylistic preferences and the fashions of the day rather than the intrinsic demands

---

[27] Bernard [sic] Häring, *Ethics of Manipulation: Issues in Medicine, Behavior Control and Genetics* (New York: Seabury Press, 1975), 63–64.

of theology herself. An effect of this attitude is that Häring makes use of many different and incompatible philosophical notions in his work. We see him using existentialism, phenomenology, Hegelian idealism, Herder's romanticism, Kant's rationalism, and even at times the philosophical teachings of Aristotle and Saint Thomas. There is no attempt at giving these disparate elements a *philosophical* unity. What unity there is comes from Häring's theology of call and response.

The use of philosophy in Häring often seems to have a primarily rhetorical purpose. He hated the dry, matter-of-fact style of the scholastic manuals, and wanted his own works to reflect the vital importance of morality. In a review of *The Law of Christ*, the English philosopher Anthony Kenny puts it as follows:

> Fr Häring thinks in superlatives and has a passion for the vertiginous. The book is full of yawning chasms and immense abysses; we read constantly of "the immensity of past and future," of "tremendous dimensions" and of "the profoundest depths" (of evil, or of the soul, or of conscience, or just of ignorance). On the other hand, he often invites us to a cosy intimacy with high abstractions: we become familiar with "the heart of reality," "the wealth of being" and with "the singularity of being in individuality."[28]

Kenny manifests this by quoting the following passage of *The Law of Christ*:

> Because of the profound harmony of intellect and will in the depth of the soul (in the substance), the intellectual power must be shaken to those very depths when the will struggles against it because of deep and sinister motives. Therefore the will in its turn must tremble in agony when it combats the clear knowledge of understanding and allows itself to be fascinated and deceived by a mere mirage of the good. The most agonizing cry wells up from the depth of the soul itself, for as root and source of unity of the powers, it is directly wounded by their dissension. Here is the profound reason for the first elemental agony, a spontaneous unreflecting pain.[29]

Häring is here referring to the Aristotelian/scholastic teaching on the unity of the soul as substantial form, but Kenny points out that the reason for bringing

---

[28] Anthony Kenny, "Recent Moral Theology," *Life of the Spirit* 17, no. 192 (1962): 33–40, at 36.
[29] Kenny, "Recent Moral Theology," 36, quoting Häring.

up this teaching is mostly rhetorical effect: "One puts the book down, awed and dizzy; then the mists clear, and one sees what he means. A man who does what he knows to be wrong usually feels sorry about it."[30] Häring could have reached the same conclusion using premises quite different from the Aristotelian ones that he employs.

Indeed, despite Häring's occasional use of Aristotle, it is clear that he does not really accept Aristotle's teleological principles. In an early assessment of Häring's work, presented as a lecture in November of 1962, Father Ernest Fortin, A.A., argued that, notwithstanding some favorable citations of Aristotle, taken as a whole, *The Law of Christ* represents a rejection of Aristotelian ethics. Häring's theology of call and response leads him to "an articulation of moral philosophy along lines that may be described roughly as those of personalism." Fortin is concerned that this feature of Häring's thought will lead to a loss of the objective element of morality:

> One cannot help wondering whether, by rejecting eudemonism or, differently stated, by refusing to base his study of human behavior on a previous analysis of man's perfection or natural end, an author can still do justice to the intellectual or objective component of Christian morality.[31]

This worry was to be borne out in subsequent years as Häring dissented from Church teaching on ever more issues—particularly in sexual morality and bioethics.

On matters of sexuality and life, Häring often uses wholistic language about the human person that sounds deceptively traditional. In fact, he understands this language in a way that makes it equivalent to a synthesis of a Herderian/romantic philosophy of subjective value and a Cartesian/rationalist philosophy of technology. Thus, in his book *Ethics of Manipulation,* Häring seems at one point to reject the Cartesian framework of nature as *res extensa* to be manipulated:

> The main problem for anthropology and ethics . . . is the overcoming of a radical objectivation that practically reduces the living person to a mere object, and limits him to a kind of knowledge and

---

[30] Kenny, "Recent Moral Theology," 36.

[31] Ernest Fortin, "The New Moral Theology," in *Collected Essays,* vol. 4 (Lanham, MD: Rowman and Littlefield, 2007), 127.

science concerned chiefly with control and utility. Where the vision of and dedication to wholeness is lost, what is identifiable becomes what can be produced. In the technical and scientific world, the principle of isolation—the isolation of a single phenomenon—is a necessity, but in practice it leads to great dangers wherever scientists transgress the boundary lines and build their philosophy and ethical justifications on that isolated reductionism. Isolation and abstraction cause "fade-out," and "fade-out" is separated by no more than a hairbreadth from dilution. The human reality cannot be divided into isolated pieces.[32]

In practice, however, Häring uses this wholistic vision to argue that man can in fact manipulate his natural faculties (reducing them in effect to "mere object"), if doing so serves the "whole" person, that is, the subjective desires of the person. This is clear in his treatment of contraception in the same book, which is worth quoting at length:

Many thought that the very fact that contraception is manipulation proved its intrinsic immorality. Others objected that it is not necessarily a manipulation. It is my conviction that we cannot deny that all forms of contraception contain manipulative manoeuvres. But the decisive question is not whether it is manipulation but whether there is an illegitimate "crossing of hierarchic boundaries." If it is a manipulation of persons and of their free will, and degrades their dignity, then our judgment cannot be anything but negative. This, however, has to be proven. There is no doubt that all forms of contraception do manipulate physiological processes. . . . This insight alone does not, however, justify a negative judgment about the method. The decisive question about all the various means of contraception is whether there is an unfavourable and unacceptable manipulation of human relationships. Each method has to be tested as to how far it manipulates the spontaneity of the marital union and endangers reciprocal love and respect. All effective means of contraception do separate the unitive end from the procreative end of the sexual act. . . . A completely contraceptive attitude is marked by a radical split of the unitive aspect from the

---

[32] Häring, *Ethics of Manipulation*, 55–56.

procreative one. In a responsible use of contraception, there cannot be only a maximum of attention to the expression of respectful and tender love; there has to be also a fundamental intentionality to preserve and foster that unity, fidelity and vitality of conjugal love which enables the spouses to fulfil their procreative and educative vocation in the best possible manner. Medical ethics shows generally that intervention in biological processes is never good in itself but is justified by a therapeutic end. There are even more reasons to assert specifically that contraception is not good in itself; but in a realistic ethics of compromise it can sometimes be considered as free from any subjective fault and can be, objectively, the best solution possible in painful difficulties to harmonize a responsible transmission of life with the exigencies of conjugal love.[33]

That is, the profound violation of the teleological order of the sexual faculty which is contraception is, according to Häring, an acceptable "manipulation of physiological processes," that is, of the Cartesian *res extensa*. It is only wrong if it becomes "a manipulation of persons and of their free will," that is, of the *res cogitans*. The key criterion ends up being a kind of Herderian expressivism, in which anything is good if it fosters the authentic expression of "respectful and tender love."

THE TEACHING OF *VERITATIS SPLENDOR*

The new moral theology pioneered by Häring and others at the time of the Council came into conflict with the teachings of the popes most visibly with the promulgation by Pope Saint Paul VI of *Humanae vitae* in 1968. And the conflict continued under the pontificate of Pope Saint John Paul II, who issued the encyclical *Veritatis splendor* in order to address in a systematic way the problems inherent in the new theology. The document addresses the problem of historicism head on:

The great concern of our contemporaries for historicity and for culture has led some to call into question *the immutability of the natural law* itself, and thus the existence of "objective norms of morality" valid for all people of the present and the future, as for

---

[33] Häring, *Ethics of Manipulation*, 93–95.

those of the past. Is it ever possible, they ask, to consider as universally valid and always binding certain rational determinations established in the past, when no one knew the progress humanity would make in the future? It must certainly be admitted that man always exists in a particular culture, but it must also be admitted that man is not exhaustively defined by that same culture. Moreover, the very progress of cultures demonstrates that there is something in man which transcends those cultures. This "something" is precisely human nature: this nature is itself the measure of culture and the condition ensuring that man does not become the prisoner of any of his cultures, but asserts his personal dignity by living in accordance with the profound truth of his being. To call into question the permanent structural elements of man which are connected with his own bodily dimension would not only conflict with common experience, but would render meaningless *Jesus' reference to the "beginning,"* precisely where the social and cultural context of the time had distorted the primordial meaning and the role of certain moral norms (cf. Mt 19:1–9).[34]

That is to say, that which perdures through all historical changes is human nature itself, the teleological principle which God placed into the human heart in the beginning. To live "authentically" is not to be governed by Herder's subjective inner nature but to live in accordance with the truth of that inner nature, which has been directed by God toward objective human perfection.

For Häring the resistance of the popes to his theology was a sign of their betrayal of the Second Vatican Council's dynamic vision of reality. But John Paul II is careful to show that the Council itself supports his teaching:

The Council warns against a false concept of the autonomy of earthly realities, one which would maintain that "created things are not dependent on God and that man can use them without reference to their Creator." With regard to man himself, such a concept of autonomy produces particularly baneful effects, and eventually leads to atheism. . . . The teaching of the Council emphasizes, on the one hand, *the role of human reason* in discovering and applying the moral law: the moral life calls for that creativity and originality

---

[34] John Paul II, Encyclical Letter *Veritatis splendor* (August 6, 1993), §53.

typical of the person, the source and cause of his own deliberate acts. On the other hand, reason draws its own truth and authority from the eternal law, which is none other than divine wisdom itself.... *The moral law has its origin in God and always finds its source in him*: at the same time, by virtue of natural reason, which derives from divine wisdom, it is *a properly human law*. Indeed, as we have seen, the natural law "is nothing other than the light of understanding infused in us by God, whereby we understand what must be done and what must be avoided. God gave this light and this law to man at creation." The rightful autonomy of the practical reason means that man possesses in himself his own law, received from the Creator. Nevertheless, *the autonomy of reason cannot mean* that reason itself *creates values and moral norms*. Were this autonomy to imply a denial of the participation of the practical reason in the wisdom of the divine Creator and Lawgiver, or were it to suggest a freedom which creates moral norms, on the basis of historical contingencies or the diversity of societies and cultures, this sort of alleged autonomy would contradict the Church's teaching on the truth about man.[35]

Human beings are therefore not the creators of the moral order but its discoverers. There exists a permanent moral order accessible to our minds.

What does it mean to say that moral order is accessible to our minds? Certainly, it is true that this order has not always been respected in practice. It is possible for conscience, in the sense of the particular judgment about what is good, to be in error. It is even possible to be habitually in error about the moral good. But there is a certain indelible conscience in man which Thomas Aquinas (together with others) calls *synderesis*, the knowledge of the good that God has inscribed in our hearts.[36] Hence moral error always includes an element of "suppressing the truth" (see Rom 1:18) that gives witness against us in the depths of the soul. This is why, contra Häring, it is important to insist on the objective norm, which the person is capable of recognizing. One can even exert "pressure," not to make someone act against their conscience, but rather to correct the judgment of their erring conscience by reminding them of the truth that is engraved by *synderesis* in the depths of their heart.

---

[35] John Paul II, *Veritatis splendor*, §§39–40.

[36] See Aquinas, *Summa theologiae* IIa-IIae, q. 47, a. 6.

I remember once getting into an argument with a distinguished moral theologian from Germany, a follower of Häring, in a seminar on Saint Thomas Aquinas. We were discussing Saint Thomas's teaching that an erring conscience does not excuse.[37] The theologian said that Saint Thomas did not take into account the "prophetic" character of conscience and was unwilling to accept that the norm proclaimed at his time might be wrong. I answered that he was not talking about the socially accepted norm of his time, but about the natural law, which is immutable. "Well," said the theologian, "how does he know about the definite content of the natural law? He accepts what is assumed in the culture of his time." This position seems to me clearly false. The issues of contraception, divorce, and "remarriage" are cases in point. The "culture of our time" tells us that it is okay to impede conception, to divorce, and to "remarry"; the Church, on the other hand, in all such regards appeals to the law written in the depths of the heart. The truly "prophetic" role of conscience is not to insist on private opinion, backed up by the custom of our time, against the perennial teachings of the Church. Rather, the truly prophetic act of conscience is to allow oneself to be led by the perennial teaching of the eternal truth.

---

[37] Aquinas, *Summa theologiae* Ia-IIae, q. 19, a. 6.

DOING HERESY: THEN AND NOW

John M. Rist

We tend culpably to evade our responsibility when we ought to instruct and admonish [evildoers], sometimes even with sharp reproof and censure, either because the task is irksome or because we are afraid of giving offence, or it may be that we shrink from incurring their enmity, for fear that they may hinder and harm us in worldly matters, in respect either of what we eagerly seek to attain, or of what we weakly dread to lose.

Saint Augustine, *City of God* 1.9

Only because of the heretics in her midst could the Catholic Church find a more exact way to express herself in words, and the orthodox were preserved in their right-thinking because of the false thinkers among them. . . . For example, was any complete account of the Trinity available before the Arians began to bay at it? . . . Nor had the unity of Christ's body been discussed in such a developed, explicit way until division [Donatism] began to trouble the weaker brethren.

Saint Augustine, on Psalm 54:22[1]

---

[1] Augustine, *The Works of St. Augustine: A Translation for the 21st Century*, vol. III/17, *Expositions of the Psalms, Ps 51–72*, ed. John Rotelle, O.S.A., trans. Maria Boulding, O.S.B. (New York: New City Press, 2001), 74–75.

HERESY, WHAT HERESY?

Heresies arise in faith and morals, though moral heresies also imply errors in faith and will only occur where the "rule of faith" applies. Heretics may not recognize themselves as such: on the tombstone of Julian of Eclanum, Pelagian enemy of Augustine, was carved, "Here lies Julian the Catholic bishop." The Church identifies heresies not because their advocates lose the argument but because she judges them objectively misguided. Schisms involve heresy actually or potentially: actually, when an accepted doctrine is rejected by a breakaway group, as many Protestants rejected the real presence of Christ in the Eucharist; potentially, when a theological advance is mooted but fails to win universal acceptance, as when the so-called Monophysites broke away after the Council of Chalcedon. Heresies affect more than the participants in the debate: those "caught in the middle" find themselves confused.

Heresies arise from *unexpected* challenges to the "rule of faith" and compel revised formulations of what the orthodox hold as implicit in existent tenets. The earliest heresies concerned such diverse questions as whether Christian males should be circumcised or whether a divine being *could* die on the Cross. One of the complaints of the Arians was that creeds should not employ language not found in Scripture: such was *homoousios* added to the Nicene creed, according to Ambrose, precisely because, being unscriptural, the Arians would not tolerate it.[2]

Heresies about circumcision and divine self-humiliation arose from a growing Christian separation from earlier cultural practices or from convictions such as the impossibility of what Paul and others defined as God's voluntary self-abasement (*kenosis*). Heresies may be "liberal" or "conservative." Conservative heresies usually develop from internal struggles within Christian communities with those whose watchword is that "we cannot change the faith of our fathers." Liberal heresies, generally of more recent date, will normally arise from the interaction of Christians with threatening external powers, such as England's Henry VIII. Pressure need not take the crude form of torture and execution; there are other, more insidious, instantiations of the axiom *cuius regio eius religio* of the pressure to conform to anti-Catholic observances. Nowadays, such threats are used rather over "moral" than "dogmatic" theology: thus, at the Lambeth Conference in 1930, the Anglicans caved in to societal pressures in favor of divorce and contraception. However, the "moral" may converge with the "dogmatic": if Christ rejects divorce and remarriage while

---

[2] Ambrose, *De Fide* 6.

Christians promote it, they are in denial of his Gospel—therefore at worst in denial of his divinity, becoming neo-Arians.

The history of Christianity may be viewed as a recurring disentanglement of Christian thought from the cultural and intellectual assumptions of its times, or rather, a gradual discernment of what in the cultural environment is compatible with Christianity. The process began with the "incredible" resurrection and is still far from complete—and, pending the conversion of the entire world, incompletable. Almost all the earliest heresies concerned the person of Jesus: Did he really die? Is he foretold by the Hebrew Bible? When will he return? More theologically, such difficulties revolved round the relationship between Jesus as Son and Logos and God the Father. Heresies about the Holy Spirit generally arose later, and their resolution tended to follow from preceding Christological disputes, which in the Patristic Age came to a decisive climax when Arius, a priest of Alexandria, contradicted his bishop: Christ, he insisted, though the first of creation, is subordinate to God the Father; he is a creature, for "there was a time when he was not."

Arianism became a problem precisely because it was a *challenge* to current Church *teaching*, or rather perhaps to current Church *assumptions*. Like the Greek Sophists of earlier days in their challenge to unexamined morality, Arius claimed that traditional accounts of the relationship between Jesus and the Father had been accepted uncritically, and many pre-Christian assumptions seemed to favor his claim: thus, a *logos*, he could insist, is the representation of a higher metaphysical level at a lower; hence if Christ is the Logos (as Saint John wrote) then (as Origen argued) he is subordinate to the Father. Though a heresy in dogmatic theology, in many ways Arianism is the epitome of all errors in theology. Even if at first sight others look very different, they turn out to have Arian implications.

And some do seem very different, being in the first instance errors about human rather than divine nature—as Pelagianism, an ever-recurring tendency, looks to be, asserting that current human nature is morally better than it has appeared to the Church (or indeed to common sense) from the times of Augustine and Jerome. But if Pelagianism, with its claims about human autonomy, is correct, then the Catholic account of the necessity of grace is mistaken; hence, it misdescribes Christ's work of salvation and therefore his nature. Hence Pelagian errors about human psychology and human weakness point to heresies about the divine nature and God's salvific action.

THE CATHOLIC CHURCH IN THE MODERN WORLD

Despite the rapid growth of the Church in many parts of the Third World, its intellectual heart remains in Europe and North America. But that heart becomes tainted with hubris—as when Cardinal Kasper referred to the Church in Africa and its theology as primitive—indicating how many European and North American prelates and theologians see themselves as intellectually, if not morally and spiritually, superior to their so-called Third-World colleagues.[3] And that spiritual "superiority" is increasingly expressed in their assimilation of the preferences of a post-Christian Europe.

Of this, rights theory provides a good example. There are solid, traditionally Catholic teachings about man's dignity as created in the image and likeness of God which can be adapted to defend basic human "rights"; yet, even in documents such as Pope Leo XIII's *Rerum Novarum* (§9), the Second Vatican Council's Pastoral Constitution on the Church in the Modern World *Gaudium et Spes* (§§26 and 41) and Pope Saint John XXIII's Encyclical Letter *Pacem in Terris* (§5), these teachings are presented as a scarcely qualified endorsement of secular (usually Kantian) theories about human *value* (note the different vocabulary) and are uncritically accepted with little correction of their theoretical weaknesses. Such unthinking subservience to secular orthodoxy advocates not virtue but rights-claims, not love but "fairness," as the foundation of morality.

Many Western thought patterns, espoused by theologians and bishops apparently ignorant of their origins in thinkers deeply hostile to Catholic doctrine, can be readily identified. The concept of autonomy, deriving (again) from Kant and other Enlightenment theorists, reveals itself as advocacy of—in religious language—Pelagianism, culminating in the desire of Western man to be a Promethean self-creator, or, in current jargon, to become trans-human. With autonomy comes the prioritizing of choice: since we are (or aspire to be) autonomous, choice overrides almost all other considerations—such as what used to be called goodness—and determines practices such as killing by abortion and euthanasia, these becoming for no small number of "Catholics," especially in public life, options too fashionable and convenient to shun. Together with autonomy and an idolizing of choice comes individualism. Our individual choices are authoritative, though we may compromise our autonomy to

---

[3] For a transcript of the interview, see Edward Pentin, "Statement on Cardinal Kasper Interview," October 16, 2014, https://edwardpentin.co.uk/statement-on-cardinal-kasper-interview/.

protect ourselves against the choices of others. The prioritizing of our choices as autonomous agents points not only to the rejection of legitimate authority, civil or ecclesial (unless accepted by contract), but to the relativizing of truth itself (as Hegel and those theologians who follow his spirit—if not avowedly his text—have recognized).

With truth relativized, there can be no fundamental authority other than the power of those able to call the moral, social, political, and ecclesiastical shots. In secular Europe and North America, these are elite groups of post-Christian relativists, deniers of any transcendental realm unless (as Richard Rorty put it) you *choose* to have one. In Latin America, they are heirs of a lingering Marxism, secular or ecclesial—now recipients of the theologically tainted financial support of bureaucratically organized Western ecclesiastical sees, where bishops see their roles as chief executive officers of a spiritually flavored, seemingly "merciful," NGO. Thus has Rauschenbusch's "Social Gospel" Christianity developed "Catholic" branches.

This is the world in which European and North American churchmen have become accustomed to live, and it provides them with a spurious professed sophistication. Yet, a challenging question confronts them: whether it is worthwhile to maintain traditional moral standards in a post-Christian culture in which money, donated by such as George Soros to corrupt Christian teaching, "talks" as powerfully as ever and where power (direct or indirect, hard or soft) will be exercised to enforce. It is not hard to see why the Church has grown indecisive about moral standards where the secular world energetically denies them and why it has fallen into brand-new varieties of heresy not immediately dogmatic but moral, though with Arian and Pelagian foundations.

Just as Augustine noted how metaphysical errors derive from attempts to justify moral failings, so with moral heresy in place, we are ripe for a new route to deny the divinity of Christ, a denial which can appear in direct and indirect versions. In the eighties of the last century, there was much debate, not least among Oxford-based Anglican clergy, about fourth-century Arianism, and there is reason to believe that underlying their disagreements were contemporary dilemmas concerning the prospects for new varieties of Arianism in the twentieth century. At an Oxford Patristics Conference, I heard one participating theologian "congratulated," only half in jest, on having moved from Adoptionism to Arianism.

THE PAPAL "COURT" AND MEDIA TEMPTATION

An unusual feature of new *moral* heresies is that by appeals in a relativist world to the "signs of the times" we are induced to misdescribe them, especially if pressure to camouflage deviation is exerted at the highest levels of the hierarchical Church. To understand this part in the drama, we must glance at the history of the papacy after the First Vatican Council.

Throughout the history of the Catholic Church, the role of the bishop of Rome has rarely—albeit increasingly in the last 150 years—been that of primary advocate of doctrinal development; more normally, it has been to scrutinize and eventually approve or reject what bishops, theologians, and others have developed—often over centuries and rarely in abstraction from the history and prospects of an expanding, specifically Christian, culture. The reasons for the apparent change are deep-seated, but some of the more significant can easily be recognized.

Before Vatican I came to an untidy end in 1870 with much of its business incomplete, it formalized part of the relationship between the pope and the bishops in council, allowing the pope, in apparently strictly regulated circumstances, to declare and promulgate "infallibly" advances in our basic understanding of Catholic truth. Though now reliant on that historic decision, such papal power has been used on only two occasions, one of which preceded the First Vatican Council itself. Nevertheless, in less regulated areas popes, especially if possessed of mediatic gifts, have increasingly become communicators, with opportunities for broadcasting their views expanding exponentially. Given that some of their utterances may look more infallible than others—infallibility itself being a somewhat confusing concept developed as being of central importance in the nineteenth century from earlier claims about *authority* (with some self-serving input from medieval Franciscans)—a new theological speciality has emerged, the effects of which deserve comment.

The murky medieval history is of intrinsic interest and may enable us to draw conclusions relevant to the current situation in the Church. It seems that the earliest question which pointed toward claims about specifically papal inerrancy—as distinct from the inerrancy of the Roman See or of the wider Church—concerned the canonization of saints. This was a comparatively minor development, with only indirect implications for papal infallibility in determining doctrines about faith and morals. The Franciscans, however, especially those guided by Peter John Olivi and later William of Ockham, called for a wider version of papal inerrancy: not so much to increase papal power but—ironically—to diminish its practical implications, and for very specific reasons.

Pope Nicholas III, especially in his bull *Exiit* of 1279, accepted that the Franciscan way of life represented the perfection taught by Christ to his apostles. That met with considerable resistance and as time passed the "Spiritual" Franciscans, following the lead of Olivi, came to fear that a later pope might cancel Nicholas's pro-Franciscan policies—as indeed turned out to be the case with John XXII. To circumvent that, Olivi argued that no pope could revoke the teachings of his predecessors on faith and morals but was bound by them since they had been taught infallibly. Popes, though infallible, were constrained by the decrees of their infallible predecessors.

But Olivi—and later in more lengthy expositions, Ockham—realized that a problem remained: suppose what a pope decreed was heretical? Olivi's radical solution was that if a "pope" proposed a heretical doctrine he was not a pope but rather a pseudo-pope who, if persisting in his errors, should be deposed. That raised in its turn the difficulty of how to determine which papal teachings were indeed heretical, and here the Franciscans ran into a brick wall. Ockham's skepticism as to how certain knowledge of the faith could be guaranteed led him not only to admit that popes could be heretical but that the same might be true of councils. It might look as though only rational theologians—perhaps only Ockham himself!—could determine which papal decrees were decrees of a true pope and therefore infallible.

In the fourteenth century, the ultimate sources from which Catholic doctrine could be *deduced* (note the word) were the subject of constant, often historically ignorant dispute, it being usually assumed that the choice was either Scripture alone or Scripture supplemented by Tradition. Then further problems appeared: how do we interpret Scripture? Which traditions, especially if supported by decisions of Councils at which a pope was present or represented, were to be deemed infallible? It might seem that Ockham's subjectivism was the only way out—which would not do. Interestingly, a third option was more or less ignored: traditional teachings implied that all apparent additions to Scripture could be deduced. But there is a further possibility: acceptably infallible teaching might be identified in whatever is *not incompatible* with Scripture. If so, doctrinal claims made by popes but incompatible with Scripture are ruled out, and by Olivi's principle, popes who persist in teaching them or condoning them are not true popes and should be removed from office by appropriate juridical procedures.

Such a position is not irrelevant to our present confusions, and returning therefore to the contemporary scene, we observe that professionals regularly attempt to determine the weight of various kinds of papal (and even more generally of Vatican and "magisterial") pronouncements, identifying which are products of the ordinary Magisterium, the extraordinary Magisterium, or infallible; while the ordinary believer, with little understanding of theological or canonical niceties, is inclined to hold that all such efforts equal an attitude far from invisible in more "primitive" times, when, regarding the pope, Catholics all knew that—as I once heard an Irishman report the contents of a sermon on the topic—"he is a good man." In more contemporary disputes about moral theology, we hear a version of this from bishops eager to evade their responsibilities as teachers of true doctrine: "After all, he is the pope."

In recent decades there has been more "informed" debate about the respective weight of an encyclical, an exhortation, or an utterance at a press conference on an aircraft. Yet few popes have gone out of their way, as did Pope Benedict XVI when writing about the life of Jesus, to distinguish their views as private theologians from those of the successor of Peter with authority to define the received rule of faith. Hence, endless doctrinal comment emerging from the Vatican has, even when compatible with traditional Catholic teaching, encouraged a new variety of ultramontanism: that seems the plausible explanation of, for example, the behavior of the Maltese bishops over Pope Francis's exhortation *Amoris Laetitia*. On this issue their attitude and acts have been at variance with their earlier insistence on traditional doctrine clearly and unambiguously formulated. Why then has their attitude so radically changed? The explanation can only be that they have followed not the traditions of the Church but the views of the current pope, forgetting that the pope is not the Church: that he is (or should be) the principal spokesman of the Church and principal guardian of its ageless teachings amid the novelties and temptations of ever-changing ages.

Thus, the revised understanding of the papal role created by Vatican I, though in some ways desirable, has opened the door to widespread abuse, not least because there is no clarity as to what is an *ex cathedra* statement but also because those who drew up the account of infallibility could not foresee how developments in the media, both secular and religious, would affect its reception. To understand such effects, we need to look at two features of the contemporary scene: one concerning the media itself—not least social media—and its ever-increasing influence for good or ill; the other the continuing reality of the Vatican as a monarchical court exercising many of the less appetizing features of the *ancien régime*.

First, then, the media, for unless we understand it better, radical adjustments to the mentality and behavior of Roman authorities—hopefully aiming to restore an updated version of conditions which prevailed in the past—can hardly be expected. Two features of modern media should be noted: the appetite for novelty, and the facility to spread a message across the globe in seconds. The decrees of Pope Gregory VII (1073–1085) took weeks or months to reach outlying parts of the Catholic world, and in some cases hardly did so at all; thus, we find his call for priestly celibacy barely reaching the shores of Iceland. Now, it takes a couple of clicks for the latest gaffe of a celebrity at an airport to go viral. Yet, speed is no guarantee of accuracy even in the reporting of gaffes.

The connection this has with the decisions of the First Vatican Council is not far to seek: Catholicism, especially if it looks (or can be made to look) reactionary, is hot copy, and in a world which assumes that a celebrity pope can answer questions at any time more or less authoritatively, it is likely that he will be tempted to tell journalists what they want to hear, or want to filter. Their reporting will, in turn, encourage people, including many of the faithful, to make their judgments as to what the Church is doing largely on the basis of reported papal activity and pronouncement. Some journalists are reasonably friendly to the Catholic Church as she presently operates and presently believes; others manifestly are not, seeing in the present reliance on papal utterances which they can publish with or without context—thus inviting "clarification"—a golden opportunity for mischief.

Such a media environment further encourages the development of an ambiguous set of behaviors that has grown up in the Church over the last 150 years. An important turning point in traditional papal activity arrived—for good reasons at the time—during the papacy of Leo XIII. His social encyclical *Rerum Novarum*, coupled with his strong encouragement of Thomism in *Aeterni Patris*, was promulgated in the hope that a combination of serious philosophy with the recovery of a revised (often patristic) Catholic social and moral agenda, based on the teaching that man is created in God's image would offer a powerful response to atheistic liberalism and Marxism. This promising agenda was promoted in Rome in the wake of Vatican I, first by Pope Leo himself, later by Popes Saint John XXIII and Saint Paul VI, and then by Pope Saint John Paul II in his Theology of the Body. Its comparative success left the new papal tendency to innovate—especially given our present mediatic background—liable to abuse, so much so that on this ground alone there is a good case to be made that popes not only should talk to the media little if at all—and with attention to the probable (even if unwelcome) effects of their words—but should consciously revert to the earlier model of the papal office: not to innovate but to scrutinize. Nor, needless to say, is it helpful for a pope to float different—even contradictory—utterances to different audiences on different days, such that if one set of comments seems "traditional" and so is welcomed with relief by "conservatives" it will be discounted by "liberals" as a convenient sop to their opponents, as it may well be shown to be, not least if followed by coarse criticism of traditional Catholics.

Although ambiguity may just leave the field open, it may also be intended to secure subversive changes, this on "Hegelian" principles. Let us call traditional Catholic teaching on sexuality and marriage the thesis (T). Let us call desired changes to that teaching the antithesis (A). Put the thesis and antithesis together and we get a synthesis (S). But in matters of moral doctrine this is a dangerous procedure: if the antithesis (A) is in radical contradiction to the thesis (T), then the synthesis (S) will itself not only be to some degree faulty but will become the basis for further ill-founded deductions.

Apart from risks inherent in "off-the-cuff" papal pronouncements in the present climate, it is clear that the more the central government in Rome is pushed into saying and doing, the less bishops will act as they should and the more they will evade their responsibilities by "just obeying orders"; this especially if they can find justification for inaction—as well as a means to protect themselves from popular hostility—by the shield of a bishops' conference. A good example was the overhasty decision of the Italian bishops to accept an arbitrary papal ruling to replace the traditional version of a petition of the Lord's Prayer by an admittedly ancient (though less well-attested) alternative designed (rightly or wrongly) to be an explanatory gloss rather than an exact representation of the Lord's original words. And servility within the Church will promote a similar mentality in dealing with secular authorities. Catholics, especially bishops, need moral courage in a hostile age.

I turn to the second important feature of the contemporary scene: namely that despite the denials by complacent theologians, the Vatican is still run as an early modern court, complete with courtiers. And though courts exist in other political and even commercial jurisdictions, the Vatican's situation as an *ecclesiastical* court is unique—albeit abuses associated with secular, authoritarian courts can be recognized there too—for in the case of the Vatican, the risks are not political or social but spiritual. This model of the Roman Curia as court situates the pope as head of an autocratic regime, whether reactionary or liberal, neither variety being appropriate, since the pope is not the Church, but first of its servants (*servus servorum Dei*). Nor should he be identified with the Church, which is the Body of Christ.

All courts, royal and ecclesiastical, prove secretive, hence open to financial misdemeanors. Everything curial, not least the power of the courtiers—ever struggling for position and influence—depends on the monarch. The corollary is that the monarch (barring a revolution) can do no significant wrong. If mistakes are made and heads must roll, they will be of courtiers who "misled" their master or got in his way, not of the master himself, who can deploy the high repute of his office to conceal the inadequacies of his personal performance. His status, whether civil or ecclesiastical, can thus resemble that of a superstar or demigod; by contrast, the Apostle to the Gentiles was at pains to point out that he and Barnabas were mere men (Acts 14:15). As for the courtiers, their dependency might seem too dangerous, potentially too humiliating, to be worth accepting, but such is the price one must pay to climb all sorts of greasy poles, and history reports how many are prepared to pay it. Popes, bishops, and theologians regularly deprecate ecclesiastical careerism; yet "scarlet fever" remains rife, generating aggressive competition flavored with the possibility of blackmail, of the smearing or of otherwise intimidating opponents guilty (or publicized as guilty) of moral delinquency—or of telling the truth about the delinquencies of others.

There are no devotional or doctrinal reasons why the successor of Peter should be surrounded by a court; other models could guarantee more continuity in the presentation of Catholic doctrine and the organization of the Church's mission while dispensing with dependent courtiers and flatterers who hardly discourage those outside the charmed circle from aping their mentality. All government may be government by elites, but there is no reason to treat elites as *ipso facto* virtuous, nor to refrain from criticizing the abuses they regularly entrain and protect. Court flattery is bad for the flatterers and for the flattered— and encourages the development of a personality cult. The present problem of such "celebrity"—though Benedict XVI tried to moderate it—goes back at least to John Paul II, whose thespian skills encouraged it; although he recognized that the role of the See of Peter in the Church should be re-examined. The context of that was relations with the Orthodox, but the question, if taken up, could hardly not extend further.

THE SEXUAL REVOLUTION

In the present Western climate, "sexual" activity of any kind is increasingly regarded as a right or as mere fun and is ideologically promoted as such. Though the rights-claim is modern, the assumption itself is age-old, though consequent behavior—often, until the sixties of the last century, only approved for men—is out of keeping both with traditional Church teaching and with the philosophical principle, going back at least to Aristotle, that we should not act just for pleasure, though we should normally enjoy performing good actions.

Sexual activity is important not only for individuals who want to enjoy it (however perversely and for whatever reason) but for any society that hopes to be renewed—under pain of elimination or radical character change—by procreation. Augustine insists that sexual sins, though not the worst, are paradigmatic in that they are curiously liable to invite sins of even greater magnitude precisely *because* we all want to justify the pleasures we receive from them: this was probably the context in which, as noted, he argued that bad morals lead to bad metaphysical construction, designed—consciously or not—to rationalize bad conduct. He would reject the contemporary notion that sexual activity, *qua* fun, is in effect the one area of human life where we need have no worries about original sin. To proclaim truth here is to be very unpopular.

The sixties of the last century, like all revolutionary periods, encouraged hedonism, especially in the form of sexual "liberation," nor is it by chance that a topless Marianne symbolizes that *Liberté* of the totalitarian revolution in France which has cast such a shadow over subsequent European history and society—which is not to deny that Marianne may also symbolize the maternal suckling of the nation. As in the French Revolution, the revolutionaries of the sixties had laudable aims jostling for prominence with the less laudable: to challenge a capitalism out of control (the "military-industrial complex") and the mindless expansion of impersonalized universities increasingly intended as production lines for cogs in the economic machine—later to provide ideological backup for (anti-Christian) liberalism. Yet many of the sixties revolutionaries were baby boomers, used to the support of Daddy's checkbook, mindless pro-moters of drug abuse (such as LSD, encouraged by such popular lyrics as "Lucy in the sky with diamonds"), aided and abetted by "the pill" as an exceptionally effective incentive for a newfound female libertinism and its self-gratifying male encouragement.

It is hardly surprising that not only did the worst features of the sixties (such as insistence on the "right" to abortion) become mainstream while many better targets were forgotten or driven back into the cultures of subgroups, but, as is customary in revolutions, the more extreme participants—not least the more extreme libertines—tended to take control, leaving the more idealistic to accept many of the old evils for fear of worse. The apotheosis of one "sexual" aspect of the whole period was epitomized by British Prime Minister David Cameron when he stated that, *as a Conservative,* he "personally [felt] very passionately about" "both changing the law and also working to help change the culture" when it came to gay marriage.[4]

The sixties were also the time of the much-needed Second Vatican Council, and it is unsurprising that its proceedings were influenced by the worse as well as the better aspects of the heated debates carried on beyond the walls of Vatican City. For, not only in the immediate area of sexual *morality* did the Church attempt to face new realities. More generally, the relations between the sexes had reached a critical point. In the West at least there was an insistence that women should no longer be largely controlled or manipulated by men (though perhaps they might be manipulated indirectly through use of "the pill"); that they should be "liberated"—though few wanted to think what "liberation" means or should mean. Indeed, the challenge of women's "liberation" was only the most recent, if a most basic one, of a series of challenges the Church has had to face since its inception. In this case—indeed with sexual liberation more generally—it was sadly unprepared, and when "enlightened," inclined to naïveté, forgetting the ubiquity of original sin.

Not that the problems of modernity at the Council were limited to sex, marriage, and the position of women—indeed, discussion of the realities in these particular areas was inhibited by Paul VI's decision to reserve to himself as pope the final decision about artificial contraception. There were other areas where traditional teachings had to be boldly developed, not least in matters

---

4 David Cameron, "Prime Minister's speech at Lesbian, Gay, Bisexual and Transgender Reception," UK Government website, July 25, 2012, https://www.gov.uk/government/speeches/prime-ministers-speech-at-lesbian-gay-bisexual-and-transgender-reception.

of religious toleration, for now that the Church was no longer in a position to repress, the Council Fathers had the opportunity to think more about what repression on religious grounds entailed for theories of human nature as created in the image and likeness of God. Here too, however, when viewed by hindsight, not only were many of the Council's deliberations finally presented as a series of compromises, and therefore in need of further "clarification," but in the rush to say something, a tendency to say something naïve could prove irresistible, especially where what was naïve was also fashionable.

It remains unclear why Paul VI took the decision to reserve to himself the problem of artificial contraception, which, from one viewpoint, summed up the difficulties of accommodating women's "liberation." Perhaps the simple explanation that he needed to listen to apparent experts, and that was not possible within the Council's necessary timeframe, is correct. In any event, the delay revealed an important feature of revolutionary situations at which we have already glanced in the political domain: that there will arise a dynamic whereby the more extreme participants overcome (in revolution may literally outgun) their more moderate colleagues.

A few of the wiser sort, most notably Joseph Ratzinger, recognized this dynamic during the Council itself—though "extremists" had developed insufficient authority to impose their views on the majority of Council Fathers. The attempt to do that was to come later, despite the steadying interlude of the pontificates of John Paul II and Benedict XVI, when debate about the "Spirit of Vatican II" broke out again. And as we should expect, the temptations of those sexual sins of which Augustine was so aware and which are so cried up by our contemporary opinion-formers, both inside and well outside the Church, were almost inevitably to lead, slowly but surely, to a free-for-all, whatever Jesus and Paul had had to say about it; for who, in the end, is Jesus—"in our day and age"?

First was divorce and remarriage among many calling themselves Christians, together with contraception on a massive scale (although some merely claimed it for married couples reasonably desirous of limiting their families), then abortion. The latter is an abstract term for the elimination of millions of unborn children, at first in extreme cases, then as a "right" and "choice," without account of the helpless victim. The "right" to sexual fun, including the varieties earlier known as unnatural, now prevailed in more than pagan form: Aphrodite/Venus still loved fertility. Homosexual acts, including buggery, once damnable, were now by no tiny a group of influential theologians and bishops—ever keen to appease if not actually to practice—held to be blessable.

In such moral heresy, the Church can be seen rotting from the inside, as can be recognized in a widely touted Vatican-inspired defensive theme. Sexual abuse by clergy is put down to "clericalism" by those who know that clericalism has few friends. Indeed, there has been and always will be clericalism, but the underlying problem about sexual abuse becomes clear when we discover that 80 percent of the abused are not children but young adult males. Clericalism may often, in Aristotelian terms, be the means, but anal penetration is the *telos*.

With his encyclical letter *Humanae Vitae*, Paul VI tried to draw a line under some forms of what he considered sexual irregularity and was apparently astounded at the reaction he provoked. He seems to have expected that his encyclical would be welcomed, not of course in the secular world, but among the faithful—not least in view of the enhanced authority which the bishops (and the journalists) had bestowed on the papacy since Vatican I. *Humanae Vitae* is a prophetic text even in senses to which Paul himself apparently paid less attention, perhaps was hardly aware of: signally that the "contraceptive mentality" has led to a demographic decline, with potentially disastrous consequences affecting many parts of the "developed" world in the last half-century.

Nevertheless, much Catholic reaction to Paul's encyclical was (and remains) strongly negative. We have not, it is said, updated ourselves; we have not completed that *aggiornamento* of which John XXIII had spoken so eloquently. And just as after Vatican II many Catholic universities, recognizing their own intellectual failings, supposed they had to choose between being Catholic and being intellectual—and chose to remain Catholic only in name and shame—so millions of Catholics ignored Paul VI's teaching, thus not only hacking away at the authority of Church and pope but opening the door to discussion of much previously unthinkable: Catholic fornication, Catholic divorce and remarriage, Catholic abortion, Catholic buggery, "gay" marriage in the Church—and why not Catholic infanticide and Catholic polygamy (of which we have been warned by Cardinal Napier), Catholic bestiality, Catholic incest?[5] There being few or no sexual sins, we all—obvious non-consensual violence as yet apart—can have fun in our own way and encourage others to do the same while remaining Catholic. Which poses the question, how many "Catholic" bishops, priests, or

5 Catholic News Service, "Cardinal Napier: Communion and Polygamy," October 8, 2014, https://youtu.be/U12-JT_pwKI.

lay authorities *are* Catholic—or, to put it specifically, how many have fallen into *moral* heresy, or worse, into mortal sin?

Many sexual sins can be put down easily enough to a cult of hedonism always liable to develop in times of radical change. But though hedonism may indeed be involved in many cases of remarriage after divorce, second marriages often have other and more problematic features, some relating to the provision of a stable environment for existing children, while others might be alleviated by a more realistic attitude toward annulment (not least in a speedier assessment where, in view of modern assumptions, it is obvious that the requirements of a Catholic marriage in the first instance have not been met). That said, there is a largely unrecognized malaise underlying the toils of contemporary marriage in an unwillingness to "commit." This may be based on a belief, usually but not always implicit, that we, especially as we tend to live longer, are "serial selves." And if that thesis were correct—which there is a multitude of reasons to deny—we are not responsible for our past actions: I am not the same person as I was (nor she as she was) when we married, so we have no reason not to separate. I am not the same person as I was when I was ordained, so I can give up the priesthood. I am different person now, so I can abandon my children. And so on. While hedonism and moral cowardice are immediate causes of the contemporary crisis in Catholic sexual morality, irresponsibility is bolstered, or overtly justified, if we subscribe even implicitly to a Humean account of the serial self.

Such being the moral climate both within and beyond the Catholic Church in recent years, it is hardly surprising that even, perhaps especially, those at the top of the hierarchy are tempted (or actually desire) to make concessions on Catholic teaching about sex and marriage, as also about abortion (where an actual life is at stake), whether from mere defeatism, uncritical acceptance of theories of progress, or aversion to asceticism. Failure to conform to the new *Zeitgeist* leads to extreme unpopularity both within and without the Catholic (indeed the wider Christian) community. We are the new prudes, the new merciless; how can we expect to be loved by the media and its clients? We might get spat on in the street if we wear clerical garb or otherwise witness to the Catholic faith. And how many of us, priests and laity alike, are prepared to object if, at a dinner party, we hear an authoritative figure declaim that the massive improvements in the lot of the Western woman depend on her being able to abort in defense of her career or social life? It was fun getting pregnant; now she must get unpregnant.

The contemporary West has become an uncomfortable place for defenders of Catholic teaching on sex and marriage. As yet, we are not tortured or executed for our beliefs, but even if you live in a clerical bubble, the pressure is there. If you live in secular society, you may be told not to wear a cross on pain of being fired. Or, if you happen to be a baker, you may be convicted of a criminal offense if you refuse to make a cake for an ostentatiously planned homosexual "wedding." Scratch a liberal and find a totalitarian. As the late Francis Cardinal George put it: "I shall die in my bed, my successor may die in prison, his successor may be executed"—that is, we should add, if he has not abandoned the Church for clerical appointment in a heretical simulacrum thereof.

And although the executioner is not immediately at work, there are, as already indicated, forms of pressure that demand much moral courage to resist. If a bishop or pope is loved and approved by our secular media, he is probably not doing his job; for to *keep* them on his side he will have to let it be known that abortion should be put on the back burner, as well as that he loves the poor and the environment—as he should, and as he knows will win him secular, if often hypocritical, plaudits. So the work of keeping the anti-Christians on his side (rather than converting them) proceeds apace. For decades now bishops, archbishops, and cardinals have forbidden the display of pro-life literature in the churches of their diocese, and, though close to prominent politicians (many of whom are nominal Catholics), have done little to persuade them to show themselves pro-life and pro-marriage.

Sometimes—increasingly—our spiritual leaders move from refusing to do the right to actively encouraging the wrong and un-Christian. I quote the response of the Society for the Protection of Unborn Children to a "sexual education" manual put out by the Vatican during the present pontificate—that is, by order of papal courtiers: "It is entirely inappropriate for children to be exposed to explicit sexual imagery, such as that contained in this course, and to be encouraged to discuss sexual matters in a classroom environment. Parents must not be under any illusion . . . [this] marks the surrender of the Vatican authorities to the worldwide sexual revolution and directly threatens our own children."[6]

---

[6] John Smeaton, quoted in Pete Baklinski, "Vatican sex ed 'surrenders' to sexual revolution: Life and family leaders react," LifeSite News, July 29, 2016, https://www.lifesitenews.com/news/vatican-surrenders-to-sexual-revolution-with-release-of-sex-ed-program-life/.

Nevertheless, things get worse: Vatican courtier organizations are encouraged to give a platform to prominent opponents of Catholic moral teachings. George Soros's associate Jeffrey Sachs has secured his invitation, and two pontifical academies have welcomed Dr. Paul Ehrlich, the long-since discredited author of *The Population Bomb*, who advocates sex-selective abortion and massive enforced sterilization; arch-abortionist Emma Bonino is, in the words of Pope Francis, a "forgotten great."[7] The Vatican that has in the past preached the civilization of life now regularly promotes a civilization of death, thereby providing substantive justification for those "Catholics" who are happy to tolerate—if not to approve—the secular abortionists and eugenicists who have killed millions of the unborn since the sixties.

One of the unhappiest recent developments concerns the once-noble Pontifical Academy for Life, founded to promote the culture of life in all its forms. Now, by an abuse of juridical power for less than spiritual ends, new members have been appointed who are "relaxed" about abortion, homosexuality, and euthanasia, while others (including non-Catholics) even favor them. We observe once again a now standard ploy developed by the Vatican court and its monarch to subvert traditional Catholic teaching: a conservative is appointed to satisfy those unhappy to query papal decisions, with a liberal—whether pro-abortion or pro-euthanasia—to secure the desired result: that is, to ensure that the Academy for Life can no longer be relied on to support life, which it is the official policy of the Vatican court to protect from conception to natural death.

It is time to ask why prominent bishops and Church organizations behave in so un-Catholic a fashion. Is it because they do not know what Catholic teaching is (as suggested by Gerhard Cardinal Müller) or that they know what it is and do not care? Or is it that in their dread of abuse from the post-Christian world, or their dream of being applauded by the secularists, they are willing to abandon what they once at least professed to believe? Is it that they never believed it and hence are happy to subvert Catholicism when "necessary"? Are some of them communist "sleepers" planted by Stalin and his successors? Or is it that many were trained by those who advocated the "Spirit of Vatican II" in full knowledge that this would increase their short-term popularity with Western elites, enabling them to enjoy "full communion" with the *New York*

---

[7] Michael Haynes, "Pope Francis again praises notorious abortionist Emma Bonino: 'I have great respect for' her," LifeSite News, May 4, 2022, https://www.lifesitenews.com/news/pope-francis-once-again-praises-notorious-abortionist-emma-bonino-i-have-great-respect-for-her/.

Times or the *Guardian*—or even Planned Parenthood International? Is it that they spend too much time with the wrong crowd, perhaps with the once-noble, now actively pro-abortion Amnesty International—thus growing too familiar with vice, what is called in labor-management circles the "chin-in-armpit syndrome"? Is it mere despair? Or is it all the above?

That is probably the right answer and, if so, indicates that something has gone terribly wrong with the education of our priests and future bishops. Many of the "Spirit of Vatican II" fraternity left the Church, disillusioned with the slowness of revolutionary change. Some of those who were priests or nuns emerged as sexual (or homosexual) "late bloomers," while in some cases retaining or securing positions as advisors to bishops. Others remained in their clerical posts and rose up the clerical pole, toughing it out in the hope that their chance to overturn traditional teaching would come, as it had among the Anglicans, Lutherans, and other mainline Christian denominations. For they realized that episcopal heterodoxy would rarely be officially and publicly reprimanded, nor would it impede promotion—provided they (like the Vicar of Bray) remained loyal, so long as he was in office, to the master of the Vatican court.

PELAGIANISM, ARIANISM, AND THE NEW SEXUAL MORALITY

Pelagianism is the ecclesial root of modern autonomy, and most non-Christian accounts of human rights are Pelagian, though also often urged upon us by Christians. But the rot goes deeper. Catholic teaching on marriage and sexual morality derives from the instruction of Jesus himself—directly, that is, not by inference, for we have his relevant words recorded in the Gospels, as also those of Paul, the Apostle to the Gentiles. So, before us are two alternatives, the first being to deny or finesse the words attributed to Jesus by the Gospel writers, which is the route taken by many members of the Scripture studies guild. If we follow it, we can all construct our own morality in the "spirit" of the Gospels. Some advanced Catholic pastors prefer that route, by sleight of mind evading its implications.

There is another, and to some more palatable, alternative: Jesus did indeed forbid his followers (for example) a second marriage after separation—but the times being now different, we are free to rewrite his commandments. The implications of that are as dire as those of its alternative, for to say that we

143

must now, as card-carrying historicists, correct the teaching of Jesus, entails that we reject his divinity; we are not Christians at all, or only insofar as Arius was Christian. Those who find both these routes unedifying will have to face the crisis in roughly the form I have outlined—and decide whether to act, and speak out, accordingly. Yet, in view of the corrosive spirit of flattery which flows from the court to the wider Church, many find no option but to drift; the Italian word *attendisti* (the wait-and-see-ers) is helpful in denoting these. The rest of us must find support in the anti-heretical Pauline text of Galatians 2:11: "I opposed [Peter] to his face."

Thus, we are confronted with the first set of strictly moral heresies; yet, analysis reveals that moral heresies entail heresies—versions of Arianism or Pelagianism—in basic dogmatic theology. Arius was confounded by Athanasius (*contra mundum*); we pray to find an Athanasius in our midst. Even so, our current moral heresies will induce thousands of laypeople to give up Catholicism. This even most within the clerical "bubble" will think undesirable.

ARIUS, PELAGIUS, LUTHER, AND OURSELVES

Present discontents in the Church can be understood in terms of earlier heresies, especially Arianism and Pelagianism, which in its secularized form now appears in an extreme version: the futile desire to be a self-creator. Further light is shed if we compare the heretical attitudes now still evading detection with the unambiguous treatment meted out to Martin Luther, thus inviting comparison of *sola fide* with *sola misericordia*. Whereas Luther was happily excommunicated and thus freed to plan the replacement of Catholic theology from the outside, our present moral heresies are internally generated by those with no intention of leaving, preferring to stay in place while by word and action undermining our moral teachings. Nor, as noted, have senior Church authorities made any serious attempt to discipline them, whether due to fear of unpopularity or because they are—to whatever degree—complicit in the heresies proposed. If we fail to recognize that present dangers are at least as great as those posed by declared enemies in the Reformation, we are doomed to sink further into the dogmatic and moral quagmire.

Perhaps the disaster which has overtaken the Church during the pontificate of Jorge Bergoglio will eventually produce good effects, not least a better understanding of traditional Catholic teachings and of the shallowness of the alternatives—always liable to point to nihilism or indifferentism—now on offer both within and without the Catholic pale. And there is also hope of a substantial "ecclesial" good. Since current moral heresies derive much power to seduce from the postures of the papal court, it may become clear that Vatican I's account of papal infallibility must be revisited. Revisited, of course, not abolished. It must be reformulated such that the endless debates about which papal teachings are *ex cathedra* and which are less substantial can be brought to an end. Perhaps we can find a clearer account of what *ex cathedra* implies and therewith a tool to deflect abuses of papal authority, whether homegrown or resulting from media pressure.

Before that can be achieved successfully, we must also recognize a major source of confusion in theology largely ignored by the medieval Church: the fact that development of our understanding of doctrine does not depend only on what can be *deduced* from Scripture and Tradition; we need also to inspect what is not incompatible with it. More generally, we must recognize that coherent theology cannot be developed without scrutiny of the poorly argued, indeed often ultimately un-Christian, reasons why such apparently faulty teachings—such as those of the Fourth Lateran Council on religious freedom—ever were adopted.

HARD CASES: A PHILOSOPHICAL COROLLARY

In current moral theology—as in parallel debates at the secular level—a seeming suasion to approve the abandonment of strict rules is presented through hard cases. This was recognized as early as Aristotle, who in the *Nicomachean Ethics* distinguishes between justice and equity: equity is the rectification (not of a law but) of a *just* law. In civil society, Aristotle's distinction must be apposite and is regularly approved: give a certain leeway to the magistrate to allow exceptions where it is impossible for the just lawgiver to foresee individual circumstances. The alternative solution—which Aristotle would reject—is to make hard cases the foundation of law: that leads to endless laxity and the inability to insist on objective principles. Indeed, for all Aristotle's distinction between justice and equity, lines must be drawn. It is absurd, he himself holds, to believe a man can justify killing his mother or commit adultery virtuously.[8]

If law cannot be built around them, then how do we handle the hard cases? That problem, difficult enough in civil law and civil morality without a slide

---

[8] Aristotle, *Nichomachean Ethics*, 1110a29; 1107b16.

into full-scale consequentialism and relativism, is more agonizing when Christ is acknowledged to be legislator—and I have sketched the consequences if he is denied that role by Christians. Augustine would warn us that the consequent agony is part of the penal condition under which we labor in "this darkness of social life" after the Fall.[9] For present guidance, however, we can turn to Jesus's words to the woman taken in adultery (John 8:11): "go, and do not sin again." Jesus is merciful; Jesus forgives; but repentance entails firm purpose not to repeat the sins forgiven.

Though the Church has often been less than merciful in the treatment meted out to sin, yet no doctrinal "improvement" is acceptable which entails denying Christ's specific commands, hence in effect denying his authority and divinity. Neither pope nor council can authorize forgiveness without demanding avoidance—or at least sincere attempt at avoidance—of the sins forgiven; far less can they "forgive" while licensing repetition with a "discerning" nudge and wink. Nor are we to suppose that nice talk ("dialogue"), in and of itself, makes all things well. On the contrary, we must do as Christ bids for fear of lapsing into Arianism or Pelagianism—even though in the end only God judges. For, as Augustine told his old mentor Simplicianus, "If I claimed to know who is eventually saved and who is not, God would laugh at me."[10]

---

[9] Augustine, *City of God* 19.6, cf. 22.22.4.
[10] Augustine, *To Simplicianus* 1.2.22.

PART TWO

MAGISTERIUM: THE TEACHING AUTHORITY OF THE CHURCH

Edward Feser

THE NATURE OF THE MAGISTERIUM

When giving to the Church her Great Commission, Christ said: "Go therefore and make disciples of all nations, baptizing them in the name of the Father and of the Son and of the Holy Spirit, teaching them to observe all that I have commanded you; and behold, I am with you always, to the close of the age" (Matt 28:19–20). We find in these words the key notes of the Magisterium of the Church. The Church is to teach all nations, incorporating them into herself as disciples; she has authority from Christ to do so; what she is to teach is what Christ taught; and Christ will be with the Church to the end so as to ensure that she does not teach error.

The magisterial authority of the Church is, then, the infallible organ through which Christ's revelation is communicated to the human race. Hence, as St. Augustine famously wrote, "for my part, I should not believe the Gospel except as moved by the authority of the Catholic Church."[1]

There is an additional crucial note of the Magisterium implicit in the Great Commission. It was specifically to his apostles, led by Peter, that Christ directed his words. And it is the successors of the apostles—the bishops, led by Peter's successor, the pope—who inherit their magisterial authority. Thus does the Second Vatican Council teach in *Lumen gentium*:

---

[1] Augustine, *Against the Fundamental Epistle of Manichaeus*, trans. Richard Stothert, in *Nicene and Post-Nicene Fathers, First Series*, vol. 4, ed. Philip Schaff (Buffalo, NY: Christian Literature Publishing, 1887), ch. 5.

In matters of faith and morals, the bishops speak in the name of Christ and the faithful are to accept their teaching and adhere to it with a religious assent. This religious submission of mind and will must be shown in a special way to the authentic magisterium of the Roman Pontiff, even when he is not speaking ex cathedra; that is, it must be shown in such a way that his supreme magisterium is acknowledged with reverence, the judgments made by him are sincerely adhered to, according to his manifest mind and will. His mind and will in the matter may be known either from the character of the documents, from his frequent repetition of the same doctrine, or from his manner of speaking.[2]

As this passage indicates, the teaching authority granted by Christ resides in what the Church describes as a "*living* Magisterium." That is to say, it is not to be found merely in documents as such but in documents considered as expressions of the "mind" of the Church's pastors, especially of the pope as Supreme Pontiff. More generally, it is to be found in the "mind of the Church" considered as a "moral person," that is, a community united by a common purpose into a single entity with personal characteristics such as rights, duties, and legal standing. Documents, whether they be conciliar decrees, encyclical letters, catechisms, or what have you, are "magisterial" because they express the mind of the Church as the moral person through whom Christ speaks. "He who hears you hears me, and he who rejects you rejects me" (Luke 10:16).

As the passage from *Lumen gentium* also indicates, not all documents have equal weight because when issuing them the Church does not always intend to teach with the same degree of finality. An *ex cathedra* papal declaration or a solemn conciliar definition is formulated with utmost precision and intended to be absolutely definitive. A remark made in the course of a papal allocution may be more imprecise, exploratory, and tentative. A papal encyclical may fall somewhere in between, with some passages closer to the definitive end of the spectrum and others closer to the tentative end. Reiterations of long-standing formulations are in the nature of the case more definitive than novel themes, and so on. Considerations about "the character of the documents, . . . frequent repetition of the same doctrine, . . . [and] manner of speaking" are among those that should guide the faithful in determining what the Church requires by way

---

[2]   Second Vatican Council, Dogmatic Constitution on the Church *Lumen gentium* (November 21, 1964), §25 (hereafter, *Lumen gentium*).

of assent. Though not all cases are equally straightforward, there are (as we will see below) nevertheless several clear general categories into which various magisterial statements can be organized.

The distinction between non-definitive and definitive teaching should not be confused with the distinction between the *ordinary* and *extraordinary* Magisterium, though the distinctions are not unrelated. Examples of acts of the extraordinary Magisterium of the Church would be *ex cathedra* declarations by a pope and solemn conciliar definitions. These are, as I have said, definitive. By contrast, the ordinary Magisterium can be either definitive or non-definitive. Examples of acts of the ordinary Magisterium would be the day-to-day preaching of a pope or other bishop, or written statements in the form of an encyclical or a document of some lesser weight. Often, statements made in such contexts are not intended to have the maximum degree of precision or definitiveness. However, a teaching that has been consistently reiterated in the course of Church history as part of the ordinary Magisterium can be definitive, even in the absence of any particular extraordinary magisterial act that has explicitly declared it to be such. As the Congregation for the Doctrine of the Faith under Joseph Cardinal Ratzinger affirmed:

> When there has not been a judgment on a doctrine in the solemn form of a definition, but this doctrine, belonging to the inheritance of the *depositum fidei*, is taught by the ordinary and universal Magisterium, which necessarily includes the Pope, such a doctrine is to be understood as having been set forth infallibly. . . .
>
> It should be noted that the infallible teaching of the ordinary and universal Magisterium is not only set forth with an explicit declaration of a doctrine to be believed or held definitively, but is also expressed by a doctrine implicitly contained in a practice of the Church's faith, derived from revelation or, in any case, necessary for eternal salvation, and attested to by the uninterrupted Tradition.[3]

---

[3] Congregation for the Doctrine of the Faith, Doctrinal Commentary on the Concluding Formula of "*Professio fidei*" (June 29, 1998), §9 and n. 17. On the topic of the infallibility of the ordinary Magisterium, see John C. Ford and Germain Grisez, "Contraception and the Infallibility of the Ordinary Magisterium," *Theological Studies* 39 (1978): 258–312; and John P. Joy, *Cathedra Veritatis: On the Extension of Papal Infallibility* (Howell, MI: Cruachan Hill Press, 2012). I have more to say about the topic in "Capital punishment and the infallibility of the ordinary Magisterium," *Catholic World Report*, January 20, 2018, https://www.catholicworldreport.com/2018/01/20 /capital-punishment-and-the-infallibility-of-the-ordinary-magisterium/.

In any event, when the Church says that Christ will preserve her from teaching error, she does not mean that every statement to be found in every document will be free from any error of any kind. What she means is rather that when she speaks in a *definitive* way so as to oblige the faithful to give their *unqualified* assent to some teaching, Christ will prevent her from thereby binding them to error.

In summary, Catholic teaching is that the living Magisterium of the successors of the apostles, and especially of the pope as successor of Peter, is the authoritative vehicle through which divine revelation is conveyed to us, that it is conveyed infallibly when the Magisterium teaches in a definitive manner, and that magisterial teaching can be binding on the consciences of the faithful even when it is not put forward definitively. The Church thereby rejects the Protestant doctrines of *sola scriptura* and "private judgment," the Eastern Orthodox position that Scripture and Tradition alone are authoritative, and the liberal Catholic position that assent may be withheld from doctrines not taught definitively.

Now, these errors all evidence a vice of *deficiency* regarding respect for the Magisterium of the Church. But it is also possible to err in this context by way of *excess*, and it is that sort of error that I want to address in the remainder of this essay. One such error would be to suppose that the Church and her pastors may in principle teach whatever they wish, including entirely novel doctrines or even something that contradicts Scripture or Tradition. Another would be to suppose that the faithful may under no circumstances withhold assent from, much less criticize, any magisterial statement whatsoever, especially a papal statement.

The Church has not only never taught such things but has explicitly taught the opposite. She has consistently acknowledged and indeed insisted that she has no authority whatsoever to contradict Scripture and Tradition or even to add novel teachings to them, but authority only to hand them on faithfully and draw out their implications. And she has acknowledged that a pastor of the Church, even a pope, who in some non-definitive statement teaches contrary to Scripture or Tradition, may respectfully be corrected by the faithful. Let us examine each of these points in turn.

THE TELEOLOGY OF THE MAGISTERIUM

To see how it can be justifiable in some cases for the faithful to correct their pastors, the first thing to understand is that this is not a matter of *resisting* magisterial authorities but rather of *assisting* them. Magisterial authority has an end or purpose, and the correction of a pastor is legitimate precisely to the extent that, both in its motivation and in the manner in which it is carried out, it facilitates rather than frustrates the realization of that end.

The nature of that end is implicit in Christ's directive to the Church to teach all nations "to observe *all that I have commanded you*." The point is to convey *Christ's* teaching, so that the Church's own teaching must never differ from his. This purpose is further elucidated by several magisterial statements on the limits of the Church's teaching authority in general and of papal teaching authority in particular. After affirming the infallibility of the Magisterium in the passage quoted above, *Lumen gentium* goes on to add:

> And this infallibility with which the Divine Redeemer willed His Church to be endowed in defining doctrine of faith and morals, extends as far as the deposit of Revelation extends, which must be religiously guarded and faithfully expounded.[4]

Similarly, precisely in the course of promulgating the doctrine of papal infallibility, the First Vatican Council makes clear:

> For the Holy Spirit was promised to the successors of Peter not so that they might, by his revelation, make known some new doctrine, but that, by his assistance, they might religiously guard and faithfully expound the revelation or deposit of faith transmitted by the apostles.[5]

Likewise, in the dogmatic constitution *Dei Verbum*, the Second Vatican Council teaches:

> The living teaching office of the Church . . . is not above the word of God, but serves it, teaching only what has been handed on, listening to it devoutly, guarding it scrupulously and explaining it faithfully.[6]

Bishops, including popes, have no authority, then, either to invent novel doctrines or to contradict the deliverances of Scripture and Tradition. Their

---

[4] Second Vatican Council, *Lumen gentium*, §25.

[5] First Vatican Council, First Dogmatic Constitution on the Church of Christ *Pastor aeternus* (July 18, 1870), ch. 4, no. 6.

[6] Second Vatican Council, Dogmatic Constitution on Divine Revelation *Dei Verbum* (November 18, 1965), §10.

duty is rather to preserve and proclaim the deliverances of Scripture and Tradition. Naturally, this does not rule out the development of doctrine, which is a matter of *drawing out the implications* of Scripture and Tradition. What it does rule out is *contradicting* Scripture and Tradition or *manufacturing out of whole cloth* some teaching that has no basis in Scripture or Tradition. Pope Benedict XVI reaffirmed this understanding of the limits of papal teaching authority in his homily of May 7, 2005:

> The Pope is not an absolute monarch whose thoughts and desires are law. On the contrary: the Pope's ministry is a guarantee of obedience to Christ and to his Word. He must not proclaim his own ideas, but rather constantly bind himself and the Church to obedience to God's Word, in the face of every attempt to adapt it or water it down, and every form of opportunism. .... The Pope knows that in his important decisions, he is bound to the great community of faith of all times, to the binding interpretations that have developed throughout the Church's pilgrimage. Thus, his power is not being above, but at the service of, the Word of God. It is incumbent upon him to ensure that this Word continues to be present in its greatness and to resound in its purity, so that it is not torn to pieces by continuous changes in usage.[7]

These passages entail that a pope would be derelict in his duty if he either failed to reaffirm traditional teaching when doing so was called for, or if he contradicted traditional teaching, or if he taught some doctrine having no basis in traditional teaching. If any sort of criticism of a pope or other pastor of the Church could be justified, it would be criticism of errors of this sort. Criticism of a pope clearly could *not* be justified if the motivation were to try to get him to *keep silent* about traditional teaching, or to *reverse* traditional teaching, or to teach some wholly novel doctrine.

FIVE CATEGORIES OF MAGISTERIAL STATEMENTS

It is well known that when a pope teaches in a definitive way, such as by means of an *ex cathedra* statement, the Church requires of the faithful an unqualified submission of intellect and will. It is also fairly well known that even when a

---

[7] Benedict XVI, Homily at the Mass of Possession of the Chair of the Bishop of Rome, Basilica of St. John Lateran, Saturday, May 7, 2005.

pope does not teach in such a decisive manner, the faithful are still required to respond with "religious submission," an inward assent that is firm even if not unqualified. Again, Catholics are not at liberty simply to pick and choose even among those doctrines not taught as irreformable.

It may be less well known that there are nevertheless some important qualifications to the submission required with respect to non-irreformable pronouncements. This is not only clear from the Tradition of the Church but has been explicitly addressed in recent magisterial interventions, most importantly in the instruction *Donum veritatis*, issued in 1990 by Cardinal Ratzinger as Prefect of the Congregation for the Doctrine of the Faith (CDF) under Pope Saint John Paul II.[8] As Avery Cardinal Dulles has noted, paragraphs twenty-three and twenty-four of *Donum veritatis* indicate that there are at least four categories of magisterial statement, not all of which are equally weighty or binding.[9] Other interventions imply a fifth category. Dulles characterizes the first four categories as follows:

1. *Statements that definitively set forth something that all Catholics are to accept as divinely revealed (such statements being dogmas in the strict sense).* Examples would be the Christological dogmas and the teaching on the grave immorality of directly and voluntarily killing an innocent human being. No legitimate dissent from strict dogmas is possible even in principle.

2. *Definitive declarations of nonrevealed truths closely connected with revelation and the Christian life.* Examples would be the teaching on the immorality of fornication and the teaching that priestly ordination is reserved to men. Here too no legitimate dissent is possible even in principle.

3. *Non-definitive but obligatory teaching of doctrine that contributes to the right understanding of revelation.* Dulles suggests that

---

8   See Congregation for the Doctrine of the Faith, Instruction on the Ecclesial Vocation of the Theologian *Donum veritatis* (May 24, 1990), §§23–24 (hereafter, *Donum veritatis*). For a more detailed treatment of the issues addressed in this section, see Edward Feser and Joseph M. Bessette, *By Man Shall His Blood Be Shed: A Catholic Defense of Capital Punishment* (San Francisco: Ignatius Press, 2017), 144–57.

9   Cf. Avery Dulles, "The Magisterium and Theological Dissent," in *The Craft of Theology*, new expanded edition (New York: Crossroad, 1995), and chapter 7 of Dulles's *Magisterium: Teacher and Guardian of the Faith* (Naples, FL: Sapientia Press, 2007).

> "the teaching of Vatican II, which abstained from new doctrinal definitions, falls predominantly into this category."[10] According to *Donum veritatis*, statements in this category must be accepted by Catholics with "religious submission of will and intellect."

However, *Donum veritatis* also makes clear that, given their non-definitive character, the assent due to statements of category 3 is not of the absolute kind owed to statements of categories 1 and 2. The default position is to assent to them, but it is in principle possible that the very strong presumption in their favor can be overridden. *Donum veritatis* says:

> The willingness to submit loyally to the teaching of the Magisterium on matters *per se* not irreformable must be the rule. It can happen, however, that a theologian may, according to the case, raise questions regarding the timeliness, the form, or even the contents of magisterial interventions.[11]

For this reason,

> the possibility cannot be excluded that tensions may arise between the theologian and the Magisterium. . . . If tensions do not spring from hostile and contrary feelings, they can become a dynamic factor, a stimulus to both the Magisterium and theologians to fulfill their respective roles while practicing dialogue.[12]
>
> . . . If, despite a loyal effort on the theologian's part, the difficulties persist, the theologian has the duty to make known to the Magisterial authorities the problems raised by the teaching in itself, in the arguments proposed to justify it, or even in the manner in which it is presented. . . . His objections could then contribute to real progress and provide a stimulus to the Magisterium to propose the teaching of the Church in greater depth and with a clearer presentation of the arguments.[13]
>
> . . . It can also happen that at the conclusion of a serious study, undertaken with the desire to heed the Magisterium's teaching

---

[10] Dulles, "Magisterium and Theological Dissent," 110.

[11] *Donum veritatis*, §24.

[12] *Donum veritatis*, §25.

[13] *Donum veritatis*, §30.

without hesitation, the theologian's difficulty remains because the arguments to the contrary seem more persuasive to him.[14]

Donum veritatis goes on in succeeding paragraphs explicitly to contrast the difficulties that a loyal theologian might have with a problematic, non-irreformable magisterial statement with "dissent" from traditional Church teaching on the part of those who "oppose the authority of Tradition" and are motivated by "the ideology of philosophical liberalism" or "the weight of public opinion."[15] As William May has noted, the clearest cases in which *Donum veritatis* would permit theologians to raise questions about a teaching would be "when they can appeal to other magisterial teachings that are more certainly and definitively taught with which they think the teaching questioned is incompatible."[16]

It is clear from *Donum veritatis*, then, that the withholding of assent from some magisterial statement that appears to *contradict* traditional teaching is not to be lumped in with the withholding of assent from traditional teaching itself. The former can be justifiable even though the latter is not. This dovetails with what we have seen about the purpose and limits of magisterial teaching authority. Again, the Church teaches that popes and other pastors have authority only to preserve and proclaim the deliverances of Scripture and Tradition, and are never to contradict those deliverances or to manufacture novel doctrines. The clearest possible application of *Donum veritatis*'s teaching about the legitimate respectful criticism of category 3 magisterial statements would be precisely to cases where a pope or other pastor seems to be overstepping the bounds that the First and Second Vatican Councils put on his authority. Such respectful criticism would amount to *assisting* rather than *resisting* lawful magisterial authority.

Donum veritatis itself implies this when it says that a theologian "*has the duty* to make known to the magisterial authorities the problems raised by [a] teaching," that this can be "a *stimulus* to both *the Magisterium* and theologians to fulfill their respective roles," and that these "objections could then contribute to *real progress*." Indeed, the instruction even goes so far as to say:

> For a loyal spirit, animated by love for the Church, such a situation can certainly prove a difficult trial. It can be a call to suffer for the

---

[14] *Donum veritatis*, §31.

[15] *Donum veritatis*, §32.

[16] William E. May, *An Introduction to Moral Theology*, rev. ed. (Huntington, IN: Our Sunday Visitor, 1994), 242.

truth, in silence and prayer, but with the certainty, that if the truth really is at stake, it will ultimately prevail.[17]

In other words, the Church explicitly acknowledges the possibility that a non-infallible act of the Magisterium can be so defective that it is *the theologian who respectfully criticizes that act who is upholding "the truth,"* so that this defective magisterial act is something from which the theologian will unjustly "suffer" out of "love for the Church." Unlike those who dissent from the Church's traditional teaching, who aim to *frustrate* the Magisterium's mission to proclaim the deliverances of Scripture and Tradition, those who would respectfully criticize an apparent departure from Tradition aim to *facilitate* the Magisterium's mission.

Now, there are two further categories of statement that do not require assent in the first place. The next one on Dulles's list is:

4. *Prudential admonitions or applications of Christian doctrine to a particular time or place.* Dulles cites as an example the Church's initial reservations, in the seventeenth century, about accepting the heliocentric theory of the solar system. Such decisions are "prudential" in the sense that they involve, not the statement of doctrinal principles, but rather the attempt prudently to *apply* such principles to contingent, concrete circumstances, such as the state of scientific knowledge at a particular point in history. Ecclesiastical authorities are not infallible in their decisions about such applications. *Donum Veritatis* remarks:

When it comes to the question of interventions in the prudential order, it could happen that some Magisterial documents might not be free from all deficiencies. Bishops and their advisors have not always taken into immediate consideration every aspect or the entire complexity of a question.[18]

Dulles points out that such decisions "require external conformity in behavior, but do not demand internal assent."[19] They generally have to do with questions about what sorts of positions theologians may in their public

---

[17] *Donum veritatis*, §31.

[18] *Donum veritatis*, §24.

[19] Dulles, *Magisterium*, 94.

writing and teaching put forward as consistent with Catholic doctrine. The concern is to ensure that theologians do not too rashly publicly endorse some idea which may or may not turn out to be true, but whose relationship to matters of faith and morals is complicated, and where mistakes may damage the faith of non-experts.

The "prudential" judgments which *Donum veritatis* addresses, and which Dulles discusses in his comments on that document, are all judgments about matters that are very closely connected to questions of doctrinal principle, even if they concern the application of principle rather than its formulation. For example, part of the reason heliocentrism was controversial is that it raised questions about how to interpret certain biblical passages. However, statements by popes and other churchmen which lack any such momentous doctrinal implications but instead concern matters of politics, economics, and the like, are also often referred to as "prudential judgments" because they too involve the attempt prudently to apply general doctrinal principles to contingent concrete circumstances. *Donum veritatis* does not address this sort of judgment and neither does Dulles in his discussion of the document. But it is clear from other statements made by Cardinal Ratzinger, while acting as John Paul II's prefect of the Congregation for the Doctrine of the Faith, that it constitutes a fifth category.

For example, in a 2004 memorandum on the topic, "Worthiness to Receive Holy Communion: General Principles," Cardinal Ratzinger wrote:

> Not all moral issues have the same moral weight as abortion and euthanasia. For example, if a Catholic were to be at odds with the Holy Father on the application of capital punishment or on the decision to wage war, he would not for that reason be considered unworthy to present himself to receive Holy Communion. While the Church exhorts civil authorities to seek peace, not war, and to exercise discretion and mercy in imposing punishment on criminals, it may still be permissible to take up arms to repel an aggressor or to have recourse to capital punishment. There may be a legitimate diversity of opinion even among Catholics about waging war and applying the death penalty, but not however with regard to abortion and euthanasia.[20]

---

[20] See Cardinals Joseph Ratzinger and Theodore McCarrick, "Vatican, U.S. Bishops: On Catholics in Political Life," *Origins* 34, no. 9 (July 29, 2004): 133–34.

Cardinal Ratzinger's point is that unlike abortion and euthanasia, war and capital punishment are not intrinsically evil. Accordingly, whether they are justifiable in a particular instance depends on various concrete circumstances and thus calls for prudential judgment. Because churchmen lack special expertise about these circumstances, their prudential judgments about them are advisory rather than binding. Hence, the cardinal says, "there may be a legitimate diversity of opinion even among Catholics" on such matters, to the extent that a faithful Catholic may be "at odds with the Holy Father" about them.

The specific example of capital punishment has become controversial in the wake of Pope Francis's statements about the subject.[21] But the more general point illustrated by Cardinal Ratzinger's remarks is *not* controversial. It has long been acknowledged by churchmen and theologians loyal to the Magisterium that at least some of the statements made by popes and other churchmen about matters of public policy and other issues of the day are not binding on the consciences of the faithful. Unlike category 4 statements, they do not require even external conformity in behavior, let alone internal assent, but only respectful consideration. Borrowing Cardinal Ratzinger's language, we might formulate this category as follows:

5. *Statements of a prudential sort on matters about which there may be a legitimate diversity of opinion among Catholics.*

Now, if respectful criticism of category 3 magisterial statements can be justifiable where they appear to conflict with the traditional teaching of the Church, then, *a fortiori*, criticism of category 4 or category 5 statements that seem to conflict with traditional teaching can also be justifiable. By no means does this give the faithful *carte blanche* to withhold assent from non-irreformable magisterial teaching. Again, *Donum veritatis* teaches that "willingness to submit loyally to the teaching of the Magisterium on matters *per se* not irreformable must be the rule." The point is that the Church herself acknowledges the possibility of exceptions to the rule, and that the clearest cases would be those in which a statement seems incompatible with Tradition.

21 Cf. Feser and Bessette, *By Man Shall His Blood Be Shed*, 183–96. See also Feser, "Capital punishment and the infallibility"; and Edward Feser, "Three questions for Catholic opponents of capital punishment," *Catholic World Report*, September 15, 2019, https://www.catholicworldreport.com/2020/10/07/three-questions-for-catholic-opponents-of-capital-punishment/.

RESPECTFUL CRITICISM CAN BE PUBLIC

Even though respectful criticism of statements in categories 3–5 can in some cases be legitimate in principle, it might at first appear that such criticisms should be raised only through private channels rather than in a public forum. For, *Donum veritatis* says that in such cases, "the theologian should avoid turning to the 'mass media,' but have recourse to the responsible authority."[22]

However, this remark is not intended to rule out all public expressions of criticism. Speaking at a press conference about a hypothetical theologian who raises such criticisms, Cardinal Ratzinger said: "We have not excluded all kinds of publication, nor have we closed him up in suffering."[23] As William May notes:

> The Instruction obviously considers it proper for theologians to publish their "questions," for it speaks of their obligation to take seriously into account objections leveled against their views by other theologians and to revise their positions in the light of such criticism—and this is normally given only after a theologian has made his questions known by publishing them in professional theological journals.[24]

Similarly, Dulles notes that *Donum veritatis* "does not discountenance expression of one's views in a scholarly manner that might be publicly reported."[25]

When read in context, the remark in *Donum veritatis* about "mass media" is clearly intended to criticize only a very specific *aspect* of modern mass media, rather than the use of mass media as such. The longer passage from which the words quoted above are taken reads as follows:

> The theologian should avoid turning to the "mass media," but have recourse to the responsible authority, for it is not by seeking to exert the pressure of public opinion that one contributes to the clarification of doctrinal issues and renders service to the truth.[26]

Furthermore, in the context of discussing the influence on those who dissent from traditional Church teaching of "the ideology of philosophical liberalism"

---

[22] *Donum veritatis*, §30.

[23] Joseph Ratzinger, quoted in Anthony J. Figueiredo, *The Magisterium-Theology Relationship* (Rome: Editrice Pontificia Università Gregoriana, 2001), 370.

[24] May, *An Introduction to Moral Theology*, 241–42.

[25] Dulles, "Magisterium and Theological Dissent," 115.

[26] *Donum veritatis*, §30.

and its pitting of "freedom of thought" and a "model of protest" against the "authority of Tradition," *Donum Veritatis* makes remarks like the following:

> The phenomenon of dissent can have diverse forms. Its remote and proximate causes are multiple.
>
> ... The weight of public opinion when manipulated and its pressure to conform also have their influence. Often models of society promoted by the "mass media" tend to assume a normative value.[27]
>
> ... Dissent sometimes also appeals to a kind of sociological argumentation which holds that the opinion of a large number of Christians would be a direct and adequate expression of the "supernatural sense of the faith."
>
> ... [But] not all the ideas which circulate among the People of God are compatible with the faith. This is all the more so given that people can be swayed by a public opinion influenced by modern communications media.[28]

Clearly, then, when *Donum veritatis* expresses reservations about the mass media, what it has in view are the secular values that dominate modern mass media and that have reshaped public opinion by means of it, and the way that dissenting theologians have sought allies in the mass media in order to reshape Church teaching in a similar way. *Donum veritatis* does not object to the use of mass media *per se*. What it objects to is trying to pressure the Church into conforming itself to the values that dominate modern mass media and public opinion.

Canon law gives further support to the legitimacy of public expressions of criticism.

> The Christian faithful are free to make known to the pastors of the Church their needs, especially spiritual ones, and their desires.
>
> According to the knowledge, competence, and prestige which they possess, they have the right and even at times the duty to manifest to the sacred pastors their opinion on matters which pertain to the good of the Church and to make their opinion known to the rest of the Christian faithful, without prejudice to the integrity of

---

[27] *Donum veritatis*, §32.

[28] *Donum veritatis*, §35.

faith and morals, with reverence toward their pastors, and attentive to common advantage and the dignity of persons.[29]

This passage makes it clear that Catholics may make their opinions known not only "to the sacred pastors," but also "to the rest of the Christian faithful." It is also important to note, however, that the passage adds some important qualifications. For one thing, it tells us that the opinions expressed ought to reflect a sufficient level of "knowledge, competence, and prestige." Neither *Donum veritatis* nor canon law gives a blank check to just any old anonymous blogger who wants to mouth off. Second, Catholics must express their opinions with sufficient "reverence toward their pastors." By no means are Catholics ever permitted to criticize the Holy Father or other pastors of the Church in a disrespectful manner.

THE TEACHING OF SAINT THOMAS AQUINAS

The teaching of *Donum veritatis* and of current canon law is not some modern novelty. It has deep roots in Catholic tradition—in previous magisterial teaching, in the teaching of saints and approved theologians, and in the historical precedent of errant pastors, including even popes, who have been rebuked by the faithful for failing to uphold traditional teaching. Let us begin with a look at the treatment of the subject found in the *Summa theologiae* of Saint Thomas Aquinas. It is worth quoting at length:

> Fraternal correction is a work of mercy. Therefore even prelates ought to be corrected.
>
> . . . A subject is not competent to administer to his prelate the correction which is an act of justice through the coercive nature of punishment: but the fraternal correction which is an act of charity is within the competency of everyone in respect of any person towards whom he is bound by charity, provided there be something in that person which requires correction.
>
> . . . Since, however, a virtuous act needs to be moderated by due circumstances, it follows that when a subject corrects his prelate, he ought to do so in a becoming manner, not with impudence and harshness, but with gentleness and respect.

---

[29] Code of Canon Law, can. 212, §§2–3.

... It would seem that a subject touches his prelate inordinately when he upbraids him with insolence, as also when he speaks ill of him ...

... To withstand anyone in public exceeds the mode of fraternal correction, and so Paul would not have withstood Peter then, unless he were in some way his equal as regards the defense of the faith. But one who is not an equal can reprove privately and respectfully. . . . It must be observed, however, that if the faith were endangered, a subject ought to rebuke his prelate even publicly. Hence Paul, who was Peter's subject, rebuked him in public, on account of the imminent danger of scandal concerning faith, and, as the gloss of Augustine says on Gal. 2:11, "Peter gave an example to superiors, that if at any time they should happen to stray from the straight path, they should not disdain to be reproved by their subjects."

... To presume oneself to be simply better than one's prelate, would seem to savor of presumptuous pride; but there is no presumption in thinking oneself better in some respect, because, in this life, no man is without some fault. We must also remember that when a man reproves his prelate charitably, it does not follow that he thinks himself any better, but merely that he offers his help to one who, "being in the higher position among you, is therefore in greater danger," as Augustine observes in his Rule quoted above. [30]

Similarly, when discussing Saint Paul's rebuke of Saint Peter in his *Commentary on Galatians*, Aquinas says that this rebuke was "just and useful" because of "the danger to the Gospel teaching," and that "the manner of the rebuke was fitting, i.e., public and plain . . . because [Peter's] dissimulation posed a danger to all."[31] Aquinas observes:

Therefore from the foregoing we have an example: to prelates, indeed, an example of humility, that they not disdain corrections from those who are lower and subject to them; to subjects, an

---

[30] Thomas Aquinas, *Summa theologiae* II-II, q. 33, a. 4. English translation: Thomas Aquinas, *Summa Theologica*, trans. Fathers of the English Dominican Province, rev. ed. (Westminster, MD: Christian Classics, 1981).

[31] Thomas Aquinas, *Commentary on Galatians*, ch. 2, lec. 3, no. 83, in Fabian R. Larcher, trans., *Commentary on St. Paul's Epistle to the Galatians*, Aquinas Scripture Commentaries, vol. 1 (Albany: Magi Books, 1966). The translation is also available at aquinasinstitute.org.

example of zeal and freedom, that they fear not to correct their prelates, particularly if their crime is public and verges upon danger to the multitude.[32]

Several aspects of Aquinas's teaching merit emphasis because they correct some common misunderstandings. First, a loyal Catholic *can* correct a prelate (i.e., someone with ecclesiastical authority, such as a bishop). Some Catholics falsely suppose otherwise on the grounds that a subject has no authority over a prelate. But as Aquinas points out, what a subject lacks is the authority to secure justice by *punishing* a prelate for wrongdoing. Only a superior can do that. That does not entail that a subject cannot *criticize* a prelate so long as the prelate really is guilty of wrongdoing, the criticism is respectful, and the subject is acting out of charity rather than pretending to exercise authority over the prelate. Note that Aquinas even says that the scriptural account of Paul rebuking Peter was meant precisely as "an example of zeal and freedom" to Christians so that they would "fear not to correct their prelates."

Second, the pope is among those who can be corrected in this way. This is obvious from the fact that Aquinas is speaking of prelates in general, and the pope is a prelate. Furthermore, the example of correction Aquinas cites is Paul's correction of Peter, and Peter was a pope. The fact that the pope has no superior on earth is irrelevant because, again, what is in view here is not a subject *punishing* a pope so as to secure *justice* (which no subject of the pope may do) but rather merely respectfully *criticizing* a pope out of *charity*.

Third, Aquinas is clear that while such correction of a prelate should in the ordinary case take place privately, there are also cases where it can and should be done *publicly*. Specifically, Aquinas says that public rebuke of a prelate would be called for "if the faith were endangered" or if his "crime is public and verges upon danger to the multitude."

Fourth, another reason such correction of a prelate can be called for is *for the sake of the prelate himself.* If a pope is guilty of serious error and of leading others into error, one does not show greater piety or loyalty to him by pretending otherwise. On the contrary, one contributes to endangering his soul. For precisely because of his greater responsibility, he is in "greater danger" spiritually, as Aquinas (following Augustine) puts it. One of the things a prelate

---

[32] Aquinas, *Commentary on Galatians*, ch. 2, lec. 3, no. 77.

is in greater danger of is arrogance, so that, as Aquinas says, correction from a subordinate can help a prelate to develop humility.

Fifth, Aquinas's remarks show that it is silly to accuse those who criticize a prelate of necessarily thinking themselves "more Catholic than the pope." For one thing, as Aquinas says, when a Catholic criticizes a prelate, "it does not follow that he thinks himself any better, but merely that he offers his help." For another, a Catholic who criticizes a pope or other prelate might in fact *be* better in some respect. As Aquinas writes, "there is no presumption in thinking oneself better in some respect, because, in this life, no man is without some fault." For example, Catholics who condemn the immoral personal lives that a number of popes of the past have had *are* in fact better than those popes *with respect to their personal moral virtue.*

Sixth, criticism of a prelate must, as Aquinas says, be carried out "*with gentleness and respect*" and *not* with "impudence" or "insolence." Sometimes Catholics who raise legitimate criticisms of a pope publicly treat him with the sort of contempt and flippancy with which radio hosts and comedians typically treat politicians and other public figures in modern liberal democracies. *This is gravely wrong.* Even when one's father is in error and must be rebuked, *he is still one's father* and the Fourth Commandment is still in force. One may not belittle him or treat him as if he were some flunky. Now, the pope is a *spiritual* father, and more than that, he is the *Vicar of Christ.* His subjects must always act in a way consistent with the high dignity of his office, even when he is not living up to the demands of that office.

The legitimacy of criticism of a pope under certain circumstances has nothing whatsoever to do with the modern liberal individualist mentality of treating authority with contempt, celebrating the rebel and the dissident, etc. Indeed, as I have emphasized, legitimate criticism of a pope is essentially a matter of *upholding* his authority by helping him better to fulfill the purpose of his office, namely, passing on the deposit of faith and teaching it to his spiritual children. The aim is to urge him to be *more* pope-like, *more* father-like, not less. As Aquinas says, it is a matter of offering "*help* to one . . . in the higher position."

OTHER VOICES FROM THE TRADITION

Aquinas's teaching is in no way idiosyncratic, but reflects a view common both before and after his time. This was true even when the medieval papacy was at the height of its power. As one author observes:

The twelfth-century canonist Gratian reproduced a statement from the previous century in his *Decretum*: "No mortal shall presume to rebuke his [the pope's] faults, for he who is to judge all is to be judged by no one, *unless he is found straying from the faith*." Even Innocent III (1198–1216), during whose pontificate the papacy reached its zenith as a spiritual-temporal institution, believed that "only *on account of a sin committed against the faith* can I be judged by the church."[33]

The eminent Dominican bishop and theologian Melchior Cano (1509–1560), a key figure at the Council of Trent, wrote:

> Peter has no need of our lies or flattery. Those who blindly and indiscriminately defend every decision of the Supreme Pontiff are the very ones who do most to undermine the authority of the Holy See—they destroy instead of strengthening its foundations.[34]

Saint John Henry Newman (1801–1890) speculated about the possibility of "extreme cases in which Conscience may come into collision with the word of a Pope, and is to be followed in spite of that word" though he judged such cases to be "very rare."[35] In support, Newman cites remarks from Saint Robert Bellarmine (1542–1621) and Juan Cardinal de Torquemada (1388–1468). Torquemada wrote:

> Although it clearly follows from the circumstance that the Pope can err at times, and command things which must not be done, that we are not to be simply obedient to him in all things, that does not show that he must not be obeyed by all when his commands are good. To know in what cases he is to be obeyed and in what not . . . it is said in the Acts of the Apostles, 'One ought to obey God rather than man'; therefore, were the Pope to command anything against Holy Scripture, or the articles of faith, or the truth of the Sacraments, or the commands of the natural

---

[33] J. Michael Miller, C.S.B., *The Shepherd and the Rock: Origins, Development, and Mission of the Papacy* (Huntington, IN: Our Sunday Visitor, 1995), 292 (emphasis added).

[34] Quoted in John Jay Hughes, *Pontiffs: Popes Who Shaped History* (Huntington, IN: Our Sunday Visitor, 1994), 11.

[35] John Henry Newman and William E. Gladstone, *Newman and Gladstone: The Vatican Decrees* (Notre Dame, IN: University of Notre Dame Press, 1962), 127, 136.

or divine law, *he ought not to be obeyed*, but in such commands to be passed over.[36]

And Bellarmine taught:

> As it is lawful to resist the Pope, if he assaulted a man's person, so it is lawful to resist him, if he assaulted souls, or troubled the state, and much more if he strove to destroy the Church. It is lawful, I say, to resist him, by not doing what he commands, and hindering the execution of his will.[37]

We find similar remarks from yet other eminent theologians and churchmen of the past. For example, Thomas Cardinal de Vio Cajetan (1469–1534) held that in dealing with a pope who abuses his office, Catholics can legitimately "oppose the abuse of power which destroys by suitable remedies such as not obeying, not being servile in the face of evil actions, not keeping silence, [and] by arguing."[38] Similarly, Rafael Cardinal Merry del Val (1865–1930) wrote:

> Great as our filial duty of reverence is towards what ever [the pope] may say, great as our duty of obedience must be to the guidance of the Chief Shepherd, we do not hold that every word of his is infallible, or that he must always be right.
> . . . Even to-day a Bishop might . . . expostulate with a Pope, who, in his judgment, might be acting in a way which was liable to mislead those under his own charge, and then write to his critics that he had not hesitated to pass strictures upon the action of the successor of S. Peter. . . . The hypothesis is quite conceivable, and in no way destroys or diminishes the supremacy of the Pope. And yet an individual Bishop does not occupy the exceptional position of S. Paul, a fellow-Apostle of the Prince of the Apostles. Even a humble nun, S. Catherine of Siena, expostulated with the reigning Pontiff, in her day, whilst full acknowledging all his great prerogatives.[39]

---

[36] Newman and Gladstone, *Vatican Decrees*, 124.

[37] Newman and Gladstone, *Vatican Decrees*, 125.

[38] Miller, *The Shepherd and the Rock*, 295.

[39] Raphael Merry del Val, *The Truth of Papal Claims* (London: Sands and Company, 1902), 19, 74.

The point found expression in manuals of theology in the period before the Second Vatican Council. Ludwig Lercher's *Institutiones theologiae dogmaticae* notes that if a pope were in a non-infallible statement to teach some theological error, "it is not unthinkable that the error . . . should be excluded by the Holy Spirit in this way: that the subjects recognize the decree to be erroneous and cease to give their assent to it."[40]

Some of the Church's greatest theologians have even held that, at least in theory, a pope could lose his office as a result of heresy.[41] Juan de Torquemada and Bellarmine held that the loss of office would be automatic, an immediate consequence of a pope's falling into heresy, with no action necessary on the part of a council or the pope's fellow bishops. By contrast, Cajetan, John of St. Thomas (1589–1644), and Francisco Suárez (1548–1617) held that the loss of office would not be automatic but would follow upon a judgment of guilt on the part of an ecclesiastical body, such as a council or the college of cardinals. According to Suárez, "if the pope becomes an unrepentant heretic, after having passed on him the declaratory sentence of his crime, by legitimate ecclesiastical jurisdiction, he ceases to be pope."[42]

It is important to note that neither theory holds that a pope can be deposed or, while still pope, otherwise punished by a council or his fellow bishops. Since he has no superior on earth, that is not possible. The claim is, rather, that *the circumstance of his becoming a heretic* is what results in the loss of his office, because it puts him outside the Church. The disagreement is over what would have to happen in order for him to *count* as a heretic and thereby lose his office. The second theory holds that a formal judgment on the part of an ecclesiastical body is necessary, and the first denies this. The Magisterium of the Church has not resolved this issue, and there is no consensus about it among theologians. But the very fact of the controversy underlines how far the Church is from holding that the non-irreformable statements of a pope are immune from legitimate criticism.

Nor is an erroneous non-definitive doctrinal statement merely a theoretical possibility. Though extremely rare, there have been a handful of cases in Church

---

[40] Ludwig Lercher, *Institutiones theologiae dogmaticae*, vol. I, 5th ed. (Barcelona: Herder, 1951), 297, quoted in Francis A. Sullivan, *Magisterium: Teaching Authority in the Catholic Church* (New York: Paulist Press, 1983), 167.

[41] For brief surveys of the main opinions, see Miller, *The Shepherd and the Rock*, 291–93; and Patrick Granfield, *The Limits of the Papacy* (New York: Crossroad, 1987), 68–73.

[42] Quoted in Miller, *The Shepherd and the Rock*, 292–93.

history of popes making such statements. Probably the two clearest examples involve Pope Honorius I (625–638) and Pope John XXII (1316–1334). Honorius was condemned for the heresy of Monothelitism by the Sixth General Council, and condemned by his successors Pope Saint Agatho and Pope Saint Leo II for at least fostering that heresy by negligence. Contrary to traditional teaching, Pope John XXII denied that the blessed in heaven immediately enjoy the beatific vision after death. He was vigorously criticized for this by the theologians of his day, and recanted on his deathbed.[43]

Saint Francis de Sales (1567–1622) provides a useful summary of traditional teaching on the sorts of errors of which a pope is capable when not teaching *ex cathedra*, and on how the faithful ought to respond to such error:

> Thus, we do not say that the Pope cannot err in his private opinions, as did John XXII, or be altogether a heretic, as perhaps Honorius was. Now when he is explicitly a heretic, he falls *ipso facto* from his dignity and out of the Church, and the Church must either deprive him, or, as some say, declare him deprived, of his Apostolic See, and must say as S. Peter did, *Let another take his bishopric.* When he errs in his private opinion he must be instructed, advised, convinced; as happened with John XXII. . . . So everything the Pope says is not canon law or of legal obligation; he must mean to define and to lay down the law for the sheep, and he must keep the due order and form. . . . And again we must not think that in everything and everywhere his judgment is infallible, but then only when he gives judgment on a matter of faith in questions necessary to the whole Church; for in particular cases which depend on human fact he can err, there is no doubt, though it is not for us to control him in these cases save with all reverence, submission, and discretion.[44]

---

[43] Under duress, Pope Liberius (352–366) temporarily acquiesced to an ambiguous doctrinal formula favored by the Arian heretics. Pope Vigilius (537–555) was condemned by a synod in Carthage for allegedly betraying Chalcedonian orthodoxy in the controversy over the "Three Chapters." Details about all of these cases can be found in reference works such as the *Catholic Encyclopedia* and J. N. D. Kelly's *The Oxford Dictionary of Popes* (Oxford: Oxford University Press, 1986).

[44] Francis de Sales, *The Catholic Controversy* (Charlotte, NC: TAN Books, 2012), 225–26.

SAINT VINCENT OF LÉRINS AND THE DEVELOPMENT OF CHRISTIAN DOCTRINE

Eduardo Echeverria

As for the time element: since time snatches away all things human, we ought to snatch from it something which may profit us unto life eternal. We are moved particularly by the terrible fear of the approaching Judgment which urges us to increase our studies of religion, and by the deceitfulness of the new heretics which requires much careful attention.

Saint Vincent of Lérins[1]

INTRODUCTION

Saint Vincent of Lérins, who died about AD 445, was a Gallic monk, the chief theologian of the Abbey of Lérins, who developed a fundamental

---

[1] Vincent of Lérins, *The Commonitories*, trans. Rudolph E. Morris (Washington, DC: Catholic University of America Press, 1949), 268. The translator informs us about Vincent and the reason for the title of his work: "Although the *Commonitories* were written shortly after the General Council of Ephesus (431), it is doubtful if they were published during his lifetime. At any rate, he used a pen name and wrote as 'Peregrinus' (the Pilgrim); he may have felt, just as we do today, that each of us is only a pilgrim, having no secure place on earth. He called his work *Commonitories* in the strict sense of the word. He wrote them, as he tells his reader, because he felt his memory getting weak and because he had observed that persistent reading of his notes helped him to see more clearly in matters of decisive importance" (259). I borrow the title of my article from the title of the book by Thomas G. Guarino, *Vincent of Lérins and the Development of Christian Doctrine* (Grand Rapids, MI: Baker Academic, 2013), 3. I am indebted not only to this work of Msgr. Guarino but also to his *The Disputed Teachings of Vatican II: Continuity and Reversal in Catholic Doctrine* (Grand Rapids, MI: Eerdmans, 2018).

theological account of the development of Christian doctrine in his chief work, the *Commonitorium* (434). His major concern in this work is about true doctrinal development in Christianity. If true development is possible, then, how does one distinguish it from corruptions of the faith? In particular, Vincent was prompted to write this work by the several disputed issues in his time regarding the Trinity, Christology, the natures and person of Jesus Christ, and the spread of heresies—to name only a few—of Donatus, Nestorius, Apollinaris, Arius, Origen, Tertullian, Sabellius, and Pelagius.

In the following, I will make some general remarks about the structure and contents of the *Commonitorium*, calling special attention to certain ideas and principles of Vincent's account. I have in mind, for example, the principle that development should preserve "what has been believed everywhere, always, and by all" (*quod ubique, quod semper, quod ab omnibus creditum est*)—but also Vincent's remarks on the way that development should be organic: "growth of religion in the soul should be like the growth of the body, which in the course of years develops and unfolds, yet remains the same as it was."[2] The purpose of the analogy is to make the point that the fundamental and essential nature of each remains the same. And, of course, there is the fundamental principle informing Vincent's distinction between doctrine and expression: *in eodem scilicet dogmate, eodem sensu eademque sententia*, that is, the differing expressions of the propositional truths of faith must keep the same meaning and the same judgment.[3] "Yet, teach precisely what you have learned; do not say new things even if you say them in a new manner."[4] Furthermore, I shall explain how Vincent's ideas and principles provide us with the fundamental key for interpreting the documents of the Second Vatican Council. Moreover, Vincent only deals with the development of *definitive* teaching such that there can never be a reversal of the key teachings of the Councils of Nicaea and Ephesus; such reversals would be, as

---

[2] Vincent of Lérins, *The Commonitories*, 270, 309.

[3] Vincent of Lérins, *The Commonitories*, 309. I disagree with Morris's translation of "*in eodem scilicet dogmate, eodem sensu eademque sententia*" as "in accordance with the same kind of dogma, frame of mind, and intellectual approach." This is not a translation but more like an interpretation. This italicized principle means to say that the meaning of a proposition is inextricably connected with its truth—regarding the status of meaning, the way things are is what makes "meaning" true or false. Put differently, a dogma's meaning is unchangeable because that meaning is true. Hence, I am following the translation of Vincent of Lérins's principle as found at Heinrich Denzinger, *Compendium of Creeds, Definitions on Matters of Faith and Morals*, ed. Peter Hünermann (San Francisco: Ignatius Press, 2012), 3020 (hereafter, cited as DH).

[4] Vincent of Lérins, *The Commonitories*, 309.

Vincent calls them, *permutationes* (corruptions), and hence quite contrary to genuine *profectus* (developments). Still, in conclusion, I will briefly consider the matter of alterations with respect to non-definitive teaching, something Vincent does not do, but I will show that this matter can be dealt with in a Vincentian mode by demonstrating that some alterations are not *permutationes* but *profectus*.

PATTERN OF THEOLOGICAL AUTHORITY

In the epigraph to this essay from the *Commonitorium*, Vincent makes one point about an approaching divine judgment. What does he mean? I think his point should be understood in the context of the question he later poses and answers: "Why, then, does divine providence often permit eminent persons, who are well established in the Church, to announce novel ideas to Catholics?"[5] Vincent answers this question: "If at any time a teacher of the Church deviates from the faith, Divine Providence permits this to happen in order *to test and try us*, 'whether we love God, or not, with all our heart and all our soul' [Deut 13:3]."[6] Furthermore, we show our wholehearted love for God by rejoicing in the truth, and the search for the truth compels one to give serious attention to religious matters. Here Vincent is referring to the search for a principle that distinguishes truth from heresy, separating sound doctrine from erroneous thinking—or more seriously, heretical corruption—so that doctrinal development occurs in the light of Christian truth, remaining "sound in the integrity of faith" for the sake of escaping "the very grave danger of losing our eternal salvation."[7]

Fundamental to maintaining the integrity of faith is, according to Vincent, adhering to the Pauline biblical principle in 1 Timothy 6:20–21: "O Timothy, keep that which is committed to thy trust, avoiding profane and vain babblings, and oppositions of science falsely so called: Which some professing have erred concerning the faith" (KJV). Elsewhere, in the Letter of Jude, this insistence is repeated, exhorting us to guard the deposit, "to contend for the faith which was once for all delivered to the saints" (1:3). However, what is the deposit? Vincent answers in the *Commonitorium*:

---

5 Vincent of Lérins, *The Commonitories*, 284.
6 Vincent of Lérins, *The Commonitories*, 303 (emphasis added).
7 Vincent of Lérins, *The Commonitories*, 269, 322.

It is that which has been entrusted to you, not that which you have invented; what you have received, not what you have devised; not a matter of ingenuity, but of doctrine; not of private acquisition, but of public tradition; a matter brought to you, not created by you; a matter you are not the author of, but the keeper of; not the teacher, but the learner; not the leader, but the follower. This deposit, he says, guard.[8]

Essentially, the deposit of faith is a revealed datum, the gift of revelation. It is constitutive to maintaining the integrity of faith. Vincent says:

That whether I or any one should wish to detect the frauds and avoid the snares of heretics as they rise, and continue sound and complete in the Catholic faith, we must, the Lord helping, fortify our own belief in two ways; first, by the authority of the Divine Law [Sacred Scripture], and then, [the former must be understood and interpreted] by the Tradition of the Catholic Church.[9]

Regarding the former, says Vincent, Holy Scripture is a sufficient condition to get at the whole truth, that is, it is "complete, and sufficient of itself."[10] Still, in light of interpretive pluralism, which Vincent suggests is nearly anarchic, he explains why we need to justify our interpretations of Scripture in light of the Church's authoritative Tradition. "As a matter of fact, [we must answer,] Holy Scripture, because of its depth, is not universally accepted in one and the same sense. The same text is interpreted differently by different people, so that one may almost gain the impression that it can yield as many different meanings as there are men."[11] Thus, Vincent rejects the monistic pattern of theological authority in which the Scripture alone adjudicates or authorizes the conflict between rival interpretations. His affirmation of the sufficiency of Scripture resembles more *prima scriptura* than *sola scriptura*. This means that Vincent opts for a pluralistic pattern of theological authority in which Scripture functions as a primary authority, but it is intrinsically and necessarily related to

---

[8] Vincent of Lérins, *The Commonitories*, 308.

[9] Vincent of Lérins, *The Commonitories*, 269, but see also 284 and 324.

[10] Vincent of Lérins, *The Commonitories*, 269. Later in the text, he says, "Not that the Canon is insufficient in itself in each case" (324).

[11] Vincent of Lérins, *The Commonitories*, 269.

Tradition and the Church as one among a network of interdependent authorities. Vincent explains:

> But, because most [false] interpreters of the Divine Word make use of their own arbitrary judgment and thus fall into various opinions and errors, the understanding of Holy Scripture must conform to the single rule of Catholic teaching—and this especially in regard to those questions upon which the foundations of all Catholic dogma are laid. We also said that within the Church itself an agreement of universality and antiquity must be observed, lest we either are drawn away from integral unity into the separatism of schism or precipitated from traditional belief into the novelties of heresy.[12]

What is the single rule of faith of Catholic teaching to which Vincent alludes above in order to "discern in Holy Scripture truth from falsehood?"[13] He answers:

> Thus, because of the great distortions caused by various errors, it is, indeed, necessary that the trend of the interpretation of the prophetic and apostolic writings be directed in accordance with the rule of the ecclesiastical and Catholic meaning.[14]

The latter refers to the authoritative and hence permanently valid formulations of the Christian faith of Nicaea and Ephesus. Vincent elaborates on the necessary rule of faith constituting normative and irreversible criteria for ascertaining truth in the content of revelation. "In the Catholic Church, great care is to be taken that we hold that which has been believed *everywhere, always,* and *by all*" (*quod ubique, quod semper, quod ab omnibus creditum est*).[15]

The obvious question to raise here is how do we get at what has been believed everywhere, always, and by all, in order to distinguish Christian truth from error? He answers, "This we shall only then do, when we follow Universality, Antiquity, [and] Consent." Vincent explains these criteria in order to answer the question: "What, therefore, will the Catholic Christian do if some members of the Church have broken away from the communion of universal

---

[12] Vincent of Lérins, *The Commonitories*, 324–25.

[13] Vincent of Lérins, *The Commonitories*, 320.

[14] Vincent of Lérins, *The Commonitories*, 270.

[15] Vincent of Lérins, *The Commonitories*, 270.

faith? What else, but prefer the sanity of the body universal to the pestilence of the corrupt member?"[16]

> We do so in regard to universality if we confess that faith alone to be true which the entire Church confesses all over the world. [We do so] in regard to antiquity if we in no way deviate from those interpretations which our ancestors and fathers have manifestly proclaimed as inviolable. [We do so] in regard to consent if, in this very antiquity, we adopt the definitions and propositions of all, or almost all, the bishops and doctors.[17]

Given, then, this pattern of theological authority, of interpretive authority, we can understand Vincent's defense that theological interpretations are justified by being in continuity with the faith of the apostolic tradition. Thus, the criterion of universality pertains to getting at the whole truth of the faith once for all delivered to the saints (Jude 1:3) that has been confessed by the universal Church. In addition, says Vincent, "it must be ascertained whether there exists from ancient times a decree established by all the bishops of the Catholic Church with the authority of a universal council."[18] He calls us to hold fast to antiquity, to the authority of Sacred Tradition, meaning thereby the ecumenical councils of Nicaea and Ephesus in which we find irreversible doctrinal formulations. Actually, three ecumenical councils preceded Vincent's *Commonitorium*: the First Council of Nicaea (325); the First Council of Constantinople (381); and the First Council of Ephesus (431).[19] However, other ecumenical councils followed Vincent's death: the Council of Chalcedon (451), for instance; the Second Council of Constantinople (553); the Third Council of Constantinople (680–681); and the Second Council of Nicaea (787).[20] These normative, binding landmarks of the faith have been laid down for the entire Church. They embody the "decrees and definitions of all the priests of Holy Church as the heirs of

---

[16] Vincent of Lérins, *The Commonitories*, 271.

[17] Vincent of Lérins, *The Commonitories*, 270–71.

[18] Vincent of Lérins, *The Commonitories*, 325.

[19] Regarding the First Council of Constantinople, according to Msgr. Thomas Guarino, "The scholarly consensus is that Vincent (as with many Westerners) did not know about this ecumenical council." Email message to author, May 15, 2020.

[20] DH 125–30; 250–71; 300–303; 421–38; 550–59; 600–603 (hereafter, *Compendium of Creeds*). The Catholic Church today recognizes twenty-one councils as ecumenical. See John XXIII, Allocution on the Occasion of the Solemn Inauguration of the Second Ecumenical Council *Gaudet mater ecclesia* (October 11, 1962), §§2, 6 (hereafter, *Gaudet mater ecclesia*).

Apostolic and Catholic Truth."[21] Vincent adds, "Novelty is to be avoided, hence, antiquity has to be respected; novelty is profane, hence, the old tradition is sacred."[22] Thomas Guarino rightly remarks, "This is why Vincent will say that the genuine Christian not only loves the truth of God and the Catholic faith but also believes only what the church has held universally and from antiquity, and will not believe that which has been introduced by someone 'other than all, or against, the saints.'"[23]

In conclusion of this section and in preparation for the next, I want to consider briefly Vincent's reflections on 1 Timothy 6:20–21: "O Timothy, keep that which is committed to thy trust, avoiding profane and vain babblings, and oppositions of science falsely so called: Which some professing have erred concerning the faith" (KJV). Vincent argues that at the root of these "profane and vain babblings" of heresy is a false view of revelation—a denial of a determinate revealed datum, revealed truth, which has been committed to our trust. Those in search of novelties of dogma dismiss the idea of being firmly founded in the faith ("completely secure harbor of the Catholic faith"),[24] putting themselves above what has been "held universally and from ancient times."[25] Vincent explains, "[they] are possessed by a permanent desire to change religion, to add something and to take something away—as though the dogma were not divine, so that it has to be revealed only once. But they take it for a merely human institution, which cannot be perfected except by constant emendations, rather by constant corrections."[26] On this view, we have no way of telling the difference between true development and a work of heresy, indeed, no way of discerning the difference between development and unacceptable change. Therefore, Guarino states, "under the guise of development, the meaning of the church's faith is illegitimately transformed, allowing heterodox ideas to be introduced."[27] According to Vincent, these changes are *permutationes* (corruptions) of the faith, as distinct from *profectus*, a proper development. Vincent's approach to the preservation of Christian truth has raised the objection that he absolutizes continuity of statically defined dogmatic truth without displaying

---

[21] Vincent of Lérins, *The Commonitories*, 275.

[22] Vincent of Lérins, *The Commonitories*, 306.

[23] Guarino, *Vincent of Lérins*, 14.

[24] Vincent of Lérins, *The Commonitories*, 305.

[25] Vincent of Lérins, *The Commonitories*, 303, 304.

[26] Vincent of Lérins, *The Commonitories*, 306.

[27] Guarino, *Vincent of Lérins*, 19.

any appreciation for the historical nature of those truths' human formulations. I turn now to showing why that objection is false.

DEVELOPMENT AND CHANGE

Preserving with care the deposit of faith in light of the irreversible doctrinal formulations of antiquity, arrived at through the "consentient determination of living tradition, particularly ecumenical councils," rather than through recreating the faith in one's own image, does not exclude development of Christian doctrine.[28] According to Vincent, history shows continuity, indeed, identity persisting from the apostolic deposit, which is a determinate revealed datum, to the developed assertions of Church dogma. It is right, he says, that those dogmatic assertions "in the course of time be thoroughly cared for, filed, and polished; but it is sinful to change them, sinful to behead them or mutilate them. They may take on more evidence, clarity, and distinctness, but it is absolutely necessary that they retain their plenitude, integrity, and basic character."[29] What, then, is development?

In the epigraph to this essay from the *Commonitorium*, Vincent makes another point that adumbrates the major issue in his account of true doctrinal development in time. He seeks to show how temporality can be of theological advantage by arguing that there is a historical dimension to the explicitation of unchangeable doctrinal truth. The core question for Vincent in chapter 23 of the *Commonitorium* is about the relationship between history and truth, a determinate truth that is indefinitely transmissible in genuine development throughout time. But in this transmissibility, Vincent advises: "Teach precisely what you have learned; do not say new things even if you say them in a new manner [*Eadem tamen quæ didicisti ita doce, ut cum dicas nove, non dicas nova*]."[30]

> This, I say, and nothing but this, has the Catholic Church, aroused over the novelties of the heretics, again and again accomplished by the decrees of its councils, i.e., what it earlier received from our forefathers by tradition alone, it has handed down to posterity by authoritative decisions, condensing weighty matters in a few

---

[28] Guarino, *Vincent of Lérins*, 14.
[29] Vincent of Lérins, *The Commonitories*, 311.
[30] Vincent of Lérins, *The Commonitories*, 309.

words, and particularly for the enlightenment of the mind, by presenting in new words the old interpretation of the faith.[31]

Here already in the distinction between doctrine and expression—*dicas nove, non dicas nova*—Vincent alludes to the distinction between propositional truths of faith and their reformulations. Indeed, the form may change but not the fundamental content of the faith because the meaning and truth of the latter remains always the same. "Hence, it must be that understanding, knowledge, and wisdom grow and advance mightily and strongly in individuals as well as in the community, in a single person as well as in the Church as a whole, and this gradually according to age and history. But only within the proper limits, i.e., within the same dogma, the same meaning, the same judgment [*in eodem scilicet dogmate, eodem sensu eademque sententia*]."[32] Although the truths of the faith may be expressed differently, they must be kept within determinate bounds. That is, we must always determine whether those reformulations preserve the same meaning and mediate the same judgment of truth, as John Finnis says, "consistent with all the propositions which the Church has at some time defined or otherwise judged to be one that followers of Christ must hold definitely." Furthermore, "restatements of the faith must retain [their] identity by retaining those same propositions, in formulations old and new."[33] Hence, Vincent insists that authentic dogmatic development must preserve the material continuity, identity, and universality of those truths, unfolding or "elaborating more distinctly and clearly" (*distinctius et expressius enucleare*)[34] or explicitly the propositional truth of this same doctrine.

At this point Vincent asks in his work the *Commonitorium*, "If this is right [preserving the old interpretation of the faith, but expressing it in new ways], then is no progress of religion possible within the Church of Christ? To be sure, there has to be progress, even exceedingly great progress. For who is so grudging toward his fellow men and so full of hatred toward God as to try to prohibit it? But it must be progress in the proper sense of the word, and not a change in faith [*Sed ita tamen, ut vere profectus sit ille fidei, non permutatio*]. Progress means that each thing grows within itself, whereas change implies

---

[31] Vincent of Lérins, *The Commonitories*, 312.

[32] Vincent of Lérins, *The Commonitories*, 309.

[33] John Finnis, "What Pope John Said," *The Tablet*, Letters to the Editor, January 4, 1992.

[34] Vincent of Lérins, *The Commonitories*, 291. See Guarino, *Vincent of Lérins*, 139n35: "Vincent's use of the *enucleare* is significant. He is 'unfolding' or 'laying open' the meaning embedded in Scripture with the help of councils."

that one thing is transformed into another."[35] Hence, Vincent does not identify development with change. True development of doctrine is not the same as a change of doctrine. Change of doctrine Vincent calls *permutatio* (corruption), and hence quite contrary to genuine development (*profectus*). How, then, does one tell the difference between development and change?

Vincent's biological analogy between the growth of bodies and the growth of religion is a clue to his understanding of development. The fundamental and essential nature of the old man and of the child, although much has changed about the person, are identical. "There remains one and the same nature and one and the same person."[36] Thus, the main point Vincent is making is about the legitimate "rule of progress" and the "order of growth": development, like bodily growth, is organic because it is an unfolding of that wisdom with which the Creator had previously imbued the infant Church.[37] Accordingly, Vincent elaborates that Christian doctrine follows the same law of progress: true progress or development of dogma should "be consolidated in the course of years, developed in the course of time, and sublimated by age—yet remain," Vincent continues, "incorrupt and unimpaired, complete and perfect in the proportions of its parts and in all its essentials (let us call them members and senses), so that it does not allow any change [*nihil . . . permutationis*], or any loss of its specific character, or any variation of its inherent form."[38] Therefore, doctrinal development means that the identity of doctrine does not change over time in the sense of being substantially transformed, implying a change in the very essence of the teaching. In sum, doctrinal development has to be homogeneous, organic development, not allowing heterogeneous ideas, and hence discontinuity, with the essential principles of the teaching.

Still, dogmatic development involves "elaborating more distinctly and clearly" (*distinctius et expressius enucleare*)[39] the propositional truth of this same doctrine. This means a restatement or clearer statement of the doctrinal content of the Gospel, of what is already conceptually possessed and known, that is, different expressions of the same truth. This is a logical type of dogmatic development in which the substance of the affirmations of revealed truths is

---

[35] Vincent of Lérins, *The Commonitories*, 309. Note that Morris translates the word *permutatio* not as "corruption" (as I have done), but as "change."

[36] Vincent of Lérins, *The Commonitories*, 309.

[37] Vincent of Lérins, *The Commonitories*, 310–11.

[38] Vincent of Lérins, *The Commonitories*, 310.

[39] Vincent of Lérins, *The Commonitories*, 291.

expressed differently in a linguistic and conceptual way but states the same thing. Congar correctly states, "When it is a matter of properly dogmatic formulas, this evolution can only mean development by way of clarification."[40] In other words, the biblical revelation "I and the Father are one" (John 10:30) is expressed in a new conceptual way—*homoousion*—which is a formally revealed truth: the consubstantiality of the Son with the Father. This new way of expressing the propositions of faith in a variety of conceptual, literary, and linguistic forms must always be—as I argued earlier—*in eodem sensu eademque sententia*, that is, according to the same meaning and the same judgment.

Vincent illustrates doctrinal development in chapters 12–16 of the *Commonitorium* by his articulation of the Christological and Trinitarian affirmations of the early councils at Nicaea and Ephesus, "elaborating more distinctly and clearly" (*distinctius et expressius enucleare*) the doctrinal content found in Scripture itself, employing concepts such as consubstantiality, hypostasis, person, nature, and many others. The formulae of Nicaea and Ephesus are a restatement or clearer statement of the doctrinal content of the Gospel, of what is already conceptually possessed and known, that is, different expressions of the same truth, *in eodem sensu eademque sententia* (according to the same meaning and the same judgment). Vincent's statements put the mysteries of the Trinity and of the Incarnation in sharper focus, limiting them within definite boundaries, and thus setting limits to further progress in Trinitarian and Christological dogma.

VINCENT OF LÉRINS AND THE SECOND VATICAN COUNCIL

Regarding the enduring importance of Vincent's thought, it is important to note that he influences Pope Saint John XXIII in his opening address to the Second Vatican Council, *Gaudet mater ecclesia*.[41] The Pope argues, like Vincent, that the Church must "*transmit whole and entire and without distortion Catholic doctrine.*" He adds, "As all sincere promoters of Christian, Catholic, and apostolic faith strongly desire, *what is needed is that this doctrine be more fully and*

---

[40] Yves Congar, O.P., *True and False Reform in the Church*, trans. Paul Philibert, O.P. (Collegeville, MN: Liturgical Press, 2011 [1968]), 232.

[41] *Gaudet mater ecclesia*, §14. I am following Joseph Komonchak's translation, which is superior to both the Abbott and Flannery translations.

more profoundly known and that minds be more fully imbued and formed by it."[42] John XXIII elaborates:

> Nor is the primary purpose of our work to discuss some of the chief articles of the Church's doctrine or to repeat at length what the Fathers and ancient and more recent theologians have handed on, things which we have every right to think are not unknown to you but reside in your minds. To have only such discussions there would have been no need to call an Ecumenical Council. What instead is necessary today is that *the whole of Christian doctrine, with no part of it lost,* be received in our times by all with a new fervor, in serenity and peace, in that traditional and precise conceptuality and expression which is especially displayed in the acts of the Councils of Trent and Vatican I. . . . What is needed is that this certain and unchangeable doctrine, to which loyal submission is due, be investigated and presented in the way demanded by our times.[43]

Importantly, John XXIII depends on Vincent as well as the First Vatican Council by implicitly distinguishing between propositional truths of faith and their formulations in reflecting on the sense in which a doctrine, already confirmed and defined, is more fully known and deeply understood.

> For the deposit of faith, the truths contained in our venerable doctrine, are one thing; the fashion in which they are expressed, but with the same meaning and the same judgment [*eodem sensu eademque sententia*], is another thing.[44]

The subordinate clause, which I have cited in its Latin original, is part of a larger passage from the First Vatican Council's Dogmatic Constitution on

---

[42] *Gaudet mater ecclesia*, §15 (emphasis added).

[43] *Gaudet mater ecclesia*, §15 (emphasis added).

[44] *Gaudet mater ecclesia*, §15. John XXIII cited Vincent's words in Latin, "*in eodem sensu eademque sententia*," when he delivered the opening discourse to the Council. These words of the discourse are quoted by the Council in the Pastoral Constitution on the Church in the Modern World *Gaudium et spes* (December 7, 1965), §62 (hereafter, *Gaudium et spes*). We have the audiotape proving, as John Finnis correctly notes, that "the one and only final version [of the opening speech] for which he took responsibility, and that therefore is authentic, is the Latin version he pronounced." Email message from Prof. Finnis to the author, April 18, 2020. See the illuminating exchange in Letters to the Editor between Finnis and his critics in *The Tablet*, December 14, 1991–February 8, 1992. I am grateful to Prof. Finnis for sending me this exchange.

Faith and Reason, *Dei Filius* (1869–1870), which is earlier invoked by Pope Pius IX in the bull of 1854, *Ineffabilis Deus*, also cited by Pope Leo XIII in his 1899 encyclical letter, *Testem benevolentiae nostrae*. And this formula in *Dei Filius* is itself taken from the *Commonitorium* of Vincent of Lérins, as I cited above: "Therefore, let there be growth and abundant progress in understanding, knowledge, and wisdom, in each and all, in individuals and in the whole Church, at all times and in the progress of ages, but only within the proper limits, i.e., within the same dogma, the same meaning, the same judgment [*in eodem scilicet dogmate, eodem sensu eademque sententia*]."[45]

What did John XXIII mean by this statement? First of all, he clearly meant to call for a suitable reformulation of Catholic teaching in light of the authoritative sources of faith, Scripture and Tradition. Second, reformulation was possible because the propositional truths of faith are distinct from their linguistic expression in different conceptual and theological frameworks. In short, there could be different expressions of the same truth, which is to say of the same proposition. Third, and most important, the differing linguistic expressions of the propositional truths of faith must keep the same meaning and the same judgment—"*eodem sensu eademque sententia*." This italicized phrase means to say that the truth of a proposition is inextricably connected with its meaning. As to meaning, the way things are is what makes "meaning" true or false. Therefore, a proposition is true if what it says corresponds to the way objective reality is; otherwise, it is false. In the words of Bernard Lonergan, "Meaning of its nature is related to a 'meant,' and what is meant may or may not correspond to what is so. If it corresponds, the meaning is true. If it does not correspond, the meaning is false."[46] Thus, a dogma's meaning is unchangeable because that meaning is true. The truths of faith are, if true, always and everywhere true; the different ways of expressing these truths may vary in our attempts to communicate revealed truths more clearly and accurately, but these various linguistic expressions do not affect the truth of the propositions.

The Dutch Reformed master of dogmatics and ecumenical theology G. C. Berkouwer (1903–1996) understood admirably well the point that "the development of dogma, which was undeniable, was not a discontinuous, but a harmonious process." Berkouwer elaborates:

---

[45] DH 3020.

[46] Bernard J. F. Lonergan, S.J., "The Dehellenization of Dogma," in *A Second Collection*, ed. William F. J. Ryan, S.J., et al. (Philadelphia: The Westminster Press, 1974), 11–32, 14 (internal quotes added).

That harmony had always been presumed, virtually self-evidently, to be an implication of the mystery of the truth "*eodem sensu eademque sententia*" [the same meaning and the same judgment]. Now, however, attention is captivated primarily by the historical-factual process that does not transcend the times but is entangled with them in all sorts of ways. It cannot be denied that one encounters the undeniable fact of the situated setting of the various pronouncements made by the Church in any given era.[47]

He pointedly adds, "All the problems of more recent interpretation of dogma are connected very closely to this search for continuity."[48] If it is a matter of development, then, there remains to face, as Berkouwer insists, "the question of the nature of continuity."[49] The Second Vatican Council faced that question in a Vincentian framework. However, it is important to consider briefly a currently influential contrary interpretation of the Council that is captivated in its discussion of doctrine "primarily by the historical-factual process that does not transcend the times," as Berkouwer puts it above.

A neo-Modernism has surfaced in the so-called "*new paradigm*," or "*pastorality of doctrine*" approach of, for example, Richard Gaillardetz and Christoph Theobald, S.J.[50] Without the Council's Vincentian approach, we are left with a so-called "principle of pastorality," which is a perpetual project of reinterpreting and recontextualizing the Gospel. For Gaillardetz, "pastoral" means "the *central values* embedded in doctrine" or in "particular doctrinal formulations mediated by the saving message of God's transforming love."[51] According to him, the affirmations of faith do not have a determinable content of propositional truth in respect of their correspondence to reality. Instead, he subscribes to an instrumentalist or functionalist view of doctrine reminiscent of the late nineteenth- and early twentieth-century modernists rather than a realist view

[47] G. C. Berkouwer, *Nabetrachting op het Concilie* (Kampen: J. H. Kok, 1968), 52, my translation.

[48] G. C. Berkouwer, *De Kerk*, vol. 1, *Eenheid en Katholiciteit* (Kampen, Netherlands: J.H. Kok, 1970), 236–37; vol. 2, *Apostoliciet en Heiligheid* (Kampen: J. H. Kok, 1972). Both volumes are translated in one complete volume by James E. Davison as *The Church* (Grand Rapids, MI: Eerdmans, 1976); see 190–91.

[49] Berkouwer, *De Kerk*, 1:236–37 [*The Church*, 190–91].

[50] The *nouveaux théologiens*—Yves Congar, Henri de Lubac, et al.—are not advocates of neo-Modernism such as we find in the "pastorality of doctrine" approach. It would take us too far afield to defend this claim here. For my defense, see my book, *Berkouwer and Catholicism: Disputed Questions* (Boston: Brill, 2013), 56–101.

[51] Richard Gaillardetz, *An Unfinished Council: Vatican II, Pope Francis, and the Renewal of Catholicism* (Collegeville, MN: Liturgical Press, 2015), 134–35 (emphasis added).

with its corresponding notion of propositional truth.[52] These "truths" are understood in a purely functional way.[53] Dogma bears no determinative relation to truth itself because the truth-status of doctrinal formulations has as such no proper referencing function to reality. Instead, the formulations are historically determined, which means that Gaillardetz historicizes the meaning and truth of dogma by expanding the meaning of pastoral.[54] "Pastoral" here has a historicist meaning, explicitly or implicitly denying the enduring validity of propositional truth. Truth itself, and not just its formulations, is subject to reform and perpetual reinterpretation. He cites fellow theologian John O'Brien to explain the historicist view that underpins the claim that doctrine has a pastoral orientation:

> [The] pastoral had regained [with Pope John XXIII] its proper standing as something far more than mere application of doctrine but as the very context from which doctrines emerge, the very condition of the possibility of doctrine, the touchstone for the validity of doctrine and the always prior and posterior praxis which doctrine at most, attempts to sum up, safeguard, and transmit.[55]

We find this approach also in Christoph Theobald, S.J., who prefers not to understand the Second Vatican Council as maintaining that the deposit of faith contains particular and plural truths to which subsequent doctrine must correspond while keeping "the same meaning and the same judgment [*eodem sensu eademque sententia*]." He prefers an approach that speaks rather of the deposit of faith "as a *whole*" (his emphasis) and "the historical form it takes at one time or another." In this way "the historical form" that the deposit assumes "at one time or another" need not be consistent with any particular truth contained in the deposit of faith.[56]

As support for this approach, Theobald adopts the frequently maintained—but erroneous—thesis that Pope Saint John XXIII only ever truly espoused what

---

[52] See Pius X, Encyclical Letter on the Doctrines of the Modernists *Pascendi Dominici Gregis* (September 8, 1907), §§11–13.

[53] See John Paul II, Encyclical Letter on the Relationship between Faith and Reason *Fides et Ratio* (September 14, 1998), §97.

[54] Gaillardetz, *Unfinished Council*, 52.

[55] John O'Brien, "Ecclesiology as Narrative," *Ecclesiology* 4, no. 2 (2008): 150, cited in Gaillardetz, *Unfinished Council*, 38.

[56] Christoph Theobald, S.J., "The Theological Options of Vatican II: Seeking an 'Internal' Principle of Interpretation," *Concilium* 4 (2005): 87–107, and 107n31.

is found in the draft Italian version of his opening discourse to the Council, as distinct from the Latin version, "corrected," as Theobald says, by the Roman Curia.[57] The draft Italian version did not contain what the Latin address as he spoke it to the Fathers and had published in *Osservatore Romano* and the *Acta Apostolicae Sedis* does contain: the crucial passage from Vincent's *Commonitorium* which speaks of plural truths expressed in various ways but always with "the same meaning and the same judgment." The draft speaks only of "the substance of the ancient doctrine of the *depositum fidei*" as distinct from "the formulation in which it is clothed." It is known, however, that the Latin text that Pope John read at the opening of the Council contained the quotation from Vincent and that he pronounced those words most willingly. This is apparent in an instruction he gave to his personal secretary, Loris Capovilla: "Of that discourse" (i.e., the opening discourse of the Council) "publish also the first draft [*prima stesura*] in Italian in order that it be known—not in order that I might be praised but as one assuming responsibility—that it [*esso*, the discourse] is mine from the first to the last word."[58]

Suffice it to say that I agree with John Finnis that "John XXIII participated fully in the preparation of all stages of the Latin Address and took full responsibility at every stage for accepting, rejecting or qualifying what was suggested to him by way of revisions."[59] In other words, John XXIII deliberately established as a governing principle of the Council the Vincentian idea that the deposit of faith contains plural truths that might be articulated in different ways, provided they express "the same meaning and the same judgment." Theobald, on the other hand, holds that the substance of the deposit of faith as a whole is "subject to continual reinterpretation [and recontextualization] according to the situation of those to whom it is transmitted."[60] This is a plea for a perpetual hermeneutics, that is, for an ongoing reinterpretation and recontextualizing of doctrinal truth. Given this principle, unlike Vincent's thought, doctrines are not absolute truths, or objectively true affirmations. Hence, the pastorality of doctrine approach denies the enduring validity of truth, and is therefore

---

[57] Theobald, "Theological Options," 107n31.

[58] Loris Capovilla, *Giovanni XXIII: Quindici letture* (Rome: Storia e Letteratura, 1970), 197.

[59] This is a paraphrase by John Finnis in an email message to me, April 14, 2020.

[60] Christoph Theobald, S.J., "The Principle of Pastorality at Vatican II," in *The Legacy of Vatican II*, ed. Massimo Faggioli and Andrea Vicini, S.J. (Mahwah, NJ: Paulist Press, 2015), 26–37.

unable to maintain the material continuity, identity, and universality of the truths of dogma.[61]

ALTERATIONS?

Vincent never deals with alterations of "non-definitive teaching." He only deals with reversals of the ecumenical councils of Nicaea and Ephesus. As I have shown above, Vincent argues that such reversals are, indeed, *permutationes*, or corruptions, rather than *profectus*, or developments, and hence, that one cannot have a reversal of such councils. In this section, I will address briefly the matter of alterations of "non-definitive teaching" in a Vincentian mode. I will argue in this section that there is a difference between change that corrupts definitive teaching and alterations that do justice to doctrinal continuity—*eodem sensu eademque sententia*—but without denying obvious doctrinal development. This is especially the case when we consider the question of alterations.[62] For we have increasingly realized that, as Berkouwer correctly remarks, "one may not explain all the differences in the process of development as simply a different formulation of the same thing."[63]

In order to sharpen our focus on the difference between "definitive" and "non-definitive" teaching, consider the variety of theological notes regarding dogmas and doctrines, their magisterial authority, and their corresponding fiducial response.[64]

1. *De fide*: dogmas of the faith. These are divinely revealed truths contained in the word of God, written or handed down, and either (a) formally defined by a pope or council; or (b) taught by the ordinary and universal Magisterium. They constitute basic truths of faith, dogmas *per se*, definitive teaching that must be believed by Catholics with the assent of theological faith since they concern matters of faith. They are called primary objects of infallibility. The Congregation for the Doctrine of the Faith

---

[61] I develop this thesis in my book *Revelation, History, and Truth: A Hermeneutics of Dogma* (New York: Peter Lang Publishing, 2019).

[62] For an important treatment of alterations or reversals, see the magisterial treatment by Guarino, *Disputed Teachings*, especially chs. 4–5.

[63] Berkouwer, *De Kerk*, 1:237 [*The Church*, 191].

[64] See Congregation for the Doctrine of the Faith, Instruction on the Ecclesial Vocation of the Theologian *Donum veritatis* (May 24, 1990), §4 (hereafter, *Donum veritatis*).

(under then Cardinal Joseph Ratzinger) gives several examples of dogmas of the faith. For example,

> The articles of faith of the Creed, the various Christological dogmas and Marian dogmas; the doctrine of the institution of the sacraments by Christ and their efficacy with regard to grace; the doctrine of the real and substantial presence of Christ in the Eucharist and the sacrificial nature of the eucharistic celebration; the foundation of the Church by the will of Christ; the doctrine on the primacy and infallibility of the Roman Pontiff; the doctrine on the existence of original sin; the doctrine on the immortality of the spiritual soul and on the immediate recompense after death; the absence of error in the inspired sacred texts; the doctrine on the grave immorality of direct and voluntary killing of an innocent human being.[65]

2. *Fides ecclesiastica*: doctrines that are infallibly and irreformably taught to be truths; they are not revealed *per se* but they materially belong to Catholic faith. They are, in other words, inseparably connected with revealed truths concerning matters required to support the faith. To deny these truths entails the denial of revealed truths. These truths are called secondary objects of infallibility; they are necessarily connected with revelation by virtue of either a *historical relationship* or a *logical connection*, expressing a stage in the development of the understanding of revelation.[66] They are (a) formally defined by a pope or council, or (b) taught infallibly by the ordinary and universal Magisterium of the Church as a *sententia definitive tenenda*, meaning thereby that this second class of truths must be firmly

---

[65] See Congregation for the Doctrine of the Faith, Doctrinal Commentary on the Concluding Formula of the "*Professio fidei*" (June 29, 1998) (hereafter, "Doctrinal Commentary"). This is the Congregation's commentary on John Paul II's Apostolic Letter Motu Proprio *Ad tuendam fidem* (May 18, 1998), by which certain norms were inserted into the Code of Canon Law and into the Code of Canons of the Eastern Churches.

[66] For an illuminating account of these truths that are historically or logically connected with revelation, see Congregation for the Doctrine of the Faith, "Doctrinal Commentary," §11.

accepted and held. This is why they are called the "faith of the Church." Both primary and secondary objects of infallibility are such that they are at one and the same time not only fundamentally irreversible, or irreformable, and hence can never be contradicted but also may need to be gradually clarified over time in order to discern what truly pertains to the *depositum fidei*.[67] Examples of such doctrines include the teaching that priestly ordination is reserved exclusively to men, the illicitness of euthanasia, and the illicitness of prostitution and fornication.

3. *Sententia fidei proxima*: doctrine authoritatively but non-definitively taught by the ordinary and universal Magisterium. "When the Magisterium, not intending to act 'definitively,' teaches a doctrine [1] to aid a better understanding of Revelation and make explicit its contents, or [2] to recall how some teaching is in conformity with the truths of faith, or [3] finally to guard against ideas that are incompatible with these truths, *the response called for is that of the religious submission of will and intellect*."[68] This judgment is proximate to the faith.

4. *Sententia ad fidem pertinens*, or *theologice certa*: pertains to theological conclusions logically deduced from a proposition of faith and taught by the Magisterium that have a high degree of certainty.

5. *Sententia probabilis*: denotes probable opinion, although in theological discussion there are many other levels operating: well-founded, pious, and tolerated opinions (with the least authority).[69]

---

67 Catechism of the Catholic Church, §88: "The Church's Magisterium exercises the authority it holds from Christ to the fullest extent when it defines dogmas, that is, when it proposes . . . truths contained in divine Revelation or also when it proposes, in a definitive way, truths having a necessary connection with these."

68 *Donum veritatis*, §23 (emphasis added). See also Second Vatican Council, Dogmatic Constitution on the Church *Lumen gentium* (November 21, 1964), §25 (hereafter, *Lumen gentium*).

69 See Gavin D'Costa, *Vatican II: Catholic Doctrines on Jews & Muslims* (Oxford: Oxford University Press, 2014), 14–15, with some adaptation. Similarly, Ludwig Ott, *Fundamentals of Dogma*, trans. Patrick Lynch, ed. James Canon Bastible, rev. Robert Fastiggi (London: Baronius Press, 2018), 9–10, §8: "Note Regarding the Theological Grades of Certainty." See also Avery Cardinal Dulles, *Magisterium: Teacher and Guardian of the Faith* (Naples, FL: Sapientia Press, 2007), 83–84; and Harold E. Ernst, "The Theological Notes and the Interpretation of Doctrine," *Theological Studies* 63 (2002): 813–25.

The first three "theological notes" intend, according to the Congregation for the Doctrine of the Faith, "to better distinguish the order of the truths to which the believer adheres."[70] Correctly explaining the authentic meaning of these truths given by the Church's Magisterium is necessary, adds the Congregation, so that they "will be well understood, received and integrally preserved."[71]

In light of the Second Vatican Council, I think it is clear that there were alterations regarding the Church's position on some non-definitive teaching; see point three above, "*Sententia fidei proxima*: doctrine authoritatively but non-definitively taught by the ordinary and universal Magisterium." For example, undeniably, the Church altered its position on ecumenism and religious liberty. Does the alteration on ecumenism—from Pope Pius XI's 1928 encyclical letter *Mortalium animos*[72] to the Second Vatican Council's teaching on ecumenism, *Unitatis redintegratio*—change (in the sense of bring about a corruption of) the Church's fundamental ecclesiology?[73] No, there is an *apparent* contradiction between the earlier and later documents rather than a *real* contradiction.

The relationship between the *one* Church of Jesus Christ that subsists in the Catholic Church, on the one hand, and the *plurality* of churches on the other is the key issue.[74] "The Catholic Church dares and must dare to take the paradoxical position of attributing to herself in a unique way the singular form, 'the Church,'" says then Cardinal Joseph Ratzinger, "despite and in the midst of the plurality she has accepted."[75] The Second Vatican Council's ecclesiology indeed affirms that the Church of Jesus Christ is a *single* reality, historically realized in a concrete, visible form, subsisting in the Catholic Church, rather than affirming an erroneous ecclesial relativism or pluralism—a multiple-subsistence ecclesiology—in which the Catholic Church is one among many churches. Yet, the Council's ecclesiology also recognizes elements of truth and sanctification

---

[70] Congregation for the Doctrine of the Faith, "Doctrinal Commentary," §4.
[71] Congregation for the Doctrine of the Faith, "Doctrinal Commentary," §4.
[72] Pius XI, Encyclical Letter on Religious Unity *Mortalium animos* (January 6, 1928).
[73] Second Vatican Council, Decree on Ecumenism *Unitatis redintegratio* (November 21, 1964) (hereafter, *Unitatis redintegratio*).
[74] I address this question at length in my book *Pope Francis: The Legacy of Vatican II*, 2nd ed., revised and expanded (Hobe Sound, FL: Lectio Publishing, 2019 [2015]), 245–97.
[75] Joseph Cardinal Ratzinger, *Das neue Volk Gottes: Entwürfe zur Ekklesiologie*, 2nd ed. (Düsseldorf: Patmos-Verlag, 1977), 149; cited in Maximilian Heinrich Heim, *Joseph Ratzinger, Life in the Church and Living Theology*, trans. Michael J. Miller (San Francisco: Ignatius Press, 2007), 309.

outside the visible boundaries of the Church. Briefly, here is the dilemma that the Council's Catholic ecclesiology avoids:

- *Either* correctly affirming that the Church of Christ fully and totally subsists alone in its own right in the Catholic Church because the entire fullness of the means of salvation and of unity, which is not found in any other church, is present in her; and then implausibly denying that Orthodox churches and the historic churches of the Reformation are churches in any real—albeit analogical but no less meaningful—sense whatsoever, such that there exists an ecclesial wasteland or emptiness outside the Church's visible boundaries.[76]

- *Or* rightly affirming that they are churches in some sense, in a lesser or greater degree to the extent that there exist ecclesial elements of truth and sanctification in them, but then wrongly accepting ecclesiological relativism or pluralism—a multiple-subsistence ecclesiology—meaning thereby that the one Church of Christ Jesus subsists in many churches with the Catholic Church being merely one among many churches.[77]

The Second Vatican Council made a courageous step forward toward the unity of all Christians, according to Ratzinger.[78] Indeed, the movement toward ecumenism, he explains, "is the genuinely ecclesiological breakthrough of the Council" and, significantly, is an important illustration of the Vincentian hermeneutics of continuity and renewal. The Council found a way forward within "the logic of Catholicism for the ecclesial character of non-Catholic communities ... without detriment to Catholic identity."[79]

Does the alteration in the Church's stance on religious liberty—from Pope Gregory XVI's *Mirari vos*[80] to the Second Vatican Council's *Dignitatis*

---

[76] *Lumen gentium,* §8; *Unitatis redintegratio,* §§3–4; John Paul II, Encyclical Letter on Commitment to Ecumenism *Ut unum sint* (May 25, 1995), §14; Congregation for the Doctrine of the Faith, Declaration on the Unicity and Salvific Universality of Christ *Dominus Iesus* (August 6, 2000), §16.

[77] *Lumen gentium,* §8; *Unitatis redintegratio,* §§3–4, 20–21, 23. For helping me to formulate this dilemma, I am grateful to Msgr. Thomas Guarino.

[78] Joseph Ratzinger, *Principles of Catholic Theology,* trans. Sister Mary Francis McCarthy, S.N.D. (San Francisco: Ignatius Press, 1987 [1982]), 370.

[79] Ratzinger, *Principles of Catholic Theology,* 232.

[80] Gregory XVI, Encyclical Letter on Liberalism and Religious Indifferentism *Mirari vos* (August 15, 1832).

humanae[81]—represent a change, that is, a *permutatio* or a corruption, in her understanding of Christ's lordship and the relationship between freedom and truth? For example, has Christ's kingship been abandoned and has Christ therefore been uncrowned or dethroned, as some critics of the Council's affirmation of religious liberty hold?[82] Moreover, does the alteration in her position on religious liberty introduce a doctrinal change—again, a *permutatio* or corruption—in the Church's traditional teaching regarding the close connection between freedom and truth so that freedom undercuts objective truth?

No, Christ's kingship has not been abandoned and hence Christ has not been uncrowned or dethroned. Moreover, affirming religious liberty does not introduce a doctrinal change, a *permutatio* or corruption, in the Church's traditional teaching regarding the relationship between freedom and truth such that freedom undercuts objective truth. In both instances, such alterations represent developments. *Dignitatis humanae* states in a Vincentian mode that the Second Vatican Council "searched the sacred tradition and teaching of the Church, from which it draws forth new things that are always in harmony with the old."[83] Briefly, here, too, there is a *surface* contradiction between these earlier and later documents rather than a *real* contradiction. These alterations represent a development of her fundamental teaching rather than a doctrinal change.

To address the questions raised here, we need to apply several principles for interpreting ecclesial texts. First, we must consider the historical context in which the document originated, particularly if its statements are polemical and antithetical. All truth formulated for polemical reasons is partial, though true. This means that what these documents fail to say is not necessarily denied; furthermore, what they do say is true, albeit said insufficiently and imperfectly, less-than-balanced or comprehensive. What is said must be supplemented and hence interpreted with respect to the "full doctrine and the full life of the church," as Yves Congar rightly stated.[84] He adds, "Ambivalence, if there is any, will be resolved positively in the direction of orthodoxy."[85]

---

[81] Second Vatican Council, Declaration on Religious Freedom *Dignitatis humanae* (December 7, 1965) (hereafter, *Dignitatis humanae*).

[82] See Marcel Lefebvre, *They Have Uncrowned Him: From Liberalism to Apostasy, the Conciliar Tragedy* (Kansas City, MO: Angelus Press, 1988).

[83] *Dignitatis humanae*, §1.

[84] Congar, *True and False Reform*, 229–64.

[85] Congar, *True and False Reform*, 232.

A corollary of this hermeneutical principle is, secondly, the distinction between the propositional truths of faith and their reformulations or restatements, reminiscent of Vincent of Lérins. The import of this distinction is, according to Berkouwer, that it "implies that the Church's *formulation* of the truth could have, for various reasons, actually occasioned *misunderstandings* of the truth itself." In other words, the formulation or expression itself of the truth could be characterized by one-sidedness such that it is not "elevated above historical relativity in its analysis of the rejected errors."[86] Berkouwer correctly explains some of the consequences of a polemically defined truth:

> An unmistakable limitation and even, in a sense, an overshadowing of the fullness of truth is created by the defensive and polemical character of dogmatic pronouncements. Thus, Trent judged the reformation *sola fide* as a vain confidence, but failed to "delineate what could rightfully have been intended by the phrase *sola fide*." The historical and polemical conditionedness of church pronouncements must be respected. It seems both necessary and almost self-evident that previous pronouncements of dogma must be interpreted in this light.[87]

Still, Berkouwer adds, "*The interpretation need not bear the character of a revision which gives a new and different meaning to the dogma in order to make it acceptable to a new era.* Dogma must be understood in the light of revelation and of the intention of the church as that intention came to expression in a given period of history."[88]

Of course, Berkouwer's point is easily understood by distinguishing between the propositional truths of faith and their formulations in a given period of history. Those formulations presuppose an *analysis* of the position under judgment that is not necessarily accurate. Later on, the analysis may be seen as one-sided and hence mistaken, without denying the enduring validity of the truth that was being restated or reformulated.

Congar helpfully suggests that the formulation or expression of the truth, as well as the analysis of the error, could be characterized by one-sidedness.

---

86 G. C. Berkouwer, *Vatikaans Concilie en de Nieuwe Theologie* (Kampen, Netherlands: J. H. Kok, 1964), 77; in English: *The Second Vatican Council and the New Catholicism*, trans. Lewis B. Smedes (Grand Rapids, MI: Eerdmans, 1965), 69.

87 Berkouwer, *Vatikaans Concilie*, 77.

88 Berkouwer, *Vatikaans Concilie*, 77 (emphasis added).

This suggestion brings us to his distinction of two types of one-sidedness. He explains: "First, there is the possibility that this formulation, made in reaction to an error characterized by unilateralism, should itself become unilateral in its expression. Next, there is the possibility that the condemnation might include in its condemnation of the erroneous reactive element the seeds of truth as well, whose original ambivalence unfortunately became deviant."[89]

Applying these principles to *Mirari vos*, the understanding of religious liberty in 1832 entailed religious "indifferentism." According to Gregory XVI:

> This perverse opinion is spread on all sides by the fraud of the wicked who claim that it is possible to obtain the eternal salvation of the soul by the profession of any kind of religion, as long as morality is maintained. Surely, in so clear a matter, you will drive this deadly error far from the people committed to your care. With the admonition of the apostle that "there is one God, one faith, one baptism" [Eph 4:5] may those fear who contrive the notion that the safe harbor of salvation is open to persons of any religion whatever."[90]

Indifferentism, then, supported religious relativism—all religions are equally efficacious vehicles of salvation, equally true—relativism about truth, a subjectivist religious epistemology, and the privatization of Christianity.

Religious relativism is rejected as erroneous by *Dignitatis humanae*. The Second Vatican Council affirms that the truth itself regarding the Christian religion is one, objective and absolute, universally valid, and unchangeable. But the Council also affirms that objective truth is not undercut by affirming religious liberty. Truth itself is distinguished from the conditions under which one comes to know that something is true. The Council says of itself:

> The sacred Council begins by professing that God himself has made known to the human race how men by serving him can be saved and reach happiness in Christ. We believe that this one true religion continues to exist in the Catholic and Apostolic Church, to which the Lord Jesus entrusted the task of spreading it among all men when he said to the apostles: "Go therefore and make disciples of all nations baptizing them in the name of the Father

---

[89] Congar, *True and False Reform*, 208–13.

[90] Gregory XVI, *Mirari vos*, in *Acta Gregorii Papae XVI*, vol. 1, ed. A. M. Bernasconi (Rome: Typographia Polyglotta, 1901), 169–74.

and of the Son and of the Holy Spirit, teaching them to observe all that I have commanded you" (Mt 18:19–20).[91]

The document states further that there is a set of duties or obligations that apply to our responsible cognitive acts, such that the individual rationally submits to the claims of reality upon him; this is an obligation regarding the truth, laid upon him by truth itself:

> On their part, all men are bound to seek the truth, especially in what concerns God and His Church, and to embrace the truth they come to know, and to hold fast to it. This Vatican Council likewise professes its belief that it is upon the human conscience that these obligations fall and exert their binding force. Truth cannot impose itself except by virtue of its own truth, as it makes its entrance into the mind at once quietly and with power. Religious freedom, in turn, which men demand as necessary to fulfill their duty to worship God, has to do with immunity from coercion in civil society. Therefore it leaves untouched traditional Catholic doctrine on the moral duty of men and societies toward the true religion and toward the one Church of Christ.[92]

Gregory XVI's reaction to the error of religious and doctrinal indifferentism and all its entailments is indeed characterized by one-sidedness insofar as he did not consider that there were elements of truth in the view that he was condemning. *Dignitatis humanae* did not suffer from that one-sidedness. We live in a free society that is pluralistic. In that society, one is free to hold religious or irreligious views. The exercise of that freedom does not entail that I am rationally justified in holding those views, nor that those views that I hold are objectively true. By the terms of our free and open society, however, there exists in principle a public forum in which I am at liberty to persuade another person that he is not justified in holding his views and that they are not true. Here are the intellectual and moral conditions under which I may discover the truth and be justified in holding something to be true:

> Truth, however, is to be sought after in a manner proper to the dignity of the human person and his social nature. The inquiry

---

[91] *Dignitatis humanae*, §1.
[92] *Dignitatis humanae*, §1.

is to be free, carried on with the aid of teaching or instruction, communication and dialogue, in the course of which men explain to one another the truth they have discovered, or think they have discovered, in order thus to assist one another in the quest for truth. Moreover, as the truth is discovered, it is by a personal assent that men are to adhere to it.[93]

Yes, "error has no rights." Rather, it is persons who have rights, who are, in other words, the subjects of rights. Congar rightly explains: "Obviously, [error has no rights], but there are persons who do have rights; and those who are in error guard the right, founded in their very nature, to remain free from constraint in matters concerning their conscience."[94] In sum, the person has the right to hold even views that we judge to be unjustified and false. We are talking here of legal rights grounded in the dignity of the person to be free from the state's constraints and not epistemic of rights. "It is necessary to distinguish between error, which always merits repudiation, and the person in error, who never loses the dignity of being a person even when he is flawed by false or inadequate religious notions."[95]

Does the affirmation of religious liberty entail the rejection of the kingship of Christ, dethroning or uncrowning him? No, the Second Vatican Council is gripped by St. Paul's vision of cosmic redemption in Christ (Col 1:9–23). In this light, the Council affirms, "The good news of Christ continually renews the life and culture of fallen man . . . as it were from within; it fortifies, completes and restores [it] in Christ."[96] This view "gives Christ, the Redeemer of man, center of the universe and of history, the scope of completely renewing the lives of men 'by opening the vast fields of culture to His saving power.'"[97] Basic to this vision is the truth that *the whole creation is recapitulated in Christ*.[98] In the written word of God, the lordship of Jesus Christ over creation and redemption is revealed (Phlm 2:11). Thus, the Council teaches, "The Lord is the goal of human history, the focal point of the desires of history and

---

[93] *Dignitatis humanae*, §2.

[94] Yves Congar, *Challenge to the Church: The Case of Archbishop Lefebvre*, trans. Paul Inwood (Huntington, IN: Our Sunday Visitor, 1976), 44.

[95] *Gaudium et spes*, §28.

[96] *Gaudium et spes*, §58.

[97] Pontifical Council for Culture, *Towards a Pastoral Approach to Culture* (May 23, 1999), §6, quoting John Paul II, Homily of the Enthronement Mass (October 22, 1978).

[98] *Gaudium et spes*, §38.

civilization, the center of mankind, the joy of all hearts, and the fulfillment of all aspirations."[99]

Furthermore, then, there is an important distinction to be drawn between the "old Christendom" and the "new Christendom." The former is the idea of an ecclesiastically unified culture and hence the state establishment of the Church. The latter pertains to the idea of a sanctified laity whose unique responsibility is to be engaged in the transformation of the full spectrum of culture for the sake of Christ's lordship.[100] This is the ecclesiology of the Second Vatican Council as found in chapters 4 and 5 of *Lumen gentium*, in *Apostolicam actuositatem*,[101] and in John Paul II's *Christifideles laici*.[102] The point here, Aidan Nichols correctly notes, "is to permeate society and culture to the degree possible with the Christian spirit, and to maximize the number of occasions in civic life where testimony to Christ and his Church might be given."[103] On this view, the new Christendom raises questions about the means and form in which the kingship of Christ should be promoted and obtained. Suffice it to say that on this score there are clear differences with the "old Christendom" insofar as the latter involved a hierarchical ecclesiastical authority over the full spectrum of culture. However, the rejection of an ecclesiastically unified culture does not entail that Christ's kingship has been abandoned and hence that Christ has been uncrowned or dethroned. What is clear is that the "Church wants to exercise an influence on persons, through persons, through the channel of their beliefs and the force of truth itself."[104]

CONCLUSION

I have considered Vincent of Lérins's fundamental theological account of the development of Christian doctrine in his chief work, the *Commonitorium*. Vincent's work bears an enduring originality and relevance for two reasons. First, he attends to the question of interpretive pluralism, which Vincent

---

[99] *Gaudium et spes*, §45.

[100] It would take us too far afield here to discuss the role that priests, bishops, and even popes play in the "new Christendom."

[101] Second Vatican Council, Decree on the Apostolate of the Laity *Apostolicam actuositatem* (November 18, 1965).

[102] John Paul II, Post-Synodal Apostolic Exhortation on the Vocation and the Mission of the Lay Faithful in the Church and in the World *Christifideles laici* (December 30, 1988).

[103] Aidan Nichols, O.P. and Moyra Doorly, *The Council in Question: A Dialogue with Catholic Traditionalism* (Herefordshire: Gracewing, 2011), 85–86.

[104] Congar, *Challenge to the Church*, 45.

suggests is nearly anarchic in his time, explaining why we need to justify our interpretations of Scripture in light of the Church's authoritative Tradition. Second, he also shows how temporality can be of theological advantage by arguing that there is a historical dimension to the explicitation of unchangeable doctrinal truth. The core question for Vincent is about the relationship between history and truth, a determinate truth that is indefinitely transmissible in genuine development throughout time such that the material continuity, identity, and universality of the truths of dogma can be maintained according to the same meaning and the same judgment—*eodem sensu eademque sententia.*

Vincent's concern in the *Commonitorium* is exclusively with definitive teaching. Nevertheless, I have given an account of the development of non-definitive teaching in a Vincentian mode. My argument is that only apparent inconsistencies exist between earlier and later ecclesial documents (e.g., *Mirari vos* and *Dignitatis humanae*) rather than a *real* contradiction. There is an underlying continuity in the alteration of non-definitive teaching, such as those on ecumenism and religious liberty. There is a difference between change that corrupts definitive teaching and alterations that do justice to doctrinal continuity—*eodem sensu eademque sententia*—but without denying the obvious development of doctrine. These alterations in non-definitive teaching represent *profectus*, or developments of the Church's fundamental teaching rather than a doctrinal change, which, in Vincent's sense, is *permutatio* or corruption.[105]

---

[105] My gratitude to Fr. Kevin Flannery, S.J., for his important help in improving my article for publication.

THE LOGIC OF DOCTRINAL DEVELOPMENT ACCORDING TO JOHN HENRY NEWMAN

Kevin L. Flannery, S.J.

Saint John Henry Newman's *An Essay on the Development of Christian Doctrine* was composed in the months leading up to his crossing the threshold, in October of 1845, from the Anglican communion into the Roman Catholic Church. But the seed of the theory put forth in that book had been sown in Newman's mind well before that time. When he was just twenty-two years of age and a recently elected fellow at Oriel College, Oxford, a somewhat senior colleague there, Richard Whately, asked Newman to assist him in preparing an article on logic for the *Encyclopaedia Metropolitana*. Newman's work on this article brought him to see clearly that reasoning involves two processes, one more basic, the other drawing upon the first, so that ideas might remain in essence the same even when elaborated logically.

These two factors—that which remains the same and its development— are associated by Newman in various places (and in different ways) with two interrelated principles found in Vincent of Lérins's *Commonitorium*: the principle that Christian doctrine concerns "what has been held everywhere, always, and by all"[1] and the principle that, even given the former principle, Church teachings develop, even while remaining in their essence the

---

[1] Vincent of Lérins, *Commonitorium* 2.5 (using the section and subsection numbering found in Vincent of Lérins, *Commonitorium, Excerpta*, ed. R. Demeulenaere, Corpus Christianorum Series Latina, vol. 64 [Turnhout: Brepols, 1985], 125–231).

same: "Small are a baby's limbs, a youth's are larger, yet they are the same."[2] These two principles and their interrelationship constitute a leitmotif in what here follows.

Newman's work on Whately's article on logic is the subject of section I of the present essay. In section II, we look at how the ideas set out in that article find their way into Newman's last sermon at St. Mary's, the university church at Oxford, preached in 1842, and also into his *An Essay in Aid of a Grammar of Assent* (which we will refer to as *Grammar of Assent*), published many years later in 1870, but very closely related to what he had learned while working with Whately. In section III, we examine the first part of *An Essay on the Development of Christian Doctrine* (which we will refer to as *Development of Doctrine*); that part lays the intellectual foundations of the theory regarding development. In section IV, which constitutes approximately half of the present essay, we examine *Development of Doctrine*'s second part, where Newman presents his seven "notes" characterizing genuine developments of doctrine.

I. NEWMAN'S PRESENCE IN WHATELY'S LOGIC AND THE PRESENCE OF WHATELY'S LOGIC IN NEWMAN

Although in his later life, after the rupture of his friendship with Newman, Whately downplayed the former's role in the composition of the *Encyclopaedia Metropolitana* article "Logic," there is good reason to believe that Newman was closely—and, to some extent, immediately—involved. The contents of the article were incorporated into Whately's *Elements of Logic*, published in 1826, in the preface of which Whately acknowledges Newman, who, he says, "actually composed a considerable portion of the work as it now stands, from manuscripts not designed for publication, and who is the original author of several pages."[3] In a letter written in 1852, Newman says that Whately originally made available to him some handwritten "analytical dialogues" on logic and proposed that he "turn them into the shape of a treatise," partly because,

---

[2] *Commonitorium* 23.4, referenced in John Henry Newman, *An Essay on the Development of Doctrine*, foreword by Ian Ker (Notre Dame: University of Notre Dame Press, 1989), 172. References in the main text and in parentheses are to this version. This volume reproduces and, for the most part, follows the pagination of the edition published in 1878 by Basil Montagu Pickering (London). In the Notre Dame publication, pages 381 and 382 contain text not appearing in that edition.

[3] Richard Whately, preface to *Elements of Logic: Comprising the Substance of the Article in the Encyclopædia Metropolitana, with Additions, &c.* (London: Mawman, 1826), viii.

suggests Newman, Whately "wished to be saved the trouble of going over the same ground twice."[4]

Sections of the *Elements of Logic* that have the ring of Newman's own elegant prose include the introduction to book 4 and the initial section (§1) of the second chapter of the same book, which is entitled "Dissertation on the Province of Reasoning." Book 4 begins, in effect, by situating the work's general approach to logic historically. When Whately (and Newman) began writing on logic, the academic climate in England was hostile to the discipline, associating it with (Roman Catholic) scholastic disputatiousness. The disputatiousness itself these same academics associated with deduction—and so with Aristotle's syllogistic—which they attempted to substitute with induction, itself linked since the time of Francis Bacon with scientific progress. Aristotle's logical writings had for centuries been called the *organon* ("the tool"); in 1620, Bacon offered to the world—and, in particular, to scientists—a *Novum Organon* ("new tool").

The problem with this general approach as it developed historically was that it tended to interpret Bacon's talk of a new *organon* quite radically: induction was to take the place of deduction, even though Aristotle himself had distinguished the two and accepted them both, each in its proper sphere. Writes Whately, by way of Newman: "I would deprecate the sophistry of striving to depreciate what is called 'the school-logic,' by perpetually *contrasting* it with systems with which it has nothing in common but the name, and whose object is essentially different."[5] In the more technical parts of *Elements of Logic*, Whately strives to place the syllogistic in a positive light. He was successful in this; his book was instrumental in making the study of logic more central to the curriculum of studies at the University of Oxford. Newman's instinctive interests were more in the other direction—toward, that is, the process of discovering truth. But they both understood the necessity—and the interlinking—of both: the discovery of truth and its logical (even syllogistic) elaboration. As we shall see, the two factors are integral to Newman's theory of the development of doctrine.

Although Whately's logic was a turning point in British academia, most of his subsequent writings took up religious themes, as was appropriate for

---

4   John Henry Newman, *Letters and Diaries*, vol. 15, *The Achilli Trial: January 1852 to December 1853*, ed. Charles Stephan Dessain and Vincent Ferrer Blehl, S.J. (Oxford University Press, 1964), 176.

5   Whately, *Elements of Logic*, 250–51 (emphasis in the original).

one who would become the Church of Ireland's archbishop of Dublin. He and Newman shared, of course, an appreciation of the essential role of reasoning—both logical and evidential—in all pursuits worthy of the adjective "human"; but eventually, it became apparent that their respective ways of understanding evidence as related to faith differed. Whately, when dealing with religious matters, chose to distinguish reasoning and faith and to give priority to reasoning as providing evidence for faith. The evidence he focused upon was the evidence of miracles as reported in Scripture. Newman, on the other hand, saw the two, reasoning and faith, once faith is bestowed, as being present together. He was acutely aware that the reasoning in which a person might have great confidence as pointing *toward* the faith might easily disappoint and so finish in lack of faith—or be misdirected and so finish in schism or heresy.

One sees how radically these two approaches to religious matters differ in Whately's book *Easy Lessons on Christian Evidences*, published in 1838. By that time, the "Tractarian Movement," which sought to bring the Anglican Church closer to its Catholic roots and within which Newman was initially a prime mover, was in full course. Whately was strongly opposed to the movement and, in particular, to its emphasis upon the doctrinal authority of (especially) the early Church. Whately saw a parallel between the latter emphasis and what he called "the pagan religions." "The Christian religion," he wrote, "was distinguished from these . . . by its resting on evidence;—by its offering a reason,—and requiring Christians to be able to give a reason, for believing it."[6]

In 1846—shortly, that is, after his conversion—Newman would come across the following remark in Thomas Aquinas's commentary on Peter Lombard's *Sentences*:

> One who knows in a scientific way [*sciens*] has both assent and reasoning [*cogitationem*]—not however reasoning *with* assent but reasoning before assent, for reason leads a person to understanding by way of resolution [that is, by linking a thesis up with principles that are known in themselves]. But the believer [*credens*] has simultaneously assent and reasoning [*assensum simul et cogitationem*], for the intellect is not brought *to* principles that are known in themselves.[7]

---

6   Richard Whately, *Easy Lessons on Christian Evidences* (London: Parker, 1838), 18.
7   Thomas Aquinas, *Scriptum super libros Sententiarum Magistri Petri Lombardi Episcopi Parisiensis*, ed. Pierre Mandonnet and Maria Fabianus Moos (Paris: Lethielleux, 1929–1947), 3.23.2.2, *solutio*

In the larger passage in which this remark is found, it is clear that Aquinas also holds that belief is not mere opinion but rather "perfect assent." He insists, however, that it is also practical and so still "open-ended," in the sense that it involves the will's always going toward the good it already grasps as its end.[8] Newman regarded in particular Aquinas's statement that the believer "has simultaneously assent and reasoning" as confirmation of what he had long thought and what—methodologically but also theologically—had separated him from Whately.

II. "UNIVERSITY SERMON 15" AND *AN ESSAY IN AID OF A GRAMMAR OF ASSENT*

This emphasis upon reasonable assent to faith as a single thing rather than upon reasoning as a distinct process that might (or might not) lead to faith may appear to militate against the possibility of doctrines developing. A content of reason embraced by faith must remain simply that, it might be argued; it cannot develop. Newman confronts this issue directly and amply in his *Grammar of Assent*, published in 1870, well after the first edition of *Development of Doctrine* (1845). But Newman was thinking about the relationship between the seed of faith and its development at least as early as 1843 when he preached the last of his university sermons on "the theory of developments in religious doctrine." Accordingly, let us begin by looking briefly at that sermon—now known as "University Sermon 15"—and then move on to the more elaborated position set out in *Grammar of Assent.*[9]

Sermon 15 was preached on February 2, the Feast of the Purification of the Blessed Virgin Mary. The verse introducing the published version of the sermon is, accordingly, Luke 2:19: "But Mary kept all these things, pondering them in her heart." One might suppose that, for Newman, Mary would represent the simple acceptance of the faith as distinct from its theological elaboration; but that is not the way he frames his argument.

---

1 (hereafter, *In Sent*). Newman's remarks on the passage appear in appendix III of David A. Pailin, *The Way to Faith: An Examination of Newman's* Grammar of Assent *as a Response to the Search for Certainty in Faith* (London: Epworth, 1969), 205–206.

8   Immediately after Thomas's just-quoted words about "the believer," he says that the person who has an opinion "has a thought without perfect assent" (*Opinans autem habet cogitationem sine assensu perfecto*).

9   References to this work are to John Henry Newman, *An Essay in Aid of a Grammar of Assent*, ed. Ian T. Ker (Oxford: Clarendon Press, 1985).

Thus St. Mary is our pattern of faith, both in the reception and in the study of Divine Truth. She does not think it enough to accept, she dwells upon it; not enough to possess, she uses it; not enough to assent, she develops it; not enough to submit the Reason, she reasons upon it; not indeed reasoning first, and believing afterwards, with Zacharias, yet first believing without reasoning, next from love and reverence, reasoning after believing. And thus she symbolizes to us, not only the faith of the unlearned, but of the doctors of the Church also, who have to investigate, and weigh, and define, as well as to profess the Gospel; to draw the line between truth and heresy; to anticipate or remedy the various aberrations of wrong reason; to combat pride and recklessness with their own arms; and thus to triumph over the sophist and the innovator.[10]

It is apparent then that Newman, although he certainly held that a development is distinct from that from which it develops, recognized too that the faithful mind that assents is the same mind—the same intellect—that formulates propositions about that to which it assents, exercising both at the first moment and then subsequently the same intellectual capacities.

Newman goes on in Sermon 15 to say things that remind one of Vincent of Lérins, portions of whose *Commonitorium* he had published in translation in *British Magazine*. Speaking, for instance, of the way in which an opinion might with time be expressed differently, Newman quotes Mark 4:28 ("first the blade, then the ear, after that the full corn in the ear") and then says that any changes "involved no abrupt revolution, or reaction, or fickleness of mind, but have been the birth of an idea, the development, in explicit form, of what was already latent within it."[11] A bit farther along, speaking more explicitly of Christian doctrine, he remarks that "particular propositions, then, which are used to express portions of the great idea vouchsafed to us, can never really be confused with the idea itself which all such propositions taken together can but reach, and cannot exceed."[12]

When he so spoke from the pulpit in the University Church of St. Mary

---

[10] John Henry Newman, *Fifteen Sermons Preached before the University of Oxford, between A.D. 1826 and 1843* (London: Rivingtons, 1880), 313. A critical edition of this same work, edited with introduction and notes by James David Earnest and Gerard Tracey, has recently been published by Oxford University Press.

[11] Newman, *Fifteen Sermons*, 321.

[12] Newman, *Fifteen Sermons*, 331.

the Virgin, he was, of course, still an Anglican; but the ideas then and there expressed would be the basis of the theory of development that would carry him into the Catholic Church. Newman was able to identify the two principles of the Church's understanding in these regards: first, that doctrine does indeed grow, but, secondly, that, over the course of this growth, there is something that remains the same. Something closely parallel occurs in animal generation and growth. The deposit of the faith received initially and pondered by the Mother of God is like the fertilized egg: even at the earliest stages in an animal's life, there is present a single, active, organic entity. We can compare Mary's "pondering" to the inherent activity of this early organic entity. This activity, informing that same organic entity, eventually produces the animal's limbs and organs. These developments, which are present potentially in the undeveloped animal, are dependent for their very existence upon the organic entity as existing earlier, but it is not so dependent upon them (that is, *as* developed), for it can (and did) exist before them and not the reverse. The developed limbs and organs serve to maintain the life of the mature animal.

Grammar of Assent is primarily about how the object of the faith gets planted in the soul of the believer. As we have seen, Newman does not regard that object as being somehow held accountable to the human process of evidential verification of the sort dictated by Whately. Ultimately it is a gift, not the merited consequence of human efforts. As he says at one point: "we need the interposition of a Power, greater than human teaching and human argument, to make our beliefs true and our minds one."[13] Nonetheless, it is important for us to understand the individual human, intellectual context within which faith arrives in order to account for (among other things) how our understanding of that object develops.

Newman says in *Grammar of Assent* that, in his basic approach to this issue, "Aristotle has been my master."[14] He quotes a passage from the sixth book of the *Nicomachean Ethics* in which Aristotle says that a young man is capable of becoming a mathematician but not a philosopher or a natural scientist. The reason for this, he says, is that "the one study [mathematics] deals with abstractions, while the other studies [philosophy and the natural sciences] gain their principles from experience, and in the latter subjects youths do not

---

[13] John Henry Newman, *An Essay in Aid of a Grammar of Assent*, ed. I. T. Ker (Oxford: Clarendon Press, 1985), 242.

[14] Newman, *Grammar of Assent*, 227.

give assent, but make assertions, but in the former they know what it is that they are handling."[15] Young men are incapable of truly assenting to the things taught to them by an experienced philosopher or natural scientist: they can just "make assertions," repeating that to which the expert assents. Since, however, mathematics does not require that sort of experience, young men can, with sufficient attention, master it.

Very important is the fact that Newman uses the word "assent" ("youths do not give assent") as his translation of *pisteuousin*, a derivative of the Greek verb *pisteuein* which means "to put faith in" or "to believe." Youths, he maintains, do not assent to—believe—the truths of (for example) biology; but biologists who have experience in the field do. Newman is speaking here about what we might call "secular faith"; but he is also in effect explaining how Christian faith makes use of—is infused into—the human soul. For, the goal of this entire volume, this "essay in aid of a grammar of assent," is to describe the Christian faith as a particular instance of faith (assent) understood more broadly. The biologist who knows animals knows something real, about which he can also speculate scientifically. The Mother of God, together with the disciples of her Son, who preserved for posterity the deposit of the faith, also knew something real, and they, together with those who encounter that same object, can and do operate scientifically with respect to that very object—which is subject, however, as is any science, to the dictates of human reason itself, especially the principle of non-contradiction.

What is of concern to Newman in all of this becomes more apparent in remarks that he makes in his 1865 *Apologia pro Vita Sua* regarding two scholars who influenced his thought as it developed and for whom he always maintained the greatest respect. The first and earlier influence was Joseph Butler (d. 1752), who "teaches us that probability is the guide of life." According to some people, says Newman, the problem with this theory is that it tends to destroy "absolute certainty" and "full internal assent."[16] The second influence was John Keble, Newman's close ally in the Tractarian Movement. Keble, relays Newman, attempted to resolve the difficulty associated with Butler's approach "by ascribing the firmness of assent which we give to religious doctrine, not to

---

[15] *Nicomachean Ethics* 6.8.1142a18–20 (Newman's translation); quoted in Newman, *Grammar of Assent*, 266–67.

[16] John Henry Newman, *Newman's* Apologia pro vita sua: *The Two Versions of 1864 & 1865, Preceded by Newman's and Kingsley's Pamphlets, with an Introduction by Wilfrid Ward* (London: H. Frowde, 1913), 121.

the probabilities which introduced it, but to the living power of faith and love which accepted it."[17] Newman says of Keble's alternative approach that it "was beautiful and religious, but it did not even profess to be logical."[18] Newman's own approach to such matters—his fusion of "antecedent probability" and faith—is not so much an alternative to the approaches of Butler and Keble but rather a combination of the two.

As Newman tells us a number of times in his autobiographical writings, constitutionally, he was not attracted to logic. He was, however, a notably self-critical man, constantly asking himself whether his attitudes and prejudices were reasonable and right or not. It was this positive character trait that brought him to the insight that, although syllogistic reasoning has its limitations, especially inasmuch as it is necessarily dependent upon knowledge acquired independently of the syllogistic itself, the act of reason that grasps a syllogism is the same act involved in the most basic assent of faith. A syllogism is simply the bringing together of two propositions and seeing that they are actually one. A holds of all Bs and B holds of all Cs. "But," the reasoner spontaneously recognizes, "that is just to say that all the Cs are A." When the disciples of Christ reflected upon and recounted the details of his life, death, and resurrection, they did not force those ideas into the syllogisms set out in the early chapters of Aristotle's *Prior analytics*. But they did reason about them, and reasoning is the very thing that those employing syllogisms do, although in a particularly self-conscious manner.

This means—this entails—that any further reflections by theologians, synods, councils, etc., upon what the disciples left to the Christian Church must maintain logical consistency with that original deposit of faith, for the presumption is that any such further reflections are united to it: they are one with it. As Newman explains in the fifth chapter of *Grammar of Assent*:

> The Catholic intellect makes a survey and a catalogue of the doctrines contained in the *depositum* of revelation as committed to the Church's keeping; it locates, adjusts, defines them each, and brings them together into a whole. Moreover, it takes particular aspects or portions of them; it analyzes them, whether into first principles really such, or into hypotheses of an illustrative character. It forms generalizations, and gives names to them. All these

---

[17] Newman, *Apologia*, 121.

[18] Newman, *Apologia*, 122

deductions are true, if rightly deduced, because they are deduced from what is true; and therefore in one sense they are a portion of the *depositum* of faith or *credenda*, while in another sense they are additions to it.[19]

He goes on then immediately to invoke the principle of non-contradiction: "If a proposition is true, its contradictory is false. If then a man believes that Christ is God, he believes also, and that necessarily, that to say He is not God is false, and that those who so say are in error."[20]

III. *AN ESSAY ON THE DEVELOPMENT OF CHRISTIAN DOCTRINE*, PART ONE

As mentioned above, Newman finished *Development of Doctrine* in 1845, just as he was converting to the Catholic Church. In 1878, he published what he called a revised edition of the work, from which a number of passages of the 1845 edition had been eliminated and some rewritten; he also reordered various sections of the work. Here we shall be following the ordering of the 1878 edition.

The first part of *Development of Doctrine*, entitled "Doctrinal Developments Viewed in Themselves" and comprising an introduction and four chapters, can be read as a disquisition upon Vincent of Lérins's principle, *Quod ubique, quod semper, quod ab omnibus creditum est* ("What has been held everywhere, always, and by all").[21] The second part of *Development of Doctrine* can be understood as an application of Vincent's other principle, which (as we have seen) has to do more directly with development.

In the introduction to the book itself, Newman speaks of "Anglican divines" who cite the first of Vincent's principles in order to defend their version of the Christian faith. "They maintain," he says, "that history first presents to us a pure Christianity in East and West, and then a corrupt."[22] Referring to the *via media* that he had formerly espoused, he speaks of Vincent's "principle" as "congenial, or, as it may be said, native to the Anglican mind, which takes up a middle position, neither discarding the Fathers nor acknowledging the Pope."

[19] Newman, *Grammar of Assent*, 99.
[20] Newman, *Grammar of Assent*, 99.
[21] Vincent of Lérins, *Commonitorium* 2.5.
[22] John Henry Newman, *An Essay on the Development of Christian Doctrine* (London: James Toovey, 1845), 10.

But, for all its congeniality, he says, the principle "as it is commonly understood by English divines" presents seemingly intractable problems:[23]

> It admits of being interpreted in one of two ways: if it be narrowed for the purpose of disproving the catholicity of the [1564] creed of Pope Pius [IV], it becomes also an objection to the [fifth century] Athanasian; and if it be relaxed to admit the doctrines retained by the English Church, it no longer excludes certain doctrines of Rome which that Church denies. It cannot at once condemn St. Thomas and St. Bernard, and defend St. Athanasius and St. Gregory Nazianzen.[24]

How then to sustain Vincent's *Quod ubique* principle in the face of these awkward facts? This is no straightforward task even for those who would invoke it favorably from within the Catholic theological tradition. Newman speaks of a council that occurred at Antioch "in the middle of the third century," describing it as the only "great doctrinal council" to have occurred before the First Council of Nicaea, which latter affirmed "the *homoousion*" or the idea of Christ's being of one substance with the Father. For all its seeming authority, however, "the Fathers there assembled [at Antioch], for whatever reason, condemned, or at least withdrew, when it came into the dispute, the word *homoousion*, which was afterwards received at Nicæa as the special symbol of Catholicism against Arius" (16). He goes on to speak similarly of a number of early theologians, including Ignatius of Antioch and Justin Martyr. If we limit ourselves "to what they expressly state," says Newman, "St. Ignatius may be considered as a Patripassian [and] St. Justin arianizes."[25] Newman's means of making sense of what thus might appear a cacophony of voices is the means he expounds more fully (as we have seen) in *Grammar of Assent*—that is to say, his analysis of the way that faith occurs in the human soul. It is not a matter of subjecting the claims of the Church to antecedent evidential verification but rather of one day—and in subsequent days—being struck by the coherence of the story that the Church tells.

This sort of thing is part of everyday life: a witness, for instance, makes a claim about something that has happened and, despite imprecision of

---

[23] Newman, *Development of Doctrine*, 15.

[24] Newman, *Development of Doctrine*, 11–12.

[25] Newman, *Development of Doctrine*, 17.

recollection and maladroit efforts to express himself, strikes a jury as "making sense." Some of the man's imprecision or even confusion might be the consequence of his struggling to explain even to himself what caused something else to occur: he is clear about the effect but vague about the cause. Accordingly, the jury might find his causal account implausible in part but accept that something brought about the effect—perhaps something of which they have some information from another source. Juries are not skeptical historicists. They realize that *something* happened in the past; having weighed the bits of evidence presented to them, they can (although they might not) agree upon an account that makes sense of it all. A similar thing happens in tracing the historical origins of a doctrine. Now that we have the doctrine, we understand how it emerged from the (presumably) well-meaning but sometimes imprecise formulations of those involved in the discussions about it.

Very often, too, understanding how a doctrine emerged involves realizing that earlier than the date at which it did emerge the historical context did not require it. Newman speaks of this with respect to the papacy itself. He acknowledges, for instance, that Ignatius of Antioch (born not long after Christ's death) "is silent in his epistles on the subject of the pope's authority"—even though he is most assertive regarding episcopal authority itself. But, Newman argues, "if in fact that authority could not be in active operation then, such silence is not so difficult to account for. . . . Christians at home did not yet quarrel with Christians abroad; they quarrelled at home among themselves."[26] "For St. Ignatius to speak of popes, when it was a matter of bishops, would have been like sending an army to arrest a housebreaker."[27] This is not to say, however, that when the need for explicitly papal authority did present itself the Church did not find its basis in the deposit of faith.

How then are we to understand the sort of reasoning that is integral to the faith? Throughout his writings, Newman cites also another passage from the *Nicomachean Ethics*, this one from the first book: "A well-educated man will expect exactness in every class of subject, according as the nature of the thing admits; for it is much the same mistake to put up with a mathematician using probabilities, and to require demonstration of an orator."[28] In the place in *Development of Doctrine* where he quotes this passage, it is apparent that

---

[26] Newman, *Development of Doctrine*, 149.

[27] Newman, *Development of Doctrine*, 150.

[28] Aristotle, *Nichomachean Ethics* 1094b23–27; quoted in Newman, *Grammar of Assent*, 266; and Newman, *Development of Doctrine*, 113.

Newman is (with good reason) associating the probabilities of which Aristotle speaks with his own concept of "antecedent probability"—such as allows one to discover sense in a historical account. This is not to say, however, that antecedent probability itself is always reliable. In the same place, Newman immediately adds: "Of course, as is plain, we may err grievously in the antecedent view which we start with, and in that case, our conclusions may be wide of the truth; but that only shows that we had no right to assume a premise which was untrustworthy, not that our reasoning was faulty."[29] As we shall see shortly, Newman recognizes that a supposed development might not be a development at all but a corruption. Those who speculate about doctrine must, therefore, avoid faulty reasoning; and those responsible for passing on the faith intact must be prepared to identify corruptions as what they are.

In the first part of *Development of Doctrine*, which we are presently considering, Newman associates the constancy of Christian doctrine with the infallibility of the Church, including the infallibility of popes. He sees an analogous relationship between conscience and Church authority. In "natural religion," he says, conscience is supreme; in revealed religion, that is, in the Church, the authority of "apostle, or pope, or Church, or bishop" is supreme. He acknowledges that conscience is not infallible; but, consistent with Aquinas, he points out that even an erroneous conscience is binding.[30] Something analogous can be asserted with respect to "the See of St. Peter": "it is not in all cases infallible, it may err beyond its special province, but it has in all cases a claim on our obedience."[31] In other words, there is good antecedent reason to assent to a papal teaching.

Within this same context, Newman quotes St. Robert Bellarmine, who maintains that "the Pope with general council cannot err, either in framing decrees of faith or general precepts of morality"—but also adds that "it is possible for the Pope, even as pope, and with his own assembly of councillors, or with general council, to err in particular controversies of fact" and that "it is possible for him to err as a private doctor, even in universal questions of right, whether of faith or of morals, and that from ignorance, as sometimes happens to other doctors." Bellarmine says also that, even in these latter cases, a pope "or his own particular council . . . is to be obeyed by all

---

[29] Newman, *Development of Doctrine*, 114.
[30] Newman, *Development of Doctrine*, 86. Cf. Thomas Aquinas, *Summa theologiae* I-II, q. 19, a. 5.
[31] Newman, *Development of Doctrine*, 86.

the faithful."[32] A Christian, and especially a Catholic, owes a papal teaching respect and obedience, for the papacy is more closely linked to Christ's promises than any other office in the Church. On the other hand, just as a person possessed of an erroneous conscience which is correctable (or "vincible") is obliged to correct it, so also is the papacy obliged to correct an erroneous or misleading teaching.[33]

Newman makes some pertinent remarks elsewhere in his writings, especially in his "Letter Addressed to the Duke of Norfolk," published in 1875.[34] They are not easy to reconcile with the remarks just considered; it is worth noting, however, that they were made between the first and the revised editions of *Development of Doctrine*. In the letter, Newman asserts that a pope is not to be obeyed if doing so would be immoral—if a politician is ordered, for instance, to violate a rightful oath or a soldier is ordered not to fight in a war he believes in conscience not to be an unjust war. In the same work, Newman cites Pope Pius IX's dogmatic constitution *Pastor aeternus* to the effect that any papal teaching "will be without any claim to be considered binding on the belief of Catholics, unless it is referable to the Apostolic *depositum*, through the channel either of Scripture or Tradition; and, though the Pope is the judge whether it is so referable or not, yet the necessity of his professing to abide by this reference is in itself a certain limitation of his dogmatic action."[35]

Although during this period of his life (that is, between the first and the revised editions of *Development of Doctrine*) Newman's position on papal infallibility is not entirely clear, it is apparent that, in that work, he was interested in showing that the often-disordered process of doctrinal development is not incompatible with the truth that the faith rests upon a solid foundation. The stable and perennial core of doctrine present within and governing the Church's developing magisterial teaching allows us, suggests Newman, to continue to invoke Vincent of Lérins's *Quod ubique* principle. In the introduction to the fourth and final chapter of the first part of *Development of Doctrine*, Newman quotes a work on mechanics in which the argument is made that, although "on account of the great nicety required in adjusting the instruments and making

---

[32] Newman, *Development of Doctrine*, 86–87; see also Bellarmine's *De Romano pontifice* 4.2. See also Edward Feser, "Magisterium: The Teaching Authority of the Church," in this volume.

[33] Aquinas, *Summa theologiae* I-II, q. 19, a. 6.

[34] John Henry Newman, *Certain Difficulties Felt by Anglicans in Catholic Teaching Considered*, vol. 2 (London: Longmans, Green, and Co., 1896), 175–347.

[35] Newman, *Certain Difficulties*, vol. 2, 329–30.

the experiments, and on account of the effects of friction, and the air's resistance, which cannot entirely be removed" such experiments can never establish an exact correspondence with the laws of motion, they do in fact confirm them. "And thus," says Newman, "a converging evidence in favour of certain doctrines may, under circumstances, be as clear a proof of their Apostolical origin as can be reached practically from the *Quod semper, quod ubique, quod ab omnibus*" of Vincent of Lérins.[36]

In the final remarks of the same chapter, Newman quotes favorably a passage by Pope Innocent I, who, in the year 417, associated his own "care of all the churches" with "the *arcana* of the Apostolical dignity" and "the form of the ancient rule, which you know, as well as I, has been preserved always by the whole world." Says Newman: "Here the Pope appeals, as it were, to the Rule of Vincentius." (Newman says "as it were" because Innocent comes a few years before Vincent.) In the same place, Newman notes that Vincent calls the pope "the head of the world."[37]

IV. *AN ESSAY ON THE DEVELOPMENT OF CHRISTIAN DOCTRINE*, PART TWO

We come now to what, in the 1878 edition of *Development of Doctrine*, is the second of its two parts. It is entitled, "Doctrinal Developments Viewed Relatively to Doctrinal Corruptions." In it, Newman discusses seven "notes" characteristic of genuine developments. In the 1845 edition, these were called "tests." It is quite likely that Newman made this adjustment in order to discourage their use as "clearinghouses" for genuine developments. Newman tells us that he began writing *Development of Doctrine* in order to assure himself that his gradually increasing openness toward Rome was well ordered.[38] What is presented, therefore, in the second part is more about the Catholic Church's status as the Church founded by Christ than about how to identify proposed doctrinal developments as corruptions. Nonetheless, many of the things he says in this second part can be employed in determining what can—and what cannot—be genuine developments of doctrine.

The second part consists of an introductory chapter (chapter 5) in which Newman identifies and explains briefly the seven notes. The introductory

---

[36] Newman, *Development of Doctrine*, 123.

[37] Newman, *Development of Doctrine*, 161.

[38] See Newman, *Apologia*, 280.

chapter is followed by seven chapters, called "applications," one for each of the notes, taken in order. These chapters differ in length, the first (chapter 6) running 115 pages, those that follow of gradually diminishing length (although chapter 10 is slightly longer than chapter 9). The last (chapter 12) runs just eight pages, including a half-page conclusion to the whole work. As Newman says in his *Apologia pro Vita Sua*, *Development of Doctrine* was "unfinished," even as it was submitted (twice) for publication.[39]

In the 1878 edition, Newman describes the first note in this manner: "First note of a genuine development of an idea; preservation of type."[40] In the table of contents, the distinction between idea and type is even more apparent: "First note of a genuine development of an idea; preservation of *its* type."[41] This is quite different from what we find in the 1845 edition, where the first "test" is called "Preservation of type or idea," or simply, "Preservation of idea." What is going on here? It is very likely that Vincent of Lérins is behind the change, but present also is a doctrinal issue Newman was made more aware of as a Catholic.

When in the 1878 edition he first introduces this note, Newman quotes the passage in Vincent we have already (partially) seen: "Let the soul's religion imitate the law of the body, which, as years go on, develops indeed and opens out its due proportions, and yet remains identically what it was. . . . Small are a baby's limbs, a youth's are larger, yet they are the same."[42] This passage comes immediately after another, now quite famous passage in the *Commonitorium* where Vincent says that "the understanding, knowledge, and wisdom" of the Church might grow, "*sed in suo dumtaxat genere, in eodem scilicet dogmate, eodem sensu eademque sententia*" ("but only in its own species—in the same doctrine, of course, the same sense, and the same purpose").[43] Although Newman neither quotes nor discusses this passage, as he wrote that first paragraph on the note

[39] Newman, *Apologia*, 325.
[40] Newman, *Development of Doctrine*, 171.
[41] Emphasis added.
[42] Newman, *Development of Doctrine*, 172; quoting Vincent of Lérins, *Commonitorium* 23.4–5.
[43] The translation of this latter passage is my own. Newman never quotes this entire passage, although in a letter of 1850 he does quote the words *in eodem sensu et in eadem sententia* from the Vulgate translation of 1 Cor 1:10. The entire passage from Vincent is quoted in the First Vatican Council's Dogmatic Constitution on the Catholic Faith *Dei Filius* (April 24, 1870), DH 3020. The phrase "*eodem sensu eademque sententia*" appears in Pope John XXIII, Allocution on the Occasion of the Solemn Inauguration of the Second Vatican Ecumenical Council *Gaudet mater ecclesia* (October 11, 1962), in *Acta Apostolicae Sedis*, vol. 54 (1962): 792, where he speaks of the *depositum fidei*. See also Second Vatican Council, Dogmatic Constitution on Divine Revelation *Dei Verbum* (November 18, 1965), §8.

"preservation of type" he certainly had it in mind. Notable about it is the way in which it begins by speaking quite generally of the Church's understanding (etc.) and then shifts its attention to particular things understood: doctrines or dogmas, each with its own sense and purpose.

Newman's word "type" corresponds to the Latin word *genere* ("*in suo dumtaxat genere*"), which specifies the proper context within which the Church's understanding might grow.[44] The doctrines, with their particular sense and purpose, we can associate with the term "idea" (more prominent in the 1845 edition). To reemploy the simile employed above, the Church's understanding must (so to speak) remain an understanding proper to the same type or species of "animal." This reading is confirmed a few lines later in a remark coming immediately after the remark about the developing body. Vincent speaks there again of a body's species: if a body's parts should so alter, he says, as to be "of a species not its own" (*non sui generis*), it is necessary that it cease to exist or that it become "monstrous" (*prodigiosum*)—a biological aberration so drastic that the entity cannot be a member of the same species of which it is an aberration.[45]

It would seem, therefore, that by the time he put together the 1878 edition of *Development of Doctrine*, Newman realized that he must make more clear the distinction between the ideas by means of which aspects of the deposit of faith might be developed and the organic entity itself, which was present—and understood—before any developments. It is quite likely that this refinement of his position is the result of his relationship, subsequent to his conversion, with the prominent Jesuit theologian Giovanni Perrone. In 1847, Newman made an articulated summary (in Latin) of his theory of the development of doctrine and submitted it to Perrone. Newman's points appear (mostly) in the left-hand column of each page of the document; Perrone, responding in the

---

[44] Newman's using as his translation "type" instead of the English word "species" or "genus" is possibly connected with Whately's indisposition with respect to the concepts species and genus. See the chapter in his *Elements of Logic* entitled "Of Realism" (especially the first couple of pages) and, in the first appendix, the entry for "same." That Newman continued to agree with Whately on this point is apparent at *Grammar of Assent*, 182.

[45] Vincent understands the word *genus* as referring to an animal species also elsewhere. See *Commonitorium* 24.9, where he speaks of *humanum genus* (the human species). The term *genus* is even more specific at *Commonitorium* 17.4, where Vincent uses it in speaking of Origen's family background: "If descent or erudition [might provide authority], what was more noble than his birth of a house made illustrious by martyrdom? [*Si genus uel eruditio, quid eo nobilius, qui primum in ea domo natus est, quae est inlustrata martyrio*]."

right-hand column, made very brief comments regarding some of Newman's points. One of Newman's points runs as follows:

> Until the Church has cast in dogmatic form this or that part of her deposit, it can happen that she is not fully conscious in her own mind [*sibi conscia*] what she thinks regarding the matter. In this sense one can say that the Church, although she possesses the whole of the deposit of the faith from the beginning, in her theology she knows now more than in previous centuries.[46]

Perrone's comment was terse: "*Hoc dicere non auderem*" (I would not dare to say this).[47]

Somewhat later in the same document, Newman, citing the first note of *Development of Doctrine* and referring to it as the principal of the seven "laws," says that any additions to the deposit are not to be "things new [*nova*] but are like evolutions of those things that were already there in place. Christian doctrine, therefore, truly grows [*crescat*]; it is not fastened together. Moreover, the true tradition continues: there comes about no refoundation [*instauratio*] of the truth."[48] Perrone (who was certainly thinking half in Italian) replies: "*Optime*" (Italian, *Ottimo*). Newman would certainly have been reassured by this exchange that he and Perrone were "on the same page." Still, given his always strong desire that his teaching and preaching be doctrinally sound, he would have wanted in his revision of *Development of Doctrine* to say clearly that he does recognize a distinction between the deposit of faith, understood and transmitted by the first disciples of Christ, and the ideas subsequently elaborated upon parts of it.

---

[46] Rev. T. Lynch, "The Newman-Perrone Paper on Development," *Gregorianum* 16 (1935): 414–15. This article by Lynch contains a brief introduction and then (pp. 404–44) a transcription of a thirty-page manuscript preserved at the Birmingham Oratory. The text of the paper, which is given the title *Utrum profecerit Ecclesia Catholica in cognitione sua fidei semel sibi ab Apostolis traditae* ("Whether the Catholic Church progresses in its knowledge of the faith once for all delivered to her by the Apostles"), is itself divided into chapters and sections, followed by twelve "theses." This remark by Newman is at chapter 3, section 4. At the end of Lynch's article (pp. 445–57) is found a brief exchange of letters between Perrone and Newman.

[47] Lynch, "The Newman-Perrone Paper," 414 (right column).

[48] Lynch, "The Newman-Perrone Paper," 430 (thesis 4). Luca Tuninetti has suggested to me that Newman's employment of the word *instauratio* in this passage could be an oblique reference to Bacon's *Instauratio magna*. Immediately before this passage (and at the very end of thesis 3), Newman has referred to the seven notes as seven rules ("regulas saltem septem vellem, quibus consuli deberet in iis accessionibus ad dogma fidei factis, quae *legitimae* censendae sunt"). He goes on then in thesis 4 to speak of the rules as laws, the "principal" one, as he calls it, having to do with the growth of doctrine (which is the key idea in the first note in *Development of Doctrine*).

Regarding the first note, Newman's typical approach is to argue that, although a historical study might turn up statements by Catholic theologians and even popes difficult to reconcile with a particular doctrine, the Church itself remains (as we might say) "true to type." Newman draws a (rough) parallel with what can occur in the political sphere:

> [A] popular leader may go through a variety of professions, he may court parties and break with them, he may contradict himself in words, and undo his own measures, yet there may be a steady fulfillment of certain objects, or adherence to certain plain doctrines, which gives a unity to his career, and impresses on beholders an image of directness and large consistency which shows a fidelity to his type from first to last.[49]

But, although this is his characteristic approach with respect to the first note, Newman is careful, particularly in the 1878 edition, to say that ideas that come into general discussion—some of which presumably are legitimate developments of doctrine—are distinct from the *depositum fidei* itself. In the 1845 edition, he says that the first note (there called a "test") "is too obvious and too close upon demonstration to be of easy application in particular cases. It implies an insight into the essential idea in which a system of thought is set up, which often cannot be possessed, and, if attempted, will lead to mere theorizing."[50] This passage does not appear in the 1878 edition; it would certainly have elicited an "I would not dare to say this" from Perrone. By the time of the revised edition, Newman's definite position is that the Catholic Church does have "an insight into" the deposit of faith, as distinct from the ideas subsequently expressed about it.

In chapter 6, the "application" of the first note, Newman draws on the historical work that had occupied him for most of his adult life. It is divided into three sections, the first on the Church "of the first centuries," the second on the Church of the fourth century, the third on the Church of the fifth and sixth centuries.

The first section speaks mostly about criticisms made of the early Church by non-Christians. The section concludes with Newman's arguing that,

> If there is a form of Christianity now in the world which is accused of gross superstition, . . . a religion which impresses on the serious mind very distressing views of the guilt and consequences of sin,

---

[49] Newman, *Development of Doctrine*, 173.
[50] Newman, *Development of Doctrine*, 65–66.

... a religion which men hate as proselytizing, anti-social, revolutionary, as dividing families, separating chief friends, corrupting
the maxims of government, ... if there be such a religion now in
the world, it is not unlike Christianity as that same world viewed
it, when first it came forth from its Divine Author.[51]

In the second and third sections, Newman is intent, somewhat similarly,
on demonstrating that, although in the immediately subsequent centuries
there arose rival entities (heresies and schisms), they were always fractious and
individualistic. They could not—and, in fact, did not—claim to be "catholic"
(lowercase). "The Church is everywhere, but it is one; sects are everywhere,
but they are many, independent and discordant. Catholicity is the attribute
of the Church, independency of sectaries."[52] "In one point alone the heresies
seem universally to have agreed—in hatred to the Church."[53] As evidence of
the Catholic Church's catholicity, he mentions that "the great Athanasius, as he
returned from his exile, made no scruple to ordain in several cities as he went
along, though they were not in his own diocese."[54]

Newman does, however, acknowledge that there was a moment in the
Church's history that might seem to undermine the Church's sole claim to the
distinction "catholic." Speaking of the moment when (as St. Jerome puts it)
"the whole world groaned in astonishment to find itself Arian," Newman says:

For a while the title of Catholic as applied to the Church seemed
a misnomer; for not only was she buried beneath these popu-
lations of heresy, but that heresy was one, and maintained the
same distinctive tenet, whether at Carthage, Seville, Toulouse,
or Ravenna.[55]

But, he continues, we find "not the faintest tendency to deprive the ancient
Church of the west of the title of Catholic; and it is needless to produce evidence of a fact which is on the very face of the history. The Arians seem never
to have claimed the Catholic name."[56] Not even the possible "minority status"

---

[51] Newman, *Development of Doctrine*, 246–47.

[52] Newman, *Development of Doctrine*, 251.

[53] Newman, *Development of Doctrine*, 253.

[54] Newman, *Development of Doctrine*, 267.

[55] Newman, *Development of Doctrine*, 275.

[56] Newman, *Development of Doctrine*, 279.

of the Catholic Church would be sufficient to declare her a corruption of the true Church.

Newman's second note of genuine development he calls "continuity of principles." We saw above that he opposes Joseph Butler's emphasis upon probability as "the guide of life"—in particular, as the guide of our religious life; but Newman frequently acknowledges that his own thinking is profoundly Butlerian. What in Butler Newman embraced enthusiastically and permanently was his recognition of multiple principles identifiable in nature but also analogically in God's relationship with humanity in religion. Newman brings principles similar to those identified by Butler from their regimented positioning prior to the assent of faith, as providing probable evidence for it, *into* that assent itself, where they lose their skeptical character. This is not to say that the person who has faith can simply move on from there as one who, employing what Aristotle called the speculative intellect, might work through a proof in geometry and then move on to other proofs. Newman—like Thomas Aquinas in the commentary on Peter Lombard's *Sentences* quoted above—is clear that the assent of faith involves the practical intellect, whose aim is always goods to be pursued and not just settled truths to be filed away in one's memory. When in chapter 5 he introduces the second note, Newman remarks: "doctrines are intellectual, and principles are more immediately ethical and practical."[57] He, of course, has nothing against doctrines; his point is simply that the principles, the continuity of which he recognizes, are about how those doctrines are applied in particular practical contexts.

By the integral accumulation of antecedent probabilities under the influence of grace, the true believer achieves the sort of certainty that Aquinas describes as having "simultaneously assent and reasoning."[58] When Newman speaks, therefore, of continuity of principles as a note of genuine development, his point is that if a group rejects the sound principles that accumulate and develop around the deposit of faith—which rejection invariably involves the group's adoption of a principle not found in the former assemblage—then that development is not a genuine development but a corruption.

What then are the principles, the continuity of which allows us to confirm that the Catholic Church is the one true Church founded by Christ? Newman lists nine of them, although in a note he also acknowledges that the acceptance

---

[57] Newman, *Development of Doctrine*, 178.
[58] Aquinas, *In Sent.* 3.23.2.2, *solutio* 1.

of developments can itself be considered a principle.[59] Of the nine, he chooses to discourse in detail upon just four: the principle of the supremacy of faith, the principle of theology, the principle of Scripture and its mystical interpretation, and the principle of dogma.

In Newman's discussion of the continuous principle of the supremacy of faith, he criticizes primarily John Locke, although the arguments he employs are similar to those he uses against Whately's subordination of faith to evidential reasoning. Locke, he says, holds that "for an individual to act on faith without proof, or to make faith a personal principle of conduct for themselves, without waiting till they have got their reasons accurately drawn out and serviceable for controversy, is enthusiastic and absurd."[60] A few pages later, Newman adds: "I do not mean of course that the Fathers were opposed to inquiries into the intellectual basis of Christianity, but that they held that men were not obliged to wait for logical proof before believing; on the contrary, that the majority were to believe first on presumptions and let the intellectual proof come as their reward."[61] To this sentence, as it appears in the 1878 edition, he appends a note saying that "this is too large a subject to admit of justice being done to it here"; he refers the reader to *Grammar of Assent* (which had come out in 1870). Indeed, in concluding this section, he makes a remark that epitomizes the approach of that work: "Arguments will come to be considered as suggestions and guides rather than logical proofs; and developments as the slow, spontaneous, ethical growth, not the scientific and compulsory results, of existing opinions."[62]

His discussion of the continuous principle of theology is an elaboration upon the former remark. He speaks very positively of the utilization of logic as "that continuous tradition and habit in the Church of a scientific analysis of all revealed truth" which applies "to all religious teaching equally, and which is almost unknown beyond the pale of Christendom."[63] But he also, as in "University Sermon 15," quotes Luke 2:19 (and 2:51): "it is twice recorded of Mary that she 'kept these things and pondered them in her heart.'"[64] Mary was

[59] Newman, *Development of Doctrine*, 325–26.

[60] Newman, *Development of Doctrine*, 327.

[61] Newman, *Development of Doctrine*, 330.

[62] Newman, *Development of Doctrine*, 336. In the 1845 edition, the wording is somewhat different: "Arguments will come to be considered rather as representations and persuasives than as logical proofs; and developments as the spontaneous, gradual and ethical growth, not as intentional and arbitrary deductions, of existing opinions" (337).

[63] Newman, *Development of Doctrine*, 336.

[64] Newman, *Development of Doctrine*, 337.

thinking both theologically and logically. Newman acknowledges too that her asking the angel how this shall be shows "that there is a questioning in matters revealed to us compatible with the fullest and most absolute faith."[65]

Newman's discussion of the continuous principle he calls "Scripture and its mystical interpretation" is a defense of the Church's use of mystical and allegorical interpretation of Scripture against those who would insist that only a literal interpretation is truly Christian. Newman quotes at length the seventeenth-century theologian John Hales, who argued that the Anglican Church ought not to follow the example of the Church of Rome, which adds "unto scripture her glosses as canonical, to supply what the plain text of scripture could not yield."[66] "This doctrine of the literal sense was never grievous or prejudicial to any," adds Hales, "but only to those who were inwardly conscious that their positions were not sufficiently grounded."[67] Hales also says of those who, in defense of the Church, would cite early theologians' employment of non-literal interpretations that even they "cannot choose but see and confess thus much, that for the literal sense, the interpreters of our own times, because of their skill in the original languages, their care of pressing the circumstances and coherence of the text, of comparing like places of Scripture with like, have generally surpassed the best of the ancients."[68]

Immediately subsequent to these words taken from Hales, Newman concludes his consideration of the continuous principle regarding scriptural interpretation by stating simply and straightforwardly: "The use of Scripture then, especially its spiritual or second sense, as a medium of thought and deduction, is a characteristic principle of doctrinal teaching in the Church."[69] The alternative—and, to faithful assent, extrinsic—principle that *only* the literal interpretation of Scripture is acceptable turns out to be a good test of true doctrine's opposite.

The fourth continuous principle, the principle of dogma, consists simply in the idea that insistence on dogma is an essential characteristic of the Church founded by Christ. Newman quotes St. Irenaeus, who praises "the Apostles and their disciples, in not even conversing with those who counterfeited the

---

[65] Newman, *Development of Doctrine*, 337.

[66] Newman is citing John Hales, *Golden Remains, of the Ever Memorable Mr. John Hales of Eaton College, &c.* (London: Pawlet, 1688), 24.

[67] Newman, *Development of Doctrine*, 345. Citing Hales, *Golden Remains*, 25.

[68] Newman, *Development of Doctrine*, 346. Citing Hales, *Golden Remains*, 27.

[69] Newman, *Development of Doctrine*, 346.

truth."[70] He immediately adds: "Such a principle, however, would but have broken up the Church the sooner, resolving it into the individuals of which it was composed, unless the Truth, to which they were to bear witness, had been a something definite, and formal, and independent of themselves." Newman also cites favorably François Guizot's remarks about the Society of Jesus which, according to Guizot, against all odds had great success in meeting the intellectual challenges of the Reformation: "Why? Because they worked from fixed principles, which they fully and clearly understood, and the tendency of which they entirely comprehended."[71] One discerns here a desire on Newman's part to counterbalance his lack of confidence, expressed with regard to the former continuous principle, in the linguistic skills of biblicists and their ability to analyze disparate biblical texts. Although he never says this, one presumes that his criticism of certain biblicists would be similar to his criticism of Whately: that for them linguistic and literary analysis is a prelude to—and a test of—the assent of faith, rather than being a component of it.

The third note of true development Newman terms "assimilative power." In introducing the note, he writes: "The very nature of a true philosophy relatively to other systems is to be polemical, eclectic, unitive: Christianity was polemical; it could not but be eclectic; but was it also unitive?"[72] Newman's appreciation of the Church's polemical character he had expressed just previously, in speaking of the continuous principle of dogma. This third note has more to do with the combination of being both eclectic and unitive. His eventual answer to his own question is that, yes, the Catholic Church does unite what it assimilates (eclectically) from other sources. It does so, he suggests, in the way that Aaron's rod "devours the serpents of the magicians."[73] The Church has always taken in ideas and practices it initially abominated, having first separated them from the ideas and propensities that made them poisonous.

Newman speaks occasionally in this chapter (chapter 8) of ideas and practices the Church has assimilated from pagan cultures, such as "the use of temples, and these dedicated to particular saints," "sacerdotal vestments, the tonsure, the ring in marriage, turning to the East," and even the *Kyrie eleison*: "all of pagan origin, and sanctified by their adoption into the Church."[74] He

---

[70] Newman, *Development of Doctrine*, 348.

[71] Newman, *Development of Doctrine*, 352.

[72] Newman, *Development of Doctrine*, 355.

[73] Newman, *Development of Doctrine*, 382.

[74] Newman, *Development of Doctrine*, 373.

mentions too that Aristotle, "reprobated by certain early Fathers," would "furnish the phraseology for theological definitions afterwards."[75] But Newman's attention is directed primarily at the way the Church has profited in this way from its polemics against Christian heretics and certain Jewish customs.

Regarding Christian heretics, Newman maintains that "the doctrines even of the heretical bodies are indices and anticipations of the mind of the Church. As the first step in settling a question of doctrine is to raise and debate it, so heresies in every age may be taken as the measure of the existing state of thought in the Church, and of the movement of her theology; they determine in what way the current is setting, and the rate at which it flows."[76] He goes on to speak of the second-century heretical movement Montanism, saying that its advocates' revelations, justly criticized as adding to the deposit of faith, anticipated the Church's acceptance of genuine developments and that "their professed inspiration" anticipated the teaching of the Church's infallibility.[77]

But more precisely indicative of Newman's understanding of this note is what he says about the Church's acceptance of practices similar to Jewish customs. He refers to St. Paul's denunciation of "distinctions in meat and drink, the observance of Sabbaths and holydays, and of ordinances, and the worship of Angels."[78] But, Newman notes, "Christians, from the first, were rigid in their stated fastings, venerated . . . the Angelic intelligences, and established the observance of the Lord's day as soon as persecution ceased."[79] How were they able to do so coherently?

There is in truth a certain virtue or grace in the Gospel which changes the quality of doctrines, opinions, usages, actions, and personal characters when incorporated with it, and makes them right and acceptable to its Divine Author, whereas before they were either infected with evil, or at best but shadows of the truth.[80]

The Church, wielding the equivalent of Aaron's rod, is always capable of adopting ideas and practices in themselves not immoral once these ideas have been separated from the sinful attitudes and ideas that make them incompatible with the life of truth in Christ.

---

[75] Newman, *Development of Doctrine*, 367–68.

[76] Newman, *Development of Doctrine*, 362.

[77] Newman, *Development of Doctrine*, 365.

[78] Newman, *Development of Doctrine*, 369.

[79] Newman, *Development of Doctrine*, 369.

[80] Newman, *Development of Doctrine*, 368.

In chapter 9, Newman considers his fourth note, "logical sequence." One would expect him to devote much attention to this note; but, in fact, in the 1878 edition it is treated in just seventeen pages in which logical issues are hardly mentioned. As already noted, the brevity of the chapter might be accounted for by adverting to Newman's own acknowledgement that the work went to press unfinished. But it is also true that the logical sequence of genuine developments is an explicit theme throughout the work, including what is said in fourteen pages of the 1845 edition that Newman transferred in the 1878 edition from what would have been their place in chapter 9 to chapter 4. Accordingly, here in chapter 9 Newman simply explains how six practices and ideas eventually adopted by the Catholic Church—pardons, penances, satisfactions, purgatory, meritorious works, and monastic rule—all "follow on the consideration of sin after baptism."[81] "Following on" is, of course, logic's core concept.

In chapter 10, Newman considers the fifth note, "anticipation of its future," by which he means that, even before the explicit adoption of an idea or practice, anticipation of the same can be found in the earliest centuries of the Church. As examples of such anticipation, he speaks of the early reverence shown to relics, the prizing of virginity, the cult of the saints and the angels, and "the special prerogatives" of the Blessed Virgin Mary. Newman explains that frequently such anticipations occurred against seemingly inimical backgrounds. The earliest Christian thinkers were often educated by Platonists, for whom matter was evil; and Jewish culture, from which Christianity emerged, regarded the touching of a corpse a defilement. And yet the early Christians, says Newman, treasured the blood, the ashes, and the bones of the saints "as something supernatural."[82] Although the early Church, against various contemporary currents, insisted that marriage was good, it also praised virginity: Newman quotes, for instance, the fourth-century Saint Methodius, who spoke of chastity as "a mighty vow beyond all vows."[83] Early Christians eschewed the proliferation of deities by the Romans, insisting with their Jewish forebears that there is just one God; and yet, very early on they honored and praised the angels and saints. Regarding the prerogatives of the Blessed Virgin, Newman does not mention countervailing ideas but simply relays the contents of early reflections upon her role in

[81] Newman, *Development of Doctrine*, 384.
[82] Newman, *Development of Doctrine*, 405.
[83] Newman, *Development of Doctrine*, 409.

redemption—an idea that might seem to, but does not, compromise her Son's status as sole redeemer.

In chapter 11, Newman considers the sixth note, "conservative action on its past." In the chapter's introduction, he remarks that "this Essay has so far exceeded its proposed limits, that both reader and writer may well be weary, and may content themselves with a brief consideration of the portions of the subject which remain."[84] But before this "brief consideration," and as is appropriate to a (hastily conceived) conclusion, Newman once again quotes Vincent of Lérins, who has been on his mind throughout the work. The piece he quotes (in Latin) follows close upon the remark we saw above, where Vincent says that "small are a baby's limbs, a youth's are larger, yet they are the same." "'Ut nihil novum,' says Vincentius, 'proferatur in senibus, quod non in pueris jam antea latitaverit.'"[85]

The instances of developments characterized by "conservative action on [their] past" are instances, says Newman, "of a great law which is seen in developments generally, that changes which appear at first sight to contradict that out of which they grew, are really its protection or illustration."[86] He mentions the prevalence of martyrdom in the early Church, which, in more peaceful times, was superseded by asceticism. When the Church, he writes, "was set free from the house of her prison, she did not quit it so much as turn it into a cell."[87] Another instance would be "the introduction of the sign of the meek Jesus into the armies of men, and the use of an emblem of peace as a protection in battle."[88] Such seemingly incongruent additions are recognized as genuine developments once it is understood that their role is to protect and preserve the more basic truth. He goes on then to make a similar point with respect to devotion to Our Lady: it does not supplant devotion to her Son, he says; rather, it augments it. "And if we take a survey at least of Europe, we shall find that it is not those religious communions which are characterized by devotion towards the Blessed Virgin that have ceased to adore her Eternal Son, but those very bodies, (when allowed by the law,) which have renounced devotion to her."[89]

---

84 Newman, *Development of Doctrine*, 419.
85 Newman, *Development of Doctrine*, 420. "Nothing new might be produced in the elderly which would not have been already latent in the young" (Vincent of Lérins, *Commonitorium* 23.6).
86 Newman, *Development of Doctrine*, 422.
87 Newman, *Development of Doctrine*, 420.
88 Newman, *Development of Doctrine*, 422.
89 Newman, *Development of Doctrine*, 426.

In the final chapter 12, Newman considers the seventh note, "chronic vigour." In speaking thus, he is referring not just to the Church's continuing to live but to its continuing to live in spite of—and even by virtue of—fierce internal doctrinal conflict such as would have brought down any other organization.

> Large portions of Christendom were, one after another, in heresy or in schism; the leading churches and the most authoritative schools fell from time to time into serious error; three Popes, Liberius, Vigilius, Honorius, have left to posterity the burden of their defence: but these disorders were no interruption to the sustained and steady march of the sacred science from implicit belief to formal statement.[90]

It is, he says, "as if some one individual and perspicacious intellect, to speak humanly, ruled the theological discussion from first to last."[91]

V. CONCLUSION

To conclude, then, it is apparent that Saint John Henry Newman's interest in and insight into the development of Christian doctrine began early in his professional academic life and, in particular, while collaborating in the composition of Richard Whately's *Elements of Logic*. Newman, however, consistently rejected the idea put forward in Whately's (and others') writings that scientific and logical rigor constitutes an antecedent standard to which the Christian faith must conform. As he would explain many years later in his *Grammar of Assent*, the assent of faith is similar to other instances of assent inasmuch as it involves the convergence of antecedent probabilities with respect to a particular thesis that at one point is perceived as making scientific and logical sense. Newman eventually came to realize that this understanding of the assent of faith can be found also in Thomas Aquinas, who held that Christian belief is a matter of having "simultaneously assent and reasoning."[92]

Newman's earliest explicit consideration of the development of doctrine is found in his "University Sermon 15," preached while he was still an Anglican. There he makes remarks reminiscent of passages in the *Commonitorium* of Vincent of Lérins comparing the development of doctrine to natural growth.

---

90 Newman, *Development of Doctrine*, 439.
91 Newman, *Development of Doctrine*, 440.
92 Aquinas, *In Sent.* 3.23.2.2, *solutio* 1.

His interest in Vincent's theory of development is also apparent in *Development of Doctrine*, the first part of which defends a nuanced version of Vincent's principle that Christian doctrine concerns "what has been held everywhere, always, and by all."[93] Nuance was necessary since Newman realized that many of his former confreres in the Anglican Church employed a certain understanding of the principle in order to argue that the Catholic Church was a corruption of the true Church.

The second part of *Development of Doctrine* has more to do, although often not explicitly, with Vincent's understanding of development as analogous to the natural growth of plants and animals. In it, Newman proposes seven "notes" characteristic of genuine doctrinal developments. The first, which he elsewhere describes as the principal note or law, he calls "preservation of type." The term "type" is most likely Newman's translation of the Latin word *genus* ("species") employed by Vincent of Lérins as part of a simile comparing doctrinal developments to the limbs of animals. In order to qualify as a genuine development, an idea cannot be something that could not belong to the species of "organic entity" that was Christian doctrine at its beginning: the deposit of faith.

The second note Newman calls "continuity of principles." The basic idea is that a proposed development's espousal of a principle inconsistent with what Newman identifies as the "continuous principles" of Christianity indicates that the proposed development is actually a corruption. Newman discusses four continuous principles: the first, which he calls "the principle of the supremacy of faith," is the idea (expounded more fully in *Grammar of Assent*) that faith is not subordinate to scientific proof. The second adds, however, that the employment of scientific methodology is by no means incompatible with the faith. The third continuous principle has to do with the Church's appreciation for interpretations of Holy Scripture other than the literal interpretation; the fourth, with the Church's constant willingness to defend its teaching intellectually—and even polemically.

The third note Newman calls "assimilative power." He speaks of the way in which the Church, wielding the Christian equivalent of Aaron's rod, which devoured the serpents of the Egyptian magicians, is able to assimilate ideas and practices from outside the faith. He mentions, for instance, sacerdotal vestments, the tonsure, and the marriage ring, the origins of all of which he finds in

---

[93] Vincent of Lérins, *Commonitorium* 2.5.

pagan culture. He mentions too Aristotle, whom early theologians reprobated but later Catholic thinkers (including Newman) drew on most willingly.

The fourth note Newman calls "logical sequence," by which he refers to the way in which certain practices follow logically from more basic Christian ideas, although not necessarily as conclusions follow from premises in a syllogism. His treatment of this note is rather brief, as is his treatment of the remaining notes; he speaks only of the way in which things like pardons and penances follow from the Church's recognition of sin after baptism.

The fifth note Newman calls "anticipation of its future," by which he means that our finding in the Church's first centuries practices and ideas corresponding to later practices and ideas constitutes evidence that these latter are genuine developments. He notes also that the earlier instances often arise against seemingly hostile backgrounds, such as the conservation of relics despite a general opinion that corpses are defiling.

The sixth note Newman calls "conservative action on its past," regarding which he quotes Vincent of Lérins: "Nothing new might be produced in the elderly which would not have been already latent in the young." Newman says that certain developments appear "at first sight to contradict that out of which they grew" but are in fact their "protection or illustration." He mentions in this regard devotion to the mother of Jesus, which does not supplant devotion to her Son but rather fortifies it.

The seventh note Newman calls "chronic vigour." As he demonstrates repeatedly over the course of *Development of Doctrine*, the Catholic Church persists as one and the same body despite periodic internal conflict regarding doctrine. It is very much as if "some one individual and perspicacious intellect ... ruled the theological discussion from first to last."[94]

94 I thank for their learned help on this essay especially Fathers Thomas Sherman, S.J., Joseph Carola, S.J., Nicolas Steeves, S.J., and Professors Luca Tuninetti and Reinhard Hütter.

SENSUS FIDELIUM:
SENSE OF THE FAITHFUL

Robert Dodaro, O.S.A.

The aim of this essay is to clarify and defend the meaning of the terms "sense of the faith" (*sensus fidei*), "sense of the faithful" (*sensus fidelium*) and "consensus of the faithful" (*consensus fidelium*) according to the teaching of the Catholic Church. Such a clarification is necessary because of the abuse of these terms—especially "sense of the faithful"—by many theologians, who misuse them as an argument in favor of changing defined Church teachings. Accordingly, the essay is divided into the following sections. To begin with, a set of definitions of these terms will be provided. This is followed by a discussion of "sense of the faithful" in relation to opinion polls, which represent the crux of the difficulty with the use of this term. Attention is then given to the specious concept of "the faithful" in some theological treatments of the term. Lastly, I present a discussion of the means of consulting the lay faithful on matters of doctrine.

DEFINITIONS

Before proceeding, I should make it clear that I am using these terms according to the definitions they were given by Herbert Vorgrimler:

> Initially we can say that the term *sensus fidei* designates a special kind of knowledge, springing from faith and embracing its fundamental features. The more precise context of the theological discussion of the *sensus fidei* is revealed by asking *who* possesses

this sense of faith, this "feeling" for faith's basic themes. As the New Testament and a long tradition testify, *everyone* who believes in God's revelation has this sense of faith. First of all, therefore, it is the individual consciousness, "illuminated" by faith and hence by God himself. In a wider sense, it refers to the collective faith-consciousness and so is also called *sensus fidelium*, the "sense of the faithful." The *sensus fidei* is to be distinguished from the *consensus fidelium*. The "consensus of the faithful" is the agreement which arises among believers as a result of the sense of faith with regard to particular items of faith, and it is also the form of expression such agreement takes.[1]

Vorgrimler's definitions have been ably summarized by Ormond Rush:

> The term *sensus fidei* refers to the instinct, possessed by the individual baptized and committed Christian, enabling him or her to recognize what is genuinely of the faith. *Sensus fidelium* refers to the communal dimension of this instinct. *Consensus fidelium* refers to the agreement and judgment, because of the *sensus fidelium*, regarding what is faithful to the apostolic heritage.[2]

It is clear, then, that the "sense of the faith" represents a source of theology since it crystallizes an instinct about what ought to be believed into a communicable form. "Sense of the faith" as a concept pertains to all baptized persons. "Sense of the faithful" expands the sense of the faith of many individual Christians into a collective feeling for the faith, which can then be used as a confirmation of what the Church believes. Saint Augustine is credited with an early usage of the latter concept when he defended the canonical status of the Book of Wisdom on the basis of the acceptance it had been shown in the Church's liturgy "from bishops to the last of the lay believers, penitents, and catechumens, with the veneration paid to divine authority."[3] In the absence of other theological testimony, Augustine pointed to the Book of Wisdom's universal acceptance over a long period of time by the faithful, both hierarchy and laity, as sufficient theological proof of its canonicity. In describing "sense

---

[1] Herbert Vorgrimler, "From *Sensus Fidei* to *Consensus Fidelium*," *Concilium* 180 (1985): 3.

[2] Ormond Rush, *The Reception of Doctrine: An Appropriation of Hans Robert Jauss' Reception Aesthetics and Literary Hermeneutics* (Rome: Editrice Pontificia Università Gregoriana, 1977), 171.

[3] CCC §92, quoting Augustine, *De praedestinatione sanctorum*, 27.

of the faith," the Catechism of the Catholic Church cites the Second Vatican Council, which draws its authority from the above quoted text from Augustine:

> The whole body of the faithful ... cannot err in matters of belief. This characteristic is shown in the supernatural appreciation of faith (*sensus fidei*) on the part of the whole people, when, "from the bishops to the last of the faithful," they manifest a universal consent in matters of faith and morals.[4]

Pope Pius IX consulted the Catholic faithful concerning belief in the Immaculate Conception of the Blessed Virgin Mary before proclaiming it as dogma in 1854. He did so by instructing Catholic bishops to report to him the belief of the faithful in their respective dioceses on the matter. Pope Pius XII similarly consulted the faithful prior to his proclamation of the dogma of the Assumption in 1950. Both cases represent a determination of the "sense of the faithful" on the part of these popes before they proceeded with their infallible *ex cathedra* definitions.

Reflecting on these decrees concerning the Blessed Mother, Pope Benedict XVI offered this meditation on the role of the laity in determining the sense of the faithful:

> Concerning the teaching on the Immaculate Conception, import-ant theologians like Duns Scotus enriched what the People of God already spontaneously believed about the Blessed Virgin and expressed in acts of devotion, in the arts and in Christian life in general with the specific contribution of their thought. Thus faith both in the Immaculate Conception and in the bodily Assumption of the Virgin was already present in the People of God, while theology had not yet found the key to interpreting it in the totality of the doctrine of the faith. The People of God therefore precede theologians and this is all thanks to that supernatural *sensus fidei*, namely, that capacity infused by the Holy Spirit that qualifies us to embrace the reality of the faith with humility of heart and mind. In this sense, the People of God is the 'teacher that goes first' and must then be more deeply examined and intellectually accepted by

---

[4] Second Vatican Council, Dogmatic Constitution on the Church *Lumen gentium* (November 21, 1964), §12 (hereafter, *Lumen gentium*).

theology. May theologians always be ready to listen to this source of faith and retain the humility and simplicity of children![5]

"SENSE OF THE FAITHFUL" AND OPINION POLLS

How, then, in the contemporary Church can the sense of the faithful be determined with regard to "what is genuinely of the faith"? Do opinion polls or surveys, whether conducted by the news media, by national episcopal conferences, or even by the Holy See reveal the "sense of the faithful"? The question is important because all too frequently theologians speak of the "sense of the faithful" in conjunction with polling results.

But polling results concerning religious matters—if they are to be believed—often reveal majority Catholic opinion at odds with defined Church teachings.[6] A 2007 Pew Research poll indicated that 72 percent of US Catholics believe that many religions can lead to eternal life, not just that *people* of different religions can be saved, which the Catholic Church teaches, but that many *religions* can lead to eternal life, a position which the Church rejects.[7] A further Pew Research poll revealed in 2019 that 69 percent of US Catholics do not accept the Church's defined teaching on transubstantiation in regard to the Eucharist but believe instead that the consecrated Body and Blood of Christ are only symbols.[8]

The same problem can be seen with reference to the global Catholic Church. An opinion poll published in February 2014, of over twelve thousand Catholics in twelve countries by Bendixen and Amandi International in partnership with the Univision Network revealed that 65 percent of Catholics

[5] Benedict XVI, General Audience, Wednesday, July 7, 2010, accessed May 16, 2020, http://www.vatican.va/content/benedict-xvi/en/audiences/2010/documents/hf_ben-xvi_aud_20100707.html.

[6] For scholarly criticism of the accuracy of religious polling in the United States, see Robert Wuthnow, *Inventing American Religion: Polls, Surveys, and the Tenuous Quest for a Nation's Faith* (New York: Oxford University Press, 2015).

[7] See The Pew Forum on Religion and Public Life, "U.S. Religious Landscape Survey: Religious Beliefs and Practices," Pew Research Center, June 1, 2008, accessed March 29, 2020, https://www.pewresearch.org/wp-content/uploads/sites/7/2015/04/US_Relgious_Landscape_Survey-Beliefs_Comparions-2007.pdf. On the Catholic Church's teaching, see *Lumen gentium*, §16; Second Vatican Council, Pastoral Constitution on the Church in the Modern World *Gaudium et spes* (December 7, 1965), §22; Second Vatican Council, Declaration on the Relation of the Church to Non-Christian Religions *Nostra aetate* (October 28, 1965), no. 2. See also John Paul II, Encyclical Letter *Redemptoris missio* (December 7, 1990), §5; Congregation for the Doctrine of the Faith, Declaration on the Unicity and Salvific Universality of Christ *Dominus Iesus* (August 6, 2000), §§12 and 14; CCC §847.

[8] See Gregory A. Smith, "Just one-third of U.S. Catholics agree with their church that Eucharist is body, blood of Christ," Pew Research Center, August 5, 2019, accessed March 29, 2020, https://www.pewresearch.org/fact-tank/2019/08/05/transubstantiation-eucharist-u-s-catholics/.

globally disagreed with the Church's condemnation of abortion. The poll also showed that 58 percent opposed the Church's teaching that forbids divorced and civilly remarried Catholics from receiving the Eucharist. However, one problem that becomes immediately apparent is that these poll results demonstrate wide geographical variances in Catholic opinion. Opposition by Catholics to the Church's teaching on abortion registered at 90 percent in France and 88 percent in Spain, whereas in Uganda opposition was at 35 percent and in the Philippines at 27 percent. Geographic divergences almost as wide occur in regard to the prohibition of sacramental Communion for divorced and civilly remarried Catholics. Resistance to this prohibition was at 82 percent in Spain, in Italy it was at 79 percent, and in France at 78 percent, while it was only at 21 percent in Uganda and at 18 percent in the Democratic Republic of the Congo.[9]

Bishops and theologians should concern themselves with determining what exactly it is that explains these diverse geographical beliefs about major doctrinal teachings. In doing so, they will want to bear in mind the consequences of a steady weakening in catechesis throughout the Church, along with the increasingly irreligious impact of secularism, coupled with the processes of individualization and religious relativism throughout the world. This global secularizing shift in Catholic thinking is encouraged by certain cinematic films and television series that condition public opinion on a range of human life and marriage/family issues such as abortion, euthanasia, divorce and remarriage, same-sex marriage, cohabitation, and sexual libertinism, in addition to religious convictions and practices such as belief in God and Mass attendance. In thinking through these factors, bishops and theologians should also avoid giving in to the pretense that Catholics in "more developed," wealthier countries possess an inevitably more mature grasp of matters of the faith than Catholics in poorer countries. Pope Francis, for one, sees this matter in exactly opposite terms.

"This is why I want a Church which is poor and for the poor. They have much to teach us. Not only do they share in the *sensus fidei*, but in their difficulties they know the suffering Christ. We need to let ourselves be evangelized by them. . . . We are called to find Christ in them, to lend our voice to their causes,

---

9   The poll was conducted for the Univision Network by Bendixen and Amandi International. These twelve countries represent 61 percent of the world's Catholic population. The overall margin of error for the global aggregated results is 0.9 percent at the 95 percent confidence interval. Univision and Bendixen and Amandi International, "Global Survey of Roman Catholics," February 2014, accessed March 25, 2020, http://bendixenandamandi.com/wp-content/uploads/2018/06/UNIVISION -Catholic-Poll-Executive-Summary.decryptedKLR.pdf.

but also to be their friends, to listen to them, to speak for them and to embrace the mysterious wisdom which God wishes to share with us through them."[10]

In conjunction with influences contributing to geographical variances over the reception of Catholic teachings, a more fundamental theological question must also be considered: namely, is it possible that the *sensus fidei*, the "instinct for the faith," as a supernatural gift of the Holy Spirit, could really diverge along national, cultural, economic, or educational lines? For example, is it theologically coherent that on any given vital moral teaching a majority of Spanish Catholics could form one sense of the faithful, and a majority of Catholics in Uganda a contrary one? Some contemporary theologians pose the dilemma of a sense of the faithful in which the lay faithful are at odds with the hierarchy, and even with the Magisterium. What, then, do they say about a sense of the faithful that is at odds with itself?

Ormond Rush, a prominent author of books and articles on this subject, suggests that there can be more than one legitimate sense of the faithful at work in the Church as a result of the promptings of the Holy Spirit, which would explain how inconsistent senses of the faithful can occur within the one Catholic Church.[11] This may be true in cases where the sense of the faithful refers to local customs of minor doctrinal import. However, it is not possible in matters involving major doctrinal and moral questions. Moreover, where in the Catholic tradition does Rush see this principle evoked?

A related question concerns certain apparent, rapid changes of perspective on key moral questions among progressivist Catholics. Can the sense of the faithful undergo dramatic change over time? Do unforeseen changes of viewpoints among Catholics—say on abortion or same-sex relations—indicate a fundamental change in the *sensus fidei*? In other words, can the "sense of the faith" be identified with one position one year, and another position later? Is "sense of the faithful" reducible to "majority Catholic public opinion" only in one particular country or group of countries, and at one particular time? The Church should consider the theological consequences of this way of thinking. For example, if it accepts the premise that the sense of the faithful as regards any significant moral question can undergo a fundamental change over a period of time, does it then conclude that the sense of the faithful

---

[10] Pope Francis, Apostolic Exhortation on the Proclamation of the Gospel in Today's World *Evangelii gaudium* (November 26, 2013), §198.

[11] Ormond Rush, *The Eyes of Faith: The Sense of the Faithful and the Church's Reception of Tradition* (Washington: Catholic University Press, 2009), 243.

has "matured" over time, perhaps as Catholics have learned more or have gained more experience? Are there no perennial doctrinal or moral truths to which the sense of the faithful is ultimately and definitively directed, but only the shifting perceptions of believers as they apply their understanding of the Catholic faith to their personal experience while they interact with pluralistic societies? Is abortion, which was condemned in the fifth century by Saint Augustine, conceivably morally acceptable in our day, or will it be so in the future?

Many contemporary theologians' understanding of the *sensus fidei* draws heavily from the value they set on experience in place of knowledge as informing Catholic faith. But theologians who embrace this approach should ask themselves what kind of "experience" brings Catholics in these different countries to adopt views at times contrary to defined Church teachings, and whether such "experience" includes moral ignorance or sin, in order to assess whether that experience constitutes a solid basis for a true supernatural instinct into the faith.

Moral questions are not the primary theological issues that involve "sense of the faithful"; the term has been applied mostly to strictly dogmatic matters. Church teaching concerned with the Immaculate Conception may not provoke objection among today's Catholics, given that many of them would erroneously regard this teaching as a pious Marian devotion which has no bearing on their own lives. Nevertheless, given the difficulty that many Catholics nowadays have with the concept of original sin, one wonders for how much longer they will continue to affirm this doctrine.

A survey conducted between 2000 and 2001 revealed that at least seven out of ten US Catholics rejected the concept of original sin, and that 62 percent believed that "truth can be discovered only through logic, human reasoning and personal experience," and not from Scripture or magisterial teaching.[12]

If Catholics do not accept the doctrine of original sin, is it likely that they would accept the dogmatic teaching on the uniqueness of the Immaculate Conception? These survey results make it clear that polling cannot be used to measure the "sense of the faithful" because the latter, as will be demonstrated below, cannot be identified with majority Catholic opinion when that opinion is at odds with defined Church teachings.

---

[12] See The Barna Group, "Americans Draw Theological Beliefs from Diverse Points of View," Barna.com, October 8, 2002, accessed March 30, 2020, https://www.barna.com/research/americans-draw-theological-beliefs-from-diverse-points-of-view/.

The concept of "sense of the faithful" is rendered all the more difficult by suggestions—advanced by some theologians—that because the term "faithful" (*fidelis*) is applicable to all baptized persons, the views of non-Catholic Christians must also be taken into consideration in determining the sense of the faithful. Yet, it is impossible to imagine a majority of members of Protestant denominations or even of Eastern Orthodox Churches embracing the dogma of the Immaculate Conception or of transubstantiation in regard to the Eucharist, to name only two significant, defined Catholic beliefs not normally shared by other Christians. This point raises the question of who, in reference to "sense of the faithful," are meant by the term "the faithful"?

"SENSE OF THE FAITHFUL" AND THE CONCEPT OF "THE FAITHFUL"

In a recently published book, Professor Wolfgang Beinert responded to criticisms I made of statements by Walter Cardinal Kasper regarding the theological concept of "sense of the faithful" in relation to the debate in the Catholic Church concerning admission to the Eucharist of divorced and civilly remarried Catholics.[13] Beinert's criticism of my understanding of "sense of the faithful" suggests that it reduces this "instinct for the faith" on the part of the laity to a mere echo of what the hierarchy teaches on its own.

Instead, I criticized the division that Cardinal Kasper implicitly posits between hierarchy and lay faithful concerning "sense of the faithful." When Kasper and Beinert write about "the faithful" (*"die Gläubigen"*) they are thinking only of the laity. Part of the difficulty with this expression is that it has two usages in Catholic theology in relation to *sensus fidei*. In common parlance, "the faithful" is used as a synonym for "the laity" as distinct from "the hierarchy." But since *"fidelis"* refers in a technical theological sense to anyone who is baptized and remains faithful, it follows that, in terms of "sense of the faithful," members of the hierarchy together with laypeople constitute "the faithful." This is the usage found in the Second Vatican Council's discussion of "sense of the

---

[13] See Wolfgang Beinert, "Einstimmen oder Übereinstimmen? Die Aufgabe des Glaubenssinnes der Gläubigen," in *Zerreißprobe Ehe: Das Ringen der katholischen Kirche um die Familie*, ed. Ulrich Ruh and Myriam Wijlens (Freiburg: Herder, 2015), 33. See also Robert Dodaro, "The Argument in Brief," in *Remaining in the Truth of Christ: Marriage and Communion in the Catholic Church*, ed. Robert Dodaro (San Francisco: Ignatius Press, 2014), 32–34. I was criticizing statements by Walter Cardinal Kasper, *The Gospel of the Family*, trans. William Madges (Mahwah, NJ: Paulist Press, 2014), 46–47.

faithful."[14] Hence, when speaking about "sense of the faithful," it is misleading to use it exclusively in relation to the laity in contrast to the hierarchy.

This is not a mere semantic problem. Is it possible to imagine a Catholic Church in which the laity hold one instinct for the faith and the hierarchy holds a conflicting one? Beinert does not propose this outcome in so many words, but he insinuates it by setting the sense of the faithful in opposition to the Magisterium, as when he asserts that the prohibitions against contraception in Pope Saint Paul VI's encyclical letter *Humanae vitae* (1968) and against the ordination of women to the priesthood in the document of the Congregation for the Doctrine of the Faith *Inter insigniores* (1976) contradict the sense of the faithful.[15]

In terms of the question of who "the faithful" in the expression "sense of the faithful" are, we can look at the designation given by Saint John Henry Newman to the phrase "*pastorum et fidelium conspiratio*," that is, a "breathing together between pastors and the faithful."[16] In this expression Newman is not talking about a *conspiratio* that unites one "*sensus fidei*" for pastors and a separate one for laity, as if the two existed independently of each other and the Magisterium had to negotiate between them in order to arrive at doctrinal truth. Instead, Newman identifies "*pastores*" and "*fideles*" as two distinct components, the breathing together (*con-spiratio*) of which constitutes the one sense of the faithful, the one instinct for the faith shared by all baptized believers, whether they are laypeople or clergy. It follows that if either of these two components is lacking, there is no sense of the faithful and consequently no consensus of the faithful. This is the understanding of these terms as explained by the Second Vatican Council in *Lumen gentium*:

> The entire body of the faithful [*universitas fidelium*], anointed as they are by the Holy One, cannot err in matters of belief. They manifest this special property by means of the whole peoples' supernatural discernment in matters of faith [*supernaturali sensu fidei totius populi*] when "from the bishops to the last of the lay faithful" [*ab episcopis usque ad extremos laicos fideles*] they show universal agreement [*universalem suum consensum*] in matters of

---

[14] *Lumen gentium*, §12.

[15] See Beinert, "Einstimmen oder Übereinstimmen?," 39, together with 43n33.

[16] See John Henry Newman, *On Consulting the Faithful in Matters of Doctrine*, ed. John Coulson (London: Geoffrey Chapman, 1961).

faith and morals. That discernment in matters of faith is aroused and sustained by the Spirit of truth. It is exercised under the guidance [*ducere*] of the sacred teaching authority [*sacrii magisterii*], in faithful and respectful obedience to which the people of God accepts that which is not just the word of men but truly the word of God [*cui fideliter obsequens, iam non verbum hominum, sed vere accipit verbum Dei*]. Through it, the people of God adheres unwaveringly to the faith given once and for all to the saints, penetrates it more deeply with right thinking, and applies it more fully in its life.[17]

The Council declares that the *effort* at discernment of the faith (*sensus fidei*), a discernment that is aroused and sustained by the Holy Spirit, is guided by the Magisterium (*sacrum magisterium*). This statement does not mean that the *sensus fidei* is discerned by the Magisterium without the consultation of the lay faithful. Nevertheless, the entire People of God is called to give "faithful and respectful obedience" (*fideliter obsequi*) to the Church's Magisterium. The final sentence in this paragraph states that through the Magisterium, the People of God adheres unwaveringly to the faith given once and for all to the saints (a reference to the "deposit of the faith"), and that through this same Magisterium, the People of God penetrates the faith "more deeply with right thinking and applies it more fully in life." These are the major points in the Second Vatican Council's most authoritative treatment of "sense of the faithful."

Many theologians intentionally downplay the role of the Magisterium in guiding the discernment of *sensus fidei* both on the part of the individual believer and collectively on the part of the whole People of God, hierarchy and lay faithful together. Beinert, for example, holds that the lay faithful are right to reject magisterial teaching when it contradicts their experience, especially in sexual and marital ethics.[18] The examples of conflict between the "sense of the faithful" and the Magisterium that he raises in his article, namely, the prohibition against contraception in *Humanae vitae* and against the ordination of women to the priesthood in *Inter insigniores*, both concern teachings that have been defined by the Church's Magisterium. Accordingly, Beinert cannot logically appeal to the Second Vatican Council's teaching in order to argue that these two doctrines are opposed to the "sense of the faithful" when the same

---

[17] *Lumen gentium*, §12.

[18] See Beinert, "Einstimmen oder Übereinstimmen?," 35–36.

Council has defined it as necessarily existing in harmony with the Magisterium. It is this conflict that Beinert posits between the Magisterium and "sense of the faithful" that most departs from the intention of the Second Vatican Council.[19] The Council represents "sense of the faithful" as the hierarchy and lay faithful being involved in precisely the kind of *conspiratio* that was heralded by Saint John Henry Newman.

Discernment between pastors and lay faithful is delicate and requires forbearance and even the passing of time on the part of all believers. Pope Saint John Paul II, writing in his 1981 Apostolic Exhortation on the Family, *Familiaris consortio*, offers the clearest statement of the principles guiding the application of *sensus fidei* that has ever been offered in papal teaching.

> Not infrequently ideas and solutions which are very appealing but which obscure in varying degrees the truth and the dignity of the human person, are offered to the men and women of today, in their sincere and deep search for a response to the important daily problems that affect their married and family life. These views are often supported by the powerful and pervasive organization of the means of social communication, which subtly endanger freedom and the capacity for objective judgment.
>
> Many are already aware of this danger to the human person and are working for the truth. The Church, with her evangelical discernment [*diiudicium*], joins with them, offering her own service to the truth, to freedom and to the dignity of every man and every woman. . . .
>
> This discernment is accomplished through the sense of faith [*sensus fidei*], which is a gift that the Spirit gives to all the faithful [*omnes fideles*], and is therefore the work of the whole Church [*opus totius ecclesiae*] according to the diversity of the various gifts and charisms that, together with and according to the responsibility proper to each one, work together for a more profound understanding and activation of the word of God. The Church, therefore, does not accomplish this discernment only through the Pastors [*pastores*], who teach in the name and with the power of Christ but also through the laity [*laici*]. . . .

---

[19] See Beinert, "Einstimmen oder Übereinstimmen?," 36–38.

The "supernatural sense of faith" [*supernaturalis sensus fidei*] however does not consist solely or necessarily in the agreement of the faithful [*consensio fidelium*]. Following Christ, the Church seeks the truth, which is not always the same as the majority opinion. She listens to conscience and not to power, and in this way she defends the poor and the downtrodden. The Church values sociological and statistical research, when it proves helpful in understanding the historical context in which pastoral action has to be developed and when it leads to a better understanding of the truth. Such research alone, however, is not to be considered in itself an expression of the sense of faith [*sensus fidei*].

Because it is the task of the apostolic ministry to ensure that the Church remains in the truth of Christ and to lead her ever more deeply into that truth, the Pastors must promote the sense of the faith in all the faithful, examine and authoritatively judge the genuineness of its expressions, and educate the faithful in an ever more mature evangelical discernment.[20]

There are many significant theological affirmations contained in this passage and they are wound tightly together. John Paul II affirms that the contemporary experience of the laity must be given serious consideration by the Magisterium. Nevertheless, and just as importantly, the Pope also warns that human freedom and objective judgment can be clouded by the mass media so that "ideas and solutions" to theological and pastoral problems can seem appealing even though they are false. The Pope terms this media manipulation a danger (*periculum*) to the human person and places the Church's discernment at the service of the many individuals who he says are working on behalf of the truth, freedom, and dignity of the human person.

The Pope then describes *sensus fidei* as "a gift that the Spirit gives to all the faithful [*omnes fideles*]." To underscore the point that *sensus fidei* applies to pastors and lay faithful alike, he adds that the Church's discernment "is the work of the whole Church [*opus totius ecclesiae*]," and that it functions through the specific gifts and charisms as well as the different responsibilities proper to each member of the Church.

At this point the Pope once again issues a warning: "the 'supernatural sense

---

[20] John Paul II, Apostolic Exhortation on the Role of the Christian Family in the Modern World *Familiaris consortio* (November 22, 1981), §§4–5 (hereafter, *Familiaris consortio*).

of faith' [*supernaturalis sensus fidei*] however does not consist solely or necessarily in the 'agreement of the faithful' [*consensio fidelium*]." What the Pope intends by *consensio fidelium* in this passage is close in meaning to a "majority view among the faithful." The Pope makes this point clear in the sentence that follows: "Following Christ, the Church seeks the truth, which is not always the same as the majority opinion [*opinio maioris hominum partis*]." He aligns "majority opinion" with power, whereas he relates "sense of the faith" with knowledge of the truth that comes from conscience. The suggestion that majority opinion smacks of power is telling. Sociological and statistical studies are useful, the Pope adds, but only when they help the Church to understand the historical context in which its pastoral activity should be developed, or when they lead to a better understanding of the truth. Hence, although their indications can be valuable, taken alone such researches do not reveal the sense of the faith.

Having said this, the Pope returns to the role of pastors with regard to the sense of the faith. Now in his strongest affirmation of the role of bishops with respect to the discernment of the sense of the faith, he insists that they "must promote the sense of the faith in all the faithful, examine and authoritatively judge the genuineness of its expressions, and educate the faithful in an ever more mature evangelical discernment." John Paul II leaves no doubt that the responsibility for discerning the sense of the faith belongs to the bishops because "it is the task of the apostolic ministry to ensure that the Church remains in the truth of Christ and to lead her ever more deeply into that truth."

It should be clear from these sections of *Familiaris consortio* that attempts to construct a sense of the faithful out of polling data or from surveys, interviews, or, worse, anecdotes conveying Catholic opinion, even those gleaned at hearings or meetings organized by the Church, or to suggest that "sense of the faithful" represents the views of the laity independent of those of the hierarchy, or that it can run counter to Catholic teaching as defined by the Magisterium, represent abuses of the concept.

Benedict XVI echoed John Paul II's position on "sense of the faith" and "sense of the faithful" when he told the International Theological Commission (ITC) that "sense of the faithful" is not to be identified with public opinion, nor can it ever be invoked against magisterial teaching.

> The *sensus fidei* is a criterion for discerning whether or not a truth belongs to the living deposit of the Apostolic Tradition. It also has a propositional value, for the Holy Spirit never ceases to speak to

the Churches and to guide them towards the whole truth. Today, however, it is particularly important to explain the criteria that make it possible to distinguish the authentic *sensus fidelium* from its counterfeit. It is certainly not a kind of public ecclesial opinion and invoking it in order to contest the teachings of the Magisterium would be unthinkable, since the *sensus fidei* cannot be authentically developed in believers, except to the extent in which they fully participate in the life of the Church, and this demands responsible adherence to the Magisterium, to the deposit of faith.[21]

In December 2013, Pope Francis renewed Benedict's invitation to the ITC to study the concept of "sense of the faithful." In his remarks to the Commission, the Pope reiterated John Paul II's and Benedict XVI's warnings about confusing "sense of the faithful" with Catholic majority opinion: "Of course, it is clear that the *sensus fidelium* must not be confused with the sociological reality of majority opinion. It is something else."[22] In a document published in 2014, the ITC then laid out criteria for establishing "those characteristics which are required of the baptized if they are truly to be subjects of the *sensus fidei*," in other words, the dispositions necessary for believers to participate authentically in the sense of the faithful.[23] It is important to know that the ITC document does not represent magisterial teaching; it is the work of a commission of theologians named by the pope to make theological recommendations. The Commission lists six characteristics and provides explanations for each. They are: (1) participation in the life of the Church; (2) listening to the word of God; (3) openness to reason; (4) adherence to the Magisterium; (5) holiness, humility, peace, and joy; and (6) seeking the edification of the Church. In terms of the first of these criteria, the ITC states that in addition to constant prayer and participation in the liturgy, especially the Eucharist, "regular reception of the sacrament of reconciliation" is required of Catholics for authentic participation in the sense of the faithful. In regard to the inclusion of "adherence to the Magisterium" as another of these criteria, the Commission points out that the Magisterium is rooted in Jesus's own teaching authority (cf. Matt 7:29), and that it is intrinsically

---

[21] Benedict XVI, Address to Members of the International Theological Commission, December 7, 2012.

[22] Francis, Address to Members of the International Theological Commission, December 6, 2013.

[23] International Theological Commission, *Sensus fidei* in the Life of the Church (Vatican City: Libreria Editrice Vaticana, 2014), §87 (hereafter, *Sensus fidei*).

related both to Scripture and Tradition. Lastly, in terms of the edification of the Church, the Commission holds that "an authentic manifestation of the *sensus fidei* . . . does not foster division and particularism within her."[24]

The German theologian Leo Cardinal Scheffczyk has indicated succinctly the answer to the question, "Who are 'the faithful' in the context of sense of the faithful?"

"We are dealing here with the capacity to judge and to bear witness in those who have faith, who open themselves to the reality of Christ and His Spirit, who live consciously in the community of the Church, which is the Body of Christ and the place where the Spirit is manifested in a unique way. People with a private faith of their own, the representatives of a 'vague Christianity,' those who are prepared to identify themselves only partially with the Church, cannot make the *sensus fidei* a reality."[25]

CONSULTING THE LAY FAITHFUL IN MATTERS OF DOCTRINE

Given the factors that have been discussed in this essay, namely (1) the Second Vatican Council's mandate of a *conspiratio* between the hierarchy and lay faithful in matters concerning the sense of the faithful, along with the Council's teaching that this sense of the faithful must be guided by the Magisterium; (2) the distinction between sense of the faithful and majority Catholic opinion; (3) the lack of adequate catechesis in the Church where doctrine and morals are concerned; (4) the increasingly irreligious impact on Catholics of secularism and moral relativism, reinforced by the mass media; and (5) the fact that not everyone among the Catholic faithful (clergy and laity) necessarily possesses authentic *sensus fidei*, the real questions to be answered are these: how does the Church discern the sense of the faithful, and the related question, how can bishops effectively consult the lay faithful over doctrinal questions?

The above-mentioned ITC document makes known various forms of consultation of the lay faithful that are expressed in official teachings of the Church and codified in canon law. At a minimum, these means should be better known. They include:

---

[24] *Sensus fidei*, §§88–104.

[25] Leo Scheffczyk, *Sensus fidelium—Zeugnis in Kraft der Gemeinschaft*, in *Internationale katholische Zeitschrift Communio* 16 (1987): 432.

particular councils, to which priests and others of Christ's faithful may be invited, diocesan synods, to which the diocesan bishop may also invite lay people as members, the pastoral council of each diocese, which is "composed of members of Christ's faithful who are in full communion with the Catholic Church: clerics, members of institutes of consecrated life, and especially lay people," and pastoral councils in parishes, in which "Christ's faithful, together with those who by virtue of their office are engaged in pastoral care in the parish, give their help in fostering pastoral action."[26]

In addition to their participation in particular councils, diocesan synods, and pastoral councils, laypeople can be invited to participate in ecumenical councils and synods of bishops convened by the pope. But they need not wait to be invited to offer counsel to bishops. The Church also teaches that laypeople can offer bishops and other of the faithful their viewpoints on matters concerning the good of the Church on their own initiative without being invited to do so, with the full knowledge that their right—and even at times their obligation to do so—is authorized by the Magisterium.[27] Moreover, bishops are reminded by canon law that they may seek at any time the expert counsel of qualified laypersons, even outside of diocesan councils or synods.[28] In short, there is no lack of opportunity for the lay faithful to offer their viewpoints to bishops.

Professional theologians in the Church, both clerical and lay, have historically been recognized as offering a service to the teaching office of the Church's pastors. The *Instruction on the Ecclesial Vocation of the Theologian*, issued in 1990 by the Congregation for the Doctrine of the Faith, and known also by its Latin title *Donum veritatis*, outlines several criteria according to which theologians can be said to participate in the work of the Magisterium.[29] According to this document, "on matters *per se* not irreformable [*in rebus quae per se irreformabiles non sunt*] . . . [i]t can happen that a theologian asks himself questions regarding the timeliness, the form, or even the contents

---

[26] *Sensus fidei*, §125, citing Code of Canon Law, can. 443, §4; 463, §2; 512, §1; 536, §1.

[27] See Code of Canon Law, can. 212, §3; cf. *Lumen gentium*, §37; CCC §§906–907.

[28] See Code of Canon Law, can. 228, §2; cf. Congregation for the Clergy, Instruction *Ecclesia de mysterio*, §2.

[29] See Congregation for the Doctrine of the Faith, Instruction on the Ecclesial Vocation of the Theologian *Donum veritatis* (May 24, 1990), §22 (hereafter, *Donum veritatis*).

of magisterial interventions."[30] When additional conditions are met and circumstances necessitate it, the theologian even "has the duty to make known to the magisterial authorities the problems raised by the teaching in itself, in the arguments proposed to justify it, or even in the manner in which it is presented."[31] *Donum veritatis* suggests that in such a case the theologian's "objections could then contribute to real progress and provide a stimulus to the Magisterium to propose the teaching of the Church in greater depth and with a clearer presentation of the arguments."[32] Commenting on these passages in the Instruction, Avery Cardinal Dulles saw a real openness to the perspective of the theologian reflected by the Congregation. "The development of doctrine has sometimes been assisted by expressions of dissatisfaction with previous deficient formulations. This observation of the CDF is noteworthy," Dulles continued, "since it is relatively new for theologians to receive official encouragement to express their problems with current magisterial teaching."[33]

With all of the above-mentioned Church structures for consulting the lay faithful in matters of doctrine, the question must nevertheless be restated, this time with a greater focus. Once the surveys have been conducted and the synods, particular councils, hearings, and meetings are concluded, once various lay theologians have offered their counsel and Catholic organizations and bloggers have made their views clear, how can bishops be reasonably certain that whatever input or feedback from the lay faithful they have garnered through these particular structures, as well as through their own conversations with lay experts on the question, expresses the "sense of the lay faithful" (*sensus fidelium laicorum*), and not the mere opinion of some of them who happened to have been consulted at a particular synod, pastoral council, or other venue? In conjunction with this question is the caution issued by the Holy See in 1997, which warned bishops to beware of those among the faithful—sometimes chosen for synods or pastoral councils through rigged selection procedures—who constitute lobby groups that push for the adoption of proposals at odds with defined Church teachings.[34]

Bishops are certainly obliged to dismiss proposals from the laity that

---

[30] *Donum veritatis*, §24.

[31] *Donum veritatis*, §30.

[32] *Donum veritatis*, §30.

[33] Avery Dulles, *Magisterium: Teacher and Guardian of the Faith* (Naples, FL: Sapientia Press, 2007), 98. CDF refers to the Congregation for the Doctrine of the Faith.

[34] Congregation for Bishops, Instruction on Diocesan Synods (19 March 1997), III.C.2.

contradict the deposit of faith or defined Church teachings as determined by the Magisterium.[35] However, the ITC document cautions that at times when Church teaching meets with difficulty or resistance on the part of the faithful, "the magisterium must likewise reflect on the teaching that has been given and consider whether it needs clarification or reformulation in order to communicate more effectively the *essential message*."[36] This statement invites close scrutiny. I take the expression "clarification or reformulation" to mean that the Magisterium ought to restate the same teaching using different language in order to communicate the "essential message" more effectively and thus to overcome the resistance among the faithful. I do not take "clarification and reformulation" to mean that the message ought to be retracted or substantively altered (otherwise how is it that the "message" is in fact "essential"?). It seems to me from this statement that what is at stake in the "clarification or reformulation" are the *verba*, the words or language used to convey the teaching, not the *res*, the essence of the matter being taught.

Another factor, rarely if ever mentioned in the spate of theological literature concerning "sense of the faithful" since the Second Vatican Council, should also be considered. If the sense of the faith of the individual believer depends upon the theological virtue of faith (*fides qua creditur*), then an individual believer's lack of faith, moral ignorance, or personal sin can also impede his receptivity to this particular insight into the faith (*fides quae creditur*) which results from grace. For this reason, the ITC is right to insist on regular reception of the Sacrament of Reconciliation as one of the necessary conditions enabling the believer (whether cleric or layperson) to apprehend the *sensus fidei*. No less an authority on sense of the faithful than Saint Augustine concluded his classic work *De trinitate* praying for divine healing from his own moral weakness and ignorance because he understood—and wanted others to understand—that his personal moral defects could impede his own perception of the rule of faith (*regula fidei*) concerning the Holy Trinity.[37]

I suggest that the question of how to discern the "sense of the faithful" is not an easy one to answer, nor should it be. In an ideal Church, this "collective faith-consciousness" might be ubiquitously in evidence, as Pope Pius

---

[35] Congregation for Bishops, Instruction on Diocesan Synods, IV.3.

[36] *Sensus fidei*, §80 (emphasis added).

[37] Augustine, *De trinitate* 15.51.

XII claimed was the case when he consulted the faithful prior to the prom-ulgation of the dogma of the Assumption.[38] But not all doctrinal questions, in particular as they concern moral issues, should be expected to achieve such a high level of visible consensus across the universal Church given the lamentable condition of catechesis, the strong cultural tug of secularism, the high level of media consumption, the low (and still falling) rates of liturgi-cal participation, and the crisis of authority that touches a wide spectrum of religious and secular institutions. These are certainly among the signs of the times affecting the manner in which the faithful today think about the authority of Church teachings, and they offer real challenges to the Church's discernment of the sense of the faithful.

Unfortunately, the ITC document offers little help in clarifying this cen-tral question. It points out that at least since the pontificate of Pius XII the opinions of the faithful have been considered necessary for the Church. It does so in the context of quoting from the Pastoral Instruction, known by its Latin title *Communio et progressio*, issued by the Pontifical Council for Social Communications in 1971.[39] No document of the Holy See has taken a more positive view of the relationship between Catholic public opinion and *sensus fidei* than this one. But even this document insists that whereas "there is an enormous area where members of the Church can express their views on domestic issues," nevertheless, "it must be accepted that the truths of the faith express the essence of the Church and therefore do not leave room for arbitrary interpretations."[40] *Communio et progressio* encourages the free expression in the Church of the opinions of the faithful, which it states "stem from" the *sensus fidei*, but then it carefully pivots back to the principle articulated in the aforementioned Second Vatican Council docu-ment *Lumen gentium* that *sensus fidei* is guided by the Magisterium.[41] Once again, the linkage between "sense of the faithful" and "magisterial teaching" is reiterated so that the expressed views of Catholics who disagree with "the truths of the faith" remain "arbitrary interpretations" and not expressions of "sense of the faithful."

---

[38] Pius XII, Apostolic Constitution Defining the Dogma of the Assumption *Munificentissimus Deus* (November 1, 1950), §11.

[39] Pontifical Council for Social Communications, Pastoral Instruction on the Means of Social Communication *Communio et progressio* (May 23, 1971), §§115–21 (hereafter, *Communio et progressio*).

[40] *Communio et progressio*, §§116–17.

[41] *Communio et progressio*, §116.

Hence, the statement in *Communio et progressio*, quoted in the ITC document,[42] that the opinions of the faithful "stem from" the *sensus fidei* has to be interpreted in the light of later magisterial statements, such as that of John Paul II in *Familiaris consortio*:

> The "supernatural sense of faith" [*supernaturalis sensus fidei*] however does not consist solely or necessarily in the agreement of the faithful [*consensio fidelium*]. Following Christ, the Church seeks the truth, which is not always the same as the majority opinion.[43]

It is unfortunate that the quotation from *Communio et progressio* in the ITC document introduces a certain ambiguity in regard to the difference between Catholic public opinion and sense of the faithful. In an earlier section of the document, the ITC is much clearer on this point:

> As the above discussion of dispositions implicitly shows, the *sensus fidei* cannot simply be identified, therefore, with public or majority opinion in the Church, either. Faith, not opinion, is the necessary focus of attention. Opinion is often just an expression, frequently changeable and transient, of the mood or desires of a certain group or culture, whereas faith is the echo of the one Gospel which is valid for all places and times.[44]

Bishops whose function it is to consult the lay faithful in matters of doctrine have the task of discerning whether what they are hearing is an echo of the truth of the apostolic faith or an erroneous opinion, even if majoritarian, and ultimately the papal Magisterium must make the final judgment. But bishops would also do well to apply the criteria offered by the International Theological Commission in regard to the dispositions necessary for participation in the sense of the faith, mindful that not all of the baptized possess the requisite dispositions.

It is for the reasons outlined in this essay that I do not believe it to be as easy to discern the sense of the faithful as do so many theologians who have written on the matter. Answers to survey questionnaires or other forms of

---

[42] *Sensus fidei*, §124.

[43] *Sensus fidei*, §5.

[44] *Sensus fidei*, §118.

consultation, no matter how professionally prepared they are, reveal opinions, and although at best they *may* give some indication of the sense of the faithful, they do not necessarily do so. Nevertheless, in spite of the fact that everyone who treats the issue of sense of the faithful admits that it is not identical to majority Catholic opinion, all too many of these theologians and journalists invariably write about it as if it were.

APOSTOLICITY AND HISTORICITY: SCRIPTURE, DEVELOPMENT, AND A TRULY CRITICAL HISTORY

John Finnis

The Church's teaching about the truth of the Gospels is a model of developed doctrine. What it transmits includes the same propositions, the same meaning and judgments—but unpacked, consolidated, and explained—as the apostles conveyed (mostly explicitly, partly impliedly) when they told listening unbelievers and believers about what Jesus of Nazareth said and did from the time he was baptized by John until six weeks after he was crucified, died, was buried, rose from among the dead, and first ate and drank and conversed with them.

The developed doctrine tells two things. First, it affirms that whatever you read in the Gospels about what Jesus said and did is—when its author's intention has been exactly understood—to be trusted as historically true. For when the Second Vatican Council's Dogmatic Constitution on Divine Revelation *Dei Verbum* (*DV*) says "the Church unhesitatingly affirms the *historicity* of the Gospels," it uses the word "historicity" not at all as it has since been employed by some theologians to mean *subject to historical change*, but instead (unambiguously, as we will see in part II) to mean *historically true*, corresponding to *what really happened*.[1] And second, the developed doctrine tells us that central among all the reasons for trusting the Gospels, and the

---

[1] Second Vatican Council, Dogmatic Constitution on Divine Revelation *Dei Verbum* (November 18, 1965), 19. Hereafter cited parenthetically in text as *DV*. Throughout this essay, all emphases in quotations are added, unless footnoted "emphasis original." Translations into English from Latin and French are by this essay's author.

Church's doctrine about them, is this: these four documents *authentically* transmit the oral teaching and preaching of the apostles. They transmit what the apostles told their hearers face-to-face in the Church's first days, weeks, and years about what the Lord had really said and done. These apostles, in risking their freedom and their lives to tell each audience what they had heard and seen Jesus actually say and do for their salvation to eternal life, always *implied* (and sometimes openly affirmed) what the Council document *Dei Verbum* says outright about the four canonical versions of their preaching and catechesis that were written up for reading: these men spoke truly and sincerely—with probity, with honesty—about *what they as eyewitnesses remembered*, or what they had been told by others who likewise saw, heard, and remembered.

As we will consider in detail, *DV* 18 and 19 spell out what the Gospel writers, too, each implied: that what they were setting down in writing was either a further expression of their own truthful, memory-based preaching, or an accurate rendering of truthful, memory-based recounting by others (say, Peter, Mary the mother of Jesus, Joseph his reputed father, Nathaniel, and other apostles) who had seen and heard words and actions of the Lord or his immediate associates or interlocutors, as recounted in these writings.

Part I of this essay concerns the importance of the apostles in the Church's understanding of doctrine's transmission and development.

Part II shows how clearly the developed doctrine distinguishes the historicity of the Gospels from the truth in the historical books of the Old Testament. Properly critically interpreted, those books—though inspired in all they say and true in all they really assert—were not intended to have what *apostolicity* (as affirmed by doctrine and vindicated by critical scholarship) entails for the Gospels: the character of testimony by or from eyewitnesses who, tested by the doubts of those they addressed, recount things said, done, and seen "among us" (Luke 1:1), that is, among the very people whom this testimony reminded or informed, *and* challenged.

Part III concerns, all too briefly, the burial of the developed doctrine as soon as its affirmation of the historical truth of the Gospels had been solemnly taught by the Council. Almost unchallenged, scholars and teachers influential in the Catholic world began and have continued uninterrupted—indeed, not rarely with high episcopal *imprimaturs*—to portray the Gospels and their formation not so much as developments as, to an extent now unascertainable, substitutions: as theologically motivated constructs of editors/redactors and their communities who redeployed but supplemented "traditional material" about the now only speculatively inferable doings and teachings of Jesus of Nazareth and his apostles. In the name of historical criticism, all such biblical scholarship and teaching ignores and defies the Church's definitive doctrine. It is doctrinal error of the gravest kind. But it is also, and first, bad history— defective because insufficiently critical. Part III enumerates a dozen angles from which to explore that failure of historical-critical method.

I.

Those who drafted and adopted *Dei Verbum* regarded it as the weightiest of all the Council's documents. Approved by 2,344 out of 2,350 bishops on November 18, 1965, its teaching on what revelation is, and how it is transmitted, is given with clarity and firmness.

Its key terms are: words, deeds, handing on (*traditio; transmissio*), and apostles/apostolic. What is done by God in history manifests and confirms both what he teaches and the realities signified by the words—the doctrines— that convey (transmit, hand on) that teaching (*DV* 2). Revealing by historical processes and events, God has manifested and communicated to us both confirmatory clarification of what reason unaided by revelation can reliably discover about the Creator's existence and goodness, and many truths accessible only by divine revelation. By the time of its completion, that revelation had disclosed more about God's nature and vastly more about the whole purpose of creation: to give access to a share in the life of God to anyone who has sought it with perseverance (endurance: *patientia*) (*DV* 1, 2, 6). The communication of this hope, a hope at first obscure though real (see Gen 3:15 and *DV* 3), was accomplished by a measured divine pedagogy through the patriarchs of Israel, Moses, and other prophets (*DV* 15). Really sufficient clarity came only with the presence and self-manifestation of Jesus Christ, by his words and deeds, his signs and miracles, his death and resurrection, and his sending of the Holy Spirit upon the apostles (*DV* 3–4). These men he commissioned to *transmit* through the rest of history that covenant of God's promise which we enter into and persevere in by the obedience of faith and by the other divine gifts: love of God and neighbor and hope in that promise of eternal life (*DV* 4–6).

The chapter on *revelation's transmission* deals exclusively with the apostles Christ commissioned and the New Testament they left us. For:

> This commission has been faithfully carried out, both
>
> > [a] by Apostles who by oral teaching, by example and by institutions have handed on what they had received—from the words, dealings and deeds of Christ or from what the Holy Spirit taught them—and
> >
> > [b] by those Apostles and associates of theirs [*apostolici viri*] who, under the Holy Spirit's inspiration, have put into writing the message of salvation. . . .
>
> And so *the apostolic preaching*, expressed in a special way in inspired books, is to be preserved until the end of time. (*DV* 7, 8)

This will be repeated, with greater specificity and doctrinal firmness, in *DV* 18 and 19. In between, the Council teaches about doctrinal development in general, and a special instance of it: how Scripture's canon formed.

DV 8 on Development of Doctrine

The "tradition that comes from the apostles develops [*proficit*, advances, progresses] in the Church with the help of the Holy Spirit" (*DV* 8). The footnote to *proficit* cites what the First Vatican Council, while teaching about reason and faith, affirmed about stability and development of doctrine (and supported by quotation from Vincent of Lérins's *Commonitorium* 23):

> For, the doctrine of faith which God revealed has . . . been entrusted as a divine deposit to the Spouse of Christ, to be faithfully guarded and infallibly interpreted. Hence, also, that understanding of its sacred dogmas must be perpetually retained, which Holy Mother Church [*Sancta Mater Ecclesia*] has once declared; and *there must never be recession from that meaning* under the specious name of a deeper understanding. . . . "Therefore . . . let the understanding [*intelligentia*], the knowledge, and wisdom of individuals as of all, of one man as of the whole Church, grow [*crescat*], and progress/develop [*proficiat*] strongly with the passage of the ages and the centuries; but let it be solely in its own genus,

namely in the same dogma, with the same sense and the same understanding [*sententia*]."[2]

DV 8 has two points to add. First, the processes by which doctrine develops:

For there is a growth in the understanding [*crescit . . . perceptio*] of the realities and the words that have been handed down. This happens through

> [a] the contemplation and study made by believers, who treasure these things in their hearts (see Luke, 2:19, 51), through
>
> [b] a penetrating understanding [*intima intelligentia*] of the spiritual realities which they experience, and through
>
> [c] the preaching of those who have received through Episcopal succession the sure gift of truth.

Second, *DV* 8 adds the reminder that all such "contemplation and study" and all such "understanding of experienced spiritual realities" must *retain* in its integrity the apostolic tradition, the revelation transmitted to, and by, the apostles, during and in the immediate aftermath of Christ's ministry:

The Apostles, handing on what they themselves had received, warn the faithful to hold fast to the traditions which they have learned either by word of mouth or by letter (see 2 Thess 2:15), and to fight in defence of *the faith handed on once and for all* (see Jude 3).

Jude, brother of the James who led the Jerusalem church after Peter had to depart (ca. AD 41–43), was one of the *apostolici viri* (approved associates of the apostles). In Jude 17 the "saints" to whom, "once for all," the faith was entrusted are identified: the apostles. It is they who were handing on the faith to believers like those whom Jude 3 exhorts to fight in its defense.

Six of *DV* 8's seven sentences refer to the apostles and their apostolic community. The Council is thus developing, by clarifying, what Vincent of Lérins doubtless meant in saying that progress (advance, development) in religion (the faith)—progress by growth in understanding (and knowledge and wisdom)—must be "solely in its own genus." The *genus* (or *kind* or, as Newman evidently translates, *type*) is, *DV* 8 implies, *apostolicity*.

---

[2] First Vatican Council, *Dei Filius*, April 24, 1870, ch. 4; cf. Vincent of Lérins, *Commonitorium* 23.

That was implicit in Vincent's several statements of the "rule" of development. For the argument in *Commonitorium* 24, is this:

> It is the sure characteristic of Catholics to keep that which has been committed to their trust *by the holy Fathers* . . . and, in the apostle's words (Gal 1:9) . . . to anathematize everyone who preaches any other doctrine than *that which has been received*.

Here, as in related passages, the first, decisive "holy Fathers" are the apostolic group. From them all subsequent "fathers" have "received in trust" the doctrine to which, in turn, all Catholics must hold fast. What grows, progresses, and can be articulated in new ways (*nove*), with new language (*novae appellationis*), is like seed of a specific *kind*, the grains of "wheat planted in the field of the Church by our forefathers [*maiores nostri*]"—which again must mean the apostles and those whose work as associates they approved. Through the course of great changes in "shape, form, variation in outward appearance," *that* same *kind* and nature is to remain: not tares or seed of any other kind, but wheat—indeed, we may add, the very wheat that the apostolic community planted.[3]

Foreshadowing the Second Vatican Council's focus and insistence, Catholic theologians like Grandmaison and Rousselot in the first decade of the twentieth century (summarized in the sixth decade by the early Karl Rahner, and resuming Newman's "University Sermon 15") had explained how doctrine can develop *without novelty* even though—or because—by the close of the New Testament *"everything was said."*[4] For "said" refers here not only to the propositions set out in the apostolically authored or approved oral-tradition writings and to already explicit doctrinal formulations crystallizable in creeds; it refers also to a "conserving envelope of analogies and figures of speech," to liturgical prayers, and to the orientations of the soul of believers implying or obscurely indicating truths, dispositions, attitudes, gestures, and rites received among the apostles.[5] The deposit of faith is *that* complex totality, and as *DV* 8 puts it: "what was handed on by the apostles includes everything which contributes toward the holiness of life and increase in faith of the peoples of God."

Development of doctrine cannot be authentic unless what is developed is "the understanding of the realities and the words which have been handed

---

[3] *Commonitorium* 23.

[4] See Léonce de Grandmaison, "Le développement du dogme chrétien—IV: Le développement proprement dit," *Revue pratique d'apologétique* 6, no. 72 (1908): 894.

[5] Grandmaison, "Le développement proprement dit," 894.

down" from the apostles (*DV* 8)—of *all* the words, and thus of all the realities, even details, that were signified by what was set down in the original canonical writing (as distinct from any mistranscription or mistranslation). Such development has often been not only possible but needed, precisely in order to defend what, once for all, was deposited with and then *by* the apostles for safekeeping and onward transmission—to defend the deposit against the fading, diminishing, or embellishing of Christ that every distortion, diminution, neglect, adulteration, or would-be supplementation of it entails.

The Canon's Formation (and Identification)

"Through the same tradition [i] the Church's full canon of the sacred books is known, and [ii] the sacred writings themselves are more profoundly understood and unceasingly made active in her" (*DV* 8). About [i], *DV* 11 is more specific:

> For holy mother Church [*sancta Mater Ecclesia*], relying on the belief of the Apostles [*ex apostolica fide*] (see Jn 20:31; 2 Tim 3:16; 2 Pet 1:19–21, 3:15–16), holds that the books of both the Old and New Testaments in their entirety, with all their parts, are sacred and canonical because written under the inspiration of the Holy Spirit.

"Relying on the belief of the Apostles": that translation, from the Holy See's website, is more specific than what it is translating: *ex apostolica fide*, "from apostolic faith." The phrase is vague because councils do not seek to settle such theological differences as that between M.-J. Lagrange (the leading Catholic New Testament scholar from 1895 to 1935) and Lucien Cerfaux (prime architect of *Dei Verbum*, especially *DV* 7–8 and 18–19)[6] about precisely how apostolicity identified the canon. Was it that the apostolic community *itself*

---

6   See Karim Schelkens, "Exegesis in the Wake of Vatican II: Lucien Cerfaux and the Origins of *Dei Verbum*," *Annali di storia dell'esegesi* 25, no. 2 (2008): 169–201; Riccardo Burigana, *La Bibbia nel Concilio: La redazione della costituzione 'Dei Verbum' del Vaticano II* (Bologna: Il Mulino, 1998). Scholarly writings of Cerfaux relevant to his work from 1960 toward *Dei Verbum*, mostly collected in *Recueil Lucien Cerfaux: Études d'exégèse et d'histoire religieuse* (Gembloux: Duculot, 1954 [vols. 1 and 2], 1962 [vol. 3]), include: "Les deux points de départ de la tradition chrétienne" (1954), 2:265–82; "La tradition selon saint Paul" (1953), 2:253–63; "La première communauté chrétienne à Jérusalem" (1939), 2:125–56; "Témoins du Christ d'après le Livre des Actes" (1943), 2:157–74; "Pour l'histoire du titre *Apostolos* dans le Nouveau Testament" (1960), 3:185–200. The complete bibliography in F. Neirynck, ed., *L'évangile de Luc: Problèmes littéraires et théologiques* (Gembloux: Duculot, 1973), 71–90, by including Cerfaux's many reviews, gives an indication of his mastery of the emergent scholarly literature across the whole field. For scholarly-popular works of Cerfaux in English, see *The Four Gospels: An Historical Introduction* (Westminster, MD: Newman, 1960); *Apostle and Apostolate according to the Gospel of St. Matthew* (New York: Desclée, 1959).

settled which writings were apostolic and therefore inspired and canonical (Lagrange)?[7] Or was it the succeeding generations who—by a development of doctrine, especially by choice of liturgical readings—settled *the same question by the same criterion* (Cerfaux)?[8] Either way, the apostles and their close associates are decisive, as *DV* 18 and 19 will make yet more certain.

II.

As we saw, *DV* 7 says that apostles and associates of theirs set down in writing what the apostles, acting in accordance with the command of Christ, had orally preached. It was reserved to *DV* 18 and 19 to articulate this more fully and with greater weight.

First, *DV* 17: salvation, the kingdom, and eternal life were revealed not to other generations but to Christ's "holy apostles and prophets ... so that they might preach the Gospel, elicit faith in Christ ... , and assemble the Church." Then, *DV* 18.1: the Gospels are the "principal source for the life and teaching of the Incarnate Word." And then, *DV* 18.2:

> The Church always and everywhere has held and holds that the four Gospels are of apostolic origin. For [*enim*] *what the Apostles preached* by Christ's command, *they themselves* [*ipsi*], *and men associated with them* [*apostolici viri*], by inspiration of the Holy Spirit *handed down* [*tradiderunt*] *to us, in writings* [*in scriptis*: in written form], the *foundation of the faith*, namely the fourfold Gospel, according to Matthew, Mark, Luke and John.

As *enim* makes clear, the first sentence's weighty affirmation of "apostolic origin" is both specified and justified by the second sentence's "they themselves," not merely associates of theirs, "handed down in writings" what they had orally preached. Of course, even if those seven words—"they themselves, and men associated with them"—were compressed to "Apostles wrote," it would not *necessarily* affirm more about what apostles (say, Matthew and John) personally did than John 19:19 affirms in saying "Pilate also wrote a title and put it on the cross" (by ordering its wording and placing), or than scholars affirm in agreeing that Paul wrote Romans (though he says "Tertius wrote the

[7] Marie-Joseph Lagrange, *Histoire ancienne du Canon du Nouveau Testament* (Paris: Gabalda, 1933).
[8] Lucien Cerfaux, review of Lagrange, *Histoire: Ephemerides theologicae lovanienses* 11 (1934): 635–37.

letter," doubtless at Paul's dictation; see Rom 16:22). "Apostles handed down in writings": the memorized oral preaching and written memoranda of, say, Matthew Levi, the customs collector—and perhaps of other apostles such as Peter and James the brother of John—were reduced to writing in a form such as we see today in Matthew, whether that Gospel results from his own editing or from another's or others' of his acquaintance, in a manner he approved or would have approved. As to the *apostolici viri* (as Tertullian called them), the drafting committee notified the Council that this refers, as "everyone knows," to "Mark, Luke, etc." Mark was closely associated with both Peter and Paul, Luke with Paul; their gospels, says *DV* 18.2, put in writing what had been preached *by apostles*. Thus, each gospel has an apostolicity more specific than simply being "of apostolic origin," and this apostolicity, the Council here affirms, is at the foundation of the faith.

Perhaps *DV* 18.2's degree of specificity—incomplete though it is—about the apostolic authorship of two gospels explains the complete silence about *DV* 18.2 in subsequent documents of the Magisterium. What the Church has always held and in 1965 still held and firmly proclaimed has fallen into oblivion—a startling hiatus in the handing on of doctrine; as a "development" in doctrine, one that fails all the tests for authenticity.

And the silence about *DV* 18.2 immediately causes *DV* 19 to be misread when it speaks of the "sacred authors" of the Gospels, as if these "authors" were neither apostles nor even companions of apostles, *apostolici viri*. Yet that is not the worst distortion in the reception of *DV* 19. Here is that whole section, reformatted and enumerated for clarity of discussion:

[i] Holy Mother Church [*Sancta Mater Ecclesia*] firmly and with utmost constancy has held and holds that the aforesaid four *Gospels, whose historicity the Church unhesitatingly affirms, faithfully hand on* [*tradere*] what Jesus the Son of God, while he lived among men and women, *actually/really* [*reapse*] *did and taught* [down to the day of his ascension: Acts 1:1–2] for their eternal salvation.

[ii] For after the Lord's ascension, *the Apostles handed on* [*tradiderunt*] *to their hearers those things that he had said and done*, and did this with the fuller understanding they now enjoyed

having been instructed by the events of Christ's risen life and taught by the light of the Spirit of truth.[9]

[iii] *The sacred authors of the four Gospels wrote them* by

[a] selecting some among the many things handed on [*traditis*] either orally or in writing,

[b] synthesizing some things or

[c] explicating [*explanantes*] them with an eye to the situation of the churches,

[d] retaining the preaching form/style—but *always* [semper] *in such a way that they [the authors] would communicate to us honest truths* [*vera et sincera*] *about Jesus.*[10]

[iv] *For* [enim] *their intention in writing was that, either from their own memory and recollections, or from the testimony of* those "who from the beginning were *eyewitnesses* and ministers of the word," we would know "the truth" of the things about which we have been taught (see Luke 1:2–4).

The Council's quotation marks around "the truth" ["*veritatem*"] are not scare quotes, but simply indicate completion of the quotation from Luke 1:2–4 (Vulgate) begun earlier in [iv].

Indeed, the first four verses of Luke provide the master idea or theme of *DV* 18–19, if not of *Dei Verbum* as a whole. For those who "from the beginning were eyewitnesses and ministers of the word" are preeminently the apostles, paradigmatically the Twelve, as Luke makes clear in his subsequent book, Acts 1:21–22; 6:4. And Luke 1:1–2 refers to the same three phases or stages as *DV* 19 [i], [ii], and [iii]: [i] the things done and said "among us" by Jesus, [ii] the handing on [*traditio*] of these by the apostles, and [iii] the compilation of this same apostolic-eyewitness-*traditio* into a "narrative" by a plurality of authors. *DV* 19 is an authentic development of the teaching in Luke (and in John) about the origins of the Gospels.

The Instruction *Sancta Mater Ecclesia* cited at the end of *DV* 19 [iii] is entitled "On the Historical Truth of the Gospels." Its primary authors, from

---

9   See John 2:22; 12:16; with 14:26; 16:12–13; 7:39.

10 The Council's footnote reads: "See Pontifical Biblical Commission, Instruction *Sancta Mater Ecclesia*, *Acta Apostolicae Sedis*, 56 (1964): 715."

its inception in early 1963 to its approval by Paul VI in April 1964, were—as consultors to the Pontifical Biblical Commission, a commission of cardinals— Cerfaux along with his former student Béda Rigaux, author of a long 1959 article on the Gospels' historicity and soon to be *DV* 19's *relator* in the Council.

The particular page of the Instruction that *DV* 19 cites, *Acta Apostolicae Sedis* 56: p. 715, finishes discussing phase [ii] of what p. 714 calls "the three stages of the tradition through which the life and teaching of Jesus have come down to us," and moves on to phase [iii]. As to phase [ii], p. 714 describes Christ's choosing of "a select group of disciples," "the Apostles," who "saw his works and heard his words" and so were well-placed witnesses to his life and teaching. They absorbed and remembered his oral preaching (phase [i]), and realized that his miracles, like other events of his life, "took place so that people might believe in him and embrace his message of salvation." So they in turn, like him, *taught orally in ways adapted to their audience*, announcing first and foremost his death and resurrection. After and because of that resurrection, they understood his words and deeds more fully—and here the Instruction's citations include those given in *DV* 19 [ii] to John, where Jesus intimates that this would be so. Repeatedly, p. 714 of the Instruction emphasizes that the apostles' memories of Jesus were strengthened, but not replaced, by the full faith they acquired after his resurrection.

Thus, the page cited by *DV* 19, p. 715, opens with the Instruction's final point about phase [ii]: just as Jesus in his post-resurrection instructions explained his own words, and those of the Old Testament, so too the apostles in their preaching "explained his words and deeds according to the needs of their audience," using a whole range of "literary genres commonly found in Sacred Scripture and the speech of that period." Their instruction "was passed on orally at first and later written down—indeed, before long [*mox*, soon], many attempted [as Luke 1:1 states] 'to draw up a narrative.'"

At this point the Instruction, since it will not touch on authorship or dates of specific gospels, starts speaking of their "sacred authors" and "the Evangelist[s]." Its single purpose, critically affirming the historical truth of the Gospels, is sufficiently achieved by stating that "they recorded *this* primitive [*primaevam*, earliest] teaching," the memory-based oral teaching of the apostles.

The cited page then articulates what *DV* 19 [iii] in points [a] through [d] will articulate, about selecting and synthesizing, and about explaining or explicating [*explanare*] in line with "the needs of the various churches." (*DV* 19 [iii]

[c] will replace "needs" with "situation.") It concludes by saying that "the truth of the Gospel account [*narratio*] is not compromised when the Evangelists report the Lord's words and deeds in different order, nor impaired when they report His words, not literally but in a variety of ways, *while retaining the same meaning* [*sensu tamen retento*]." The last words of p. 715 are Augustine's, and again imply that memory was crucial: "It is quite probable that each Evangelist felt duty-bound to narrate his particular account in the order which God suggested to his memory . . . at least where order would not affect the Gospel's authority or truth."

Historical criticism, and especially "form-criticism," had been discussed in the Instruction's preceding pages. In summary, that method is helpful, even necessary, but not when deployed as it commonly is on erroneous presuppositions such as those listed on p. 713: faith does not depend upon or care about historical truth; God does not intervene in the world by revelation, miracles, or prophecies; the creative power of the primitive Christian community was more important to the formation of the Gospels than the apostles were. These principles and opinions, says the Instruction, lack scholarly foundation and "are *inconsistent with the sound principles of historical method*" (714).

Sound exegesis uses all the sound elements of "form-criticism." Constantly searching for the original writers' intentions, sound exegesis attends rigorously to their literary genres and native patterns of expression. "In short, the exegete will use any and every means to acquire a deeper insight into the nature of the Gospel tradition, the religious life of the early churches, and *the meaning and value of the apostolic tradition*."

DV 19 and *Sancta Mater Ecclesia* are fully concordant. They were drafted largely by the same two or three scholars. The same cardinal-exegete, Augustine Bea, presided over the adoption of the Instruction and was Paul VI's personal emissary in the settling of *DV* 19's final version. Later, the leading American exegete on the postconciliar Pontifical Biblical Commission, Raymond Brown, systematically slighting *DV* 19, would put about the myth (repeated by his colleague Joseph Fitzmyer) that *DV* 19 depended on the Instruction so extensively that it even took its opening words from the Instruction's title.[11] In readily accessible truth, those words headed up *DV* 19's drafts long before the Instruction; both documents took it from the First Vatican Council's teaching (quoted

---

[11] Joseph A. Fitzmyer, *The Interpretation of Scripture: In Defense of the Historical-Critical Method* (New York: Paulist Press, 2008), 10.

above) on scriptural revelation and from the Council of Trent's teaching on "that meaning [*sensum*] of sacred Scripture which holy mother Church [*sancta mater Ecclesia*] has held and holds."[12]

The Instruction's more immediate reception may, however, have stimulated a final, reinforcing tweak to *DV* 19. By early fall 1964, the young Jesuit exegete Joseph Fitzmyer had translated and commented on the Instruction in *Theological Studies*, a leading American theological journal. In doing so he had disclosed how far he and doubtless many others were straining to abandon Catholic exegesis as understood in the tradition articulated in *Dei Verbum*. He noted, above all, that "historical truth" appears only in the Instruction's title (and in its discussion of philosophically misguided versions of form-criticism), not in its own positive teaching. According to him, its authors, by this (alleged) silence and by their acceptance of redactional "selecting, synthesising and explicating," implied that the Gospels, besides any historical truth (historicity) they may (!) contain, contain other kinds of truth: poetical, rhetorical, perhaps even mythical truth, which all together make up the inspired *Gospel truth*. According to Fitzmyer, the Church is affirming no more than "Gospel truth" and, therefore, that is all the Instruction need mean when it speaks of "the truth of the Gospel account." He used a rhetorical question to imply that, because of its "admission of . . . redactional work" such as the exception that Matthew "added" on divorce, the Instruction can scarcely be taken to have meaningfully affirmed the Gospels' "historical truth" or (synonymous) "historicity."[13]

Such statements and insinuations will have been read in Rome in late 1964, not least (we may suppose) by Bea, whose own commentary on the Instruction, building on his 1962 pamphlet for all the Council Fathers, was translated (by Fitzmyer!) in 1964 (and the title greatly changed from *La storicità dei vangeli* to *The Study of the Gospels*). As agent for Paul VI, Bea ensured that, at the drafting's very last stage (November 1965), *DV* 19 [i] came to include "whose *historicity* the Church unhesitatingly affirms."

In Bea's, Cerfaux's, Rigaux's, *and* Fitzmyer's writings, "historicity" meant historical truth. And the drafting commission made this explicit: "historicity," they said, is an unambiguous word that refers quite concretely to the reality of

---

[12] Council of Trent, First Decree Concerning the Canonical Scriptures, Session 4 (April 8, 1546); DH 1507.

[13] Fitzmyer, *The Interpretation of Scripture*, 38, 44, 49–50. Originally published as "The Biblical Commission's Instruction on the Historical Truth of the Gospels," *Theological Studies* 25, no. 3 (1964): 387–88, 395, 400–401.

the actions or events about which the Gospels tell. *Thus DV 19 affirms what Fitzmyer claimed the 1964 Instruction does not*—wrongly claimed, because the Instruction's affirmations leave no room for the opinion that the writing of the Gospels included elements conveying what Jesus did not do or teach but the writer(s) thought the churches needed to believe he taught and did.

But plainer still, there is *DV* 19's last sentence. This excludes all theories claiming that the redactors/editors active in stage [iii] allowed themselves to depart from eyewitness memories by adding statements or actions invented or created to make, illustrate, or explain some theological or moral point. Plainly, in selecting among their memories, and in articulating them, the Gospel writers were responsive to the interest they and their earliest audiences had in the ful-fillment of the Old Testament's histories and prophecies; and very occasionally they made some other comment (e.g., Mark 7:19b). But they invented nothing, whether to fabricate the fulfillment of prophecies or for any other motive of persuasion. *DV* 19 [iv], present as *DV* 19's final sentence in identical form and place from before work began on the Instruction in the spring of 1963 all the way to *Dei Verbum*'s approval in November 1965, is the Council's rejection both of Rudolf Bultmann's theses about the Gospels' relation to history and of any redaction-critical theses that defend similar conclusions.

For *DV* 19 [iv] affirms that the Gospel writers in their redactional work had an overarching *intention (illa enim intentione scripserunt)*. That intent is essential to *DV* 19's affirmation that these redactors/writers were *always* com-municating *true and sincere* things about Jesus—historically true things. For that intention was, 19 [iv] affirms, that the solid truth of Christian preaching and teaching be demonstrated *by honest and accurate recounting*, if not *of what was remembered* (recollected) about Jesus by the Gospel writers, then of what was reported ("testimony") to them by eyewitnesses who themselves remembered what Jesus had said and done.

And the connective "For [*enim*]" unequivocally signifies that what is affirmed in 19 [iv] is the foundation for what *DV* 18.2 calls the foundation of the faith.

The affirmation in 19 [iv] also tells why 19 [i] uses "the Church *has held and holds*" instead of "has believed and believes." It is to show, the drafting commission explained, that the Church, in saying that the Gospels faithfully hand on what Jesus actually said and did, is stating what ought to be held as a matter not just of faith but *also of reason*.[14]

---

[14] Emphasis original.

In all these ways, *DV* 19 carefully indicated the Gospels' straightforward kind of historicity. It is the *historicity that is intended in advance by honest eye-witnesses in testifying, and that then results when this testimony is understood, accepted, and handed on*, and that can be supplemented by the testimony of those who, like John Mark, and Saul, and even Luke, heard it from them and, like all their first hearers, could cross-examine them and verify what they said by commonsense reference to facts of time, place, and circumstance.[15]

As Lagrange says in one of his last lectures—after forty years studying and commenting upon the Gospels in their historical concreteness, with the intent always to be more critically historical than the "historical criticism" of his era: for a Jew (or a Gentile) to believe the claim of Jesus to be Christ and Son of God, after his crucifixion in humiliation for making that outlandish claim, there had to be miracles, and words that strike mind and heart as simply true. "The faith's foundation is the reality of *facts*" (and therefore the honesty of reports of them).[16]

The Old Testament and History

About history, theology, and the Old Testament much needs saying, but not here. There are indeed *various kinds* of "historical" discourse and writing, as *DV* 12 indicates in its programmatic statement about critical study of Scripture:

> To search out the intention of the sacred writers, attention should be given, among other things, to "literary forms." For truth is set forth and expressed differently in texts which are *variously histor-ical* [*vario modo historicis*], prophetic, poetic, or of other forms of discourse.... [D]ue attention must be paid to the customary and characteristic styles of feeling, speaking and narrating which prevailed at the time of the sacred writer.

But history, as the historian-exegetes Lagrange and Cerfaux emphasize, is a *science*, a critical, disciplined set of judgments about evidence. So what the First Vatican Council (following Justin, Aquinas, and the whole Catholic tradition) taught about the sciences applies also to history. Any appearance of conflict between "reason"—the disciplines of the human arts *and sciences*—and "faith" must arise either from someone's misunderstanding or misinterpretation of the

---

[15] Gal 1:18; 2:2; 1 Cor 15:3–7.

[16] M.-J. Lagrange, "Le réalisme de l'Évangile selon S. Jean," *Revue biblique* 46 (1937): 321–41.

Church's apostolic faith, or from prematurely taking some proposition to be scientifically (that is, critically) established. So these disciplines and sciences should be encouraged, and if they are freely pursued according to their own principles and methods, they will not trespass on what belongs to the faith.[17]

What belong *both* to the faith and to the science of history are the realities of those actions and words of Jesus that the apostles' preaching and teaching narrated, including his resurrection and his activities with them over the succeeding forty days. Their reports are historical even though selected, shaped, and worded so as to indicate *also* the place of these realities in the sequence of God's gradual disclosure of preparatory information to the particular people chosen to be its bearer.

About the records of this people that are included in the books of the Old Testament, Cerfaux had conveyed something of what *DV 7* means by its phrase "variously historical" in his 1951 "Revelation and History":

> God leaves to men the task of writing their own history. He has not willed to reveal either primitive history as such—everything that happened down to the kings of Ur of the Chaldees—or the secular history of the kings of Israel. When the author of *Kings* wants to write a page of history, he looks to the annals of the kings. Are these more reliable than the annals of the Assyrian kings, or than our newspapers today? . . . they may lead him into an error on details that are irrelevant to his purpose; he reproduces them as he finds them. God does not have this responsibility; it is not for him to change the truth-value [*valeur*] of the ordinary sources his secretaries have at their disposal.[18]

Any secular history in the Bible is there merely as frame for revelation's disclosure of God's project, past and present, of assimilating human persons to himself. Indeed, it is not even the Bible's primary purpose to be a history, not even sacred history or history of the revealed religion. Thus, Cerfaux in 1951. Fifty years earlier, Lagrange said much the same, with worked-out detail, concluding: in the Bible there is "less history than was thought when history was less well known."[19] This met with opposition, but the recently

---

[17] *Dei Filius*, ch. 4.

[18] Lucien Cerfaux, "Révélation et Histoire" (1951), in *Recueil* 1:345–46.

[19] Marie-Joseph Lagrange, *La méthode historique, surtout à propos de l'Ancien Testament*, (Paris: Lecoffre, 1903); *Historical Criticism and the Old Testament*, 2nd ed., trans. Edward Myers (London:

founded Pontifical Biblical Commission, with Pius X's approval, replied: if solid arguments conclude that sometimes "the sacred author did not intend to recount true history properly so called, but rather—though with the outward appearance and form of history—to propose a parable or allegory or some meaning different from the strictly literal or historical meaning of the words," then even the duly cautious should accept that conclusion.[20]

The main question always is what the finally responsible author or editor *intended to assert*, to take *full responsibility for the truth of*—not merely to set down as a framework assumed or accepted from "sources." Luke, thought Cerfaux, did not take full responsibility in relation to the dating of the reign of Tiberius (Luke 3:1). (Perhaps so, though Fitzmyer's case for concluding that Luke 2:2 mistook the date of the census absurdly *assumes* the Lucan inaccuracy he is trying to demonstrate, against the *certainly possible* translation that eliminates inaccuracy.)[21] But Luke manifestly did intend to take the responsibility of asserting virtually everything else—claimed by him as being certainly true (Luke 1:1–4) because it is a narration of what he accepted, after himself taking everything into account from the beginning, as the testimony of reliable eyewitnesses genuinely remembering what they had seen and heard.

And that is why *DV* 19 [iv] is so significant. *DV* 12 states the primacy of *intention*, divine and human, in the interpretation of all parts of Scripture:

> Since God speaks in Sacred Scripture through men in human fashion, the interpreter of Sacred Scripture, in order to see clearly what God wanted to communicate to us, should carefully *investigate what meaning the sacred writers really intended*, and what God wanted to manifest by means of their words.

DV 19 [iv] affirms the judgment of reason, and tenet of the faith, about the *intention* of the Gospels' authors when they present the words and deeds of Jesus. Even when they present them in selected, synthesized, and explanatory form, the intention always was to take the responsibility of asserting historical truth by conveying eyewitness memories of what Jesus really (*reapse*, 19 [i])

Catholic Truth Society, 1906), 14. See also his "Introduction au livre des *Juges*," *Revue biblique* 11 (1902): 5–30.

[20] Biblical Commission, *De narrationibus specietenus tantum historicis in S. Scripturae libris qui pro historicis habentur* [On narratives only apparently historical in the biblical books considered to be historical] (June 23, 1905), *Acta Sanctae Sedis,* vol. 38 (1905): 124–25.

[21] See Joseph A. Fitzmyer, *The Gospel according to Luke* (Garden City: Doubleday, 1981), 401.

said and did. About relatively little in the Old Testament, it seems, could any such affirmation be made—or need be made for the Old Testament to have its intended meaning and its prophetic and *pesher* value for Jesus and his mother (Luke 1:46–55), for the apostles, and for those who follow them.

III.

Since 1965, the Magisterium has allowed Catholic doctrine about the nature of the Gospels to be obscured and neglected, to the practical oblivion of some elements necessary for the solidity and truth of Christianity.

The Catechism of the Catholic Church omits any reference to *DV* 18.2, and in quoting *DV* 19 (CCC §126) omits 19 [iv], the foundation of the Catholic faith's foundation. John Paul II's *only* citation of *DV* 19 is in his Apostolic Letter *Novo millennio ineunte* (January 6, 2001); its paraphrase conveys 19 [iv] scarcely if at all, and then disconcertingly (and incompatibly with *DV* 19) contrasts the life of Jesus on Easter Day (and the next forty days) with his "historical life." Pope Benedict XVI, who as Joseph Cardinal Ratzinger was involved in the preparation of *Novo millennio ineunte*, intervened in the 2008 Synod of Bishops on Scripture to express his dismay that the exegetical mainstream now "denies that the Lord instituted the Holy Eucharist and says that Jesus's corpse remained in the tomb. The Resurrection in this view would not have been a historical event but a mere theological view."[22] Yet his Post-Synodal Apostolic Exhortation *Verbum Domini* (September 30, 2010), while citing almost every other section of *Dei Verbum*, did not cite *DV* 18 and 19, included no perceptible response to the mainstream's defection from the apostolic faith, and made no reaffirmation, however muffled, that the Church believes the Gospels' statements about what Jesus said and did are always honest and true because what they transmit are accounts directly or indirectly from apostles drawing on their memory of what he said and did.

The Pontifical Biblical Commission, converted in 1973 from magisterial to consultative status, was addressed by each of those popes in terms giving no hint that the doctrine so solemnly taught in *DV* 19 had since 1965 been

---

[22] Address of His Holiness Benedict XVI during the 14th General Congregation of the Synod of Bishops, October 14, 2008, penultimate paragraph: https://www.vatican.va/content/benedict-xvi/en/speeches/2008/october/documents/hf_ben-xvi_spe_20081014_sinodo.html (official translation; in the Italian original, and all the translations provided by the Holy See, the word "mainstream" was in English and quotation marks). With superabundant caution, the Pope referred to the mainstream "in Germany."

treated by mainstream Catholic Scripture scholars with disdainful silence, or that the Commission members they appointed included scholars such as Raymond Brown who openly held that, as a matter of history, the resurrection came down to some sort of never-described experience of Peter, probably in Galilee, some indeterminate time after the crucifixion and death of Jesus. In 2014, the Commission, addressing questions about truth and inspiration that *Verbum Domini* implicitly passed off to it, quoted selectively from *DV* 18 and 19, omitting 18.2 and 19 [iv]. Unwilling to hand on the integral doctrine of the Church, or the testimony of John's Gospel about itself, or the apostolic testimony in Luke and John about the tangible, proof-supplying bodily reality of Jesus on Easter Day (and other days before Pentecost), the Report—along with many internal inconsistencies—fails to draw the essential distinctions between the Old and New Testaments' relation to history and offers no critical reason for its shunning of the hypotheses available to show that the Gospels harmonize with each other and therefore can convey the reality of historical facts.

Cerfaux died in August 1968, Bea in November. Early in 1970, the new *Revue théologique de Louvain* was launched with the magisterial "Progrès et continuité dans la critique des Évangiles et des Actes [Progress and Continuity in the Historical Criticism of the Gospels and Acts]" by Cerfaux's successor in Louvain's chair of exegesis, his former student Msgr. Albert Descamps— soon to be appointed the first secretary of the new-style Pontifical Biblical Commission. Descamps surveys Gospel criticism from the period of "the old school" (*les anciens*), through source-criticism, form-criticism, and finally, "from the mid-1950's," redaction-criticism. Gospel criticism (says Descamps) has been progressive: each stage *rationally* supersedes its predecessor(s) while absorbing the progress already made. The old school had held (he goes on) that the Gospels, being directly or indirectly (Mark, Luke) by eyewitnesses, are transparent for the words and deeds of Jesus. Then nineteenth-century source-criticism "virtually traumatized" exegetes by establishing that the Gospel writers neither were nor had interviewed eyewitnesses: this, he says, is one of historical-criticism's *definitive acquisitions*. The Gospels' composition followed a long process of tradition, and relied upon sources that are essentially the "testimony" of Christian *communities*, communities about whom nobody knows whether or how far they had any *evidence*—could in a strict sense *testify*—about Jesus. Such sources, moreover, we can neither reconstruct with any confidence nor say how freely they, and the traditions they may transmit, had been interpreted by those unknown persons who transmitted them. For historians, Descamps concludes, there is a black box or no-man's land between Jesus and the Gospel authors/redactors, and we know not how much is redactional in origin.

Throughout, Descamps argues merely from exegetical *consensus*, estimating its degree or scale at each point. Cerfaux goes unmentioned, save for a claim that his posthumous *Jésus aux origines de la tradition* ascribes little value to study of oral traditions. Actually, however, the pages cited, foundational to Cerfaux's book, stress such study's value.[23] Oral preaching and teaching, testifying to Jesus's words and deeds, could indeed be composed, says Cerfaux, with a view to a memorization sufficient to carry, right down to the Gospels' redaction, all that the apostles and other disciples wanted transmitted. No black box. This and similar historically probable theses about the stability of the apostolically supervised preaching enable us to see that it was a fallacy, not a definitive acquisition (traumatic or otherwise), for source-critics to infer that if a Gospel writer was not an eyewitness but a redactor using sources—a premise that may be granted but should not be conceded—his Gospel does not convey eyewitness testimony. To this day, the sophisticated exegetical techniques celebrated by Descamps have yielded no real evidence against the affirmation of Luke 1:1–4 and *DV* 19 that, throughout the Gospels, we are hearing the preaching or catechetical voice of apostles or, in a few passages, of others who remembered what Jesus said and did.

DV 19, unmentioned in Descamps's lecture, is indeed the position of the "old school," as authentically *developed* by historian-exegetes like Lagrange, Cerfaux, and Rigaux. It distilled high scholarship that had fully understood and engaged with the whole sequence of methods—source-criticism, form-criticism, and redaction-criticism—and it included all that those methods had actually established. Whether Descamps was recalling it or not, Cerfaux's 1927 response to the leading form-critic, Bultmann, was composed expressly to vindicate, by rethinking, the working assumption of *"les anciens"* (Cerfaux's phrase before Descamps's): confidence in the probity (sincerity, trustworthiness) of the Gospel tradition.[24] Rigaux's 1958 defense of Gospel historicity pointed, *inter alia,* to form-critics' "original sin," the assumption that differences of form

---

[23] Lucien Cerfaux, *Pour une histoire de Jésus: Jésus aux origines de la tradition* (Bruges: Desclée de Brouwer, 1968), 38ff.

[24] Lucien Cerfaux, "La probité des souvenirs évangéliques" (1927), in *Recueil* 1:371.

correlate with differences in historicity.[25] And Cerfaux's 1957 sample exercise in redaction-criticism displayed the redacting of Luke 8:15 and 21:19 (on endurance [*hupomonē, patientia*] and persecution) as illustrating a wider conclusion: "throughout his Gospel, Luke rises to a challenge that would have defeated others: he has remained literally faithful to the authentic words of Jesus and to their fundamental meaning [*signification fondamentale*], and has at the same time managed to adapt them to a Church situation that has gradually evolved."[26]

But it was Descamps, and other members of the Pontifical Biblical Commission of 1973 and after, who spoke for what suddenly (among Catholic scholars) became the scarcely challenged mainstream. Even their relatively few Catholic critics have hardly alluded to *DV* 19, either as the authoritative doctrine it is or as a distillation of sound historical-critical investigations.

The effect on the holding and handing on of the faith has been more devastating than anything since, at latest, the Arian heresy of the fourth century. But unlike that other great contest between truth and error, this one is, unfortunately, little noticed—in its causal essence, as distinct from effects—or at least little discussed by defenders of the faith.

And, for all the peer-reviewed scholarly skills of its authors, the mainstream body of work that has silenced *Dei Verbum*'s key teaching fails the main tests of authentic historical-critical method. Here are a dozen among the many points that should be made about those tests, in their bearing on the Gospels.

1. Historical judgments are not critically warranted unless they best explain, or contribute to best explaining, the data, the evidence both about what was done (or said) and about why other competent persons now decline (if they do) to affirm it.

2. None of the so-called "criteria of authenticity"—adopted for a few decades (with scant attention to the ambiguity of the term "criterion") by most mainstream scholars after, or as part and parcel of, their premature decision that the Gospels are not by or from eyewitnesses—was ever a necessary or a sufficient basis for a sound historical judgment. Each is no more than a commonsense consideration relevant, but never like a

---

[25] Béda Rigaux, "L'historicité de Jésus devant l'exégèse récente," *Revue biblique* 65 (1958): 481–522, at 505; at 511 a position essentially identical to *DV* 19 [iv] is stated, and on the following pages is defended against objections of the kind that Descamps in 1970 would treat as decisive and well-founded.

[26] Lucien Cerfaux, "Fructifier en supportant (l'épreuve)" (1957), in *Recueil* 3:120.

decision-controlling rule, to the rational acceptability and soundness or probable soundness of the hypothesis articulated in a historical proposition, and none is of decisive importance in relation to credible testimony of witnesses whose honesty can be assessed by other considerations.

3. Every explanation of data/evidence (and therefore every judgment of fact) depends on presuppositions about the basic structure of reality (e.g., that time runs in one direction). An explanation cannot be the best unless it is attentive to those presuppositions. Regarded in a really fully critical way, the reality known to us by observation, natural sciences, and history cannot be explained altogether sufficiently without inferring that it is entirely dependent for its initial, historical, and present existence on a transcendent, intelligent Creator, on a potent choice that it begin to be, and then develop, in the *forms* imparted, by transcendent causing of natural causalities, to the universe and all its contents (an imparting somewhat analogous to what contemporary biologists call the transmission of *information* by and between cellular, molecular, and submolecular processes and the entities thereby given form). This existing universe, in due course, by a kind of leap in such forms, began to include living entities and, much later still, beings not only animate and sensitive but also intelligent and therefore able to share propositions and reasoning with each other, and to receive *and understand* intelligible information from the transcendent Creator. The name for that last form of imparting information is (divine) revelation.

Like the evolving of the universe under divine creation and providence, so divine revealing has been a process. That process of revelation culminated and verified itself in the life, actions, and words of Jesus of Nazareth. These together convey the information that Jesus was (and is) truly man and truly God, intervening in history to communicate efficaciously, and begin giving effect to, the *further* information that this whole created universe has a supranatural purpose: that those human persons who have been and are *willing* to accept and live in accord with the Creator's purposes can, even after death, live forever by a kind of participation of their whole being in the life of the Creator. To disclose something of the content of this covenantal offer, and to demonstrate its authenticity and truth, Christ gave a variety of signs of transcendent power over ordinary nature, even over human death, culminating—after his own exemplary submission to death in fidelity to the mission willed by the Father—in his own resurrection in wholeness of life: bodily as well as spiritual, but "glorified" in a spiritualized bodiliness surpassing yet including ordinary eating and drinking.

4. Anyone who says (as mainstream post-Vatican II exegetes regularly do) that the science of history—historical investigation and judgment in line with the best and most critical methods—cannot include an affirmation of the activities of the resurrected Jesus of Nazareth as presented in the Gospels (and summarized abstractly in the previous paragraph), *misconceives historical investigation and judgment.* If Jesus in fact met and ate fish with his disciples on Easter Day, in anything like the way described by Luke and John, that fact, like any other past occurrence, can be investigated by historical methods and—as part of a best explanation of the evidence about this fact along with many other alleged or verified facts—can be affirmed, critically and responsibly, to much the same degree of probability as countless other historical judgments about one-off events more or less remote from us in time. The same goes for other miracles of Jesus (and indeed of some of his first and later followers).

5. So too, with his prophecies. To assume, like leading German Catholic bishops in their preface to the 1970 and all later editions of a New Testament retranslation, that he could not or did not prophesy the fall of Jerusalem, and that—as their preface asserts—*therefore* the Gospels attributing such prophecies to him were completed after AD 70, is to adopt a presumption lacking sufficient exegetical basis, and—all things considered—incompatible not only with the Catholic religion but also with critical-historical investigation and judgment.

6. For all these reasons, mainstream reliance on at least a presumption that *consensus* among competent Scripture scholars is a reasonable basis for making judgments about the Gospels' dating and reliability (and indeed their genre and intent) is radically unsound. Since very many competent contemporary Scripture scholars decline to postulate either that there has been divine imparting of existence and information by transcendent Creation, or that there has been communication of

intelligible information by revelation attested by miracles and prophecies, consensus is neither necessary nor sufficient for—and indeed is incompatible with—best explanation and sound historical judgment on many exegetical issues—perhaps most issues beyond the purely philological (linguistic).

7. Mainstream late dating of the Gospels, ignoring or discounting the entire absence from the New Testament of any reference to Jerusalem's and the Temple's having been recently burned and destroyed, rests on scholarly opinion that has tended to rely on three presumptions: that Gospel prophecies of Jerusalem's fall were fabricated (or at least resurrected) after the event; that "high Christology" such as in Matthew 11:25–27, Luke 10:21–2, and John 1:3, 14, and 20:28 takes decades to develop; and that the *silence of Paul's* and other New Testament epistles about the Gospels and much of what they recount shows that no accounts such as the Gospels existed during Paul's ministry. The first two presumptions are unsupported by evidence, and are incompatible with the self-consciousness, words, and works of Jesus presented in any New Testament writing; the decisive development of doctrine could as well have occurred before the end of the crucifixion year as during any later period of years or decades.

And this argument from silence—like many others in mainstream New Testament scholarship—does not bear the weight put on it. If deviations and disputes in the Corinthian church had not gotten the response that survives in 1 Corinthians, we would have scant evidence that Paul ever told his congregations anything much about what Jesus taught or said in establishing the Eucharist, or anything concrete about sequences of events like his resurrection and subsequent "presentations of himself alive" to his apostles (Acts 1:2–3). Like a single searchlight suddenly switched on, 1 Corinthians—alone among surviving first-century Christian letters—discloses that Paul had orally handed on much that overlaps with what the written Gospels say Jesus taught (in this case about marriage and divorce) and said and did at the Last Supper, and about his post-resurrection appearances to the apostles and many disciples.[27]

And if the author of Acts had not already written a most detailed and extensive Gospel, we would infer from the silences of Acts that its author/redactor

---

[27] 1 Cor 7:10–11; 11:23–26; 15:3–7, 11.

had slight interest in Jesus's public ministry and, beyond a few slogans, knew little about it.

And from three gospels' silence about all but one of Jesus's four Passover visits to Jerusalem during his public ministry, anyone might readily, yet quite mistakenly, infer a one-year ministry. The proper inference is quite different: the apostles, or many of them, decided immediately[28] to present the public ministry in one vast, simplified, easily pictured, sweeping motion from the Jordan to Galilee and the north, and back south to Jerusalem, a presentation affirming no specifiable duration but *as if* recounting a single year, and matching, soon if not immediately, a one-year calendar of liturgy and catechesis.

8. Mainstream exegesis among Catholics since the 1960s (and among non-Catholics since the 1920s) uncritically neglects to acknowledge the antecedent improbability that the faith, in its first three decades, could have spread to as many as it did—or that, early in its fourth decade, Roman Christians could have gone in "immense numbers" (as the secular Roman annalist tells)[29] to hideous deaths rather than renounce it—*unless its converts had been evangelized* with accounts of Jesus's teaching and prophecies *about as detailed* as *Matthew's*, and of his signs and wonders, passion and death *about as detailed* as *Mark's*, and of his resurrection *about as detailed* as *Luke's*. Nor does the mainstream consider with critical attention what is likely to have actually been involved in, and yielded by, the apostles' announced dedication to "ministry of the word" (Acts 6:4; Luke 1:2) in Jerusalem in the first years or indeed the first months of the first year after the Lord's departure. Predisposed to dismiss in advance as novelistic, romantic, or imaginary every working hypothesis that has the specificity of real-world, historical causation in human affairs, mainstream positions uncritically take the immense gaps left in the apostolic community's records (by Jewish, Roman, Muslim, and heretical Christian depredations) as license for concluding—given further assumptions about the time needed for development of doctrine and about the "silence" of Paul—that the writings now in our hands acquired all or most of their specificity of form and content only forty, fifty, or sixty years after that self-dedication of the apostles.

---

[28] See Acts 1:21; 10:36–40; 13:23–25, 27–31; Gal 1:18; 2:2.

[29] Tacitus, *Annals* 15.44.5.

The most reasonable presumption and working hypothesis is that, in those few earliest months and perhaps years, they were settling[30] the topics and much of the content of most if not all of the highly selected pericopes such as are now found (sometimes differently arranged) in our three synoptic gospels and, with some differences, in John. Each such memorizable unit and sequence of units would be fit to help wider circles of preachers and teachers launch and carry forward the venture—memorialized in Acts and Revelation as an astounding, cosmically significant adventure—of constituting a new Jerusalem and a new, living Temple comprising Gentiles and Jews to the ends of the earth by handing on to them, one by one, by word of mouth as if hand to hand, the memories and testimony *of each or several of those apostles* (or sometimes of those close associates of theirs). Those memories would be a source of even the detail— perhaps flexibly articulated afresh in varying preaching occasions—of each unit and each set, even when the need to relate these recent events to the history and prophets of Israel would also count for much in selecting and shaping each sequence and its units.

Perhaps, as Cerfaux came to think, the composition/redaction of the Gospels themselves was delayed until three or four decades after the creation of the stable and more or less complete collections (oral or written) of sets of oral units—he thought that the parts of Matthew conveying Jesus's teaching had been near-finalized, orally and probably also in writing, by AD 40 but that biography came in with Mark. But when historical probabilities and data are considered with less deference to tides of scholarly consensus than even independent-minded Cerfaux eventually gave, it can be responsibly judged that the missionary, liturgical, and catechetical needs of Christian expansion out from Jerusalem led, much earlier than the 60s, to the making of written Gospels such as those we now have. After Cerfaux's death, critiques of the mainstream-consensus dating, by John A. Robinson (1976, 1985), John Wenham (1991), Philippe Rolland (1994), Hans-Joachim Schulz (1993, 1997), and others, have advanced various counter-hypotheses, all more probable, historically, than any version of the mainstream presumption embraced representatively by Descamps—the presumption that the Gospels' redaction was after the outbreak of the Jewish War or the fall of Jerusalem, largely as the work of unknown theologians (of genius) creatively "redacting" "traditional materials"

---

[30] This is neither to contest nor accept Lagrange's judgment that the fixing of themes was essentially by Simon Peter: *Evangile selon saint Matthieu* (3rd ed.: Paris, 1927), 552.

emergent in now scarcely identifiable Christian communities without warrant of any Apostle or other eyewitness. Against that consensus-based presumption, the transition from phase [i] through to phase [iii] of the formation of the Gospels as described in *Sancta Mater Ecclesia* and *DV* 19 should be presumed to have taken not thirty-three plus thirty-three years (as asserted by Brown and Fitzmyer) but about one or two plus about ten to eighteen.[31]

The core narratives of Matthew, a Galilee-focused Jerusalem gospel, incorporating notes or oral teaching such as the apostle Matthew Levi might set down or adopt from one or more associates among the apostles, need be substantially shaped no later than the first year after Easter. Its completion during the next one or two decades may have involved, as Lagrange and Cerfaux thought likely, some awareness of Mark.

John Mark of Jerusalem, an attendant for both Peter and Paul, witnessed his Cypriot uncle Joseph Barnabas, along with Saul, efficaciously present the Lord's teaching to Cyprus's able Roman proconsul, Sergius Paulus, ca. AD 45, and may well have composed his Gospel very soon afterwards. It is a Roman/Latin-oriented, action-focused, preacher's manual style, Petrine account (but not without Pauline traces): a version of the Jerusalem preaching notably shorter than Matthew's but richer in many eyewitnessed details. Its doubly meaningful opening words, "Beginning of the gospel" (Mark 1:1), refer equally to itself and to what Jesus announced. Since Mark was known by the early fifties to nascent churches "up and down Pontus, Galatia, Cappadocia, Asia, and Bithynia" (1 Pet 1:1; 5:13), he may well have been the unnamed man whom Paul commended to the Corinthian Christians as "praised/famous for the gospel" (2 Cor 8:18) among "all [those same] churches," and as trusted by those churches to supervise their collection for the Jerusalem church (8:19). From Paul, Luke, and Peter we get converging glimpses of Mark as an outstanding trustee, a stalwart in all-round mission service.[32] And his Jerusalem family base[33]

---

31 For example: Joseph A. Fitzmyer, S.J., "The Word of God, Magisterium, and the Historical Character of the Gospels," in William Madges and Michael J. Daley, ed., *Vatican II: Fifty Personal Stories* (Maryknoll, NY: Orbis, 2012), 164–66 at 165–66: "*Dei verbum* distinguished in effect, as did the Biblical Commission before it, three stages of the Gospel tradition: (1) what Jesus of Nazareth did and taught (A.D. 1–33); (2) what the apostles proclaimed with postresurrection faith and clarity about what he did and taught (A.D. 33–65); and (3) what the evangelists selected, synthesized, and explicated from stages one and two in their literary productions that we call the Gospels (A.D. 65–95)." Likewise Fitzmyer, *The Interpretation of Scripture*, 49; Raymond E. Brown, S.S., *An Introduction to the New Testament* (New Haven: Yale University Press, 1997), 107–109 ("first third . . . second third . . . last third of the first century").

32 2 Cor 8:19; 2 Tim 4:11 (cf. Acts 11:29; 12:25); Acts 13:5; Col 4:10.

33 Acts 12:12; cf. Mark 14:15; Acts 2:2.

would easily make him a hearer, at least, of the apostolic "ministry of the word" throughout its earliest years (cf. Acts 12:25), and allow him to insert into his version of it the trace of his own presence at the Gethsemane dénouement of Jesus's ministry (Mark 14:51–2). Much suggests that writings or recitations by him were primary sources for Acts 1–15.

Luke, arranged with a close eye to Mark and in contact with John's Gospel (in oral form?), draws upon various additional eyewitness accounts from that pool of Jerusalem witnessing and teaching of which in Matthew we find a first, highly selective, and structured sequential overview (and in Mark an even more selective one). Written to circle out from and back to the Temple, Luke like those other synoptics is completely silent about many things certainly known to its author, Luke. The widespread assumption that Luke could not have known Matthew's genealogy and infancy narrative, or the numerous other details in which the Synoptics overlap but differ, is historically unrealistic. More likely, each Gospel writer trusted his own memory or his own eyewitness sources; none treated any other existing Gospel as his *source of information*. Rather, each considered that both the apostolically accepted pool of eyewitness testimony (the pool to which his own sources contributed), and any apostolically accepted "Gospel" version in existence when he wrote, were or transmitted honest and informed testimonies true to historical fact, and that *therefore* all would be found to be harmonizable—in all their components and across each of those versions.

John, a Gospel handing on Jesus's deeper teachings for (but not reserved to) elders and theologians,[34] is equally insistent on historical facts and true to the geography of Jerusalem and Samaria of the 30s. It neither refers to "Gentiles" or any mission to them nor adapts to Gentiles what it says and presupposes about Jewish institutions and practices. It may well have been virtually complete (including chapter 21—probably never, despite superficial appearances, an afterthought—and awaiting, if anything, only a prologue), in oral and rigorously memorizable Jewish-feast oriented arrangement, *before AD 40*, even if not *finally published* in writing until considerably later. In the Church's earliest days and years, Peter and John in tandem taught in a Temple portico and in other public or private places in Jerusalem, preaching across Samaria not much later.[35] Traces of an early course of tandem preaching by them seem detectable

---

[34] See Marie-Joseph Lagrange, *Évangile selon saint Jean* (Paris: Gabalda, 5th ed. 1936), esp. lxxvi–xc, cxxxvi, clxiii, clxvi, clxx–clxxii, 519.

[35] For a sense of "in tandem," consider "their" speech in Acts 4:19.

in fifty pericopes[36] originally making up five interwoven sets now distributed across the parts of Mark (with a few elements now clearer in Luke) and John where those gospels are perceptibly complementary: (i) John the Baptist and the call of the apostles; (ii) ten matching miracles; (iii) the bread of life; (iv) the passion; (v) the resurrection. That preaching's aim was the aim now stated in John 19:35 with 20:8; 20:30–31; and 21:2: that everyone who hears or reads this Gospel may *accept* its discourses and prologue—about Jesus as true God and true man and the eternal life he makes available—as having God's authority and truth, an acceptance that is full and rational in its reliance on the historicity of its speaker's eyewitness testimony both about Jesus's miraculous power over nature—from Cana through to his resurrected encounters with apostles and disciples in Jerusalem and Galilee—and about his to-the-death conforming with God's will.

Hypotheses such as these explain and fit the historical data—and confirm the doctrine handed on in *DV* 19—better than alternatives. And nothing critically warranted precludes an expectation that further historical-critical work on the Gospels and on the authenticity and dating of the epistles[37] may develop authentically the historical judgments underpinning *DV* 18 and 19—judgments that track those made by many whom the apostles addressed, face-to-face, in Jerusalem while Pontius Pilate still governed Judea.

9. Mainstream source-criticism and resolution of the Synoptic Problem tend to presume—rashly—that abbreviation of a proto-Matthew would be senseless; that where matter found elsewhere in the Gospels is absent from Mark it was matter unknown to Mark's redactor/author; and that where Luke and Matthew overlap with Mark (the Triple Tradition) they have Mark as their source, so that here whatever one or other adds to Mark is "redactional," "secondary," "*theologoumena*" ("invented" and its cognates are strategically left unsaid). Each of these pervasive assumptions is improbable, and they regularly contribute to such total-loss

---

[36] 5 × 5 = 25 in Mark, 5 × 5 = 25 in John.

[37] The same may well prove true of critical investigative work on the date, authorship and occasion of Revelation, and on its witness to the public ministry of Christ: cf. Bernard Gineste, *Les quatre chevaux du Messie: Apocalypse 5–6: un conte initiatique* (Paris: BoD, 2019), 59–83; Gineste, *Préhistoires du cheval noir: Apocalypse 6:5–6 et le printemps du christianisme* (Paris: BoD, 2022). It will not be utterly amazing if investigations of Apocalypse (Revelation) more detailed, critical, and evidence-led than Cerfaux's (and countless others') disclose the mind and hand, soul and visions, of "John who was called Mark" writing on Patmos and at Laodicea a few months or weeks before Paul's captivity in Jerusalem and Caesarea.

shipwrecks in logic, interpretation, and historical judgment as John P. Meier's scholarly 135-page attempt to establish that the events and sayings in Mark 7:1–23 and Matthew 15:1–20 (the unwashed-hands controversy) "do not go back to the historical Jesus" and so in Mark are somebody's invention and in Matthew are mere redaction.[38]

Much more likely is what has been outlined above: behind each of the four Gospels is the network of apostolically stabilized and approved oral preaching, topically articulating already structured and organized memories of apostles and other eyewitnesses. From this network a first narrative reassembly was made as a proto-Matthew. Before very long, this was abridged—but with rearticulations and detailed supplementations (evidently with the authority of Peter's memory) and an extra handful of Septuagint allusions—as Mark.

10. A mainstream assumption is that *les anciens,* down to the Second Vatican Council, took the Gospels as always giving Jesus's *ipsissima verba.* In truth, Augustine, Lagrange, Cerfaux, etc., all held what *Sancta Mater Ecclesia* restates: even when not *ipsissima verba Iesu,* the Gospels convey what he meant, or what he would accept as equivalent to what he meant, its gist (at very least—for the testimonies deployed in them were by listeners with acute memories and reverence for every word of expositions repeated *and varied* from place to place). And of what he did, too, they give accurate accounts, with *great selectivity* and doubtless some forgetfulness of detail, but again *no invention.* The entire Gospel tradition all the way through its composition was under the eyes both of Apostles who by the end of the forty days after Jesus's resurrection understood him well, and of other persons of probity who had seen him—and whose acceptance of the spirit of Gethsemane and the Cross excluded advancing the Gospel by fictions.

Mainstream positions entail that between the apostles and the composition of our Gospels there intervened not so much a development as a revolution, changing events and teachings (history and doctrine) into a superstition—transforming, by cult, an inspiring and honorable but simply human prophet

---

[38] John P. Meier, *A Marginal Jew: Rethinking the Historical Jesus,* vol. 4, *Law and Love* (New Haven: Yale University Press, 2009), 342–477. Meier cites three hundred scholarly books and articles in his first footnote. Cf. John Finnis, "From the Heart Come Forth Words and Deeds that Defile" (Notre Dame, IN: Center for Ethics and Culture, 2017), 3–11, https://law.nd.edu/assets/256941/cec_paper_10_nov_rev_online_pdf.pdf.

crucified under Pontius Pilate into the divine, preexistent figure of the Son of God through and for whom all things were made (John 1:2–3 and 10:38; Col 1:19; Phlm 2:6; cf. Matt 11:27; Luke 10:22). There is no reason to doubt that, as Acts summarizes in terms whose unsurpassedly archaic character Cerfaux among many others demonstrated, the apostles from the June/July following the April crucifixion were proclaiming not only (and above all) the Lord's resurrection but also his preceding "miracles, wonders, and signs," and his status as Son of God (Acts 2:22, 24, 31; 3:1, 26; 4:2, 10). The cult came with or soon after, not before, this teaching and evangelizing.

11. When *DV* 19 [iii] refers to the Gospel authors [a] selecting, [b] synthesizing, and [c] "explicating with an eye to the situation of the churches," it points, among other things, to the profound interest of the earliest faithful in *pesher*, a showing that some text or pair of texts of the Scriptures ("the Old Testament") illuminate (and are illustrated by) present or recent events. The *pesher*s articulated expressly by Peter in his first Pentecostal sermon (Acts 2:16–36), and by the apostles and others after release by the Sanhedrin (4:24–28), were preceded by the teaching of Jesus (Luke 24:27, 44–45). But they track, too, his prophetic design in choosing to *act* by miracles and wonders that equally were signs, illuminating his authority and power but also his purpose not only of immediately doing good (say, by feeding first the five thousand, Mark 6:30–44) but also of foreshadowing (say, by then feeding the four thousand in the non-Jewish Decapolis, Mark 7:24–31; 8:1–9) an imminent world-historical mission transforming Israel from a single nation to the universal Church, the new Jerusalem where earth and heaven, this world and eternity, really (including, for a time, sacramentally) meet and interact (cf. John 1:51).

12. Finally, there is the other kind of data that needs explanation: the massive fact that the mainstream, the guild, refuse the doctrine of *DV* 19 and the historiographical and historical theses and hypotheses just outlined. And such an explanation can indeed be given. For without postulating any discreditable motivations extrinsic to scholarly inquiry, it is easy to draw up a list[39] of fifteen or more attitudes, dispositions, and habits of mind on display in this mainstream scholarship, tending to make

---

[39] See Finnis, "From the Heart," note 54.

it insufficiently critical and prone to error about fundamentals of the discipline. Not least among these habits of mind is the complacency that takes for granted the massive historic and—though fast depleting—present reality of Catholic institutional, liturgical, sacramental, intellectual, and spiritual life, and the profusion of theological subdisciplines, all distracting attention from the dependence of the whole edifice on the precise, narrow set of facts affirmed in *DV* 18 and 19 to be foundational to the faith.

EPISCOPAL CONFERENCES AND THE LOCAL RENEWAL OF SACRAMENTAL DOCTRINE

Guy Mansini, O.S.B.

The teaching authority of national conferences of bishops—organizations like the United States Conference of Catholic Bishops (USCCB)—is once again in the theological spotlight, something that has not been the case since the 1980s. Why is there any interest in what seems to be so abstract an issue? The answer is that national conferences are thought by some to be a possible instrument unto the end of a renewed Church. The nature of the proposed renewal will perhaps make the question about national conferences less abstruse. So this essay begins there—the context in which to insert the question about the teaching authority of national conferences, the context that may make the question lose its abstract character.

I. A PROPOSAL ABOUT SACRAMENTAL PRACTICE AND DOCTRINE

Sacramental Practice and a Contemporary Church

The Church cannot be present in the contemporary world unless she is herself contemporary. And she cannot be really contemporary without welcoming contemporary people to her worship, her prayer, and her action in the world on behalf of the poor and disadvantaged. This welcome is a sacramental welcome because the Church is a sacramental reality. Now, a significant portion of the

contemporary world in the West is divorced and remarried. Another significant cohort is in homosexual unions. Furthermore, different religious, even
deeply religious, cultures are given to estimating the religious significance of
the married and the celibate quite differently. Moreover, women are far more
likely to be religiously interested and committed people throughout the whole
course of their lives than are men.[1]

So, if the Church is to be a real presence of the grace of Christ in the world
today, it is often urged, she cannot invite women to join her but then deny
them positions of sacramentally ordained leadership. Then too, she ought to
recognize the goodness of mature and steady homosexual couples and so invite
them into her fold as *holy* couples, couples who are nowise different from het-
erosexual couples except for some details of how they pledge their embodied
love one to another. Again, she cannot tell the divorced and remarried that they
really and truly belong to the Church by their baptism, but then deny them a
place at the Communion table to which we are admitted by baptism. Further,
the Church cannot restrict the priesthood to celibates and yet realistically
promise to ensure pastoral care for local churches that have no positive estimation of celibacy. So, the renewal of the Church, the contemporaneity of the
Church, the effectiveness of the Church as herald of the Gospel and dispenser
of the mysteries of Christ to all those he wishes to save—which is, we must
remember, *all* men and women—all this depends on a renewal of sacramental
practice, which depends on a renewal of the sacramental doctrine that governs
sacramental practice. Such is the proposal.

Alleged Resources for the Renewal of Sacramental Practice and Doctrine

What are the theological resources for negotiating this renewal? They are supposed to be many.

First, there is the priority of the particular to the universal Church, since
the universal Church has actual existence only and exclusively in particular churches—the diocese of Toledo, the diocese of Louisville, the diocese of
Bologna, and so on are the instantiations of the universal Church without
which it would not exist. Particular churches must be let to find their own way
in the changing and various cultural conditions in which they exist without

---

[1] This is a common perception of the postconciliar American church. For hard and much more detailed
data, see "The Gender Gap in Religion around the World," Pew Research Center, March 22, 2016,
https://www.pewresearch.org/religion/2016/03/22/the-gender-gap-in-religion-around-the-world/.

threatening their communion with the universal Church. What is suitable for Africa and the memory of the Ugandan Martyrs may not be suitable for North America in the ecclesial reception of homosexuals. Again, what makes sense in the Amazon basin may not make sense in Central Europe.

Second, there is the fact that the baptismal equality of all Christians is foundational to the Church and supports whatever hierarchical differences there may be in the Body of Christ in virtue of the Sacrament of Holy Orders. This means in practice that the *sensus fidei fidelium*, or sense of the faith enjoyed by all the baptized faithful, has a sort of preeminence and priority relative to the more refined, scholarly, abstract knowledge of the faith possessed by bishops or priests (or theologians). In other words, there is a sort of authority of the faithful prior to that of the hierarchy. This sense of the faith, moreover, is conditioned by the varying cultures in which the Church is planted. We should not expect it to speak the same word throughout the whole world at the same time, or the same word throughout the whole of time.

Third, there is the witness of history to the fact of the independent and autonomous functioning of episcopal authority in local assemblies of bishops, the "synodical" structure of the Church. This is to say that the Church has within her memory the instruments for arranging and explaining practices suited to a particular cultural space.

Fourth, there is the understanding that office in the Church is ministerial—that is, official people, bishops and priests, are servants of the People of God who are that people simply in virtue of their baptismal dignity. It is this fact that Pope Francis reminds us of when he proposes to invert the pyramidal image of the Church, at the top of which there are the bishops and whose apex is the pope. Stood on its head, the image reminds us that pope and bishops are "under" the faithful as servants.

Fifth, there is the contemporary action and inspiration of the Holy Spirit. It is not just that the Holy Spirit helps us remember the words of Christ. Also, he teaches us new things, what eye has not seen nor ear yet heard (1 Cor 2:9).

Last, there is such a thing as the development of doctrine, which all recognize in the Church since the time of Cardinal Newman if not since the time of Vincent of Lérins in the fifth century. The only novelty now being urged is a greater recognition that development can be begin in local, regional gatherings of particular churches and, indeed, that the diversity generated by such development may continue to be merely local.

When we put all this together, and particularly when we remember Pope Francis's exhortation, especially in view of the *sensus fidei*, that everyone in the Church must be first a listener rather than a teacher, then it emerges that we should no longer speak of *the* teaching authority in the singular, referring to pope and the universal consortium of bishops. Rather than speaking of *the Magisterium* and just supposing that it can be but one, we should recognize that there are *many "magisteria,"* many authoritative voices in the Church. Considered as a whole, this view supports the claim that regional assemblies of bishops, bishops who listen to the voice of their faithful people, can be expected to be centers for that adaptation of Church practice and Church teaching that will make the Church contemporary—that will make the Church actual and vital in today's world. Thus, we see the expectations many have for a renewed and untrammeled functioning of episcopal conferences, the national assemblies of bishops that the Second Vatican Council called for and encouraged, and more generally, for the synod of bishops provided for by Pope Saint Paul VI, and for the regional synods that the Apostolic See calls for from time to time. And in fact, this very centrality of episcopal conferences to a decentered, "synodal" Church has been adverted to by Pope Francis himself. He is by no means to be associated in a simplistic way with all the proposals listed in the above paragraphs. And yet, he seems sympathetic to thinking about the Church, and the churches, and the renewal of doctrine and practice in just such a way that these proposals could be thought to be real possibilities through the action of local churches, which is to say, through consortia of particular churches or dioceses at the various peripheries of the one Church.

Episcopal Conferences

Unfortunately, the free and untrammeled exercise of the capacity to teach on matters touching faith and morals and sacramental practice by national conferences of bishops is something very much "trammeled" by the existing legislation of the Church, and this has been thought by some to impede the effort to make the Church contemporary by making the churches that compose her and that are organized in national conferences like the USCCB contemporary.

This existing legislation is to be found in *Apostolos suos*, an apostolic letter issued "motu proprio" by Pope Saint John Paul II on May 21, 1998, on the Theological and Juridical Nature of Episcopal Conferences. This letter, including as it does juridical norms, regulates the teaching authority of national episcopal conferences, which "must always be in communion with the head of the college [of bishops] and its members" (§22). (The head of the college of bishops is, of course, the pope.) A conference so constituted may teach authoritatively in such a way that all the faithful of the pertinent territory are bound to the teaching only if certain conditions are met. If the teaching is unanimously approved by the bishops who are members of the conference, "the faithful are obliged to adhere with a sense of religious respect [*religioso animi obsequio*] to that authentic Magisterium of their own bishops" (§22). If, however, such unanimity is not present but at least a two-thirds majority approves of the teaching, the teaching can be presented as the authentic Magisterium of the conference provided that the "*recognitio*" of the Holy See has been obtained.

Absolute unanimity within a large national episcopal conference is, to be sure, not easily achieved and, in fact, quite rare. In the end, therefore, this legislation prevents the peripheries of the Church from finding their own ways—"ways" in the plural, note—in the effort to contemporize the Church. This legislation rather keeps the national conferences tied relatively strictly to the Roman center, the Roman apex of the pyramid. Law that has once been made, however, can, it may be urged, be unmade. Why cannot there be a short and sweet juridical fix to unleash the powers of the many *magisteria* in the Church, the regional and synodical structure of the Church, and therefore the voice of the Spirit speaking through the *sensus fidei* of the faithful baptized of the many churches?

The devolution of doctrinal authority to national conferences or regional synods desired by many seems therefore easily to be within the grasp of the Church.

To see why this in fact is not so will require us to back up a few steps and insert the contemporary questions about such devolution of teaching authority into a broader theological context.

II. REVELATION AND THE CHURCH'S CUSTODY OF REVELATION

Christian Revelation Meets Us as Revelation

Christianity is a revealed religion, and the truth it announces is a revealed truth. Just in itself, this does not make Christianity very special according to Saint John Henry Newman. He thought fallen human nature was weak and weak-minded enough always to stand in need of revelation, the word of God illuminating our mind and giving guidance to our will. And he thought God was good enough always somehow to provide this illumination. So, to Newman's mind, we should reckon that there is revelation in many places and many times and many forms, and especially, we should suppose that there is revelation in the form of each person's moral conscience, whose voice is an echo of the voice of God.

What then did Newman think *is* special about Christianity? He thought that in Christianity, revelation, God's revelation of his mind and will, meets us *as* revelation. Christianity possesses God's revelation as revelation—that is, in knowing that it *is* God's revelation and in recognizing it just as such. We know that we find God's revelation in Christianity because here God's word meets us *as* God's word, and it comes with sufficient credentials for us to take it as such.

What Newman means here is very simple. Revelation comes to us as revelation when the Old Testament prophet begins his message with the introduction "thus saith the Lord." Revelation comes to us as revelation when the Lord Jesus says in the Sermon on the Mount, "You have heard that it was said [through Moses] . . . but *I* say to you" (Matt 5:21–22), where the "I" that teaches is the "I" of one who claims to be the heir of David, the Messiah, the Son of God. When Christ speaks, therefore, we encounter revelation as revelation. And then, to complete the picture, revelation meets us as revelation when the Apostle says to the Corinthians and also to us "I decided to know nothing among you except Jesus Christ, . . . the power of God and the wisdom of God" (1 Cor 2:2; 1:24), or "God [is] making his appeal through us . . . be reconciled to God. . . . For . . . now is the acceptable time; behold, now is the day of salvation" (2 Cor 5:20; 6:2).

The prophets speak to us through the word of the Old Testament and Christ speaks to us through the word of the canonical Gospels. But the apostles speak to us not only through the word of their testimony recorded in the New Testament as a whole but also through their successors, the bishops whom they sent out after them, even as they were sent out by Christ to preach the Gospel to everyone and baptize those who believed. So, for Catholics, it is very easy to find revelation as revelation. We can look things up in the Bible, reading it as does the Church. Reading it as does the Church means reading it according to the creed, "the rule of faith," and according to the Catechism of the Catholic Church and other such warranted proposals of the word of God. And again, we can tune in to the word of Christ by tuning in to the living voice of the successors of the apostles, the bishops, and to the priests the bishops accredit in our parishes, and to the catechists the priests accredit in our schools.

The Church's Custody of Revelation

But now let us make trouble. Or rather, let us take account of the trouble of the sometimes-difficult questions about what the word of God really is and really means, questions that arise and must arise because, although the word of God does not change, we do. The word of God has therefore to be received from age to age, in varying cultures, in varying conditions of human achievement and sinfulness. Now, as it happens, the Lord Jesus himself anticipated just this situation. He told Saint Peter that whatever he bound on earth would be bound in heaven (Matt 16:19). He told Saint Peter that his reading and recollection of truths concerning faith and morals would be a true reading and an accurate recollection and that therefore he could give absolutely trustworthy witness to the word of God, the revelation of God in Christ. It would be true, and known by us to be true, just because Peter is the rock on which the Church is built and just because of this promise of the Lord to him. And the Lord Jesus, taking no chances, built in some redundancy to the promise that his word would not pass away and could always be found in its pristine purity and sense (Matt 24:35). For he told the ensemble of the apostles together, as a unit including Peter, the same thing (Matt 18:18). So, he left the Church with two instruments that would ensure we can meet his revelation as revelation. There is the pope, who succeeds to Saint Peter's chair. And there is the whole ensemble of bishops, the "college" of bishops including the pope, that succeeds to the ensemble of the apostles.

The common teaching of the Church for ages and ages has therefore been that, when the pope discharges his Petrine responsibilities to the full, his teaching is guaranteed—by God fulfilling Christ's promise through the work of the Holy Spirit—to be true. In addition, when the universality of bishops teaches the same thing in a matter of faith and morals or even touching on the faith and moral truth delivered to the Church by Christ, then that teaching, too, is divinely guaranteed to be true. The bishops can teach the same thing, moreover, whether they are gathered together in one place, in an ecumenical or general council, or whether they are scattered to the ends of the earth across the globe in their particular churches or, as we usually name them, dioceses.

All of this machinery for preserving the word of revelation as revelation— knowable and apprehensible as such—came to nice expression in chapter 3 of the Second Vatican Council's Dogmatic Constitution on the Church.[2] This Council completed the work of the First Vatican Council, which had limited itself to speaking only of the primacy of Peter and the magisterial authority of the pope, by speaking also of the supreme episcopal ruling power over the Church and the supreme episcopal teaching authority. This teaching does not mean there are two supreme powers in the Church, the pope on the one hand and the collection of bishops on the other, since the collection of bishops, their "college," always includes the pope as its head. It means that there is more than one way the one supreme authority of the Church, located as it is in the pope and in the consortium of bishops including the pope, can act.

The Second Vatican Council not only asserted the ruling power and teaching authority of the entire college of bishops and clarified its relation the successor of Peter, however, but also encouraged more particular and so limited exercises of joint episcopal action as applications of "the spirit of collegiality."[3] Furthermore, the Council sought to revive the earlier Church practice of local councils—local and limited because not inclusive really or virtually of all the bishops of the whole Church, which would make for a general, ecumenical council—and did so once again by way of encouraging the establishment and operation of national episcopal conferences.[4]

III. BACK TO NATIONAL EPISCOPAL CONFERENCES

So now we are back to the question of the teaching authority of national episcopal conferences. Can the encouragement of the council extend to giving such conferences, or regional synods, an authority to teach, like that of the entire college of bishops with and under the pope, in such a way as to bind everyone to the same teaching? That is, just as the entire college, or the pope acting on his own as head of the college, can bind all the bishops and all the faithful to a

---

[2] Second Vatican Council, Dogmatic Constitution on the Church *Lumen gentium* (November 21, 1964) (hereafter, *Lumen gentium*).

[3] *Lumen gentium*, §23.

[4] Second Vatican Council, Decree on the Pastoral Office of Bishops *Christus Dominus* (October 28, 1965), §§36–38.

definitive teaching, can a conference of bishops bind everyone in the conference to an authoritative teaching?

The answer is no. And the answer is no because no national group of bishops can exercise authority in the same way as can the entire college of bishops when they find themselves to be in moral unanimity on the truth of some teaching (one or two dissenters do not count). And there are three reasons for this. First, the New Testament is silent about such intermediate authorities between a bishop and the entire college with its head, the pope, or between a bishop and the successor of Peter. Since the New Testament knows no such intermediate authorities, neither can the Church whose charter is the New Testament. These intermediate authorities are erections of positive law for the good of the Church by legislative act of the pope. It cannot be, therefore, that a bishop, who exists by the Lord Jesus's institution and so by divine law, has the same relation to the college of bishops as a whole, also a dominical institution and so of divine law, as to his national episcopal conference. *Apostolos suos* notes this.[5] The moral unanimity of the college can bind an individual bishop in both his ruling and teaching. The moral unanimity of a national conference can do no such thing, and the idea that it can do so is contrary to the nature and natural rights of an institution of divine law, namely, that of the individual bishop itself.

To put this last point again: just as it is a matter of divine right that the authority of an ecumenical council or of the pope *cannot* be resisted by a few dissenting bishops, it is also a matter of divine right that the moral unanimity of a local episcopal assembly *can* be resisted by dissenters, however few they may be. In the end, moreover, both of these exercises of "divine right" serve the unity of the whole Church.

Second, the legislation of *Apostolos suos* is nothing more than an application of the teaching of the Second Vatican Council on the authority of national conferences to the *teaching* authority of such conferences. For, in the first place, the Dogmatic Constitution on the Church (*Lumen gentium*) knows nothing of any intermediate doctrinal authority between the college as a whole and an individual bishop, and in this is faithful to the New Testament. In the second place, there is the Decree on the Pastoral Office of Bishops in the Church (*Christus Dominus*). As we have seen, this decree encourages national conferences of bishops to act collectively for the common good of the churches in their land.

---

[5] John Paul II, Apostolic Letter Issued *Motu Proprio* on the Theological and Juridical Nature of Episcopal Conferences *Apostolos suos* (May 21, 1998), §13 (hereafter, *Apostolos suos*).

The Council has in mind the exercise of the pastoral office of bishops. For its pastoral decisions to have binding force on all the bishops, however, they must be passed by at least two-thirds of the bishops and receive the *recognitio* of the Holy See.[6] *Apostolos suos* establishes the same arrangement for the exercise of the teaching authority of such conferences, for, although it specifies that a doctrinal declaration unanimously approved by the bishops of a conference "may constitute authentic Magisterium and be published in the name of the conference itself," as we have seen, it also specifies that the conference is "in communion with the head of the college and its members."[7] It may fairly be said that *Apostolos suos* simply applies the legislation of the Council more expressly to the teaching authority of conferences.

Third, there is the nature of each particular church and the nature of the responsibilities of each bishop. This will take a more extended word of explanation. But it provides the theological intelligibility of the above factual arrangements of governing and teaching authority in the Church.

What is a particular church? It is most fundamentally a *Eucharistic* assembly, a Eucharistic community. It is just because it is a community that celebrates the Eucharist that its members belong to the Body of Christ that is the Church. Without the Eucharist, there is no full incorporation into the Church. The Eucharistic Body of Christ inserts those who receive it into the ecclesial Body of Christ. What makes a particular church a true and genuine particular church is just this possession of the Eucharist. This is to say that the authenticity of a particular church depends on just this real possession of Christ in the very act by which, in the memorial of his sacrifice, he fulfills the prophecies and promises, establishes the new and eternal covenant, offers us to his Father in the Holy Spirit, and gives himself to us in his Body and Blood as the pledge of immortality.

It is just because a particular church is a Eucharistic assembly, moreover, that it is presided over by one of the successors of those who were present at the original Eucharistic assembly, the Last Supper, and to whom the charge was given "Do this in remembrance of me" (Luke 22:19). A Eucharistic assembly is an episcopal assembly. Now, just because of this Eucharistic character of the particular church there are certain demands that it must respond to, and which the bishop must ensure are met by his people.

---

[6] Second Vatican Council, Decree on the Pastoral Office of Bishops in the Church *Christus Dominus* (October 28, 1965), §38.4.

[7] *Apostolos suos*, §22.

Each particular church—the church at Ephesus or Corinth or Toledo or Paris—is under strict obligation to be open to all the other particular churches. This is not an obligation of positive law merely. It is not an obligation of practical organizational wisdom. It is an obligation that is constitutive of the particular church. To fail in this openness is to fail to greet the same Christ that this church celebrates in the *other* churches that celebrate the same Christ. It is to be not merely inchoately schismatic, but formally schismatic. But the demand of openness is itself demanding. In order for a particular church to maintain this openness and so in actuality to be a particular church, the Gospel must be preached and embraced whole and entire, and the sacraments must be celebrated just as they came from the hand of Christ, and the moral discipline of Christians must be in conformity with the two great commandments of love. Like recognizes and loves like, and no particular church can be welcoming of all the other particular churches unless it is like them in doctrine, worship, and discipline. This means, correlatively, that it cannot decide a matter of faith on its own, independently of the confession of faith of other churches. This means that it cannot settle matters of sacramental practice that touch on the substance of the sacrament independently of the practice of other churches. It means that it cannot determine a pattern of moral action independently of the patterns lived out in other particular churches.

Just so, each bishop of a particular church has not only to guard the unity in faith and sacramental and moral practice of his own church, but must do so with an eye to maintaining the unity of his church with all the other churches. This double responsibility, guarding the faith and practice of his own church and keeping an eye out for the faith and practice of other churches besides his own—of all the churches, in fact—is something written into the very form of the institution of the college by Christ. The same concern for the whole as was given to Peter was also given to the college, as it were, *in solidum*. So, whenever a bishop teaches truly in conformity with the Gospel, and whenever he maintains the practice of his church in conformity with apostolic practice, then he builds up the whole Church by building up his own. And whenever he looks beyond his flock to act for the good of other particular churches, by way of advice or letter or consultation, then he is looking to the good of his own church. That this unity in communion is also the concern of the successor to Saint Peter does nothing to relieve the individual church and the individual bishop from their responsibilities in the same vein. The conspiration in truth and love is not the breathing of one man. The joint—and consciously joint—activity of minding the truth and enacting apostolic practice is the responsibility of all the bishops.

This obligation of openness to other churches, this obligation of the bishop to keep an eye on the communion of his church with other churches, is an obligation that answers the two chief things that the Lord Jesus left to his disciples. He left them the revealed truth of the Gospel, the mind of God as to our supernatural end and the means to attain to that end. And he left us the charity by which we may commend ourselves to that truth and to the way of life commensurate to it. The openness of one church to another, therefore, is by no means a matter of conveniently keeping to a juridical standard extrinsic to the Gospel. It is a matter of keeping the Gospel itself in its integral truth, and a matter of keeping fellowship in charity with all other Christians gathered in their own churches. In the end, it is a matter of keeping the one Christ, keeping in union with him, the Head of the Church.

No individual particular church, and no collection of such churches, can therefore decide some matter of faith or sacramental or moral discipline for itself without taking account of the whole Church. Just as each bishop teaches authoritatively in his own diocese, the conference can teach authoritatively for its own region and in its own name if all agree. But even so, it cannot teach anything that varies from the faith and practice of the whole Church. It cannot, for instance, decide in its own name and unanimously to revise the Apostles' Creed or change the substance of the sacraments or throw out one of the Ten Commandments.

IV. ALLEGED RESOURCES FOR THE DEVOLUTION OF TEACHING AUTHORITY REVISITED

Particular Churches within the Catholic Church

In the light of the above, it is easy to see that particular churches are by no means prior to the universal Church. The requirement that each particular church be open and so offer hospitality to all the others indicates rather the contemporaneity of the universal Church and the particular church. So it cannot be that the particular churches precede the Church as a whole and constitute her by some federative act of foundation. No, here the whole is rather prior to the parts, because the whole is the reality of Christ—and Christ just as he has shared himself in his teaching and his grace first with the apostles as a whole.

The whole Church is manifest already in Jerusalem on the day of Pentecost, where representatives of all the nations hear the preaching of all the apostles. This is the root theological fact behind the legislation of *Apostolos suos*. It is the root theological fact behind the document of the Congregation for the Doctrine of the Faith, *Communionis notio*.[8]

Theological reality requires us to say that, just as particular churches are "in" the universal Church, and this is a manifest sociological fact, so the universal Church is "in" each particular church. This mutual inherence occurs first in virtue of the presence of the Head of the Church made real and operative in the celebration of the Eucharist, and second in virtue of the presence of a member of the apostolic college convoking and governing that church, one of the successors of the apostles, a bishop in communion with Rome.

The Sensus Fidei Fidelium

a. The *Sensus Fidei* and the Alleged Priority of Baptism in a Theology of Revelation

A large part of the argument for the devolution of teaching authority to national conferences or regional synods rests on an appeal to the *sensus fidei fidelium*, the sense of the faith of the faithful baptized Catholics and the priority of such a sense of the truth of the Gospel to the teaching authority of the bishops.[9] The idea is that this *sensus fidei* will function as a sort of font of revelation, that the Holy Spirit will speak through the sense of the faith of the baptized to bring forth new teachings, adapted to the circumstances—cultural and political and social and economic—of the particular churches that comprise the conference. Thus, some people speak of the *sensus fidei* as consisting of a kind of intuitive insight into divine realities themselves, and the authority of Saint Thomas Aquinas on what he calls "connatural knowledge" is invoked here. It is readily granted by the proponents of this view that this insight into divine things may be inarticulate; nonetheless, it is taken to be a vehicle of the Holy Spirit speaking to the churches.

There are several things wrong with this scenario. First, while the *sensus fidei* can be construed as an instance of what Saint Thomas means by connatural knowledge, the above explanation does not really present his teaching on

---

[8] Congregation for the Doctrine of the Faith, Letter to the Bishops of the Catholic Church on Some Aspects of the Church Understood as Communion *Communionis notio* (May 28, 1992).

[9] See Robert Dodaro, O.S.A., "Sensus Fidelium: Sense of the Faithful," in this volume.

this mode of knowing and in fact deforms it. Second, the *sensus fidei*, which in its own right is correctly described as authoritative, is not and cannot be epistemologically prior to the magisterial authority and teaching of the bishops. Third, it is not independently active but reactive to proposed formulations of teaching and practice, and so in that way "proactive," but only, to repeat, on the basis of its prior formation by the word of God. Each of these points needs a word of explanation.

By connatural knowledge, Saint Thomas means the kind of knowledge exercised by someone conformed to a morally significant and even divine reality. By the love of Christ and the love of Christ's virtues, for instance, one is conformed to Christ and his virtues. One therefore becomes conformed to the chaste and pure Christ by one's possession of and living by the infused supernatural moral virtue of chastity (Thomas's example). Such possession of and living according to chastity does not give intellectual insight into the nature of chastity. What it does do—more importantly for the personal holiness of the chaste Christian—is make the chaste person an immediate measure of what actions are chaste and what actions are not. The measure is immediate in that it relies on no argument, no syllogism with one premise defining the nature or properties of chastity. The chaste person himself knows by a sort of instinct what is in harmony with his own virtuous reality, which is to say what is in harmony with the chaste Christ to whom he is conformed, and what is not. He may not be able to say why this is so; he may not be able to express it with any insight; but he *knows*, and indeed, he knows with a sort of supernatural certainty. There is an authority evidenced here, the authority of a life knowingly and intelligently conformed to Christ and Christian virtue.

The *sensus fidei* for all Christian matters, moral and doctrinal, is therefore something acquired by conforming oneself to the teaching of the Church, which is to say the teaching of the bishops and priests and catechists and Catechism. It is dependent on learning doctrine, credal and moral, and living according to it in reverence and holiness, and is therefore quite dependent on the prior word of the Gospel, the Scriptures recorded in the Bible and hammered out in Church teaching. So, across the board, the *sensus fidei* is an authoritative witness in the Church. But its authority is derived from the prior authority of the words of the creed and Catechism.

When the general outline of revelation was sketched out above, there was a certain emphasis on the fact that revelation takes place by means of human words: the word of God gets itself into human words. It takes place exclusively by means of such words and the historical events that explicate and corroborate them.[10] So whatever the *sensus fidei* is and however it is imagined it operates, it brings no new hitherto unheard-of truth into the consciousness of the Church. It is strictly a fruit, as it were, of these prior events and words of revelation and of the evangelization and catechesis that report and explain them.

Just so, the *sensus fidei* is a reactive knowledge, not an independent font of Christian revelation. When it meets some doctrinal or sacramental or moral proposal, it measures what it understands by its own immediate reaction to it, as something that is in accord with Christian reality or not—the Christian reality installed in one's own person by conformity to Christ. In this respect, furthermore, it is simply a confusion and an obfuscation to speak of many *magisteria* in the Church. To be sure, if bishops and priests do not learn the pastoral lay of the land from their people, they are not doing their job and will be bad communicators of the Gospel. But the sort of pastoral ignorance that ensues from such misfeasance is not to be confused with an ignorance of the Gospel.

The idea, therefore, that a careful canvassing of the *sensus fidei* could independently revise or remake some aspect of sacramental practice or doctrine is therefore entirely mistaken. The idea that it can speak such a word of revision or revocation stems from the confusion of the *sensus fidei* with "religious experience" and the Liberal Protestant and Catholic Modernist understanding of religious experience. This bears a word of explanation.

For Liberal Protestants such as Auguste Sabatier and Adolph Harnack, for Catholic Modernists such as George Tyrrell, and for the grandfather of this position, Friedrich Schleiermacher, revelation is purely and originally experiential. This is to say it is prelinguistic and even preconceptual. The words of the prophet or of the Christ or of the Christian evangelist are human inventions: they do not share the authority of a divine word to us—the idea of which is purely metaphorical—but are the prophet's or the mystic's own formulation of what the ineffable experience of the presence and closeness of the divine means for him or her.

Every Catholic who thinks that the *sensus fidei* is going to radically alter Christian doctrine—as the Catholic Modernists at the beginning of the twentieth century hoped—fundamentally misunderstands what revelation is. When

---

[10] See Second Vatican Council, Dogmatic Constitution on Divine Revelation *Dei Verbum* (November 18, 1965), §2.

the prophet begins his message to the People of God with "thus saith the Lord," that is not a metaphor. Moreover, the "deposit of faith" which St. Paul tells Timothy and Titus to keep in the pastoral letters is a deposit of doctrine, not of experience. It is a deposit whose form is a matter of "sound words" (1 Tim 6:3). This means that any further explication of the content of revelation is an exposition of, or an interpretation of, or an inference from, those words.

To my mind, forgetfulness about how the *sensus fidei* is established in the faithful, by episcopal preaching and the sacramental and moral practice of the faithful, allied with the understanding of revelation current in Liberal Protestantism and Catholic Modernism—this fundamental theological confusion, or confusion about the nature of revelation, is at the root of many quite fanciful hopes in the Church today.

b. The *Sensus Fidei* and Different Cultures

There is another important mistake bound up with the appeal to the *sensus fidei fidelium* that needs to be aired, however, and that is how the *sensus fidei*, taken as religious experience, is allied to a local culture. That is, there is a further deformation of the traditional meaning and functioning of the *sensus fidei* when it comes to considerations of the contribution of culture to contemporary forms of the expression of doctrine. If the *sensus fidei* is confused with religious experience as understood in Liberal Protestantism and Catholic Modernism and so becomes itself a sort of font of revelation, or a *locus theologicus*—a place where theological formulation and understanding finds its building blocks—and if, as seems only fair to observe, all foundational human experiences including religious experience are embedded in cultures, enacted in cultures, and expressed in cultural forms, then we should expect episcopal conferences and regional synods to find in the culture in which they are situated a contemporary formulation and contemporary modification of doctrine. It is not just that the evangelist or bishop, in order to speak effectively to them, has to know the culture of those he teaches and to whom he preaches. He will now draw out some of the content of what he teaches from the surrounding culture. The various cultures of man will themselves be fonts of revelation, fonts, that is, of how to speak the presence of God to all men, all of whom God wishes to save.

This is a radically different picture of the relation of the Gospel—of revelation—to culture than we find in the New Testament. St. Paul tells the Galatians that when we are baptized into Christ, there is neither Jew nor Greek, neither slave nor free, neither male nor female (3:28). And he tells the Colossians that when we put on Christ, there is neither Greek nor Jew, neither barbarian nor Scythian (3:11). Being a Christian is something independent of cultural forms insofar as they distinguish us one from another. Insofar as different cultures unite us by way of some development of natural theology, the resources for which are a part of human nature, this is not so (see Acts 17:22–30). "Pagan" ideas can be pressed into the expression of the Gospel in doctrine, and the idea that this is so is by no means abhorrent or even surprising to a Catholic. After all, this seems to be verified already in Scripture itself, in the Book of Wisdom in the Old Testament, and according to some scholars in Saint Paul's own articulation of Christological doctrine.[11]

Insofar as different cultures produce contradictory and therefore divisive views of reality, however, they cannot be subsumed into the effort to express Christian truth without correction and emendation. In Christ, to be sure, we are above all these differences, having found a new and final unity of the race in the second Adam. And it should be remembered, moreover, that the Old Testament teaches that cultural difference is a result of sin (Gen 11). God can by his providence draw good things from distinct cultures, of course, as the Church has always recognized—the gold of the Egyptians was to be despoiled, and the seeds of the Word bore fruit in all lands and nations. But the new order of a synodal Church, of a Church where the "encultured *sensus fidei*" and precisely as encultured becomes a font of revelation, reverses the teaching of Saint Paul. Now, baptized into Christ, there is still slave and free, male and female; there is still Jewish Christianity and Greek Christianity; there is, or should be, a Scythian Christianity and a Berber Christianity. The trouble, however, is that just as the original cultures, taken in their full strength and individuality, are incompatible with one another, so also will these various forms of Christianity be discordant and make for a chaotic and incoherent Church.

In short, the Gospel corrects, it is not corrected by, cultures. One supposes that underneath the quite contemporary celebration of different and distinct cultures there is the old cultural relativism of post-Enlightenment European thought. Whatever one culture says is true, is true for it, but there is no trans-cultural truth, and even God can supply no higher point of view, no higher truth, to which all cultures, all men and women, are called and to which they

---

[11] For the Book of Wisdom, see John Bergsma and Brant Pitre, *A Catholic Introduction to the Bible* (San Francisco: Ignatius Press, 2018), 1:678–79, 681–82. For Christology, see Anthony Giambrone, O.P., "Primitive Christology as Ancient Philosophy," in *A Quest for the Historical Christ: Scientia Christi and the Modern Study of Jesus* (Washington, DC: The Catholic University of America Press, 2022), 210–44.

are bound. Christianity itself, on this view, becomes just one more "culture," in itself something negotiable, in itself something to be altered and modified to suit the tastes and desires of whoever wields power. The so-called "empowering" of indigenous peoples and peripheral cultures rather in fact hands them over, with whatever truths they have indeed managed to hammer out in their experience, to nihilism.

The Ancient History of Local Synods in the Church

But what of the early history of the Church? Local synods such as that of Carthage (419) or Second Orange (529) certainly exercised teaching authority. And the sign that the teaching was authentic and of God was the reception of this teaching by the whole Church, Rome included. Nothing has changed. Today, the authority of the teaching of a particular episcopal conference is signified by the *recognitio* of the Holy See, a sign that can now be immediately asked for and swiftly given. In the early Church, the authentic character of the teaching of a local synod was manifested more slowly, but no less surely, by its universal reception.

The Inverted Pyramids

In Pope Francis's challenging image, we stand the pyramidal Church on its apex. This is to remind us that priests and bishops and pope stand "under" the baptized faithful in order to serve them. They are ministers ("servants") not only of the Gospel and of Christ, but of Christ's people. The Holy Father's point is doubtless true and imaginatively expressed. But in what does this service consist? This should be obvious from what was said in the second part of this essay. Stand the Church on its apex as you will, this does not alter the dependence of the Church as a whole on episcopal teaching authority, itself dependent on the authority and word of Christ, which is the perfect embodiment of the word of God and which alone is the foundation of faith.

The Continuing Role of the Holy Spirit

Proponents of the devolution of teaching authority to local synods and episcopal conferences, in addition to their appeal to the *sensus fidei* and the manifestation of revelation in the religious experience of various cultures, also invoke the continued working of the Holy Spirit as an agent of revelation. Here, the operative text is the observation of Christ on the night before he died that he had many things to tell the disciples, and although he said to them that "you cannot bear them now," he promised them that "when the Spirit of truth comes, he will guide you into all the truth" (John 16:12–13). What is this except a promise of continuing revelation in the age of the Church?

It is, of course, nothing of the kind. For the passage continues, "He will glorify me, for he will take what is mine and declare it to you" (16:14). Revelation remains radically Christocentric in the Fourth Gospel: it is not complete without the gift of the Spirit, but its object remains the Word made flesh. The Spirit, indeed, will teach the disciples "all things" (14:26b). But the "all things" are precisely the teaching of Jesus: "the Holy Spirit, whom the Father will send in my name, he will teach you all things, and bring to your remembrance all that I have said to you" (14:26c).

The continuing role of the Holy Spirit in helping the Church understand the meaning of the Scriptures he first inspired does not contradict the truth that revelation is "closed" with the death of the last immediate disciples and apostles of Jesus, just as the Letter of Jude has it, since the faith has been "once for all delivered to the saints" (Jude 1:3).

Development of Doctrine

Doctrine develops. This is a fact recognized by all. Whatever we think is possible in the immediate moment, does not this fact presage a greater openness to the proposals outlined in the first part of this essay? It does not. Development means change. But we must ask what kind of change is at stake.

Let us go back to the requirement that a particular church must be in doctrinal union with the others. This is a matter not only of what all the churches now assert and teach in communicating the Gospel ("synchronic" unity). It is also a matter of union with what has already been taught in the churches from the time of the apostles ("diachronic" unity). Hence the intelligibility of Vincent of Lérins's formula: "*quod ubique, quod semper, quod ab omnibus.*" When we want to know what to hold as Catholic truth, we look for what has everywhere, always, and by everyone been believed. Eucharistic openness demands union of faith now with all the churches everywhere. But since it is a union in apostolic faith, the demand extends to union with the Church in the fifth century, the thirteenth century, and so on. That is, we look for—and to—what has always been believed.[12]

---

[12] See in this volume, Eduardo Echeverria, "Saint Vincent of Lérins and the Development of Christian Doctrine;" and Kevin L. Flannery, S.J., "The Logic of Doctrinal Development according to John Henry Newman."

Dogmatic development may clarify what has previously been confessed; it may re-express it in different terms; it may draw consequences from it. But what it cannot do is contradict it. To think that it could is to discount apostolicity as a necessary mark of the Church, just as to deny that now in this moment we must all be on the same page is to deny the catholicity of the Church. Teachers must teach the same doctrines as were taught in the past. And the *sensus fidei* of the faithful must keep the same shape from age to age for the simple reason that it is conformity to Christ, and Christ is the same yesterday, today, and forever.

V. THE IDEA THAT SACRAMENTAL PRACTICE CAN BE ISOLATED FROM CATHOLIC DOCTRINE

We must last take up the idea that sacramental practice and doctrine are somehow independent of Catholic doctrine as a whole, for this lies in the background of the supposition that, without prejudice to the Catholic expression of revelation, the Church or some local part of it can change who is admitted to orders, who is admitted to the Communion table, and who is to be considered married in the Lord—and all this without implying any denial of core Catholic doctrine.

It is true, of course, that the ordination of married men to the priesthood and dropping the discipline of celibacy for some sections of the Latin Church is on the surface a matter of discipline and can be changed without any implication that the doctrinal teaching of the Church about orders is being altered. This is true, but in fact, the implied message, or the message to be read between the lines, in allowing indigenous peoples to have married priests is unacceptable for two reasons. First, it supposes that the peoples of Africa or the Amazon are incapable of appreciating the spiritual good of celibacy. It supposes they are incapable of hearing and understanding and taking to heart the very words of Jesus in the Gospel that, for the sake of the kingdom, it is better not to marry. It supposes they cannot understand the excellence of being exclusively concerned with the Lord's affairs, as Saint Paul puts the point. Human nature is one thing across time and throughout space, and the Gospel call perfects this nature wherever it is found. So it is not true that these peoples are less capable of understanding this Gospel and the excellence of Jesus's call to celibacy and virginity than ancient Greeks or Syrians, than contemporary Europeans or North Americans.

In the second place, the permission for married priests right now and in this age of secularism in the West, a secularism that touches indigenous people quite as much as it does Western suburbanites, would in the end be an endorsement of the secular understanding of sexual expression, sexual relations, sexual reality. And that understanding, that estimation, is that no human life is worth living without an active sexual life, without actively engaging in sexual relations. The message would be that the Catholic Church has at last begun to understand this implication of the Enlightenment rejection of Christianity. The message would be that, really and truly, there is nothing in this world to live for that does not include active sexual experience and pleasure. The message would be that, finally, Catholics have caught up with the times, the times as defined by the expectations of the sociologists and psychologists of secular man. There is nothing in the world to live for that is transcendent to the values of the world, or in other words, there has been no incarnation of the word of God, and there has been no demonstration in his life of a charity that surpasses the good of marital love.

The other suggested changes can be dealt with more straightforwardly and directly. Both the "ordination" of women to the priesthood and gay "marriage" are not celebrations of sexual difference and sexual identity, but denials that naturally given sexual identities are intrinsic to the human person. They are denials, then, that there is any point to the masculine sex of Christ in whose person the priest acts and to the feminine persona of the Church. And it is the nuptial relation of Christ and the Church that every Christian marriage images and imitates and is sustained by. To "redefine" marriage and ordination gives us a Christian reality in which sexual difference is not a potential signifier of divine things, and sexual difference cannot as such be taken up into the sacramental order. The sacramental order turns out, in reality, to be indifferent to sexual difference as a gift of the creator God.

In other words, the ordination of women and gay marriage give us a world in which the Jesus of the Gospel of Thomas speaks truly. There the disciples ask him whether they shall enter the kingdom as children, that is, as prepubescent and in that respect sexless human beings. He answers in part: "When you make the two one, . . . when you make the male and the female into a single one, so that the male not be male nor the female female . . . then you will enter [the Father's kingdom]" (no. 22). Right. Holy transcendence is something indifferent to sexual differentiation, and such differentiation is an impediment to entering the kingdom of God. On these terms, the Christ who will bless such marriages and acknowledge such ordinations is a Gnostic Christ, not the Christ of the fourfold Gospel that St. Irenaeus confessed.[13]

---

[13] See, for example, Irenaeus of Lyons, *Adversus Haereses* 3, 11.

Last, there is Communion for the divorced and remarried. Since no adulterer can approach the Communion table, admission of such people to Communion is to imply they are not living in adultery. And this is to imply they have truly been divorced and their prior marriage dissolved. Now, marriage as understood by Catholics is a sign of the nuptial relation of Christ and the Church. Moreover, it is just because the bridegroom is the Second Person of the Trinity, the Logos of God, that the Church is confident that she can never be abandoned by her groom, never be issued a bill of divorce. Rather, she is confident of his pledged love and knows herself to be abidingly safe in the charity of Christ, which is the charity of God. But divorceable Christian marriages imply that the Church's bridegroom is precisely not immediately the Son of God, but is some additional person who, like the men of the Old Testament, could write a bill of divorce. In other words, divorceable Christian marriages imply a Nestorian Christ. The Son of God is not born of Mary nor does the Son of God betroth the Church to himself. It is another person, a created person. Just as the Nestorian Christ cannot rightly be worshipped in his humanity, since it is no longer sacred by its immediate union with the Second Person of the Trinity, so no marriage is holy with the holiness of divine fidelity which is to find expression and actualization in both mind and body. What God has united in marriage can therefore be put asunder by a Nestorian Church.

In this way of viewing things, we are still in the Old Testament, because the Word has not, in fact, really become flesh. We are still under the regime of Moses, who allowed divorce because of the hardness of our hearts. That hardness is taken away only by the Christ of Saint Cyril and taught by the Council of Ephesus, who rejected the double personhood of the Nestorian fiction.

In sum, there is no way to separate sacramental practice and doctrine from the creed. As G. K. Chesterton observed, Catholic doctrine, like the Lord's tunic, is woven from top to bottom without seam.

VI. CONCLUSION

We must ask to what end the Church would contemporize herself in the ways suggested in the first part of this essay. As was acknowledged there, the Church is a sacramental Church. Sacraments, however, are instituted by Christ. They have the shape he gave them. They are not re-shapable by the Church. Did the Church try to do so, she would cease to be contemporary with Christ and the apostles. This is an impossibly high price for a relevance that, moreover, will be fleeting, since it is worldly.

As to ensuring contemporaneity with Christ, the contemporaneity that saves, it is the peculiar responsibility of the bishops, a dominically instituted responsibility, to maintain the shape of his sacraments, just as it is their peculiar responsibility to maintain that fullness and integrity of evangelical truth that declares their intelligibility.

Each bishop has a special responsibility for maintaining his diocese in the truth of the Gospel. All bishops together have a catholic responsibility for maintaining the Church as a whole in the truth of the Gospel. At this level, whether in council or scattered throughout the world, the one voice of all the bishops may speak infallibly. Between these two poles there are episcopal conferences and synods which, by their nature as partial gatherings of episcopal authority, cannot usurp the voice of the whole, or pretend to speak to their local churches, nationally or regionally gathered, in the way the whole of the college can speak to the whole Church.

Why is this? Just as it is not good for man to be alone, so it is not good— it is not possible—for a particular church, a diocese, or a local assembly of churches, to be alone. Such loneliness destroys the ecclesial character of the particular church from within. The adventure of Catholicism is inscribed in our very name, "Catholics": we do not want to be alone; we want to be with the whole, because only then can we be with the one Lord who died for all and therefore for the whole. Otherwise said: there is no private joy for Catholics; that our joy may be complete, we have to have fellowship (*communio*) with all the churches, because only then do we have fellowship with the Father and with his Son, Jesus Christ (see 1 John 1:3–4).